P[raise for Find the Perfect College for] You

"Ros[alind Marie and Claire Law have written an im]pressive volume that [...] e of the tools for under[standing ...]

[...] D., author of
Looking at Type: The Fundamentals and Looking at Type and Careers

"This book is long overdue! At last two premier experts have combined qualitative research and their decades of experience with matching students with the right colleges to produce an insightful guide for students, parents and guidance counselors.

"In today's economy, mistakes can be costly, and parents are looking for a sure strategy to match their student to a college that fits them.

"Hats off to these two—They hit the bull's-eye!"
—*George de Lodzia, Ph.D., Emeritus Professor
of Business Administration, University of Rhode Island*

"Students, their parents and their advisors will gain from the insights provided here. This is new and valuable college planning territory. Take a look. These pages take college planning to a new level."
—*Steven R. Antonoff, Ph.D., Certified Educational Planner,
Antonoff Associates, Inc.*

"No one other than Rosalind Marie and Claire Law could have written this book. They know students, and they know colleges. They tell you why and how a student's MBTI® personality fits well at specific colleges.

"Through the lenses of the MBTI® personality preferences, the authors reveal how students' personality and learning style fit at specific colleges. The authors researched and merged student attributes with what the college offers. Students will find ready-made lists of colleges that are likely to be a solid match for them.

"The process of choosing a college through this method is an entirely more self-directed, conscious way of going to college. Students will get to know themselves better and will understand the ethos of the college after reading this book.

"By opening any given page, students will get a fascinating view of the college of their dreams—the idyllic four magic years of living and learning."
—*Sue Bigg, MPH, Certified Educational Planner, educational consultant*

"This book presents a proven, effective tool for the job of finding a college! Each one of our high school seniors has been able to pick their major and find a college by working through this process. What a relief!"
—*Lori Pohly, parent, Huntsville, AL*

FIND *the* PERFECT COLLEGE *for* YOU

82 Exceptional Schools That Fit Your Personality and Learning Style

ROSALIND P. MARIE
and C. CLAIRE LAW

Find the Perfect College for You: 82 Exceptional Schools That Fit Your Personality and Learning Style
Second Edition By Rosalind P. Marie and C. Claire Law

Published by SuperCollege, LLC
2713 Newlands, Belmont, CA 94002
www.supercollege.com

Credits: Cover: TLC Graphics, www.TLCGraphics.com. Design: Monica Thomas
Layout: The Roberts Group, www.editorialservice.com

Trademarks: All brand names, product names and services used in this book are trademarks, registered trademarks, or tradenames of their respective holders. SuperCollege is not associated with any college, university, product, or vendor.

Disclaimers: The authors and publisher have used their best efforts in preparing this book. It is sold with the understanding that the authors and publisher are not rendering legal or other professional advice. The authors and publisher cannot be held responsible for any loss incurred as a result of specific decisions made by the reader. The authors and publisher make no representations or warranties with respect to the accuracy or completeness of the contents of the book and specifically disclaim any implied warranties or merchantability or fitness for a particular purpose. The accuracy and completeness of the information provided herein and the opinions stated herein are not guaranteed or warranted to produce any particular results. The authors and publisher specifically disclaim any responsibility for any liability, loss, or risk, personal or otherwise, which is incurred as a consequence, directly or indirectly, from the use and application of any of the contents of this book.

ISBN13: 9781617600036

Manufactured in the United States of America
10 9 8 7 6 5 4 3 2 1

Library of Congress Cataloging-in-Publication Data
Marie, Rosalind P.
  Find the perfect college for you : 82 exceptional schools that fit your personality and learning style / Rosalind P. Marie, C. Claire Law.
     p. cm.
  Includes index.
  Summary: "This book matches students' personality type to colleges that best fit them. It provides detailed descriptions of the academic, physical, and social environments of each campus"-- Provided by publisher.
  ISBN 978-1-61760-003-6 (pbk.)
  1. College choice--Psychological aspects--United States. 2. Personality. I. Law, C. Claire. II. Title.
  LB2350.5.M344 2012
  378.1'98019--dc23
                                   2012001453

ACKNOWLEDGEMENTS

We would like to thank the following individuals who have supported our vision in this book through to its completion. First and foremost, our husbands, John Krawiec and Chip Law who accepted the book's considerable commitment and demands on our energy with grace. We want to thank our earliest supporters Steve Antonoff and Sue Bigg, who believed in our ability to bring a new idea to the table. Dr. Charles Martin, Richard J. Puhek, Esq. and Dr. Delodzia gave us critical and much needed feedback during the writing and composition stages in their area of expertise. Bill Dingledine, President Elect of SACAC 2009-10, (Southern Association for College Admission Counseling), the first professional educator to look at the finished manuscript, gave us a Bravo, along with insightful comments that influenced further editing. Our seven, twenty-something reviewers, Sheila Khan Judkins, Adam F. Khan, Saima Majid, Katherine Olaksen, Andrew Inglis, Cord Briggs and Anne Krawiec, brought their youth and recent collegiate experience to the manuscript. Along the way, Anne Newton, Janet Seif, Leigh Anne Spraetz, and Virginia Short helpfully responded to our queries for feedback. Our appreciation goes out to the twentieth century psychologists whose research influenced us lastingly and remained our constant inspiration while advising high school students. We thank the several authors of books within the stable of Personality Type literature and whose work provided checkpoints to our own manuscript, Gordon Lawrence, Paul Teiger, Barbara Barron, Earle Page and Alan Brownsword.

NOTE FROM THE AUTHORS

This book was born out of the authors' personal experience while advising college-bound students. Our philosophical perspective strongly points to starting the process by helping students better understand themselves through assessments, interest inventories and personal interviews. With those emerging student profiles we call upon our knowledge of individual campuses and their unique academic and social environments. Throughout each advising session, telephone discussion and meeting with student and family we seek to match and interface the student personality preferences and learning style with college and universities that support and appeal to those student profiles. We set out to capture that advising process in this book and elected to enter our individual, subjective views of college campuses into a qualitative research design.

Over the period of ten years, we consulted with professional educators and psychologists to develop and move forward with the methodical framework that resulted in this book. Our observations and advising are heavily based upon, and follow much within the theories of student development and environmental theories which encompass the physical and social environment. The research and theories of Alexander Astin, 1962, 1968; and Astin and Holland, 1961; Holland (1973) and Myers (1980), Michelson, 1970; Moos, 1979, Pascarella, 1985; Stern, 1986; Strange, 1991 and Kurt Lewin, (1937) have influenced our work in this book. The *Myers Briggs Type Indicator*®, emanating from Jungian Psychological theory, is the foundation of our college advising process and lays the fundamental groundwork for this book.

CONTENTS

THE COLLEGES

FOREWORD

As you will come to appreciate, there is much depth and perspective in this book. We thank you for investing time and energy moving through the written words and sometimes demanding concepts. Remember, however, that this book is not a field directive. We want the best for you as you may take direction from its pages. It is a privilege to enter your life and we do so with suggestions, not mandates. Ultimately your parents and you have the credentials to determine the right college and the right educational major.

Do These Situations Look Familiar?

"My son is in high school and we were hoping that he could find a college on his own. He's done some research, has taken standardized tests twice and seen a couple of schools, but he still has no direction."

"Sarah dropped her books on the kitchen table on the way to the fridge, and said, 'I'm not going to apply to that college. None of my friends are going there.'"

"Tristan is a top student at a very strong independent school. Each semester the high school class ranking and his place in the rank seems to draw energy away from exploring colleges and determining the type of education suited for him."

"Heather wants a different type of college than her friends and the students in her high school often choose. We want to help her define what that 'difference' means while visiting a cross section of colleges, but we don't have any idea how to accomplish this."

"Jason, our son, wants to go to a large university, preferably public. We would like him to keep an open mind and include smaller universities and liberal arts colleges on the list of prospective colleges to visit. We are having little luck getting this idea across to him."

"Leah is a strong student in her class and she will be the first to attend college in our family. We are depending on the school counselor but also want to understand and help her with the final selection of a college and her major."

These are fairly common experiences for parents of college bound high school students. This innovative book will help you open up the student's vision while talking about college. Those conversations can enhance their potential and personal success in college using the student's Personality Type as the key.

CHAPTER 1

WHAT'S IN THIS BOOK?

The College Search

Starting the search for the right college with the high school student can be both exciting and unsettling for families. Students are about to start an unfamiliar journey. Parents may or may not have much experience with the college application process. Over the years, family, friends and neighbors have been good sources of help along with books on raising children. Past visits to Barnes and Noble or similar bookstores were frequent and pleasant. Now parents and students find themselves back in the aisles, but this time in a new section called College Guides. There are a lot of choices on the shelf, more than expected. The college guides offer many statistics and opinions about the process of applying and selecting a college.

So why would you select this book? Because it is the *only* college book that matches the student's Personality Type in reference to the Myers-Briggs Type Indicator® instrument, and therefore their learning style, with the teaching philosophies at a college or university.*

Our book offers this original perspective for students, parents and high school guidance counselors because the focus is on the student learning style primarily and the college descriptions secondarily. You will be able to use our very successful method to select colleges that match the individual student. Within these pages you will find 82 of our favorite colleges that run the gamut from the most selective to more or less open admission. By following our planning suggestions throughout the search, parent and student will begin to recognize learning environments. You will then be able to match the students' Personality Type and learning style with the colleges. As you do this, you can start with the colleges we suggest for your student's Personality Type. The value in doing this is to confidently add new colleges to your list

1

for serious consideration. At the same time, the process can lead you to drop others from your current college list. As you understand more about learning style and how it plays out in the lecture halls and classes, you will also more accurately assess colleges that are not listed in this book.

Personality Type

So exactly where does this Personality Type research come from and how reliable is it? The concept grew out of the work of early 20th century psychologists Carl Jung and Katherine Briggs with her daughter, Isabel Myers who developed a complex theory of human personality and the concept of personality preferences. Their understanding of human personality was put to practical use during World War II when GIs were successfully assigned to work tasks, based on their answers to questions developed by Myers. Those questions, updated to reflect modern society, are in constant use today, in business, government and education. Our book highlights the career fields favored by each of the sixteen types as identified in the research. We then recommend the educational majors and minors that prepare undergraduates for those fields. We have found that high school students like to talk about majors surfaced by this research for their type and are less interested in talking about others.

In Chapters Two and Three you will explore and then uncover the student's likely Personality Type**. With this selection, you can get started using our book to expand or slim down your college list. In the process you will become quite knowledgeable about three powerful tools in college planning. They are the student learning style, educational majors favored by each Personality Type, and the college environments. We highlight each of these three tools as they appear on the individual college campuses. They are the heart and soul of our book.

Learning Style

Learning style is so important because it frees the student to be more creative and more open to exploration if they are in a learning environment that works for them. The learner is more motivated when there is a good match between campus educational approach and their individual learning style. Undergraduate college students use a lot of emotional and intellectual energy in the classroom to understand information presented by the professor. The student who is taking in knowledge with their preferred learning style can focus wholly on the subject at hand. The student who is not so well matched to the learning style is doing two things: learning the information and then rearranging it into ways that can be remembered and utilized. Therefore, the student who learns best by working with others in pairs or small teams learns quickly and soundly if the professor requires student teams. The undergraduate who learns best by mulling over ideas in their mind without interruption learns well if the professor relies heavily on reference documents at the library or online documents. These two study methods utilize two of the eight potential learning preferences that make up a student's learning style. The primary use of our book is matching your student's learning preferences with the colleges that support them through educational practices in and out of the classroom.

Exploring Educational Majors

The second powerful planning tool is the multiple short descriptions of majors and minors that may be especially rewarding for each Personality Type. Once again, this is the *only* book that connects the dots between learning style and educational majors currently offered on college campuses. How many times have we heard about students who don't know what to declare for their major in the last two years of college? How many times have we heard from graduates who can't get into a career field or advance because their degree has little relation to the job they want? A great way to avoid this outcome is to take advantage of the research that identified distinct occupations favored by each of the Personality Types. In our book, we recommend major and minor fields of study that pair up with the preferred occupations of each Personality Type as recorded in the archives of MBTI® career research. This can be a great tool for most high school students who are undecided. For those who have a major in mind, our specific suggestions give them complementary studies for a minor or concentration that also appeals to their Personality Type.

College Physical and Social Environments

Our concept of identifying Personality Type and learning style at the colleges is original. Yet, there is also the more familiar and really important campus social culture to consider when choosing a college. It is explored through the Social and Physical Environment and they comprise the third tool in our book that is so useful for finding the right fit. Person Environment theories examine how people react to certain physical spaces such as college campuses. Taken together, the social and physical environments have a strong influence in shaping student body values, beliefs and behaviors.

More specifically, social psychologists such as John Holland describe how certain people shape a social environment and are attracted to like minded individuals. Lawrence Kohlberg, another preeminent social psychologist, offers a foundation for understanding the development of college student morality. Research by pioneers, such as these two theorists, has influenced key practices in collegiate environments like the Honor Code. Environmental psychologists, such as Kurt Lewin, describe how the physical attributes can also shape specific behaviors. This is further explained in the next chapter.

You would witness the Person Environment Theories in action when students march for or against oil exploration. Individuals on any particular campus tend to be like-minded, and would likely hold similar views or at least be sympathetic with each other on an issue like oil exploration. These important theories helped frame our observations of the illusive nature of campus social life that is so important during college selection.

82 Colleges

So why did we select these 82 colleges as a 'primer' for matching learning style and Personality Type with college environment? The simple answer is because these 82 colleges have very cohesive and well crafted educational environments. These colleges are consistently on target with their educational beliefs. They put their understanding into action every day, each semester. They have administration and faculty perspectives that fit a clear cluster of types among the 16 learning styles. These 82 colleges translate their beliefs into a cohesive curriculum and residential life. The core courses required for graduation harkens back to the philosophy of their founders. The course curriculum is notable for what it offers and what it does not offer. The undergraduate time spent on and off campus, in internships or study abroad trips, reflects how the administration and faculty view acquiring knowledge. The option to double major or combine a single major with other minors reflects the administration's view of societies needs in the workforce. The advising for post graduation options points to how the college expects its graduates to contribute to society. All of these reflect and support specific learning styles and define educational culture on the campus. This is why we selected these 82 excellent colleges.

Three Powerful Tools

The solid match between undergraduate student and college can launch the young adult into their first professional position with personal satisfaction and success. Learning style, best fit majors and minors and college environment are three powerful tools used to find the right match. Yes, they are not quickly absorbed, but the advising method as presented in this book capitalizes on them. It lays out the basic concepts and hundreds of specific examples that you can access by tables or by reading the individual college reviews. We hope you will agree.

*Myers-Briggs Type Indicator®, MBTI®, and Myers-Briggs® are trademarks or registered trademarks of the MBTI® trust, Inc., in the United States and other countries.

**www.mbticomplete.com is recommended by the Association of Psychological Type as the official website for completing the MBTI® survey on line.

CHAPTER 2

THREE POWERFUL TOOLS VIEWED IN ACTION ON COLLEGE CAMPUSES

In this chapter, we present a layman's description of Personality Type with learning style and the benefits of exploring educational majors and minors for each type plus the key features of the physical environment and social life.

Why is this important information to have? As the student, you will understand your personality preferences and honor them. Your preferences come naturally to you because they are better developed. You will choose your college with more confidence because you know why you enrolled. Even though your choice may be very different than that of your friends, you will feel secure about your decision to enter a particular college or technical school. You can get a sense or gut feeling about a college fairly quickly when you know your personality preferences which will point in the direction of college majors and minors.

Some students will also naturally gravitate toward a social group that shares some of their personal values, simply because such a social group will give them more opportunities to express themselves. Other students who wanted to be in the more "diverse" large city campus might realize after a semester or two that the broad variety of ethnic backgrounds feels like a fire-hose experience in relating to the world. Another group of students may really need to know what they will major in before they enter college. Those colleges that offer fields of study and the pathways to a definite career will likely attract students who need surety. Students who wonder what they will major in when they go to college are likely to prefer a college where they can remain open and undecided for the first two years. Here a student has the time to take many subjects and explore many options. There are so many reasons why the social culture is important.

The Physical Environment offers a concrete snapshot of the college location and campus layout. An urban campus located in the center of a city like Boston offers an entirely different college experience than one located in northern New Hampshire. In our experience, the relationship between the student and the physical attributes of the location are extremely important. We will alert you to the quality of the college campus in the mountains that makes hiking possible, or, to a location near other colleges that often results in students being able to cross-register. We remind the reader that a college near snowy mountains may offer a ski pass to its students who together socialize on the bus to the ski slopes every weekend. Contrast this with the indifference of the typical subway ride even though students attend the same university.

Finding the perfect college match depends on understanding oneself, and entails choosing courses, majors and careers that suit one's innate personality preferences. This helps students develop their sense of purpose and find satisfaction in college and in life.

Personality Type and Learning Style in College

Each Personality Type has its own characteristic learning style. The learning style can be thought of as how each individual takes in information and retains it for use.

There are eight distinct preferences as to how we interact with our world. In the examples below, you will discover that an individual college can cater to and support several of the preferences depending on the college's academic philosophies. As we surveyed and visited colleges, we would come across a number of factors that seemed to point to certain preferences. When several factors surfaced to honor and support a particular preference, such as S–Sensing, it would then become one of the determinants we used to identify Personality Types compatible with that campus. We typically found that colleges serve a range of two to four distinct preferences quite well through their specific educational practices, curriculum and academic philosophies. The eight preferences are organized into four pairs. An individual student can be one or the other within each pair but not both. Therefore, each student will have four preferences that make up their Personality Type.

Extravert and Introvert Learning Styles

College students with the extravert preference would like professors who require active and frequent participation or teaming with other students on projects. The opposite choice is Introvert. Students with the introvert preference would like coursework that requires internet research and reading a list of selected journals on reserve in the library. These are examples of educational practices that honor two preference opposites: Extraverts (E) and

Introverts (I). Most colleges have educational features that serve both of these preferences. However, some colleges tend to lean toward one or the other.

Sensing and Intuitive Learning Styles

The next pair of preferences includes the Sensing (S) preference and the Intuitive (N) preference. The Sensing student prefers to learn by collecting all the facts and then arriving at a conclusion. The needs of this Sensing student would be met in a college freshman year course like "Introduction to Experimental Biology." This is taught in a step by step, building block approach through lab techniques. These same techniques then would be used in upper class courses. On the other hand, a freshman course like "Foundations in Biology" that starts first with the theories central to understanding the subject meets the needs of the Intuitive learner. This Intuitive learner likes to get the big picture first and then discover the facts. A student will have either the preference for sensing courses or intuitive courses.

Colleges may offer both types, sensing and intuitive courses. Sensing and intuitive preferences are the predominant preference pair that underlies collegiate academic philosophies. Colleges tend to lean heavily toward one or the other: sensing or intuition. Educational practices influenced by these two preferences interface with all majors and minors as well as some extracurricular activities.

Thinking and Feeling Learning Styles

The third pair of preferences includes students with a Thinking (T) preference and students with a Feeling (F) preference. Objective analysis and logic rule within the preference for thinking. A college emphasizing the thinking preference would lean more toward analytical and precise subject matter with advising for undergraduates to explore career fields. On the other hand, a college that mentors and advises with an orientation for the feeling preference would emphasize humanistic content and career exploration by defining personal beliefs and values. Educational advising influenced by the feeling preference would call attention to values during an open ended, discussion based process between professor and student.

Many college courses are quite grounded in objective analyses as a preferred way to acquire knowledge which reflects the thinking preference. A lesser number of colleges heavily emphasize exploratory, values driven learning. The reader should know that each of these opposite learning preferences can lead to an exceptionally fine acquisition of knowledge and understanding. Despite leaning toward thinking or feeling, colleges tend to acknowledge the opposite and also provide curriculum honoring the other preference. Students will be one or the other of these preferences.

Judging and Perception Learning Styles

The last set of preferences is that of Judging (J) and Perception (P). Again, an individual undergraduate student is one or the other of these preferences. The student who likes a course syllabus that is well organized with a list of to-do's and clear cut-offs for grades favors the judging preference. The undergraduate who likes a paragraph on the course objective leans toward the perceiving preference. College professors often utilize a little of both preference orientations in how they organize the course objectives. However, the college administration policies outlined in the catalogs often lean toward one preference or the other. It will be reflected in the requirements for graduation, the regulations for residential housing, registration, research participation and more. This preference tends to influence both the social and academic life on the campus.

College Educational Majors and Minors and the Best Personality Fit

As noted in Chapter One, there are preferred occupations for each of the sixteen Personality Types. Many decades of research with the MBTI® instrument support the correlation between personality and occupation*. It is our premise that the student who is familiar with their Type's preferred careers/occupations will have a clearer, chartered path through their four collegiate years. The value of this book is to identify educational majors and minors that naturally suit the student's strengths and inclinations.

Within this book, the reader will find suggestions for paths of study at each of the colleges that are reviewed. The purpose of each short description is to pique the interest of the high school student and encourage the exploration of that educational major or minor. We strongly recommend that all students read through each of the educational majors listed for their Personality Type. That exercise alone will likely trigger new ideas about how to evaluate other colleges. It is not intended to be a directive for declaring a major at that college or any other college. Rather, it is one of the powerful tools in this book that will help high school students start to think about the purpose of their collegiate education.

College Physical Environment

The environment is what you experience when you first visit and then move to a college campus. You look at the campus landscape and the views, flower beds, trees and buildings. Some buildings become an easily recognizable icon. You see how the undergraduates dress. You hear the sounds of city noise traveling across the campus. You hear what students are talking about. You feel the energy level across the campus on the day of your visit. Everyone notices the environment in some way. We believe that two features of the environment are particularly important for making the right college selection: the physical and the social environments.

During a visit to a college, some students will begin to see themselves on a campus and some will not. They will notice the distance between the classroom buildings and the freshman halls. They may envision themselves using a bike to ride to class. They may notice the location of fraternity houses if the college has them.

The last few decades have seen a lot of construction on college campuses. These newer buildings are designed with careful attention to how students will use them, because colleges are aware that building layouts and floor plans play an influence on students. New buildings are designed to blend in with the established architecture. Also, they are configured with specific goals for student behavior. The external building of residence halls is often planned with a view to form a sort of village community where students can easily socialize and engage in learning and extra-curricular activities. New residence halls are likely to be suite-style apartments with a common area, where students can meet and greet one another. Semi-circular classrooms with smart boards are spaces that encourage discussion among students and professor and make note-taking easier. A college coffee shop with comfortable couches and a snack bar tends to encourage students to sit and read while sipping the latest flavor of chai. Over a cup of coffee some will seize the opportunity to discuss the upcoming exam. Many colleges have also elected to build professional level theaters and music practice rooms with high quality acoustic stage and sound equipment. When this occurs, students who might otherwise drop their musical instrument at the last high school concert may take up their flute again.

As colleges use physical space across the campus in new ways, professors are moving their offices into the residence halls. Campuses with this new concept offer more access to professors. This is especially attractive to students who want to continue a discussion that started in class. This increases the student's options for their free time when not in the classroom. It shows how the physical environment can play a huge influence on the student experience. These changes are supported by the theories of twentieth century psychologists, from Kurt Lewin (1936) to Alexander Astin (1984) and George D. Kuh (2004). This research examined the effects of campus environments and studied the variables that keep students more engaged on campus. We note these attributes at each college we visit. The physical environment has the potential to generate academic engagement and friendships, thus contributing to student success in college.

In these ways, the physical environment influences the behavior of students in subtle and often unnoticed ways. Taken as a whole, this is often referred to as the Environmental Press. Since students could miss the degree to which it will challenge them, we refer to the effects of the Environmental Press throughout our book to give students another lens by which to explore and evaluate a college. It is often at work when students live in a specific "house." The "house system" originated at the Universities of Oxford and Cambridge in England. In these residences students not only sleep and eat. They also form intellectual communities serving just about every need of students, from elegant dining to academic and social mentoring. In fact, at some universities, students identify more with their house or residence hall than the college itself.

We also consider the subtleties connected with a college's location. The "city drain" is a documented effect on student life. Generally, the city can take students away from on-campus activities. What will be the nature of the contacts made off campus? Most large American cities are multi-cultural and many students will experience this diversity. Some will have dinner at the Korean restaurant while others will dine at the local pizza joint and will see each other on the streets. Along with academic work, these variables associated with the location of the college will impact students.

College Social Environment

The social environment describes the human characteristics that shape the distinctive social life at a particular college. When we visit colleges we note the groups and individuals that inhabit that campus and seem to color the social scene. By describing the social environment we offer the reader another set of lenses with which to look at the collective groups of students at a particular college. The authors examine what makes them tick, what makes them different from students of another college. At some colleges the academic experience is competitive in nature while at others it's an "all for one and one for all" mentality. While each student is different and unique, together they influence one another and define the college atmosphere. The differences in social climate among colleges can also be a result of the particular policies, structure, restrictions and rules. The college mission often factors in our review of collegiate atmosphere since it points to the nature of the social experience.

We sometimes noted the clubs, often indicative of the student's interests, in capturing the nature of the social environment for our readers. For example, on some campuses political activism can be the prime organizing factor for many of the clubs and organizations. On other campuses students may form many clubs and activities around volunteer service or religion. The environment may be the major concern at yet another college. On this last campus, the administration and faculty may respond by bringing noted lecturers in the environmental debate to campus and students might monitor the groundskeepers' use of fertilizer and water.

While assessing college social environments we relied on the framework provided by social psychologist John Holland, who proposed a classification based on the simple concept that groups of a feather flock together. His work is familiar to many educators and is known as The Holland Typography. It's comprised of these groups: realistic, investigative, artistic, social, enterprising and conventional. It predicts that realistic individuals are attracted to those who, like themselves, want to see concrete results from their efforts. Realistic students in college tend to engage in activities that are practical and may yield secure careers. These students together create a realistic college environment. On the other hand, artistic individuals may want to express their creativity in unique ways so they may seek out a college where the students do just that.

Each of these defining social and physical features is so important that they melt together like a cake, once it is baked, to comprise the campus culture and environment. They are critical because students need to know before they apply to college whether they like chocolate, caramel or marble cake. Parents and students will note the flavors of the campuses they visit after they study the sections on physical and social environments. More importantly, with this book they will learn to recognize the physical and social press of the environment. You will decide which environment fits best.

In the next chapter, we offer an exercise that allows parents or students to choose their preferences that form a Personality Type.

* The MBTI® instrument has been the subject of hundreds of research projects studying the links between personality type and different aspects of life. The Center for Applications of Psychological Type™ (CAPT®) maintains the largest single collection of research about the MBTI® instrument in the world. (In the 1940s and 1950s, Isabel Briggs Myers first recorded her research notes on thousands of index cards, which are now part of the archives at the University of Florida in Gainesville, Florida.) www.capt.org

CHAPTER 3

UNCOVER YOUR PERSONALITY PREFERENCES AND TYPE

With a basic understanding of all the preferences you can move forward by making a choice on four scales. When you make your selection within each of these four pairs you might be just slight or you could be very definite, it doesn't matter at this point. Students and/or their parents will select their choice on these four scales and in doing this, they will identify their likely Personality Type. Then you can proceed to chapter six for a list of the colleges that support your learning and social inclinations.

Keep in mind, however, that any student can find success at any college. Adaptability, capability, strength of high school academics, motivation and other factors come into play. Yet students who know their type are more likely to visit and hone in on campuses that really fit them.

Extraversion and Introversion

The first scale is between **E**xtraversion and **I**ntroversion. Please read and react to the information below. Which one sounds more like you? Which has more of your behaviors? Which describes you better?

Extraversion, referred to as **(E),** appeals to those high school students who want to socialize with a large group of friends, from casual acquaintances to middle and best friends. The social butterfly gets energized by meeting many people and being involved in many clubs and extracurricular activities. Extraverts are the first to say hello in the hallway and one of the first to raise their hand in class, volunteering to give answers. They could be attracted to the debate team, the mock trial or student council. Extraverts are often visible in activities, sports and projects and familiar to teachers and staff in the high school. They like to be expressive conversationalists. Others think of them as participants and supporters of the school community. Extraverts are usually chatting in the lunch room and sometimes getting in trouble for chatting in class too. Easy to know, extraverts often think out loud and easily throw their personal thoughts into the classroom discussions.

Introversion, referred to as **(I),** appeals to those high school students who want to have a few, select friendships. Introverts could possibly lose interest and enthusiasm in some of the rah-rah high school activities like pep club. Yet, the math team or cross country team meet the introvert's needs because it basically involves others, but nevertheless is mostly an individual effort. They rely on their own gathering of information and reflect with care and time as they reach conclusions or act on information. They appear to be reserved and sometimes may even seem withdrawn. They enter the hallway quietly, without swaggering or gesturing, possibly absorbed in earnest conversation with a classmate or a teacher. Introverts prefer to do homework alone. They typically communicate with other classmates who are deeply interested in the subject too. Art class may appeal to them because they can express themselves without excessive conversation. Introverts are pondering and thoughtful, often seeking a deeper explanation than the teacher provides.

Extraversion (E)	Introversion (I)
I love pep rallies and find them rarely boring.	Pep rallies are required, OK, and sometimes interesting.
Moving through the halls to next class is for catching friends.	Moving to the next class is best done quickly to avoid the crush.
Lunch time is to find friends and make plans.	Lunch time is to eat with a friend.
Planning for and working on the Homecoming Float is a definite.	Going to Homecoming, if friends are going too, works for me.
Teaming in science labs is helpful and improves grades.	Teaming in science lab is required mostly and could be limiting.
I know the answer; my hand is up pretty much immediately.	I know the answer, think it over, then maybe I raise my hand.
What is your choice?	
❑ **Extraversion (E)**	❑ **Introversion (I)**

Sensing and Intuition

Sensing, referred to as **(S),** students love to study subjects that have a practical connection to the world. They use structure to assure that their facts are categorized and correct. They like step by step directions and feedback that is definite and measurable. Sensors in high school prefer not to have many open ended questions from the teacher that require guesswork or interpretation. This preference learner tends to like subjects such as earth or life sciences and physics. Their memory is an asset which helps them get good grades on fill in the blank and matching quizzes in high school. They follow instructions accurately. They are first class observers of what they can see, hear, and smell. Generally speaking, they are not looking for hidden meanings and do not enjoy reading between the lines. If a teacher does not move rapidly through the material or jump around, these students will get a solid understanding of the subject and accept the concepts. Sensors might challenge a teacher if the facts in a lesson plan don't jive with their knowledge of reality. They can be good at athletics because they focus on today's game, tuning all their senses to the sport during the play. They are present and attending, happy with the organized teacher who covers what they need to know.

Intuition, referred to as **(N),** students prefer to explore theoretical information and abstract knowledge. They are driven by possibilities. They love to develop big ideas and random thoughts that can catch a teacher or classmate by surprise. They are imaginative, global learners who appreciate the big picture and may dislike too many nitty-gritty details. Intuitive students are able to see beyond the information presented by the teacher during the class period. They anticipate the subject matter and look forward to the next chapter. They like to read books that have heroes or fantasy orientations or anything else that stretches the imagination. They rely on their hunches and can build connections between seemingly unrelated topics. These students like to add to the information presented in class. They are future oriented and would like the model United Nations if their high school should offer it. They like a teacher who moves along quickly and offers choice in doing homework assignments. Intuitive students are ready to move on to new material and will automatically connect it to earlier knowledge. They prefer variety and new materials in the classroom; it brings excitement and interest to sequentially-based knowledge.

Sensing (S)	Intuition (N)
Teachers who introduce new material in steps and building blocks are best.	I like a teacher who starts out with the big picture first.
High school classes cover most of what I need to know for the first year of college.	High school classes don't expand enough or read between the lines.
Teachers should be very clear and stick with direction on assignments.	It is best when a teacher gives choices on homework.
Practice labs prepare me for tests, and the second time around works.	Practice labs slow me down, it's better to move along to new stuff.
Memorizing information is the way to the best test score.	Class discussion and learning ideas with words and notes is best.
If I were to study trees, my first choice would be to examine several leaves for their structure.	If I were to study trees, reading about the leaf structure of different trees is the best way to start.
I'd like to join groups like the baseball, basketball or cheering squads.	I'd like to join the yearbook, science Olympiad, debate team or student government.
Which side do you prefer?	
❑ **Sensing (S)**	❑ **Intuition (N)**

Thinking and Feeling

Thinking, referred to as **(T)**, students who prefer thinking are analytical and logical. They often enjoy analyzing ideas and information with an objective point of view. They try to bring a "cause and effect" clarity to a free-roaming, off-task class discussion. They need logical principles and order. Thinkers would respond well to a teacher who presents complex issues without emotion and reveals underlying principles. These students would not respond well to a teacher who tells daily stories about their own life experience as a way to bring understanding to the subject. Thinkers can simmer down a complicated problem because of their ability to logically organize complex situations. They can examine an event from the outside. Their precise conversation can even seem like a critique, yet it originates from the need to objectively catalog reality. Occasionally, their logic can rule over more gentle viewpoints that rely on instinct or intangible information. Students with the thinking preference really expect and focus on fairness through order in the high school administration. They are motivated by assignments and accomplishments that lead to an objective.

Feeling referred to as **(F).** Feeling preference high school students often place the greatest importance on the personal connections with the teachers and students. They gain energy through their friendships. They are aware of others' feelings. Feelers can seem diplomatic, capable of sizing up situations and able to avoid stepping on toes if deemed appropriate by them. They find something to appreciate in most of their friends and not-so-friends. They need harmony at home and in the high school social groups in order to function well. The feeler brings human values to the subject and likes teachers who bring their life stories into the class discussion. They shine with appreciation when the teacher compliments their contribution. Small group work in the class is a hit with them. They are supportive of their friends and would like each and every friend to reciprocate in return. Therefore, it is not surprising that we find them working in summer jobs where they can express care and empathy, such as camp counselors. They can be very persuasive in both academic and extracurricular activities if they choose because they understand the emotional needs of others. They like a high school principal that pays attention to the energy and needs of the learners rather than the credits and grades.

Thinking (T)	Feeling (F)
Teachers who concentrate on reasons for historical events are best.	Teachers focused on people in history explain it best.
The class should move through material with organization and purpose.	The class should move through material in tune with the class mood and desire.
I like looking closely at readings for cause and effect or mistakes.	I like reading people's experiences and perspectives.
I prefer classes that run like a humming machine, on track to the finish line.	I prefer classrooms that have a comfy, calming and personal side.
Designing or putting together the theater backgrounds suits me.	Trying out for high school drama productions suits me.
Drama with friends is kind of boring, and I stay out of it.	Drama is part of my group. I want to help my friends.
I use my cell phone to check with friends and set up plans.	I use my cell phone to see how my friends are doing.
Which is most appropriate for you?	
❑ **Thinking (T)**	❑ **Feeling (F)**

Judgment and Perception

Judgment, referred to as **(J)**, students like to plan their week, their school day, and other activities in an orderly and complete manner. Their day follows a routine if practical and possible. As high school students, they usually like to finish their chores or homework, closing the book, figuratively and literally. Those of the judging preference see homework and class assignments as serious business that should be completed and turned in on time. Once they have made a decision about class schedules, electives or extracurricular clubs to join, they are confident and are unlikely to second guess that decision. They can ignore surprising information in the college search process if it doesn't fit into their predictions about that college. The list of colleges they initially settle on is not likely to be amended. After the applications are turned in, the wait until April of the senior year is unpleasant for a student with this preference. However, once the decision envelopes arrive or the email is opened, it's over. Now this student will comfortably move forward with plans for the upcoming freshman year. They like high school administrators who are consistent and ensure a predictable calendar of activities.

Perceiving, referred to as (**P**), students like to gather information and explore at length and without deadlines or time limits. Perceiving students are often curious. They are turned off when high school counselors start the process in a formulaic way. They appreciate a high school teacher who responds positively to second viewpoints or alternative viewpoints. They enjoy spontaneity in the classroom and like the discovery method to move suddenly forward in understanding. During the junior and senior year in high school, they explore many colleges, seeing the possibilities in each. This allows them to keep the college list open, flexible and able to accommodate a last minute, good discovery. They often enjoy and have fun visiting many campuses even though they may remain unsure. Helping them out, however, are their research skills which uncover fascinating information about all the colleges on their list. Their final selection, though difficult to reach, will be well supported as they arrive on campus in the fall. This student will always appreciate the teacher or administrator who changes it up, brings in some new material or adds excitement to the traditional pep rally in high school.

Judgment (J)	Perceiving (P)
Teachers who post their outline and class goals for each week and stick to it are best for me.	Changes to the weekly plan when something interesting or important pops up are okay.
Class lesson plans with just one objective at a time for the week are my preference.	Class lesson plans that work on several projects during the week are my preference.
I will persist with the class work even if I'm tired and it's rainy.	I will take it slow and easy if I am tired and it's rainy.
Teachers should design most lesson plans for giving students knowledge.	Teachers should usually put fun and excitement in most lesson plans.

Clearly marking the end of a unit of study before moving on is best.	Connecting the end of one unit with the next, overlapping assignments is best.
Lunch is pretty much with the same friends, same table, etc. I'm not late.	Lunch might be at a different place or with different friends. I might arrive last.
I know when homework is due and get started on time.	I don't often focus ahead or start early on homework.

Okay, which will it be for you?	
❏ **Judging (J)**	❏ **Perceiving (P)**

Now circle your preferences on this grid:

Extraversion (E)	**Introversion (I)**
Sensing (S)	**Intuition (N)**
Thinking (T)	**Feeling (F)**
Judgment (J)	**Perception (P)**

Remember, each of your four chosen letter type preferences could be slight, moderate or clearly defined. It is okay to be just 51 percent sure of your choice. Now—write down each of your four letter preferences in the order completed. This is your likely Personality Type. Now you can move forward and use this book to its best advantage*.

*Students can also formally confirm their selections in this chapter by completing the MBTI® assessment. It is available through a large number of professionals from psychologists to educational consultants or through www.mbticomplete.com.

CHAPTER 4

DESCRIPTION OF PERSONALITY TYPES IN HIGH SCHOOL

Each of the sixteen Personality Types is the focus of this chapter. To illustrate the Personality Types, they have been summarized specifically as students in the junior year of high school. The sixteen descriptions highlight the four core courses in high school, math, English, science and history and how each Personality Type relates to the curriculum and typical teaching methods in high schools across America. The reader will find that each of the sixteen types reacts differently to the core subjects based on their type's preferred learning style. In addition, the teacher's own Personality Type plays into the way the material in the course is delivered. By describing personality and behavior within an 11th grade English class, parents can appreciate their teen's reaction to the subject and teacher. Teens may find out why they react to some teachers in a certain way.

Nevertheless, it is important to remember that innate ability always plays a defining role in how students like or dislike a subject. Teacher personality and teacher interest in the individual students also has a great influence on the student experience in a particular class, regardless of Personality Type. However, learning style is innate and doesn't typically change. So we ask the reader to consider the high school descriptions below. Students or their parents can then compare and further confirm the Personality Type that was selected in chapter three. Are you still unsure of your Personality Type? If so, you can access and complete the MBTI® assessment tool, widely available through psychologists, educational advisors, and at www.mbticomplete.com.

ENFJ Learning Style in High School

English: English is likely to be a favorite subject. A teacher who presents literary figures along with the reasons for their behavior in the novel is a favorite. This type can read between the lines and understands the motivations of the characters in novels like *Robinson Crusoe.* They often love to participate in class. They must have harmony in the class to feel positive and will actively participate in discussion where values are front and center. If the teacher plays favorites and allows the class to become divided for any reason, this type will shut down. The teacher who encourages study groups will appeal to this type.

Math: A teacher who assigns nightly homework in precalc and covers the answers the next day in class really works for this type. These daily exercises will help this student meet their personal goals within the semester precalc curriculum. The teacher who actually assigns a grade or a point value to daily or weekly work will gain their appreciation. Teachers will get a thumbs up if they offer markers or milestones that track completion and academic progress throughout the semester. Teachers who only give periodic tests will get a thumbs down because this type likes to know where they are at in the class.

History: This type will probably like history, but may not get the best grade because sometimes they let their personal opinions count more than the facts. The teacher who brings out the human interest in historical narratives really plays to their learning style. The teacher who devotedly follows the chronology or focuses on the objective reasons for a war may not get their approval. They might view the Pilgrims' perilous Atlantic crossing through the survivor's tales and emotional scars. They are much less interested in the actual year that the Pilgrims landed than the drama of it all.

Science: The ENFJ will like a science teacher who assigns projects that require outside work with other classmates. They especially like anatomy classes because they are connected to human health. The "knee bone connected to the leg bone" makes for the orderly, structured way they prefer to learn. The teacher who acknowledges their skill and ability to be a team player will best develop this student's potential. The teacher who assigns technical lab reports that only require recording observations will be hard for this type. Daily or weekly quizzes centered on data will also not appeal to this type if it is the primary method for the final grade.

ENFP Learning Style in High School

English: English is likely to be a favorite subject. This type likes teachers who help them clarify their ideas. They will enjoy just about any novel, short story, or poem the teacher assigns. They really like to have a personal relationship with their teachers. The English teacher is likely to appreciate this type's quick mind and solid ability to identify human emotions in the literature. As a result, the teacher might encourage participation by this type for help inspiring class discussions and ultimately become a friendly mentor or counselor. The ENFP will happily offer insightful comments if they actually read the assignment on time. Typically doing homework at the last minute, they may drag their feet on actually capturing those insightful comments on a paper. They are likely to get a B or a C in this subject if the teacher does not help them out.

Math: This type likes teachers who use humor and variety in the class, but also stick to the lesson plan and always explain the steps within each problem. This student gets the overall nature of the formula, but because they miss the details, the steps must be pointed out to them. This student is a big picture learner and loves the teacher who can teach with an imagination which stimulates the class. The teacher who scores big for this type makes time for informal problem solving and fun during class.

History: Teachers will get the best work from the ENFP if the homework assignment directly matches the information presented in class. The teacher who enthusiastically talks about Bismarck and Germany gets their attention and will get the best work from this type by assigning a paper that follows the classroom discussion to be turned in within the next few days. The teacher who speaks about Bismarck in class but changes the topic for homework that night will discourage this type. Variety in the assignment and extra credit projects are welcomed by this type.

Science: This student likes teachers who start with the adult insect to explain the process of metamorphosis in biology. The remaining steps in the process should have some fun and negotiation. A teacher who allows for a self designed project will definitely please them. This type likes "minds-on" and "talking it out" with others rather than solo, pencil and paper, observational reports. They relate to the spoken word, especially if the teacher has developed a personal relationship with the class. Short answer, projects and verbal reports best reveal this type's knowledge in chemistry versus multiple choice and fill in the blank.

ENTJ Learning Style in High School

English: The ENTJ likes a teacher who is fair and rewards students who turn in homework on time and gives extra credit for lengthier reports. They are curious and like complex literature but also want it to be related to reality. They would like biographies and literature that explains how great minds and important figures came to be. They like a teacher who encourages a lot of classroom discussion. They like to speak up and will raise their hands to relay the continuous ideas that come into their head during class.

Math: This type wants to be right and often likes precalc because there is a clear and finite answer to each problem. A math teacher who organizes a little competition between student groups will score a touchdown with this type. They like to do problems that others may not be able to complete. They like to invent their own way of working a math problem calling on their broad understanding of the formula. They will take the time to explore different solutions to get the same right answer. If the teacher is organized when presenting new material, the ENTJ will rise to the task.

History: This student will like history if the teacher can present the subject through class projects like dramatic reenactments, oral presentations and class discussions. A teacher who would assign team projects and offer a chance to lead a project would be a favorite. This type will not like a teacher who primarily uses a lecture format to teach history. At the same time, they do like an orderly, chronological march throughout the semester and appreciate a teacher who reminds them if they seem to be missing important details in their search for the big picture.

Science: The ENTJ likes the way chemistry, biology and physics teachers give the class a structured, sequential outline at the beginning of a segment or chapter. The ENTJ will be interested in learning facts and objective information about the brain if the teacher uses ferrets or gerbils to illustrate the application of that knowledge. They may dislike the physics teacher who passes up this type of experiment that offers the opportunity to use insight. Memorizing facts and cramming to cover one more chapter before the semester ends gains their dislike.

ENTP Learning Style in High School

English: This type likes the fact that literature is open to many interpretations. The ENTP explores the possible motives and reasons why a protagonist may act in a certain way. Poems are also something that triggers their imagination. They will like teachers who invite student discussion and include multiple points of view. They will not like teachers who do not deviate from a structured interpretation of book. The ENTP can deal with opposing points of view. When this type has an assignment, such as writing a book review, they are not likely to make an outline. They will like a teacher who gives multiple short stories or poems to read, as opposed to a teacher who stays on one novel all semester. Teachers may find that this student's original interpretation of a poem is not clearly supported in writing and find it difficult to assign a "C" to the most original paper turned in.

Math: The ENTP may have a hard time following the formulas and prescribed teaching in precalculus because there is little room for creativity. However, the teacher who shows different approaches to solving a problem will pique their interest. The teacher who gives an open ended math test, such as "tell how you would build a bridge using math formulas" will be their favorite. If the teacher only offers one kind of math exam all year long, it could become the tedious, ho hum class of the day. The ENTP quickly tires of rules and could make careless, small mistakes. They tend to prefer conceptual math, where they can apply new ways of solving problems.

History: This student likes a fascinating teacher who ties in past events with today's world. They like to read and teach themselves. The teacher who speaks of the numbers of horses and soldiers and hours involved in the battle of Gettysburg will lose this type. The teacher who speaks of Lee's battle plan and Grant's hunches will have them raising their hands to join in with their unique opinions. On a test, they are likely to miss the starting date of the Phoenician wars but the reasons for it will be understood by them. For that reason, an essay test in history is preferable to a multiple choice test.

Science: The ENTP loves asking questions, figuring out how scientists discovered a new vaccine and knowing why milk is best drunk when pasteurized. Teachers in the subject of biology who really ask the "why" questions are favored by the ENTP. The teacher who makes them work hard to memorize the species and specific functions of cells is not a favorite. The teacher who gives students ten chemicals in the lab and rewards the student who made the most compounds brings out the best of their creative learning style.

ESFJ Learning Style in High School

English: This student will like the teacher who requires a chapter to read in the assigned novel and then follows it with a quiz, all the better if this is done on a weekly schedule that is predictable. The ESFJ does not like teachers who skip around and grade with different methods. They do not appreciate surprise assignments or quizzes. This student's written reports however, will likely be well prepared and reveal more insight into the material presented in class. If the literature is about values and compassion, their own passion for helping others will shine through because of their own, often deeply held values. This type will not mind a lecture on the various types of poetic cadence and will take detailed notes.

Math: This ESFJ likes to use graphic calculators because of the step by step sequences. Teachers who use this as a primary tool will be appreciated by this student. Typically very responsible and earnest, this student will remain on task during difficult algebraic explanations. The ESFJ could ask for clarification on behalf of the class. They are going to be a full participant in the classroom and could be very helpful to fellow students who are less willing to acknowledge their confusion. But no matter how far behind the class or an individual student gets, the ESFJ will be socially appropriate and not likely to disrupt the class or give up.

History: This type will often put forth their ideas in class discussions because they quickly recognize and appreciate facts. They will be well informed and freely share that information to help others in the class reach the same conclusions. They appreciate the teacher who gives them compliments and will do better when they receive positive comments about their work. Their clarity of thinking will shine when the teacher keeps the lessons concrete. They like that practical movement toward the knowledge expected for the coming tests and quizzes. They do not appreciate abstract, theoretical possibilities that require making assumptions about history. They will gladly help other students in the class.

Science: The ESFJ is likely to understand and appreciate the formulas because they can be demonstrated. In other words, this could be the favorite subject during the class day. Concrete concepts and application of those ideas is a favorite activity at which they often excel. Their lab work is very thorough and their lab grades may improve their overall subject grade. Mastering the individual concepts of meticulous lab work is their specialty, and they could earn the highest lab average in the class because of this. They like to work with their peers in a group in the classroom, preparing for the next day's lab experiment.

ESFP Learning Style High School

English: The ESFP is very social and often gregarious, they may enjoy literature that describes social conventions such as *The Great Gatsby*. They usually support social traditions and may not appreciate literature with an abstract, philosophical bent. A highly detailed book that describes the social scene well will really bring the story alive for this type. Literature that defies social conventions may offend their sense of values. They could shine giving an oral book report on a subject in which they are interested. Their preference for step by step learning will allow them to give a sound, thorough report that other students may learn from and come to appreciate.

Math: This type does well with a structured math presentation, and they will especially learn well from applied math lessons that relate to a real situation. They will need those frequent spontaneous energy bursts sometimes to get through the semester in abstract algebra. If the teacher is organized and personable, the teacher will bolster this student's confidence in acquiring and mastering the math work. The teacher gets a thumbs up who regularly encourages discussion of the math problems while the class together works out the answer. Plotting, graphing and geometric designs make sense to them. Classroom management that discourages active discussion or allows one or two students to frequently provide the answers won't work for this type. Follow through with after class assignments and practice may be difficult for them because it is a solo activity and may not necessarily be fun.

History: This student will do well with a history curriculum that allows for hands-on activities like dramatic reenactments or interactive videos. Group activities, such as poster sessions for history day, where this type can study with others, will really bring history alive and pique their interest. They will prefer history taught through significant historical figures versus the traditional chronological time and events approach. They can be fascinated by the lives of people. They could become anxious if they are not encouraged by teacher and this could happen because they are typically sensitive. They are likely to procrastinate on turning in assignments unless they are passionate about the topic. Remembering specific facts and historical details is often a gift of this type who typically does not like highly abstract concepts.

Science: This type will like the teacher who presents the theory of radioactivity through Marie Curie's own research. Science must be connected with reality and purpose for this type. The hands-on nature of environmental science could be a favorite subject, especially if the teacher takes the class to the river to test water samples. They need a certain framework to assignments but also need some elbow room to test and try out their own ideas. The teacher who takes the lab outside of the classroom to identify rocks, collect and identify plants, find animal traces and monitor atmospheric instruments should make this student very happy. Group work and student pairing for class assignments is satisfying because of the personal relationships.

ESTJ Learning Style in High School

English: Papers will be written clearly in a journalistic style, handed in on time without any wandering sentences. The typical literature studied in the classroom is likely to be somewhat mysterious to them such as *Beowulf*. Nevertheless, they will persevere and remain on task in reading the entire assigned list of books. They will also give their opinion in class especially if the book blends facts with a good story, like *The DaVinci Code, Nickel and Dimed: On Making it in America* or detective novels. The teacher who centers a reading list on books like *Beloved* by Toni Morrison may activate the impatience of this type because the story line is metaphorical. They will not easily suspend their disbelief to move along with a story line that intertwines fantasy with reality.

Math: Where order reigns and the teacher is well prepared and follows a predictable, sequential lesson plan the ESTJ will likely appreciate the class and the teacher. They prefer clarity in explanations of math work. They will want to be sure that they are right or present themselves well prior to raising their hands to ask a question or give an answer. Yet they will speak up even if they are alone in their opinion. They will not feel comfortable revealing a lack of understanding. They prefer tangible results so ongoing problems with answers the next day is not their favorite way to learn. They will appreciate being asked to mentor other students, if requested by the teacher. They gravitate toward finite math because solving the equations will yield correct or incorrect answers and their strong observational skills will identify small mistakes along the way.

History: Since these students are impressed by proven knowledge, history is likely to make perfect sense to them. This tradition bound type likes the straight forward, historical records because they are factual events without hypothetical queries, and history offers fewer opportunities for abstraction than other subjects in high school. The ESTJ student can sit and learn from a dry presentation of the topic if it includes concrete examples. Clear expectations and homework assignments are preferred by this student. Conversely, abstract or opinionated teachers could possibly energize the student who would ask for clarification in a respectful and appropriate way. Typically, they will turn reports in on time, follow through with homework and take a leadership position in the class.

Science: They tend to like this subject because they are learning something useful and real to them. Opinions, interpretations and nebulous ideas are rarely interfaced in the high school science classrooms, so this student is more comfortable with this quantifiable subject. There is no room for argument on how mitosis occurs or at what temperature water boils. The ESTJ's attention for detail, conscientious approach and willingness to take charge helps them excel in the lab assignments. They respect the teacher who presents this subject traditionally, with a syllabus and well organized. They also enjoy being publicly recognized for good work in the classroom because competence is an important milestone for them. The teacher who gives this independent learner the responsibility to lead others will find an enthusiastic student leader because leadership is an important milestone for them.

ESTP Learning Style in High School

English: This type will like literature which emphasizes, describes and is grounded in the physical environment, real things and people. The teacher who assigns reading that is primarily abstract and emotional in its story line will not hold the attention of this student. Hemingway's *Old Man and the Sea* and readings of Mark Twain are right up their alley. Homework that emphasizes variety in assignments and subject matter helps them stay engaged with abstract literature. Their contribution in class discussion is often summarizing or expanding on earlier comments so that the lesson can move forward. They're appreciative of the multiple points of view in literature and really enjoy the films and videos that illustrate the novel they are reading.

Math: The concepts involved in higher maths such as precalc can give this student pause and possibly stump ESTP who has previously done well in understanding discrete math and concrete problems. Their typical strength of collaborating with other students is not often seen in math. High math requires and rewards mastering the abstract concepts embedded within the formulas. The math teacher who brings in practical, real world examples of the math problems will make inroads with this student.

History: History may be the favorite subject of the school day if the teacher uses project-based activities such as documentaries, pictorial exhibits and dramatizations that liven up and add variety to this fact-based discipline. They could be strong contributors in class discussion because their recall of historical facts is a comparative strength in the typical history class. They find historical figures to be compelling if the teacher offers study methods that physically engage their senses. Curiosity is a very real learning tool for this type. Written assignments will likely avoid the 'would of, could of, should of' line of reasoning. They prefer instead to prove their understanding of the subject by revealing a logical thread without unnecessary theory.

Science: This student is likely to prefer the days spent in the lab verses the days spent in listening to lecture and preparation. They will be comfortable with lab partner assignments that include three to four students over the typical two assigned to an experiment because they are often gregarious. They are likely to be the enthusiastic member of the group and will move the experiment forward if it stalls, even if it requires a blunt direct comment from them. They prefer to experiment informally and explore with the least fuss and muss. The teacher who leans too heavily on book and lecture will garner their disfavor. Visible, concrete results, often a part of high school sciences, gives them a chance to excel through active, direct and assertive participation.

INFJ Learning Style in High School

English: This student could be quiet and unassuming about this subject that really speaks to their hearts, but they are shy about revealing this to others because they are private people. They do not like a teacher who would call on them, unless they raised their hand with a carefully thought out answer. They like a teacher who understands that they are listening and are on task, even if they do not speak out in class and answer questions. They may especially do well in a home schooling experience for a year or two because they need time and quiet to process their thoughts and prefer to teach themselves. Idealism and heroism such as is portrayed in *The Perfect Storm* by Sebastian Younger will appeal to this type.

Math: The INFJ prefers a teacher who is very well prepared. The teacher who offers a steady, even presentation of the big picture and the theory that underlies the numbers gets their respect. An equation will make more sense to this type even if it is not plotted on a graph because they can picture it intuitively. They thrive on careful analysis and the freedom to search for their own math solutions. They are independent learners and may need gentle guidance from a teacher to get back on the right track. They rely on their insights about math to be correct, but will ask a question of the teacher to confirm that they have the right answer.

History: This type is usually fascinated by this subject. They are excited to learn how the colonies came together to form a union. An assignment that required a full length examination of John Calvin would be right up their alley. Calvin is a complex figure and clearly impacted the pilgrim's motivation. INFJ would love to examine the puritan ethic. They prepare very well for all history tests even if the teacher doesn't teach to their style. This student loves to read and will do extra credit for the learning itself.

Science: They will do well in this subject. They will thrive with a demanding teacher who requires the students to be organized, good with time management and planning a semester projects and the accompanying paper, projects and reports. They will relate positively, through reason, to certain science issues like sustainability unless their personal belief system does not support that view. If they make a small error in judgment during a project or lab and the teacher calls attention to it, they will take it personally and be really hurt because of their high standards.

INFP Learning Style in High School

English: The INFP does well in class because INFP is usually interested in literature. They probably are avid readers of the *Harry Potter* series because it is richly metaphorical and depicts relationships and human values. They may also like science fiction books that stimulate their curiosity. They easily take on additional reading that is not required for class. They may find it hard to tear themselves away from a favorite novel. Their interests in literature range far and wide. They write their best papers when inspired and the topic relates to their own beliefs. They want the teacher to appreciate and compliment their work as well as coach and mentor them.

Math: In class, the INFP may be deeply invested in learning if math is taught in general concepts rather than preplanned, linear lessons and repetitive homework problems. For example, the INFP likes to know how the story of how Mr. Pythagoras discovered the Pythagorean Theorem, and how this can be applied to understanding how the universe works. A teacher who is always rational, objective and to the point, who doesn't let emotion enter the class discussion, may be upsetting to the INFP.

History: They like to use their inquisitive mind while working or studying solo. They typically like history if there is stimulating discussion in class and it is not abrasive or argumentative. Lectures might be considered boring, especially if it's a monologue by the teacher. INFP seeks to understand reasons for wars and is likely to look for a universal reason that explains all conflict. They prefer harmony in the classroom and will dislike a teacher who cannot earn the respect of the class. They may have trouble finishing their history report because the details can bog them down. The teacher who provides structure with some wiggle room does well with this student.

Science: This type sometimes gets bored with studying traditional biology or physics. They want science to relate to the human experience. The study of light and lenses make more sense to them if the teacher talks about people who suffer from cataracts. INFP needs broad concepts and big pictures first to spark the interest otherwise they may not incorporate the facts which they receive as too monotonous and boring. INFP would rather write about metamorphosis and life cycle in a short answer test rather than fill in a list of stages on a matching test.

INTJ Learning Style in High School

English: The INTJ loves the teacher who is competent and knows their literature. They would not like a teacher who accepts multiple interpretations of a novel. They want the teacher and class to settle on the best and most accurate interpretation that can survive the INTJ's analysis and critique. They do not like a teacher who moves from novel to short story to a poem in one lesson plan on a whim. They like an organized, logical review of each assigned reading.

Math: They challenge the teacher because they are quiet and learn privately. They often avoid group assignments and choose not to volunteer answers. They will complete math homework almost with resignation because the formulas do not give them freedom with the outcome. Sometimes they work so hard in trying to perfect the answers on their take-home precalc exams that they get down on themselves. Generally, INTJ is comfortable in the math classroom. This subject utilizes INTJ's love for analysis. Solving a problem is like getting to the finish line, an important milestone for this type.

History: This type will challenge the teacher's position on the Vietnam War. They like a teacher who will allow them to ask pointed questions. They ask questions to learn about the subject. They risk being not liked by the teacher and possibly others in the class because they learn by challenging the views presented in history classes. A teacher who follows the textbook interpretations regularly is not their favorite. They like a teacher who presents history in conceptual frameworks that encourage student insight.

Science: This student finds that teachers who start with the big picture in chemistry or physics are right up their alley. They are ok with missing a few of the steps and details because they will fill in the gaps later. Some teachers may like it when the INTJ challenges a few of their statements. They like a teacher who moves quickly through the chemistry chapters verbally explaining and highlighting required concepts for the upcoming AP exam. INTJ has an inner vision of how chemistry composes the world. The teacher syllabus must interface with the INTJ's vision.

INTP Learning Style in High School

English: The INTP may be reticent to speak up although they have may have an opinion. INTP can get very absorbed in a novel if it interests them. If the short story or poem does not interest them, they are likely to get bored. If the novel includes puzzles, mysteries, riddles or science fiction it is a winner as far as they are concerned. They connect the unrelated hints and clues to find the solution.

Math: This student is often on the honor roll. They may shine in pre calculus because they have the thinking power to hang in there and get the abstract theory behind the formulas. They are likely to enjoy the derivatives in higher level calculus. They really can tap in the coordinates and numbers on their hand held T-83 graphic calculator. They like this little instrument. For those who do not like math, their tendency to overlook details may trip them up on exams. Their uneven surges of energy could drain their overall effort. If the teacher negotiates with this student on the grading to include math problems that seem to be riddles, then INTP's impressive concentration kicks in.

History: Teachers that connect historic events with current problems and policy will really get INTP to pay attention. If teachers dwell on event upon event to build a chronological timeline, they are likely to lose this type. INTPs may not get appreciation by the teacher because they can become totally absorbed in connections between the past and future, with little bearing on current class discussion. History may be a favorite or a loathed subject depending on the teacher's approach. This type may come across as skeptical in their questioning as they explore and satisfy their exceptional curiosity.

Science: This type likes the pure science that teachers talk about in the classroom, and they can listen and learn while moving a concept around in their head. They may actually enjoy or not enjoy the lab experiments. They certainly don't care for the group and collaboration often assigned by the science teachers. They will shine at memorizing the formulas and enjoy the complexity of the problems in science. Sometimes they become so absorbed in their lab work that they lose sense of time and place.

ISFJ Learning Style in High School

English: The teacher who is clear and highlights the moral issues helps them figure out the various shades of gray in the story line. They will be comfortable reading Jane Austin's *Sense and Sensibility* because is pretty straight forward yet deals with common family issues. This author feeds the type's compulsion to make mental scrapbooks, rich with people details. ISFJ will be paying very close attention to everything said in the class so that they can be accurate in forming their judgments. They value the establishment and social conventions more often than not because it helps them know where they stand. Inferences made by students or the teacher in class may not be understood or accepted because they hear things literally. However, they are not likely to speak up and challenge the teacher or fellow students.

Math: Their usual mastery of the facts and their great work ethic will let them shine in the more sequential math tasks. The nature of abstract concepts in math may frustrate and wear them down so that test grades could be inconsistent sometimes. They complete all of their homework ahead of time even at the expense of play. They will like a teacher who applies the Pythagorean Theorem to figure out distance, which is a practical, hands-on concept for this type. They will like the teacher who offers a familiar routine to the lesson plan throughout the school year. They don't like to be rushed. The security of an orderly classroom that is evenly paced is very helpful to them.

History: Studying history through the social and human side is a favorite way to get into this subject. They can bring history alive, for themselves, by wondering what historical figures thought and believed at that time. They will even pass judgment on the morals or decisions made by those historical persons. Only when they ask will the teacher find out that the ISFJ has some unique and interesting insights. If a history teacher includes historical dramas in the course, they will make it easy for ISFJ to learn. Teachers who approach history in terms of facts, dates and events are less liked by this type, especially if the teacher calls attention to them in class.

Science: Mastering the facts in the sciences and then devising practical applications in the lab will be a natural and preferred learning experience for them. They will like the definite outcomes of experiments which leave little to guess about. Experimental teaching in the labs will work well for them if the teacher gives specific direction and identifies what is the end result of the lesson. ISFJ have their exceptional observation and retention skills. They are likely to be the best prepared lab partner and conscientiously accept responsibility for the exercise.

ISFP Learning Style in High School

English: The ISFP likes a teacher who is crisp and direct in discussing the storylines in literature and avoids shades of grey morality. What really drains this type's reserve is drawn-out explanations and hypothetical insights into what an author might have meant by a certain phrase or poem. In this high school class, ISFPs would rather watch a Shakespearian play on DVD first, and figure out the rest on their own. Usually, ISFP in English class hesitates before contributing opinions. They want to please the teacher. They are just as happy to observe rather than to propose an interpretation that they fear might be farfetched.

Math: This type appreciates the clarity of this subject. However, because they are not assertive and prefer to remain unnoticed, they could fall through the cracks if they don't have a caring teacher who coaches them along. They will put in extra effort if math interests them. They are cautious until they feel supported by the teacher at which time they can become energized in the classroom. Math teachers who don't seem personally interested in the students will not be their favorite. The precalc teacher should give examples of practical nature when presenting formulas to this type. The teacher who injects humor into the class lesson or is willing to make a game out of learning math could be their favorite.

History: This student is likely to excel and enjoy history if the teacher encourages them to informally come up with their own interpretations of the facts and events. They appreciate a teacher who pauses and gives the class enough time to process new information and their individual thoughts. If the history topic really piques their interest, they will go all out and turn in a seven page report. They will excel at a project that requires cut and paste historical mosaics. On history day, they will use posters to illustrate historical figures, complete with pictures and illustrations of clothing and dwellings. The teacher who notices them in a personal manner will be a favorite.

Science: They really understand and learn from those labs where there are animal samples and skeletons and specimens. Learning comes easier to them this way. They will learn from film or video presentations about the natural life cycles and the chemistry involved in those cycles. Sometimes the teacher does not understand their informal, impulsive interest in learning. At the same time, these students do not appreciate the big picture, relying instead on memorization of the facts. A teacher who pairs them up with another socially sensitive, down to earth, student will get ISFPs best work.

ISTJ Learning Style in High School

English: This type will be suspicious of the many possible meanings to a metaphor. The inferential reasoning required to interpret literature could be a riddle to them. Deep inside they don't trust all the positions and interpretations because in their view, only one is correct. They will listen quietly, not complaining, and likely not reveal their discomfort with the open ended and exploratory class discussion. They are likely to write clearly, with organization and free of flowery prose. They do well with book reports gathering factual information that would support a position. They could submit well written papers and call on their previous knowledge of grammar and English structure that they learned and enjoyed via drills in earlier school years. ISTJs want to reach the learning objectives set by the teacher and if they don't get this in class they will sort it out later by themselves.

Math: They are able to grasp the theory and concepts in advanced math by building up their math knowledge sequentially over the years. Math takes advantage of their logic-based approach and so they can solve complex problems especially if the teacher is clear about the foundational steps. They will pay attention to formulas presented on the board with intense concentration especially if there are graphs, tables and illustrations involved. They will accurately pinpoint errors that they identify. On math quizzes and tests there will be no small careless mistakes. When they are solving equations they will remember to use the right laws of properties and numbers.

History: They will be accurate on dates and facts with reports they turn in on time. If the history teacher assigns a wide-ranging topic that is not broken down into a clear outline, they will not like it. They will like the class if the teacher offers the material in an organized fashion and sequentially leads to the big picture. The ISTJs make for very good students, carefully observing and following the teacher's directions. They don't want to call attention to themselves so they appreciate the teacher who acknowledges their due diligence quietly. They are keen observers of what is. Their excellent memory is like the hard drive in a computer. Group work is not their favorite way to learn because ISTJs will step in and finish what others did not complete. As a result of doing this heavy lifting, they become aggravated. When it comes to answering questions in class, they will be thoughtful with a planned answer. Sometimes the conversation will have moved on to another point and they will not volunteer that thought they were preparing. The teacher will often come to know this student's mastery of the subject through their written work.

Science: Biology, chemistry, or environmental sciences are enjoyable because they allow for logic and reasoning to arrive at a definite conclusion. These sciences move toward the big picture typically after introducing facts and information followed by a building block sequence. ISTJ likes this approach. Hands-on lab work will provide them an opportunity to demonstrate their competency and awareness of safety issues. They will not blow up the lab. Through their senses, they are very grounded in the lab assignment. Occasionally, they will volunteer to do a demonstration, taking responsibility for carrying the experiment to the end and making sure it gets done. They won't forget to come back to the lab to shake up the vial or check up on the growth.

ISTP Learning Style in High School

English: This type will prefer literature that is in a journalistic style of writing: what, where, when and how. This satisfies their need to know what makes things tick. They will like clearly descriptive essays, short stories and novels about what is, in the non-fiction category. If the teacher prefers novels with high emotional content and allegory this student will likely be turned off. They are likely to find themselves out of synch with the English class during poetry study. However they might like the haiku poetry because of its short, clear presentation with more concrete words. The teacher who is touchy feely and highly creative will be a puzzle to them. This student is likely to be passive in class and if the teacher requires participation, the grade could suffer.

Math: They usually like this subject especially finite math like algebra I, statistics and geometry. They are often orderly, paying attention to detail, and carefully print their numbers on the page so they won't make mistakes. They will adore math teachers who present lessons clearly. There are two types of answers, right and wrong, and this student is likely to willingly retrace their steps if they made a mistake. The short cuts in math formulas and most efficient proof to verify the correct answer is like duck soup for the ISTP. They like the objectivity of math. The sequential, step by step teacher will keep the attention of this student. The occasional math teacher who gets lost in their own presentations is not going to work for this student because they crave clarity. Math helps this type understand technical material which is what they are really interested in.

History: The teacher who presents this subject with emphasis on facts in categories and logical classifications will be a favorite teacher and likely to get this student to raise their hand in class. A teacher who covers the chapter with multisensory learning tools like video, graphs, posters, maps and text will allow ISTP to look for that practical thread that pulls it together. For that reason it may take the teacher several months or perhaps the semester to understand what this student has to offer to the class discussion. A teacher who flavors their history with social, religious or political random threads will not be their favorite. If the history topic piques their curiosity, they will want to know the material clearly and objectively as it relates to their present circumstances.

Science: They are likely to shine in physics, chemistry, biology and earth science because these subjects impact their lives today. This type really enjoys the many hands-on experiments and learning assignments, like dissection, because these make practical things clearer and are basically like play. The classification and systems of science are very appealing to them. Enjoying and excelling in their observations of experiments, ISTPs are likely to become participants and leaders in this class. Their papers and written work will highlight the accumulative, factual nature of the sciences. It is likely they will be engrossed by class projects.

CHAPTER 5

THE COLLEGE DESCRIPTIONS

The reader will find our three powerful tools for finding the right match college addressed in each of the campus descriptions. We hope you will become very familiar with your learning style and utilize it as a backdrop while reading these descriptions. You are likely to find much at each college that appeals to you within the list of colleges recommended for your Personality Type. We hope you will be introduced to several new educational majors and open to exploring them regardless of the college you attend. We also hope you will be alert to college environments and determine what suits you best, thereby freeing up emotional and academic energy to learn and enjoy the upcoming four years. Pay close attention to the bolded words in the Physical and Social Environment descriptions. We believe they characterize strengths on the campus. Remember that these descriptions are intended to supplement and guide your decision making—This book is not a field directive.

In addition to the identified Personality Types, the college descriptions highlight individual personality preferences that we found to be in high evidence on each campus. For your quick review, the following abbreviated descriptions should be helpful. As a reader, when you see reference to a Preference, such as S—Sensing, you can refer back to these brief definitions*:

E—Extraversion
Focus on the outer world of people and things

I—Introversion
Focus on the inner world of ideas and impressions

S—Sensing

Focus on the present and concrete information gained from the five senses

N—Intuition
Focus on the future, with a view toward patterns and possibilities

T—Thinking
Form decisions on logic and on objective analysis of cause and effect

F—Feeling
Form decisions primarily on values and on subjective evaluation of person-centered concerns

J—Judging
Prefer to have things settled and tend to plan and follow an organized approach to life

P—Perceiving
Prefer to keep options open and tend to follow a flexible and spontaneous approach to life

* copyright CPP, Consulting Psychologists Press, inc., 3803 E. Bayshore Road, Palo Alto, CA 94303

AGNES SCOTT COLLEGE

Office of Admission
141 East College Avenue
Decatur, GA 30030
Website: www.agnesscott.edu
Admissions Telephone: 800-868-8602
Undergraduates: 862 Women

Physical Environment

Agnes Scott College is located a few miles from the center of Atlanta, in Decatur, a very cosmopolitan and welcoming suburb. The vibrant pace of the capital infuses energy and opportunities into the lives of the women at this college. The public subway line, MARTA, starts at the airport and makes the city accessible. Students stop at the Decatur station to get to the Agnes Scott campus or travel to and from an internship in the city. A few blocks from campus there are vibrant small businesses and boutiques. There are coffee shops that make comfy study spots off campus. The Starbucks and Java Monkey often appeal to students who want their latte while reviewing the umpteenth chapter of Organic Chemistry before a final exam.

Once on campus, the 100-acre treed setting feels quiet, cool and comfortable. The campus was established around the 1900s and has a mix of collegiate architecture and Victorian-style buildings, some of which are slated for a sustainability update. It has a deep sense of history. In 1886 Agnes Scott College started out as the Decatur Seminary for Women and certain buildings have a clear spiritual feel, especially Main Hall and Rebekah Scott Hall, connected by a charming outdoor passageway. These were the first buildings on campus. Some of today's students may still have future seminary aspirations.

The academic buildings are located on a long rectangular stretch of land that ends with a pond, used for researching birds and wildlife and their habitat. Many women here are **ecologically minded** and care about protecting the environment.

The weather in Atlanta is warm most of the year, and so swimming and tennis are two very popular sports at Agnes Scott College. Many "Scotties" participate in Division III sports.

Social Environment

"Scotties" like to learn, to express the truth and to make the world a better place for everyone. They accept the Honor Code which allows them to schedule their exams when they want to take them. "Scotties" are encouraged to behave **honorably**. This is part of the Agnes Scott experience. The college takes in high school graduates and expects them to become a force in society. The end result is critical here. They don't expect graduates to become a vice-president immediately, but they sure want you to become somebody eventually—they are interested in the reality of you doing something important with your life. Thus they like helping others while taking care of themselves as well. There is an implicit sense that excessive stress should be avoided. They may join the meditation group, or go to the dance studio for some exercise or yoga, or may prepare a social dance. Many become active in volunteer efforts, others join the women in business group. There is a wide variety of women here, some looking for that classic liberal arts education, others for liberal arts with an exposure to business or the pre-med, pre-teacher education.

Some undergraduates are members of academic honors organizations such as **Phi Beta Kappa** and Dana Scholars. Religious organizations, including the Baptist Student Union and the Fellowship of Christian Students, are well received by the student body. Undergraduates are very involved on campus and assert themselves in a polite manner. **Leadership** is valued by the entire community with students taking a stand on many issues, from politics to ecology. Their clubs and organizations function to benefit the entire college campus. They actively make their views known in the school paper. The process of becoming is as important as the end goal itself. "Scotties" believe in themselves, and so they are able to assert themselves, to **speak out** for the purpose of making improvements, whether in their life or at the college or in society. They do so actively yet avoiding the most radical of positions. Bright, competent, mindful women graduate Agnes Scott.

Compatibility with Personality Types and Preferences

Undergraduates at Agnes Scott College are often activist in their approach to learning. The women come to this campus to secure professional skills and gain entry into the marketplace. The student body might define competency as expertise within a field. Competency is also defined as communication and persuasion to enact new processes (P) in a discipline. Undergraduates look to traditions but embrace change here. Faculty and administration follow a similar trajectory. Most areas of study are familiar, traditional (J) subjects found at liberal arts colleges, yet, there is a strong program to interface students with fast-paced Atlanta. Neither students nor professors shy away from the dynamic enterprise of this rapidly growing city.

The directional factors that propel this small, unique women's college in the 21st century seem to center on justice and access. Religious tradition and faith, originally the centerpiece in founding Agnes Scott College, have found their voices through study of these contemporary American issues (E). Students are accepting of ideas that encompass the unknown (N). Graduates expect to become actively engaged with their communities. They anticipate opportunities to solve tomorrow's problems. They expect to bring talent and leadership to the table for this purpose. Agnes Scott graduates are measured and confident at the same time.

In the following listing of college majors it is important to remember that students can fit into any college and can be successful in any major. We have found that the Personality Types below fit very well at this college. The course-of-study chosen for each Personality Type corresponds to MBTI® research and is presented as an example favorable for that type.

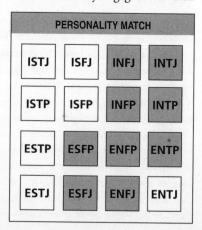

PERSONALITY MATCH			
ISTJ	ISFJ	INFJ	INTJ
ISTP	ISFP	INFP	INTP
ESTP	ESFP	ENFP	ENTP
ESTJ	ESFJ	ENFJ	ENTJ

INFP likes to ponder and examine their own values and those of others. This habit is going to be an asset at Agnes Scott. The campus is a blend of modern day American social currents and traditions of past years. It is an environment in which diverse social viewpoints are welcomed. INFP will take notice and appreciate this. The minor in Educational Studies prompts discussion about the best ways to develop critical thinking and provide high school graduates with a basic foundation of knowledge needed in society today. Sensitive INFP will find a real appreciation of both the children and the challenge during the internship semester offered in a public school.

INFJ is very inclined to follow their beliefs into a profession or work setting and often it is one that helps or cares for others. They have a passion for understanding the human condition, theirs and others. The faculty at Agnes Scott College offers a major or minor in **Religious Studies** that reveals the foundations of religions across the world. Spirituality naturally lends itself to introspection and INFJs prefer to mull their thoughts over with others as they incorporate observations into personal beliefs. Never fear, INFJ is more than up to this challenge and likely to find other passionate undergraduates on this campus excited to talk about life's meaning.

INTJ will likely enjoy the very abstract nature of studying **Biology** at Agnes Scott College. Students approach studies in this major through the lens of process, advanced technology and evolution. Very little is static in the curriculum, and facts are accumulated to find their way into the big picture. Courses in biology at this college require a great deal of intuition in addition to the sweat equity associated with comprehending basic, essential biological processes. The department offers a selection of courses across this growing discipline from evolution, genetics, and ecology to botany. INTJ will take advantage of this variety to identify a focus for the likely graduate studies they will pursue after graduation. It is ideal for INTJ to study biology in this manner.

INTP is drawn to the impossible, well at least the hard-to-understand. The degree in **Physics** should suit INTPs for this reason. The labs and intense logical, objective reasoning within this science are comfortable arenas for this type. The unknown, at least unseen, nature of the physics generates plenty of abstraction. There is tolerance to dwell on the process within this discipline of physics. There is much less dwelling on the resultant loud bangs, hissing sounds or clouds of unpleasant odors. Again, this is just right for INTP who wants to focus on the how-it-happened rather than the after-the-fact collection of hisses, bangs and odors.

ESFP can be very coordinated usually. This combined with their penchant for entertaining others, including themselves, points to the Agnes Scott major in **Dance.** The college offers an enviable selection of courses in this department. They include lesser known dance concepts such as the Laban which focuses on movement as an art form with analysis of the physical movements. The curriculum includes a balance of dance forms, dance history, techniques and expression. ESFP will appreciate the versatility of study within this degree at Agnes Scott as well as the career options for performance, teaching and possibly choreography after graduation.

ENFP often desires freedom and intellectual space to pursue their ideas. Business environments that offer this will bring out the entrepreneurial spirit in this type. The degree in **Economics** at Agnes Scott College allows ENFPs to study economic theory and application through the big picture lens. The type's insight and creativity is very helpful with the abstract nature of courses focused on resource allocation. Spontaneous and enthusiastic, with little patience for getting bogged down, their participation will be positive in college and on the job in the dynamic world of finance.

ENTP can look to the **Mathematics** major to take advantage of their strengths. Mathematics professors are actively connecting math with the power the discipline brings to society and humankind. ENTP is all about these kind of very large concepts and important positions within society. Given this motivating presentation of mathematical prowess and an inclination for math, ENTP will be willing to declare the math major. Along the way, any number of interesting applications and careers will fly through their active mind. This degree combines nicely with ENTPs natural confidence. It is likely to give them entry to important work environments and mathematical research applied to improving everyday life.

ESFJ and the **Chemistry** major at Agnes Scott is a duo that can work. The department is focused on practice and development in research design. It is a hands-on experience course of study that is very practical. The major prepares graduates for entrance into medical diagnostic specialties, teaching or pharmaceuticals. Each of these fields can bring ESFJs together directly with those in need of their knowledge and skills. Agnes Scott actively includes research experimental design in their curriculum. This approach often requires collaboration with others and conscientious follow through. Both of these are characteristic strengths of the ESFJ.

ENFJ could be quite happy with the quality and variety of course work in **English** offered at Agnes Scott College. This type is fond of gathering insight and information that leads to the understanding of others. The study of literature is excellent training ground for this since human motivation and human awareness are the focus of most literature. ENFJ is a skilled facilitator, often leaning on their warm interpersonal relationships with others. Reading between the lines comes naturally for ENFJs as well as analysis of literature. Polished and decisive, they will likely move into the world of journalism and persuasive communications with success.

AMERICAN UNIVERSITY

Office of Admissions
4400 Massachusetts Avenue, NW
Washington, DC 20016
Website: www.american.edu
Admissions Telephone: 202-885-6000
Undergraduates: 6,130; 2,529 Men, 3,601 Women
Graduate Students: 1,599

Physical Environment

Located in the northwest part of the nation's capital, American University takes advantage of its location to observe **Washington's politics**, press core and socio-economic issues affecting our nation and the world. The campus architecture features many square and rectangular cement buildings that remind us of government structures. The lawns between the buildings are free of flower beds and other frills, except for the occasional bench. In this setting, undergraduates are likely to wear business attire to class on occasion. Yet they work out in the well-equipped health club without need for well known sports fashion. The setting is inviting to the serious student who is interested in understanding **substantive issues** that can be acted upon. These issues are political, social or environmental.

There are seven residence halls on the main campus to choose from themed housing to a volunteer service floor, Honors floor and **international/intercultural** hall. The school of Public Affairs on the Ward Circle Building has high-tech classrooms. Kogod School of Business bulked up with high end tech features in its newest expansion. The nearby Kay Spiritual Life Center draws undergraduates of various religious beliefs.

The nation's capital is AU's extended campus. Taking a short bus ride and then the METRO, students are soon at Dupont Circle. American University does not fight or ignore **the pull of the city**. The university career office has contacts with 500 internship providers in the area. Students will gain job exposure in Washington and many seek to secure permanent jobs in DC.

Social Environment

Students who fit in well at American University are **independently motivated** and can achieve their goals. They are not shy and typically take advantage of all that American U and Washington, DC have to offer. Students will likely be at venues with well-known speakers. They will participate in events around the capital, from attending political debates to demonstrations. Students' goals are usually connected with journalism, broadcasting, political science and national and world politics.

Undergraduates often come with established leadership skills and direct their academic and social experience with purpose. They start establishing their network with students hailing from all corners of the world, children of dignitaries stationed in Washington and American students from across the country and socioeconomic spectrum. Students have access to strong departments of foreign languages often seeking out off campus study to become proficient in their foreign language.

Upon graduation, some will become government employees, secret service agents, economists or journalists.

The undergraduate student at AU will experience some competition in securing internships in DC. However, they are typically up to the task. This may entail scouting out internships and making personal contact with professors who may also have other government jobs besides lecturing. AU is for students who like to study democracy in a practical way, such as analyzing a system of ballot collection. They enjoy visiting historic monuments, partaking in rallies and journalistic events.

In the dorms, students create a home away from home as they forge relationships by introducing themselves to others on their floor. Sports at AU don't monopolize the social scene nor do they define the school spirit. AU is a Division 1 member of the Patriot's League. It has no football but the Eagles basketball and volleyball teams are sufficient to keep fans entertained.

Compatibility with Personality Types and Preferences

American University is strategically and culturally placed in the diplomatic neighborhoods of Washington, DC. For all educational purposes, there is a permeable boundary between this University and the power offices in DC. Prospective students are alerted to the fact that professors often have positions in policy making throughout the government. The faculty and staff assertively take advantage of their proximity to the nation's capitol. The university has a long established network which it activates on behalf of its undergraduate students.

Happy students at American University can't wait to step foot in the office (E) of their first internship. Many of these positions are within the halls of the congressional offices but the city also hosts hundreds of national offices for business and other enterprises. Students are exposed to multiple worldwide ethnicities by venturing into the city for entertainment The American University curriculum is designed for those with a passion plus a driving need to accomplish (J). Those drawn to this university are pretty sure of their convictions. Most desire a career track at international policy levels or within U.S. governmental departments that play across the international scene. Starting out as freshmen they search out the major or minors that move them toward their interests in health, politics, business, communication, social science, etc. Prior to graduation, students will have well explored and likely settled in on a career goal (S) such as campaign manager or nonprofit executive. Their international perspectives are refined through the university's academic philosophies and the amazing international presence in the nation's capitol.

In the following listing of college majors it is important to remember that students can fit into any college and can be successful in any major. We have found that the Personality Types below fit very well at this college. The course-of-study

PERSONALITY MATCH			
ISTJ	ISFJ	INFJ	INTJ
ISTP	ISFP	INFP	INTP
ESTP	ESFP	ENFP	ENTP
ESTJ	ESFJ	ENFJ	ENTJ

chosen for each Personality Type corresponds to MBTI® research and is presented as an example favorable for that type.

INTJ is compelled to privately generate new concepts and ideas. The Bachelor of Science degree in **Economics** at American University with an emphasis in theory will be ideal for this type. The coursework is rich with options for theoretical interpretation. It has multiple points of entry to determine an economic perspective. INTJs will take this as an invitation to develop their own scenarios as they carefully grasp information presented in class lectures. This type can do both at once.

ISTP is attracted to facts, details and information that have a practical use. The degree in **Anthropology** at American University has a reality based focus which suits ISTPs who ordinarily shy away from this abstract field. Looking a few layers deeper, ISTPs realize the discipline has the potential to be an excellent fit. The archeologist, a subfield of anthropology, searches for hard, specific clues that could reveal much about an ancient city or culture. It is a strongly featured discipline within the department at American University. Internships and work experience in national research libraries such as the Smithsonian and National Museum of American History offer ISTPs the reality base they prefer.

ISTJ is going to like the looks of the Bachelor of Arts degree in **Justice**. It thoroughly surveys all the types of social institutions that deal with criminal behavior. At American University, the curriculum leans heavily toward the policy of dealing with criminal activity. Course work focuses on justice as public government functions and enforces criminal policy. ISTJ is practical in their daily work habits and attitudes. They honor fairness and following procedure, and each of these characteristics is quite desirable for a civil service careers in justice. ISTJs understand that supporting the criminal justice system is also protecting and serving the community. It is all very appealing to this type who is often dependable and conservative by nature.

INTP can be drawn to mathematics if their endeavors can be used as a tool to solve problems. Considering this, INTP will like a degree such as American University's **Applied Mathematics.** This type is always thinking, always defining and analyzing subjects of interest to them. Undergraduates in this math degree can follow their interests and bring the power of math analysis to the research in important national agencies—all within walking or subway stop distance. The National Archives would present innumerable options for a research design. This type would probably also enjoy looking at the rare, historical math volumes in the university archives. This collection will surely spark a few minutes of INTP thought about the lives of those earlier mathematicians.

ESTP could go for the **Law and Society** degree at American University because this type has the ability to meet others and quickly establish a working rapport. ESTPs will also find fascinating options for co-op and internships across the DC governmental agencies. This type's desire to learn in a fast-paced, experiential environment affords them the possibility to troubleshoot or bring about a settlement through their skilled negotiation. At American University there is a balance between academic study and hands-on experience. The curriculum is crafted for those desiring to go on to law school and it offers an American as well as international perspective in legal studies. As a result, ESTPs may also explore and could pursue international legal services.

ESFP is well suited for the 24 hour news cycle. The degree in **Public Communication** at American University is chock full of arguably the best foundation courses. ESFPs need only to turn on the computer or TV to study the government releases moving across the airwaves in this capital. ESFPs live and work in the present day and the current week. They are not inclined to give much attention to the distant future. Instead, they superbly pick up on what is going on around them, not missing a beat. They typically relay that observation with enthusiasm and social finesse. This degree—at this university—for this type—is a stellar choice.

ENTP loves to look into the future with other interested students and a professor willing to speculate. This speculation is an ENTP's forte. Without much effort, they take in the spectrum of any discipline, indulge their curiosity by taking a random class and write an odd, original paper. Variety and complexity is the key to success for this type. The major in **American Studies** at American University has both. The curriculum moves toward understanding complex American culture by highlighting historical cause and effect that can be put to use today. ENTPs might enter any of several different career fields: business, journalism, cultural art, teaching and foreign service or a graduate school with this degree.

ESFJ is most often the cheerleader for an organization. They reliably pull for the team rewarding both the fans and players for their participation. Students in the elementary classroom thrive with a teacher who so rewards and appreciates traditional effort and duty. The degree in **Elementary Education** at American University has an exceptionally fine program for future teachers. Undergraduates will spend considerable time observing and practice teaching in urban and suburban DC schools. The ethical emphasis for public educators in our society to empower and enlighten the next generation is a focus of American's curriculum. Very social, almost always pleasant, ESFJs bring stability and caring to their classrooms, yet it will be their curiosity about others that might draw them into educational research.

ESTJ wants to live the responsible and sensible life—in the dorm, in college classes and thereafter. Order is a need and usually a talent for this type. Take charge ESTJs would enjoy the precise nature of the scientific courses in the medical health fields. The Bachelor of Science in **Health Promotion** is bolstered with strategic internships in DC such as the Department of Health and Human Services. ESTJs will find the interdisciplinary nature of the curriculum helpful because of the systematic exposure to all the options for specialization within the broad health field. The degree also leaves open the door for graduate work in medical research. The university sponsors research in human performance with a state of the art laboratory that focuses on diagnostic practices.

ENTJ with a political passion quickly recognizes that American University has several degrees tailored specifically for their strengths and interests. The degree in **Political Science** has a rich and unique curriculum. Unusual courses in the curriculum include Ancient Political Thought that examines the world of Socrates, Plato, Aristotle and ancient Roman law not from the philosophical perspective but from political, civic views. Metropolitan Politics covers the political nature of the city with its suburbs rather than the social nature of the city. ENTJs are power players themselves and would not shrink from the deterministic nature of this discipline. The Peace and Conflict Resolution semester held at American University will also help ENTJ prepare for a career in politics or government.

AMHERST COLLEGE

P.O. Box 5000
Amherst, MA 01002-5000
Website: www.amherst.edu
Admissions Telephone: 413-542-2328
Undergraduates: 1,795; 886 Men, 909 Women

Physical Environment

The beautiful Amherst campus spreads out over 1,000 acres, overlooking the Holyoke mountain range of western Massachusetts. Students enjoy the sweeping views and use the many hiking trails. The first year orientation program generates **friendships** among the students who come from many different backgrounds. Plants and well-aged trees on the campus create a similar garden feel as Emily Dickinson's nearby home. The Lord Jeffrey Inn, a fixture of the college and the town of Amherst, was renovated in 2011, retaining its historic charm. Some of the Amherst students are drawn away from their books by this type of natural setting. The sheer beauty of the college compels 98 percent of the students to stay on campus all four years. Some will take advantage of the charming, artsy town right outside their door. A few others will be attracted to the hustle and bustle of social activates at the large state university in town. A small number take the shuttle bus to the other five colleges in the consortium that offer a limited number of cross registration opportunities.

Social Environment

Amherst College is an ideal setting for students who like to be a big fish in a small pond and love to learn. There are many **talented equals** on this campus, and yet all are noticed. Students will leave their brand and legacy. They are interested in almost everything they learn to become proficient at problem solving and easily draw **logical conclusions**. They have a strong sense of culture, so they like visiting art galleries, planetariums and discussing projects and assignments together in their dorm rooms. Students are most likely to throw a party to celebrate others' nationalities, customs and religious holidays. The international perspective cannot be underestimated on campus with faculty coming from around the globe.

The heavy academic rigor channels the social life of the student body, composed primarily of high school valedictorians. Comfortable in the **world of ideas**, these bright and self-directed students form a vibrant and diverse community of leaders. Bright, underprivileged students are well represented at Amherst. Amherst students are comfortable socializing across varied social and economic backgrounds as well as addressing multi-cultural issues. This shapes their perspectives as they chart their individual course of liberal studies. Amherst students can be super-studious and **intense,** even overly-invested in their tasks, yet always efficient finding time to analyze the broad issues facing the world's future. They present outstanding academic qualifications and individual accomplishments.

Compatibility with Personality Types and Preferences

With its orderly approach to offering a unique and wide ranging curriculum, Amherst appeals to personalities that are comfortable with structure and accountability (J). At the same time, there is a wide, free range of choice within the pathways of any particular major or course of studies. A personality that prefers to rationally analyze (T) all the alternatives may be annoyed, especially in the first few semesters with the tight 'channeling' of curriculum selection, but in the long run, they will have great freedom within their chosen major with the amazing courses offered at this college. Students with a love of facts and details (S) will find this strength helps them with the 'accountability' piece and the sheer academic production that will be required at this most selective liberal arts college.

Students on this campus learn by lively discussion and free exchange of ideas. They equally converse with each other and faculty. They observe, read, discuss, observe some more, read some more and exhaustively survey the foundations within a discipline. Then there is an internal mandate within the undergraduate student body that each individual will analyze the heck out of that foundational information, the point of this analysis being to plumb the depths and to create new knowledge, to synthesize a personal understanding.

The administration and faculty believe this process takes place primarily on campus. The libraries, coffee shops, dormitories, lecture halls and professor's offices are all fair game for learning locations. Basically at Amherst learning occurs anywhere that is sufficiently free of distractions which could sidetrack the student from reaching the most comprehensive understanding of their discipline. Undergraduates are expected to sample and secure individual interface with the Amherst curriculum as it represents the sum of current knowledge in academia today. Undergraduates must master their own major as well as develop an intense awareness outside of their declared discipline. On the journey through this very reasoned learning environment, students receive sufficient, occasional reminders of the difficult world that awaits them on graduation. Their ability to deal with unsettled, dynamic America is secured through their intense preparation for an intellectually purposeful life.

In the following listing of college majors it is important to remember that students can fit into any college and can be successful in any major. We have found that the Personality Types below fit very well at this college. The course-of-study chosen for each Personality Type corresponds to MBTI® research and is presented as an example favorable for that type.

PERSONALITY MATCH			
ISTJ	ISFJ	INFJ	INTJ
ISTP	ISFP	INFP	INTP
ESTP	ESFP	ENFP	ENTP
ESTJ	ESFJ	ENFJ	ENTJ

ISFJ with a spiritual bent will like the **Religion** major at Amherst College. This very caring and attentive type will find the structure they need to comfortably work with their advisor in this abstract field. Three areas are required for mastery that allows undergraduates to successfully pursue graduate study. They are precise knowledge of one particular religion, general knowledge of a second religion and the skills for prescient research in this historical discipline that strikes at the heart and soul of mankind.

ENTP will be attracted to the **Law, Jurisprudence and Social Thought** major. They like to jump into difficult wide ranging discussions that are elusive of finite truths. In the course titled Law, Speech, and the Politics of Freedom, Amherst students attempt to make sense of the multiple interpretations of the words 'free,' 'speech' and 'speaker' in an attempt to define dangerous, anarchic, politically correct speech and public discourse, the understanding of which is critical for civilizations.

INTJ with a penchant for mathematics will probably make room in the schedule for **Philosophy of Mathematics**. This course explores the three philosophies of math that evolved in the 20th century—logicism, intuitionism and finitism. This personality preference is great at mulling over the possibilities privately, in their mind, as they stroll across a quadrangle to dinner. Perhaps during dessert they will come up with experimental algorithms for pushing math philosophy forward in the 21st century.

ENFJ finds that no matter what major they select, their idealism will be honored in the **Five College African Studies** Certificate Program. It complements any major selected at Amherst and will establish credentials for caring, organized ENFJs to work for world organizations providing services to the African continent. Improving and focusing on community and generating basic human services would come naturally to this type.

INTP can become absorbed in the **Physics** Department approach. Their course offerings delve into the past, recreate landmark experiments by masters such as Faraday, allow students to discover the results and interface their observations with the current and emerging theories in physics today. New technology in laser application and photonics is clearly something that would appeal to this curious, flexible deep thinking type.

INFJ could conclude that **American Studies** is a delightful course of studies at Amherst. This type might observe that the major attempts to refine and reach a whole, meaningful description of American society. Coming to understand America is a large job, with its multicultural society and constitution that guarantees the rights of all peoples. The course The City: New York studies this resilient metropolis as a culture representative of urban life in America. INFJs will arrive at their own internal perspective of September 11th as well as of the memorial to the victims and the grave harm inflicted on our nation.

ISTP might like the **Film and Media Studies** curriculum. The courses which explore film and video are compelling and allow this technical personality preference to delve into the digital representations and techniques in producing the moving image. Marching to their own drummer, ISTPs want freedom to wrap these courses into their declared major at Amherst. The college is supportive since film and video courses appear throughout the curriculum such as the Weimar Cinema: The "Golden Age" of German Film in the German department.

ESTJ will be on time to make the required early declaration in the **Neuroscience** major at Amherst College. This type understands and approves of preplanning with a goal. The elbow grease and interdisciplinary nature of the courses in this major work perfectly as preparation for post graduate study in medicine, law and the sciences. ESTJs can see the sense in the well structured, somewhat conventional and somewhat novel work involved in this major.

ISTJ could find that **Psychology** at Amherst is going to work because of the academic depth and breadth in the department. ISTJs like to become masterful in their selected courses and the alpha to omega is covered by the Amherst curriculum in this fast evolving field. Courses reach beyond senior year academics and run from the study of memory, to the psychology of leadership, to the rigorous research methods and more. The way psychology is taught at Amherst is ideal for this type because of the extensive exposure and preparation to successfully pursue the PhD level of studies. ISTJs find research in the psychological discipline rewarding because of its precise nature.

ENTJ will appreciate the extraordinary breadth and currency of the curriculum offered through the **Economics** department at Amherst. From game theory to the economics of poverty to the nuts and bolts of micro and macroeconomics, the faculty and courses present a sweeping look at this complex discipline. ENTJs rarely shy away from complexity or large concepts. In fact, they thrive on elements inherent to demanding social movements within our society. Studying the human weave between politics, policy and resources is likely to compel young, energetic ENTJs.

BATES COLLEGE

23 Campus Avenue
Lewiston, ME 04240-6098
Website: www.bates.edu
Admissions Telephone: 207-786-6000
Undergraduates: 1,725; 796 Men, 929 Women

Physical Environment

Bates College is located in the Lewiston area, about 35 miles north of Portland. These are former mill-towns that grew on the banks of the river during the industrial revolution. Although most students stay on campus during the weekend, there are restaurants and malls within a short distance where students buy top quality winter clothing. There are many opportunities for **outdoor recreation** and students participate and compete in alpine and cross-country skiing. Students like hands-on experience and utilize the **coastal Maine environment** to conduct chemistry and geology research and experiment to learn from nature. The 109-acre Bates campus is surrounded by a residential neighborhood and a lake in the center. This pond is referred to as "the puddle" where students skate and play hockey during wintertime. The architecture is a mixture of modern and historic buildings. The Dining Commons hall, a starkly modern building, has multi-story windows with pretty views of the alumni walk and the trees on campus. This new and imposing student center supplanted Memorial Commons in Chase Hall, an old, well-worn facility that felt soft and warm in comparison to the new architecture on campus. The Hedge and Roger Williams Project furthers Bates academic philosophy by providing social learning spaces designed for faculty and students to informally cross paths.

Creative students are drawn to the Olin Arts Center, by the pond, which has an art museum, a theater and the music and fine arts studios. The sofas and lounge areas add a comfortable feel to this building for the eclectic, imaginative Bates student.

Social Environment

Bates students are uniquely **different from one another**. They arrive on campus with surprisingly different interests and an insatiable curiosity. They are seekers. They don't exactly follow the status quo. They leave high school personas behind and become socially and intellectually sophisticated students in an alternative style. Those students who were into intellectual Goth or Anime in high school find that on this campus they are embraced and accepted for their open and unique artistic qualities. Many undergrads get involved in community service. On the edge of being ironic, students here are comfortable criticizing the status quo, even to their professors with whom they become close. Students often drip with **tongue in cheek humor.**

These students were not likely to have bought into traditional or conventional social activities in high school. Here they want to do something new, different and exciting, while handling an intellectually rigorous course of study that shapes their beliefs and time on campus. Students appreciate using their **fine-tuned writing** and computing skills. There is a certain sense of relaxation in students here, who are laid-back, comfortable in their skin and free to be what they want. There's also a spiritual thread across the curriculum and the students want to apply moral principles to what they learn. They **examine their purpose in life**. Students embrace the ideals of freedom and equality. Bates was founded by the Abolitionists prior to the Civil War and students of color and international students are quite comfortable here. The majority of undergraduates are service oriented and volunteer in local, state, regional and/or national venues.

Over half of the students rank in the top 10 percent of their high school class, and the rest rank in the top quarter of the class. This is an SAT optional college and only 50 percent of students submit their scores. Professors form very close relationships with the students.

Compatibility with Personality Types and Preferences

Bates College is bold. The $\underline{B}$ equals Bold $\mathbf{X}$ Bates^2. In many ways it is like a formula, a straight forward campus. The students, however, are on the cutting edge of straight forward. Unconventional and grounded, Bates undergraduates are in your face if you care to stand in front of them. They are confident in their edginess (P). The courses of instruction here are very interesting. One could say the courses are bold too. The titles keep your eyes glued to the catalog page: Cancer, Extreme Physiology, Plants and Human Affairs, Insects and Human Health and Avian Biology. The above are offered in addition to traditional coursework for the degree in biology, and this humor is typical of other course titles. The faculty and administration have constructed numerous service learning options (F) and tied these together with moral perspectives. It's a win-win situation because so many of the students are involved in service work. The campus environment seems devoted to the future (N). As a result, the compelling nature of the learning environment is to construct a better future. Bates undergraduates would likely agree that the present world conditions are simply not acceptable. Bates College provides the platform to recognize international societal needs and the belief in disciplined improvements for the future

In the following listing of college majors it is important to remember that students can fit into any college and can be successful in any major. We have found that the Personality Types below fit very well at this college. The course-of-study chosen for each Personality Type corresponds to MBTI® research and is presented as an example favorable for that type.

ISFP and the major in **Biology** move in tandem together nicely on this campus. This type likes to mix it up outside with activity and variety. The courses of instruction on this campus are unconventional with many hands-on labs in the open fields and forests of Maine. The quiet and accepting ISFP will fit well into the unconventional ways. At the same time, this type has a real need

PERSONALITY MATCH			
ISTJ	ISFJ	INFJ	INTJ
ISTP	ISFP	INFP	INTP
ESTP	ESFP	ENFP	ENTP
ESTJ	ESFJ	ENFJ	ENTJ

to develop their deeply held values. Bates' philosophy of education interfaces with moral perspectives.

INFP might like the **African American Studies** at Bates College. The courses of instruction are particularly rich here. This reflects the administration philosophy which is strongly tolerant, almost, but not quite, Quaker-like. Regardless of ethnicity, the INFP will delight in the depth and breadth of this course of study. On graduation, they would be exceptionally well qualified for organizations pursuing African American perspectives in the work place.

ENFJ has a penchant for the dramatic. This type's fine ability to connect with others could be further fine tuned with Bates major in **Rhetoric.** At Bates, the undergraduate can select a concentration in theory and criticism or film and television studies. Either way, the ENFJ will naturally excel at presenting information in a way that helps others. Supporting others, as in Be All You Can Be, is important for this type.

ESFJ is likely to enjoy the course Community Education/Community Action. It reviews the nature of the full service school in American neighborhoods. Being organized and delivering personal services to large groups of children is right up the alley of this type. The minor in **Education** at Bates College looks at the provoking issues in elementary and secondary education. This minor in education presents a rich selection of educational courses for ESFJ who is always curious about others and genuine in helping them move forward.

ENFP would likely excel as a research assistant in academic environments. How about the **American Cultural Studies** as a potential major for this fun-loving type? The broad nature of this degree really appeals to this big picture type. It is an interdisciplinary program and ENFP gets to pick the exciting courses in each field at eclectic Bates College. Maybe they will register for The Age of the American Revolution, 1763-1789, The Photograph as a Document, or Gibbons, The Decline and Fall of the Roman Empire. This last as it relates to western civilization and American history.

ISFJ will probably like the expansive courses available in the **Religious Studies** major. There are representative courses of religions around the world with more emphasis seemingly placed on cultural expressions of faith. Mystic literature, medieval religious practices, Greek and Roman Myths and ancient gods all lend a historical perspective to the religious studies at Bates College. Humanistic perspectives are woven into the comparative approach to this major. Reflective and calm, ISFPs will likely gather in the information and quietly construct their spiritual and religious thoughts into a personal, cohesive belief.

INFJ with artistic interests will find the **Art and Visual Culture** major quite desirable. The studies are likely to be dripping with symbolism here at Bates College with its emphasis on international culture. With this major, the INFJ might move into the world of visual design. This type's independence and creativity will be strong assets for developing public and private events at galleries, museums, corporations and civic associations.

INTJ will find academic roaming room in the **Psychology** major at Bates College. There are four content areas: biological-health, developmental-personality, cognition-emotion, and cultural-social. These four allow the undergraduate INTJ to survey the discipline while looking for that exploratory nook within the expanse of human personality. While pondering, INTJs are also likely to come up with new avenues for research along the way to a PhD in psychology or perhaps neuroscience.

INTP who was fascinated with the night sky in elementary school might just decide to major in **Astronomy** at Bates College. The courses in astronomy also work nicely with the **Geology** major. These two fields together, as double major, have more than enough unsolved puzzles to keep INTPs busy searching for patterns and answers throughout their lifetime, and it will be the INTPs who stay with it until they have solved at least one of the mysteries in our universe.

ENTP has a pretty deep reservoir of energy for their projects. This type with some talent for numbers will enjoy studying **Economics** at Bates College. With the basics of micro and macroeconomics completed, the ENTP can further focus with the course, international financial stability. It is the optimistic ENTP, very capable of impersonal analysis, who might be working for an economic institution in the coming years. Charged with finding ways out of financial crises could become a career for this type!

BELOIT COLLEGE

Office of Admission
700 College Street
Beloit, WI 53511
Website: www.beloit.edu
Admissions Telephone: 608-363-2500
Undergraduates: 1,397; 569 Men, 755 Women

Physical Environment

"You don't voluntarily move to Wisconsin" says a Beloit student who comes from California, however, this is where she felt **compelled to come**. The college is on the Wisconsin-Illinois line and is accessible from the airports of Chicago, Milwaukee and Madison. The city of Beloit is rather quiet, recalling its earlier paper and pulp industry now transitioning to artistic and niche industry. The campus is located in a residential neighborhood near the town center. Beloit College was designed by a group of prominent folks from New England and hence it has a northeastern look to its architecture.

Many students live in **"theme" houses** around the perimeter of campus in old Victorian and Colonial homes, and form their own small communities bound by common interests. There are a few Greek houses as well, and they focus on community service initiatives. First-year students reside at 840 College and 609 Emerson Street, where the lounges are ideal places for students to congregate, to watch shows and to bond together for the four years. The administration's emphasis is on creating an environment where students can live and learn at the same time. To this end, a state of the art modern science complex was built between the living and academic areas of the campus. It bridges the social spaces with learning laboratories and promotes collaborative work.

The Beloit art and anthropology museums offer students a real life experience as curators as well as exhibiting artists. These museums are open to the community and add an intellectual and **artistic influence** to this small community composed of college and city. The Hendricks Center for the Arts, opened in November 2010, is a delight for musicians, dancers and artistic technophiles complete with a lighting design studio.

Social Environment

High school students who moved outside of the conventional high school social groups like Beloit College because here it's perfectly all right to have "your own sort of interests" and to express them in "your own way." Undergraduates here want to continue avoiding the status quo. They mostly embrace a **very crunchy and artsy lifestyle** or politically express themselves by leaning to the left of center. Students accept that everyone is honored for their different talents here. Some within the community look for common ground with society and seek harmony through their educational studies. A good number choose the vegetarian way.

Incoming students might declare a passion for Faulkner while enrolling in other courses with little relation to his literary themes. The reality is that these students are scholarly and proud of it. If they are reading Machiavelli they engage the text and seek to make connections between theory and practice. They may link 11th century Chinese wisdom with management problems in the 21st century. There is a strong desire to live and practice what they learn so they become engaged in political campaigns or volunteer with Big Brothers/Big Sisters and Habitat for Humanity. Students at their core are **sensitive, caring and open** to other possible ways of living and understanding. The smallness of this community helps them try out and practice those concepts.

The college supports this personal examination by reintroducing familiar texts but with completely fresh levels of interpretation. Beloit College is likely to open up many options for students so it's not unnatural for them to change their majors while moving forward to integrate and apply new knowledge. The small town, Beloit experience is nicely juxtaposed with the openness in their social environment on campus. The interesting student personalities add spice to the educational studies. Graduates will be shaped by their desire to make a difference and change this world for the better.

Compatibility with Personality Types and Preferences

Beloit College is dedicated to reasoned learning. While the faculty and administration remain open to many perspectives (P), students are expected to arrive at their own cohesive view of the world. There are many avenues that provide encouragement to examine national and world perspectives for this purpose. Students explore their beliefs through the lens of their academic courses and outside of the classroom. Often the topics will be addressed from a humane point of view (F). Many become socially active and bring their perspectives into campus clubs and events. There is a hands-on, observational approach to the course work. Students move through their educational studies with a measured process, observing, collecting and arranging information into meaningful knowledge. The campus academic energy channels this type of analysis in a way that is thoughtful, articulate and caring. Conversations can be free-wheeling and oriented from many directions, but students are definitely reaching for a position, a justifiable observation. At Beloit, there is an ever present undercurrent in learning and purpose to education at large that often translates to political or social positions. Undergraduates tend toward the unconventional because it offers another filter to understand what they observe. The successful student at Beloit College is one who does not feel bound to the traditions and longing for their hometown. Instead, there is commitment to listening to fellow students who are each on their quest to build an individual view of the world. Graduates have a sensitive, reasoned and reflective approach to life and life's work.

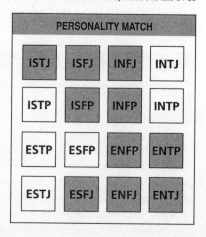

PERSONALITY MATCH

ISTJ	ISFJ	INFJ	INTJ
ISTP	ISFP	INFP	INTP
ESTP	ESFP	ENFP	ENTP
ESTJ	ESFJ	ENFJ	ENTJ

In the following listing of college majors it is important to remember that students can fit into any college and can be successful in any major. We have found that the Personality Types below fit very well at this college. The course-of-study chosen for each Personality Type corresponds to MBTI® research and is presented as an example favorable for that type.

INFP should find the study of **History** truly designed with their learning style in mind at Beloit College. The department approaches history as an explanation of human motivation and human endeavors. Undergraduates search for patterns that created stability and security for the historical period. This is an ideal approach for INFP who delights in plumbing the depths of abstract information. Studying history in this way also allows for originality and insight, both of which INFP has in abundance.

INFJ doesn't often relate to classic entrepreneurial business coursework. However, at Beloit College this type will find the major in **Economics and Management** suits them well. The department keeps the curriculum flexible. Undergraduates must reach their own perspective of world economies and learn of ways to interface their understanding in the world of business, profit or non-profit. The INFJ is fine with this. They can be creative, caring and proud of their work. All three are pretty important for this type.

ISTJ will find the **Molecular, Cellular and Biology** major focuses on proposing and probing hypotheses. It is an orderly, structured discovery of what is there for the observer. This is an ideal way for ISTJs to learn. This type is considered and reasoned in their approach to learning and Beloit is a fine collegiate environment for their learning style. Though they are not inclined to be alternative in thinking, the ISTJ will relate to the reasoning process which is so prevalent on this campus. This major will give them a traditional preparation for graduate school in the health sciences.

ISFJ wants to express their convictions in a low key way. This type is also a master at details with a fabulous memory for them. The major in **Science for Elementary Teaching** at Beloit College is an excellent choice for this type. Their content course work in the biology department approaches learning through analysis of what can be observed. This type's appreciation of fine detail will be such an asset in this precise environment. Their inclination to find personal meaning through quiet reflection will be rewarded on this campus of searchers for life's truths.

ISFP will find the art department at Beloit College particularly rich with expansive thinking. The **Studio Art** major is very much connected to process learning. Students study the process of communicating at length. Written and oral communication underlies the technical courses in drawing and design. The foundational work in communication is supplemented by peer student feedback. Well, that is just swell for ISFP who wants to be a loyal and cooperative member of the community. At Beloit, where individual perspectives are encouraged, feedback will be measured and supportive of meaningful art. Again, this is just swell for ISFP.

ENFP can keep the options open with the unusual major in **Education and Youth Studies** by selecting Track 3—Youth and Society. This concentration prepares students for graduate study in a surprising number of fields, law, social work, mental health, art, coaching, adolescent health services and family research. The ENFP will probably want to sample coursework in most of these. Beloit College requires a full term of field work. ENFP will look on this as an opportunity to select the most interesting research connected with youth services. This type has the vision to align their educational goals with pertinent research in the fields of interest to them.

ENTP could be attracted to the major in **Business Economics** at Beloit College. Typically, the core course work required of business majors would not excite ENTP. However, Beloit College combines the fundamentals found in business with economic theory. Add in the touch of required international courses, developing written communication to convey business analysis and experiential education and you may capture the ENTP imagination. This type will look for creative, innovative applications of those skills in their start up of an off campus organization or search out those flexible internships giving them experimental license.

ESFJ will really like the approach to learning **Chemistry** at Beloit. The department is determined to bring the abstract nature of this field into the labs. Much of the course work is based in inquiry and experimentation using sophisticated instruments found in newer research labs. By replicating recent research designs, students at Beloit follow the chemical pathways through the processes. The department brings together those actual experiments with the abstract learning and microscopic behavior of materials. ESFJ will appreciate this practical, real avenue of learning for the detailed, yet abstract world of chemistry.

ENFJ can be a rather holistic person when it comes to health. They prefer to look at the person's entire environment for the source of illnesses. The major in **Health and Society** at Beloit ensures that undergraduates explore cultural practices, emotional energies and social inequalities as influencing disease processes and treatments. ENFJ appreciates nontraditional health perspectives and Beloit is just the environment to encourage reasoned study of alternative medical practices around the world. This degree is a springboard to graduate studies in the fields of health policy and medicine. At Beloit and in health career paths, ENFJ's warmth and creativity at problem solving will be in much demand.

ENTJ could really appreciate the foundational approach to the expanding, interdisciplinary field of **Psychology.** This field is growing by leaps and bounds looking to explain human behavior in connection with other more traditional sciences like biology, chemistry and sociology. This expansive thinking is exactly what ENTJ does very naturally. This type likes to wrap-it-up after a meaningful exploration of the issue at hand. Not spontaneous by inclination, they will however calculate and skip over information along the way. At Beloit the major in Psychology will prepare this type to move on to graduate study. It also refines ENTJ's natural ability to reason through human behavioral patterns, asking meaningful questions and arriving at meaningful positions.

BOSTON COLLEGE

140 Commonwealth Avenue
Chestnut Hill, MA 02467
Website: www.bc.edu
Admissions Telephone: 617-552-3100
Undergraduates: 9,088; 4,252 Men, 4,836 Women
Graduate Students: 4,818

Physical Environment

All it takes is just a walk through the campus of Boston College for most high school juniors and seniors to fall in love with this university. The view from the main entrance is dotted by the mature trees lining the way to the tower of Gasson Hall, renovated in 2010, which beckons at the end of the road. In 1913, it was the first classroom building on campus, and students studied "recitation," the art of memorizing and public speaking. The collegiate Gothic architecture is repeated in other buildings such as the Burns library that houses rare manuscripts and antique books. The campus physically has a **spiritual feel** parallel to the presence of the Jesuit fathers, many of whom teach classes, hold mass services and interact with students.

The football stadium holds over 44,500 spectators and is a popular place for these **sporty students** and alumni who go all out for their teams and have fanned many victories since the football team joined the Atlantic Coast Conference. The Flynn recreation center is also a favorite place for many students who like intramural sports and want to **keep fit**. Slated for completion in Fall 2012, Stokes Hall adds classrooms for the Humanities departments and new meeting spaces for students to socialize.

Boston College has a self-enclosed campus surrounded by a mature neighborhood of upscale homes and estates. There is public transportation outside the entrance to upper campus. It's the last stop and turn-around for the T, a trolley that runs down the middle of **Commonwealth Avenue**, packed with students from other nearby universities, the Boston Common, coffee shops and rented apartments along the way.

Over the last decades Boston College has experienced significant enrollment growth in both its undergraduate and graduate programs. Despite new residences such as Voute' Hall on the main campus, a second campus in nearby Newton was needed and built. The college provides regular bus service for undergraduates to and from Chestnut Hill. The 40 acre Newton campus supports the law school, a center for conferences and the undergraduate residence halls. Although some students might prefer to reside on the **Chestnut Hill campus**, others are happy enough to live in the **Newton residence halls**. In fact, they claim the food is better there, it's easy to make friends and the bus becomes a meeting place for getting to class together with a friend.

Social Environment

Students at Boston College were high achievers in high school. They carry their ambitions on to college and add an intense and dynamic feel to the classroom and social life. Students from a Catholic background are comfortable here, as are others who are open to taking religion as part of the required core of classes. There are many students whose parents graduated from Boston College, although being a legacy is not enough to gain a spot on the admitted list.

Students come to this college to **study and play hard**. Irish and Italian ethnic perspectives run strongly throughout the student body. Social life is active, vibrant and abundant, yet students here very much care about their grades, their preparation for a well respected and rewarding career and expect to be successful on graduation in the world of work or graduate studies.

The Jesuit presence on campus sets the tone for tolerance and moral conduct. An ethical education is part of the curriculum and student life. **Service to the community** is very important here and virtually no one graduates without having done a considerable amount of work to benefit others in the community. It may be why BC graduates remain a close-knit group of people who support one another up to and after graduation.

Compatibility with Personality Types and Preferences

Boston College with its four undergraduate divisions delineates academic disciplines (T) in a traditional manner for undergraduate students. In our world that is becoming more cross disciplinary, the college offers a unique advising program that helps students identify potential careers. At Boston College the advising process occurs throughout four years of education. Through one on one discussion with student and professors information is offered (S) for exploration. Faculty offering their experience and knowledge is the advising focus for first year students. Off campus retreats and programs specifically for students also connect academic majors with potential careers.

The city of Boston also plays a large part in the nature of academic advising and career exploration. The city lures prospective students for its limitless activities. Once they arrive on campus as freshmen, the undergraduates live in a figurative and literal city noise that permeates their college experience. The frequent trips on the green line to downtown and the excitement of city life must be woven into the traditional academic coursework. The successful Boston College student is one who can weave these two together while incorporating spiritual and moral perspectives with their educational studies. Students come with the expectation that traditional values supporting society will be honored, valued and interfaced with their education.

In the following listing of college majors it is important to remember that students can fit into any college and can be successful in any major. We have found that the Personality Types below fit very well at this college. The course-of-study chosen for each Personality Type corresponds to MBTI® research and is presented as an example favorable for that type.

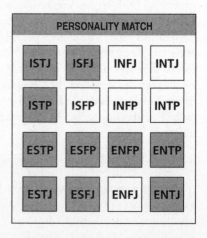

PERSONALITY MATCH

ISTJ	ISFJ	INFJ	INTJ
ISTP	ISFP	INFP	INTP
ESTP	ESFP	ENFP	ENTP
ESTJ	ESFJ	ENFJ	ENTJ

ESTJ will find the **Accounting** major at BC very well tuned to organizations, public and private, international and local, that require sophisticated audits. ESTJs approve of accountability and responsibility so this is a natural fit. They are also objective and typically capable of cutting to the heart of matters efficiently. The School of Management is well resourced and ESTJ's study in accounting will be bolstered by the other majors. Socially, ESTJ is likely to summon their no nonsense approach to filter which enticing Boston events should be sampled each weekend.

ISTJ after college graduation will not likely mind putting on the professional garb and providing accurate, organized and timely services to the customers. The concentration in **Finance** offers the very opportunities which ISTJs excel at— understanding large organizational systems and serving the larger community efficiently and with practicality. Boston College offers a solid array of introductory and advanced classes in this important discipline that ever-prepared ISTJs will want and jump right into from the first day of classes. Relying on their sense of loyalty and fabulous memories, they move through the cumulative courses and secure a financial body of knowledge they so need and prize on graduation.

ENTJ will make good use of the concentration in **Corporate Reporting and Analysis** if they are inclined to management. This type is skilled in leadership and capable of good intuitive observations applied to the near term future. The sequence of courses in this major will prepare often savvy ENTJs to navigate the crucial monetary patterns in financial corporations. Socially, this type will want to be where the action is occurring and that is in the vibrant financial district in downtown Boston during the day and lively suburbs on the weekend.

ENFP might find the **Communication** major at BC very well suited to their style. The curriculum is a solid and somewhat unusual combination of theory and some practical course work. ENFPs are abstract thinkers that need variety. Lectures addressing the theory of how information flows will be enticing for this type. Courses that interface the nuts and bolts of TV productions provide the fun they need too. At BC, discourse on ethics of the media will also rivet ENFP attention if combined with the direction of future marketing practices. ENFP will be energized by fun activities in the city, yet will often remain on campus as frequent participants in student life.

ISFJ will appreciate the degree in **Nursing** at BC with so many top notch hospitals within subway distance. Internships are accessible and this type will appreciate the one-on-one contact with patients during their collegiate years. The degree includes a strong curriculum in diagnosing, therapy and ethical considerations. The ISFJ with their deeply held personal values will strongly relate to the moral perspectives at this Jesuit college. There will be ample opportunities to discuss medical ethics at the off campus retreats offered to undergraduates. When time permits, this type will step out into Boston life, but only after all other responsibilities are completed!

ESFJ can take advantage of the major in **Secondary Education.** All of Boston is available for three required teaching pre practicum followed by a senior year practicum in teaching. This is a strong program and the graduate will have a solid grounding in classroom management. The requirement to double major allows this conscientious type to be thoroughly prepared in the High School classroom. ESFJ is also likely to support and participate in formal BC social events on campus. This type is loyal to the organization. As an undergraduate, they will want to be supporting BC in volunteer community service or cheering at the football games.

ENTP will like the flexible nature of the **General Management** program at BC. ENTPs can select two areas from among accounting, information systems, finance marketing organization studies and operations technology management. The field research options within the city's financial district are exceptional. With this type of experience, ENTPs graduating with this concentration will have credibility to enter financial management careers. ENTP vision can be pretty clear when it is resting on accurate information. Their exciting, risk-taking nature also works well in the world of business.

ESFP will call upon their strength in personal negotiation with the **Human Resource Management** concentration at BC. Students' explore and incorporate concepts of leadership, ethics and organization during the course of studies. This type prefers a career that calls upon their sincere interest in others which is clearly required in national and global enterprise today. Recognizing the here and now details of varied work environments and requirements is necessary and quite doable for ESFP.

ISTP has the option to pursue employment or research with the **Geological Sciences** major at BC. In either case, ISTPs get to head straight for the labs. They enjoy getting their hands around practical projects. They are likely to look for technical solutions to the environmental issues. This type will volunteer to head out to the field with all the instruments, set them up and live in a tent next to the gadgets until the data is recorded accurately. In respect to Boston social life, they are likely to head into town with a few close friends and show up for the major BC social activities. Otherwise, catch them jury-rigging gadgets in the dorm room.

ESTP and **Operations and Strategic Management** are a good fit. Competition and fast-paced markets demand across-the-board acumen in manufacturing and service organizations. This type understands the competition and the fast pace. They are excellent at networking and troubleshooting. ESTP is also excellent at pulling together a deal among competing team members. The actual reading and lectures might tax some ESTPs, yet there will be good opportunities to get out into Boston's businesses for outstanding job training. While they are putting in a full day at the office, they will also likely join the office staff for after hour socializing. The line between learning, working and socializing is intermittent for this gregarious type!

BOSTON UNIVERSITY

121 Bay State Road
Boston, MA 02215
Website: www.bu.edu
Admissions Telephone: 617-353-2300
Undergraduates: 18,714; 7,701 Men, 11,013 Women
Graduate Students: 14,013

Physical Environment

Boston University stretches along Storrow Drive which flanks the Charles River, and the Mass Pike on the south side. Commonwealth Avenue crosses the campus from Kenmore Square on the east side to Babcock Street on the west side by the university track and tennis center. This is a **very urban campus** and students who love it, **love Boston**. They develop an appreciation for culture, sports and the many enjoyable activities available by living with 300,000 other students in city. There is a lot to do in Boston and students often jog along the Charles River, where there may be free concerts, or head for an Italian restaurant at the South End.

Transportation is available on the bustling city side. The T (city trolley) runs aside the campus and students board at the College of Arts and Sciences and get off six stops later at the west campus residences, thus avoiding the chilly winds that blow along this route in winter. Nearby Fenway Park, home of the Red Sox, Newbury Street and Kenmore Square attract high school graduates who want to dress with flair and build their city smarts. Undergraduates **learn to navigate Boston quickly**. When it's sunny and warm, they may go to the "beach," an area by the law school that flanks the Fenway with the heavy flow of cars substituting for the sound of waves.

At BU students live in a variety of residence halls. First years often reside in the Towers which are classic cinder block dormitories. Then there are four city blocks of impressive brownstones which are much desired by the upper class students. A new student village was completed next to the sports complex and the ice-hockey arena. It's an 18-story high rise where up to 2,500 students live in apartments. Although the trolley runs frequently on Commonwealth Avenue, students must be **hardy and strong** to walk into the wintry winds to get to and from class. Some upper class students opt to live off campus in Brookline or other nearby areas.

The university, tightly constrained by the city, aggressively approaches renovations and construction. Renovations to the Metcalf Science Center, the Walter Brown ice rink and the Green Computer Center are eye opening. In addition, a new building on east campus scheduled to open in late 2012 will feature a state of the art, one stop, student center six stories tall.

Social Environment

BU students work hard and play hard. They **balance academics with socializing** just about every week. Most were at the top 10 percent of their high school class, learn by collaborating with other students and desire clear cut plans that support realistic goals. About eight percent are international students adding to the cosmopolitan educational experience. Students here are **independent** thinkers and manage their lives and activities in this busy and varied environment.

Students do well to research the course offerings ahead of time and pursue what clearly interests them. Students who take several semesters to declare a major risk lengthening the time to graduate. Once they declare a major, students start to gain a greater sense of community on this college campus. They can participate in undergraduate research if they collaborate with a professor to submit a grant proposal and secure approval. Students at BU are **go getters**. After the "core" requirements are fulfilled, students may design a course of interdisciplinary studies, where they study interrelated subjects such as philosophy and physics, or urban studies and public policy. Others follow well defined, demanding courses of study in traditional subjects.

At night students might go out into the city with their friends from the dorm, yet the following night, they may join another group of undergraduates for yet another adventure. They may not know each other by name but there is still a sense of camaraderie. The BU experience is a **smorgasbord of social activity**: living in a certain tower, exercising in the new sports center, cheering for the Terriers, watching a Red Sox game. All of these are part of this unique college community.

Compatibility with Personality Types and Preferences

Boston University is for the high energy student who is pumped up by the city's fast pace. However, success takes a lot more than just being attracted to this dynamic city. BU students usually have the endurance and sharpness needed to secure an undergraduate degree while juggling lots of alluring and exciting activities (P). Both endurance and a sharp wit serve them well as they navigate the requirements for graduation in the required core courses, divisional studies, concentrations and minors. For those who move through the academic system efficiently, there is the additional reward of acquiring city savvy skills. At Boston University, the administration clearly directs the students toward self responsibility with sometimes Byzantine administrative and academic policies. Students are intellectually challenged. Administratively, they must watch their progression (S) through the required courses in their desired field of study. The faculty expect a level of maturity that coincides with confidence and intellectual brightness. Looking around the campus during any season of the year, you will find exactly these types of students. They are strong students, willing to take a risk, who know what they want in respect to fun and work.

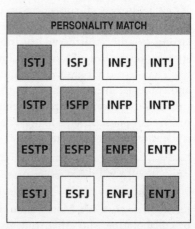

PERSONALITY MATCH

ISTJ	ISFJ	INFJ	INTJ
ISTP	ISFP	INFP	INTP
ESTP	ESFP	ENFP	ENTP
ESTJ	ESFJ	ENFJ	ENTJ

In the following listing of college majors it is important to remember that students can fit into any college and can be successful in any major. We have found that the Personality Types below fit very well at this college. The course-of-study chosen for each Personality Type corresponds to MBTI® research and is presented as an example favorable for that type.

ISTJ makes a good choice with the **Environmental Analysis and Policy** concentration because it is an evolving field, yet one laden with specifics, like quantitative environmental modeling. This works well for ISTJs who will definitely drive policy decisions in the future. This type is comfortable with cataloging facts to memory and then using those facts to form decisions with logic. Fortunately, this will work well at Boston University which is rule and policy oriented.

ISTP will make positive use of the degree and concentration in **Human Physiology** which is not often available at smaller liberal arts colleges. This degree will provide the gateway for ISTPs to move on to further training and graduate schools. They are likely to choose from the allied health specialties that require technical expertise and independent analysis. This type is comfortable with spontaneous decisions of a technical nature especially if it involves machines.

ESTP with knowledge gained from the minor in **Advertising** at BU could be dynamite in a business setting. They are well suited to BU's approach to educating students since ESTPs will mix it up as much as possible with hands-on experience for credit in the city. ESTP confidence will be handy as they promote ad copy ideas with faculty. Surrounded by visual images and advertising on Boston's sidewalks and vistas from the T, fun and excitement is readily available and attractive to this type.

ESTJ likes the facts and the tradition associated with teaching science. Science labs are a well known and permanent feature of chemistry that is not going to change. This suits ESTJ and BU offers a degree titled **Chemistry: Teaching** that fits right into ESTJ views of the world. What high school principal wouldn't be comforted by ESTJ's appreciation of standard operating procedures? This type's natural skill for leading and affinity for people combines nicely in this career.

ISFP who works in the field of **Archeology** gets to play outside in the dirt and stick with the facts, essentially the artifacts. Leaving the abstractions and theories to others, this type will enjoy piecing together real finds, and once done move on to the next field! BU's concentration in Archeology, not often available in liberal arts colleges, is a hidden gem and strongly supported by the active archeology club.

ESFP is a good bet for physical therapy. BU offers a strong undergraduate degree in **Health Science** for admission to competitive physical therapy graduate programs. This type revels in helping others, especially if it involves repetition of complex skills the ESFP has learned. This degree also offers exploration and entry into emerging health specialty careers other than physical therapy. As medical treatment advances through technology, new careers are opening.

ENFP likes to be creative and the concentration in **Nutritional Science** at BU definitely offers a wide perspective. Nutritionists will be important in the future not only as dieticians, but also as researchers and policy setters. Boston has amazing medical resources from Tufts New England Medical Clinic to Boston's Children's and Brigham and Women's Hospital plus so many more. This environment is designed for creative, fun loving ENFP to dash over on the T and build the social network for further study after graduation.

ENTJ is going to reach for the stars at BU with the **Mathematics Specialty in Statistics** program. They can further blast through the stratosphere, so to speak, by combining this precise major with a minor in Business administration and management. ENTJs have an entrepreneurial side to their personality that nicely mixes with professional positions. Boston will be more than happy to surround ENTJ with the high finance environments that demand mathematical analysis.

BOWDOIN COLLEGE

5700 College Station
Brunswick, ME 04011-8448
Website: www.bowdoin.edu
Admissions Telephone: 207-725-3100
Undergraduates: 1,762; 870 Men, 892 Women

Physical Environment

Bowdoin College is located on the **coast of Maine**, 26 miles from Portland. Brunswick is a quaint town of 20,000 people, with cobblestone streets and many restaurants that are friendly to students. Bowdoin owns Orr Island, 13 miles away on the coast, where students frequently participate in geology and marine research. Nearby Freeport, with its designer outlets, attracts students who have a taste for function with fashion outdoor clothing. Bowdoin's 225-acre campus has **forested areas** with walking trails where **athletic** students run or cross-country ski. Here the nature of the Maine environment attracts students who like to be very physically active.

The main campus is built around the 1855 Congregational Church, which now serves as the meeting place for various religious groups on campus. Two museums of art and modern theatres bring out the musician and actor in these students. The campus has a **balanced feel,** almost spiritual, to the environment and students relate well to this. The issue of **sustainability** is addressed daily here, as these students want to impact and address in their own way natural resources that are perceived to diminish in the 21st century. Students reside in green residential halls, which were built with recycled materials, using natural sources of light and heated by geothermal means. In order to save potable water, rain is collected to flush toilets. Without a doubt, students here are or become activists for issues currently in the public square.

Social Environment

Eighty-five percent of students are out of state and bring a strong high school resume hailing from public and independent schools. They are likely to be **creative** thinkers or performers in dance, theatre, music and fine arts. They are excellent writers and speakers and write many **provocative** articles for literary magazines published at Bowdoin. After all, Henry Wadsworth Longfellow, Nathaniel Hawthorne and Franklin Pierce were in the Bowdoin class of 1825, and we know the rest of their stories.

The common denominator here is that students are very concerned about sustainability, not only for Bowdoin but also for the world. They love to explore alternative forms of energy such as wind mills in order to protect nature and take stewardship of the environment.

Although there are no fraternities or sororities, many students belong to outing clubs and are skilled at outdoor sports. They also socialize around themed parties in their residential houses on Friday night. Some really identify with the house they were assigned to by Bowdoin in the freshman year and continue to socialize with that group through the four years. Others like to socialize by joining clubs, like the swing club, and attending those social events in the student center.

Almost everyone on this campus is attracted to and loves the **visual and performing arts** even if they are not talented themselves. On this campus almost every student is politically-inclined or has a political opinion about issues of the day. There are a solid number of bright, under-represented students who add to the socio-economic mix of this community.

Bowdoin students are **bright,** passionate, athletic, artistic and high achieving. Approximately 80 percent rank in the top 10 percent of their high school class and are the high school students who juggled a heavy academic load and many extracurricular activities. They are thirsty for knowledge and so they are willing to work hard as they engage in intellectual pursuits at this college that focuses exclusively on teaching undergraduates. Students typically respect each others' point of view and freely express their opinions which mirror trends in society. This concern for others' ideas and opinions forms an essential element of living in this peaceful, **non-competitive, intellectual community**. Students enjoy each other's talents and gifts whether they are modest or exceptional. They exchange information and wide-ranging thoughts.

Compatibility with Personality Types and Preferences

Bowdoin College brings to mind the words "laid back" and "intense" at the same time. The Bowdoin undergraduate is in pursuit of acquiring very large, sweeping ideas as they apply to society. It's a demanding endeavor so there is plenty of stress relief in the campus environment starting on Friday night. Faculty question students by making observations of what "is." Student answers could be more complex questions. Bowdoin undergrads become accustomed to ambiguity and discovery as paths to learning (P). It is OK to delay and get lost in the process before a good answer appears, maybe even more than one right answer will surface. This open, intuitive, approach (N) is nicely applied in the physical sciences at Bowdoin. Their philosophy in the sciences is to approach the studies through stewardship and conservation which calls for creative problem solving. At the same time, there is another notion very much present on campus, referred to as the 'common good.' It seems to drive a wedge of utility into all the academic majors. Students become attuned to purpose and outcome (T). They accept the role of change agent and prefer to do this with others in collaboration. The faculty and administration very much assumes that sweeping societal changes are not initiated as solo events, but take a community of committed and knowledgeable individuals working together with a plan. Being connected with others (F) on campus seems to promote a natural brotherhood. Moving forward into their careers with confident expectation is a good description of the Bowdoin students on graduation day.

In the following listing of college majors it is important to remember that students can fit into any college and can be successful in any major. We have found that the Personality Types below

PERSONALITY MATCH			
ISTJ	ISFJ	INFJ	INTJ
ISTP	ISFP	INFP	INTP
ESTP	ESFP	ENFP	ENTP
ESTJ	ESFJ	ENFJ	ENTJ

fit very well at this college. The course-of-study chosen for each Personality Type corresponds to MBTI® research and is presented as an example favorable for that type.

INFJ brings insight to the world of art. The **Visual Arts** major at Bowdoin is wonderfully supplemented by the natural beauty of the Maine coastline and rolling forests and a strong technical curriculum. It will be so enjoyable for this type, often searching for life's meaning, to reach for that technical perfection in a calming landscape that pulls an emotional response from the viewer.

ISTP enjoys getting out of the classroom or any similarly four-sided enclosed space. The **Earth and Oceanographic Science** major at Bowdoin offers fascinating and boots-on opportunities to study bedrock and coastline geology. This technical type will happily take scientific instruments out to measure waves and tides. The broad nature of geology also gives ISTP wiggle room to explore and select a specialty that interests them, critically important for this type.

ENFP may be attracted to the teaching minor in **Education**. The Bowdoin preparation for teaching is exacting and selective. Many parents would wish that their child could be taught by a Bowdoin-educated teacher. The course titled **High School** looks at the purpose and nature of secondary school in today's society. Students are charged with designing a model charter school as part of their preparation. ENFP will be enthusiastic about this assignment and will identify with the cheerleading culture of American charter schools.

ENTP is fascinated with power and doesn't mind thinking about moving into power circles. The study of power is well viewed through the lens of Eastern Europe. At Bowdoin, the **Eurasian and East European Studies** interdisciplinary major provides the large pair of glasses in this allegory. Conflict, past and current, in this pivotal part of the world could assure ENTP many opportunities to apply their knowledge in an advisory or consulting role after graduation.

INTP will find the **Computer Science** major at Bowdoin amusing as well as sufficiently deep. The course, Computing Tools and Issues, is classic Bowdoin College. This is the college that asks question after question about computing and what purpose it is serving for mankind. Along the way, INTP will also pick up skills to start employment at any of the social media conglomerates. Prior to graduation, INTP will track and compare the latest smart phone release for everyone in the dormitory.

INTJ and **Mathematics** is a good platform from which this focused personality can launch into the world of advanced studies. At Bowdoin College, math is studied for its pure logic and for its utility for mankind. The course titled "Optimization" teaches the original thinking INTJ that math formulas are made to solve the world's social problems too. At Bowdoin, this type will be exposed to the idea of using math beyond releasing more statistics and databases. This would be the math department's contribution to Bowdoin's common good.

INFP with a good ear can devote themselves to a career in music. At Bowdoin the **Music** majors often follow one of four tracks: General Music, Music and Culture, Composition or European and American Music. For the INFP with their penchant for adaptability and insight, the fifth option in a self-designed music major is an alluring choice too. Perhaps they will want to connect music directly with people and the concept of service. It will be INFP who can tie these three together with meaning and utility.

ENTJ is a dynamite consultant in the business world. At Bowdoin, the interdisciplinary major titled **Mathematics and Economics** will allow this hard charging type to enter into the most selective financial houses and consulting companies. The wide ranging discourse of this major as related to the linear world of money and math are covered quite nicely. ENTJ smiles with anticipation as they look into their consulting future with this preparation.

ENFJ and **Psychology** makes good sense for this type that is gifted with seeing human potential in individuals and organizations. The Bowdoin College environment is a good fit for this personality preference. Often gifted with a good sense of humor, ENFJ's interaction with clients in therapy will help individuals recognize their weaknesses and strengths.

ISFP often likes careers in the health services field. Their exceptional powers of observation combine nicely with the many practices and techniques involved with diagnosing illnesses. The major in **Biology** at Bowdoin naturally follows the college philosophy to improve the body of knowledge for the "common good." This works for ISFP since they very much want to use their skills while working one on one with people. This major will allow ISFP to launch into any advanced medical training.

BRANDEIS UNIVERSITY

Office of Admission
415 South Street
Waltham, MA 02454-9110
Admissions Telephone: 781-736-3500
Website: www.brandeis.edu
Undergraduates: 3,341; 1,564 Men, 1,877 Women
Graduate Students: 1,500

Physical Environment

Brandeis is located on the beltway surrounding Boston, Route 95, formerly called Route 128. A commuter train stop is located near the Brandeis athletic fields on South Street, so students explore Boston and vicinity. The campus is built on 235 acres of rolling hills, referred to as an **upper and lower campus**. The buildings are modern, rectangular structures, with the exception of the circular theatre building and the **Usen Castle**. The castle is an iconic building that houses sophomores and is located on a higher elevation overlooking the campus. With a softer architectural contrast, the new Mandel Center for the Humanities seems to be purely glass, (Cinderella's slipper?) and shining metal with neon light bars suspended in thin air. The new Shapiro Science Center offers a sobering, geometric presence that is akin to its advanced research laboratories.

There are three distinctive architectural **houses of worship** which visually relay the spiritual egalitarian views that exist on this campus: a Catholic, Jewish and Protestant chapel, in addition to a Muslim prayer room. The academic calendar is arranged so as to permit students of a particular faith to celebrate their holidays. Jewish holidays and Chabad services are celebrated. Students appreciate the open acceptance of Jewish lifestyle, philosophy and religion. The dining room has a distinct section for kosher dining and another section for American-style food. It's typical to see a Rabbi mingling with Jewish students during lunch. This is part of the Brandeis experience.

Social Environment

This college was founded in 1948 and is named after the first Jewish Supreme Court Justice, Louis Brandeis. This university offers an excellent education and opportunities for undergraduate research in many fields under the watchful eye of professors. Enterprising students may conduct neuroscience research at one of the hospitals in Boston and secure employment options at graduation. Others continue scientific research in graduate school or will enter medical school. Many volunteer with AmeriCorps and other service organizations.

The college does not track the number of students who enroll who are Jewish but the general sense is that approximately half are Jewish. The Jewish religion is observed in a wide range of historical and contemporary traditions. All members of the student body will be familiar with the impact of Jewish traditions and beliefs on contemporary and world society.

Even before arriving at Brandeis students understand what it means to promote **social justice** and equal rights for all races. Students who attend Brandeis are committed to diversity. Students typically develop a solid **ideology** and become politically aware and active. **Reconciliation** in the study of Jewish-American history is viewed from several cultural perspectives, as well as traditional **Jewish perspectives**. Oppression of African Americans in the singular historical sense of civil war perspective is supplemented in conversation with an uncommon depth of understanding. Historic African American figures of strength and leadership would be equally acknowledged as well as honored. Students are typically passionate about issues and the full Brandeis experience can offer a bright light of awareness from several perspectives. The college has no core curriculum except for some distribution credits. Students can graduate from Brandeis without taking any religion courses.

Students who do well at Brandeis ranked in the top 10 percent of their class and have SAT scores in the high 600s or low 700s. Approximately 90 percent of accepted students present this profile. They must handle challenging academics and excellent professors. Many students are interested in becoming medical doctors, veterinarians or lawyers. Approximately 75 percent of students come from outside of Massachusetts. **International** students bring their customs and perspectives to campus contributing to the global feel of suburban Boston. Brandeis students look well cared for and quite happy. Many are driven to be successful. Administration and faculty guide and mentor the undergraduate students similar to their experiences in their hometown extended families.

Compatibility with Personality Types and Preferences

Brandeis University is exceptionally accommodating in connecting academic studies with student interest and exploration. The faculty is quite active with their own independent research, yet at the same time they seem to solicit students interested in their particular research to join in. There is careful, consistent and practical (S) advising for identifying majors and career tracks, advanced study and research after graduation. University programs and career mentoring are excellent.

Extracurricular activities and clubs reveal the exceptional interest and study of social justice issues in its broadest sense. The study of other ethnic cultures is solid. It is supplemented with the universities strong outreach across the globe. Brandeis admits international students for their two-way perspectives. International students learn firsthand about American Jewish perspectives and American students with Jewish orientations learn of world cultures other than American.

As a result, Brandeis students are able to view the concepts of Jewish nationality through other cultures. The terrorist attack in Mumbai, in late 2008, highlighted this significant international perspective within

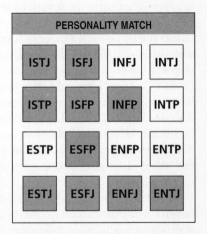

PERSONALITY MATCH

ISTJ	ISFJ	INFJ	INTJ
ISTP	ISFP	INFP	INTP
ESTP	ESFP	ENFP	ENTP
ESTJ	ESFJ	ENFJ	ENTJ

the student body. This terrorist attack formed an immediate response from Brandeis students. Their outreach included direct support to the devastated overseas Mumbai community.

The city of Boston also adds awareness of universal humane themes (F) with many Brandeis undergraduates attracted to city culture that is familiar to them. This university has an international flavor that runs throughout accompanied by a perspective of what is good in our own nation. Humane justice and rationality (T) are highlighted at Brandeis through the lens of many nationalities. Undergraduates here arrive with an affinity for other cultures and openness to transcending boundaries.

In the following listing of college majors it is important to remember that students can fit into any college and can be successful in any major. We have found that the Personality Types below fit very well at this college. The course-of-study chosen for each Personality Type corresponds to MBTI® research and is presented as an example favorable for that type.

INFP could elect to declare the **Studio Art** major at Brandeis University. Their personal vision is drawn out through the encouragement and sensitivity of this department. There is an underlying theme that requires students to look at art as an expression of the individual message. Theory and current day issues are subjects of focus in the intermediate courses. INFPs excel at relating their personal beliefs through their creative work. At Brandeis University, both the beliefs and the creativity are expected and nicely combine in this major.

ISTP likes to be efficient with the resources at the disposal of a student team or class project. The major in **Computer Science** at Brandeis University requires coordination and efficiency. How else would you explain a class in Machine Learning? This techno type is definitely going to sign up for this class. ISTPs enjoy team work and controlling chaos when their trouble shooting can save the day. The degree in computing here has wide options for focus and ISTP loves the spontaneous nature within this department.

ISTJ will like the historically based curriculum and the unusually large number of course offerings in the **American Studies** major at Brandeis. Academic courses and perspectives within this curriculum seem to focus on the American experience minus today's trendy political and social filters. The minor in **Legal Studies** is a swell combo with this major. ISTJs will be headed toward a career in justice or law and be very well prepared between these two courses of study.

ISFJ is often a natural leader in the field of education. This type has a comfort level with administrative procedure and attention to detail. The combination is really desirable for a major in **Education Studies**. Brandeis offers a robust degree with access to a variety of educational environments through internships in the city of Boston. The department is very focused on directing undergraduate students to understand the ethical purposes of education. There are many Why and How questions here for ISFJ to ponder.

ISFP has a thoughtful side to their daily habits. The degree in **Environmental Studies** will provide enough rumination for a full bodied ISFP career. This type gets lots of energy from being outdoors and being productive with a meaningful environmental student project. The faculty commits to undergraduates exploring the relationship between environmental policy and practice as directed by government and industry. Since ISFPs are quite adaptable to change, this dynamic career field is quite suitable

ESFP more often than not has an affinity for animals. The major in **Biology** at Brandeis University has several lines of study that actively explore animal behavior. The marine biological semester at Woods Hole is a good example. Since ESFPs also prefer to be physically active with lots of variety, it is ideal to include the hands-on nature of studying and working with animals. ESFPs natural rapport with others in social settings will be an asset in zoological careers that essentially care and/or train animals on behalf of public education.

ESFJ definitely is a supporter of community such as high school traditions, local celebrations and educational programs for senior citizens. The major in **Health: Science, Society and Policy** is an extensive study of the health field across society, from the individual through to global health. ESFJs are quite comfortable with the field of health. They want to support others and reduce the negative effects of disease and environmental stress. At the same time, this type is a supportive member of organizations and excels at delivering services within large bureaucracies. Brandeis has a hands-on component in the internships of this major that really appeals to ESFJs. This Field-based Senior Research option immediately interfaces the undergraduate student with patients needing health related services.

ESTJ likes the idea of a solid, no frills undergraduate degree. ESTJs interested in science will be attracted to the degree in **Chemistry** since it is well received and appreciated in the job market. ESTJs must determine which focus within this broad degree to follow after graduation. At this university, the chemistry major can lean toward solid credentials to enter the fields of biochemistry, environmental sciences, pharmacology, medicine, dentistry, law or business. ESTJ usually struggles to makes these types of decisions. The extraordinary lab resources and visiting faculty in Colloquia certainly provide amplification of the options.

ENFJ is a master at oral communication. Words certainly can intrigue this type as tools that carry multiple meanings, some of them persuasive. The major in **Language and Linguistics** has both variety and underlying structure that is appealing to this type. For the ENFJ who can be a computer geek, Brandeis has a nice complementary line of study that connects linguistics with computation. This field has multiple avenues in graduate study from anthropology and sociology to computer science. Faculty in the department pursue strong linguistics research from artificial intelligence to mathematical properties of linguistic formation.

ENTJ is one to come up with innovative and logical steps for solving problems. **Neuroscience** offers application for these two ENTJ characteristics. This emerging field is well positioned at Brandeis University for study of the brain through its neural systems. A full complement of faculty research includes chemical, biological, genetic, computational, perceptual, memory, spatial and behavioral lines as applied to the brain. ENTJ likes to be on the leading edge of an evolving career and Brandeis research in this field introduces this undergraduate to a huge array of research and follow on study options.

BROWN UNIVERSITY

45 Prospect Street, Box 1876
Providence, RI 02912
www.brown.edu
Admissions Telephone: 401-863-2378
Undergraduates: 6,380; 3,042 Men, 3,338 Women
Graduate Students: 1,971

Physical Environment

The city of Providence provides a sophisticated and lively environment for Brown students. It's like a mini-Boston minus the hustle and bustle of a large city. City streets like Thayer run through the university area and offer interesting diversions in an **eclectic atmosphere**. There's a one screen movie theatre which often runs foreign language films, many recently released from the Cannes film festival. There are internet cafes, ethnic restaurants and street musicians in good weather.

The prominent hill in Providence is home to Brown University along with historical homes and buildings with some on the national register including the first Baptist Church in America from 1600s. The federal style old homes speak to social upper class living. The train station is within a few minutes of the university and it connects students with Boston and New York. Prospective bright students with considerable artistic talent are drawn to the possibility of a dual degree from the Rhode Island School of Design, adjacent to Brown's admission office.

Many of the Brown buildings retain the look and feel of the late 1800s and Brown undergraduates like New England's old customs and ways, reminiscent of England which they have likely visited. Many of the 220 buildings on the hill were built more recently. The large Life Science complex joins the "Walk" an interconnecting network of walkways and parks. Landscape architecture and tradition are also enhanced by the Van Wickle wrought iron gate which opens and closes for incoming and graduating students. It gives the feel of closeness and options with so many pathways to get to classes. It is representative of the **academic freedom** here. Students drawn to Brown love the possibility of experimenting with courses and enjoy the pleasing physical landscape for its originality. The entire environment speaks to a classy intellectual lifestyle. Students here want to be in the midst of it.

Very much in tune with recent collegiate architecture, the new Granoff Center for the arts contains collaborative spaces for artistic production and reminds one of a toddlers attempt to square up three building blocks, yet gets them off center. It is amusing and delightful to look at from a distance. With the 2011 renovation complete, the Metcalf Center for Research provides collaborative space for the cognitive, linguistic and psychological disciplines. Another major spruce up finds a glass arched interior in the Faunce House Campus Center, now a vibrant area for study and undergraduate snack time.

Social Environment

Brown University's founding mission gave license to students studying what they wanted, to the depth they wanted and without taking other "prescribed" classes. This still holds true today, since there are **no core** requirements. Students identify courses in conjunction with their advisors and design their own concentration.

Students who love Brown University truly love it. The admission process is rigorous as are the classes. The educational philosophy appeals to these free-thinking, **idealistic** students who are also extraordinarily bright. Brown's administration continues to require that students chart their own course of education. The faculty expects students to learn from each other and bring new information to the classroom experience. In fact, there is a sense that Brown University is relying on its students to be the trailblazers who will move the common body of knowledge forward. Students here are self directed to the "nth" degree. They are referred to as Brown's primary resource. Often nurtured by their professors, at times they are **treated as equals** with creative insights to share. Brown students are genuinely **single-minded** about something, and often they get lost in that "something."

In addition to handling a heavy work load, these students get intensely attracted to unique, original activities. Most will become loyal in friendships by identifying with the themes of love, peace and happiness. Some would have been described as "nerds with a social personality" in high school. Others are children of free thinkers who are identifying with their parents' ideals. There are also conservative thinking, conventional students here who will be tested in their views. Most are relaxed despite the **heavy academic demands**. Students are likely to collaborate and help each other. With a plurality of individuals, the common denominator is commitment to changing the social or physical environment in some way, shape or form for the better of all. Brown students are oriented to the future. It accommodates their originality well.

For these students who seek to express themselves and explore without limits, the campus is paradise. Brown graduates will know how **knowledge is interconnected and relative**. These graduates are likely to contribute and broaden the base of knowledge in any field, not just their selected concentration. They remain active within the educational process after graduation. They are wary of the transience of present day information. They find less use for ordinary, commonly known facts. Some are very well grounded and become extraordinarily successful. Others choose to apply their expertise and acumen without thought of practical worldly concern.

Compatibility with Personality Types and Preferences

Brown University is a study in diffusion (P). Simply said, there are no hard lines or sharp edges in this intellectual environment. Instead, synthesis, discovery and expansion seem to rule. Students who find Brown University a comfortable place are those who want to see beyond and behind what is currently known: the future and the past. Their motivation may be intense curiosity, or they may be compelled to help others (F) as the primary way of defining themselves. Regardless of their motivation, these students are willing to jump into the unknown at some level (N) with the confidence that they will surface with personal abilities which will be used productively. They have many personal definitions to nail down in four years. They are likely to search for their own meaning of "productivity." They come expecting to find the academic climate that will welcome these very abstract questions. They are optimistic that their personal connections with people and their intellectual acumen will translate into humanistic accomplishment. They have much less admiration for the practical, expedient world. Rather, Brown students will devote their intellectual energy to learning how to ask the questions. It is almost certain that the answers will expand the body of knowledge in their academic fields.

In the following listing of college majors it is important to remember that students can fit into any college and can be successful in any major. We have found that the Personality Types below fit very well at this college. The course-of-study chosen for each Personality Type corresponds to MBTI® research and is presented as an example favorable for that type.

PERSONALITY MATCH			
ISTJ	ISFJ	INFJ	INTJ
ISTP	ISFP	INFP	INTP
ESTP	ESFP	ENFP	ENTP
ESTJ	ESFJ	ENFJ	ENTJ

INFJ would potentially find the concentration of **Human Biology** at Brown University a desirable approach to the discipline. In fact, they might choose the theme of health and disease. This type is not likely to accept conventional practices. Their intuition easily kicks in and they will not shy away from the huge difficulties facing our nation as the population ages and expands. Their own enthusiasm can translate into exceptionally fine leadership when they believe in the work at hand. Brown University is an ideal setting for this type to let their inspiration help define the future of health delivery systems in a nation and world of limited resources.

INTJ is truly a type where still waters run deep. Their friends and associates often are amazed at the originality and depth of their thinking when INTJ chooses to reveal it. The educational philosophies at Brown University will be ideal for this type. In four years, they will be encouraged and rewarded for making those revelations. Although many classmates will be comfortable with the process and the evolving nature of learning, INTJ has the chutzpah to charge on and find the definitive answer. Definitive answers are part of their larger than life visions. So who else to tackle such a revolutionary and intense concentration as **Cognitive Neuroscience**? The additional complexities that occur at freely floating Brown University simply call out louder to INTJ.

ISFP will appreciate the **Visual Arts** concentration at Brown University since a sense of beauty is innately a characteristic of their personality. This warm fuzzy type is quite comfortable communicating through the arts and is likely to be drawn to the hand-crafted, three dimensional pieces that speak through their simplicity. ISFP is very good with the here and now, with what can be seen and touched. It is this preference for the observable that allows them to excel in the fields of design. At Brown, this type will find the encouragement they need to reveal and translate their inner convictions through artistic craftsmanship and design.

INTP doesn't actually believe that problems are insolvable. It is not in their nature to grant you that position. At the same time they are pretty skeptical. They might give you less agreement than you expect when you offer a solution to that insolvable problem. The concentration in **Computational Biology** will give them a proper tool to be skeptical and yet seem reasonable. With the tremendous leaps in quantitative information coming our way through genetic and DNA studies, there is a huge need for big, long-range thinkers. INTP doesn't get bogged down in the details and never forgets the original problem to be addressed. So as they get deeper into the data bits, when many of us mortals would have difficulty recalling what 1 or 0 meant, it is the INTP who stays on track with an internal compass. Theories and innovation mix naturally with their afternoon Coke break.

INFP will find their inner ideals and beliefs likely in synchronization with Brown's **Community Health** concentration. INFP can fashion a strong foundation for law school and a subsequent career in medical law. This type has the patience to research the difficult and complex such as the recent husband in Florida pitted against the parents of an adult woman reliant on machines and 24-hour care for her life. These ethical medical queries will be familiar territory for INFP. They are willing to labor long hours if the work contributes to human well being. Brown's great openness in curriculum offers this type the autonomy they thrive on when learning. They are excellent at collaboration when in a cooperative environment where others see the value they bring to the table.

ESFP just knows that once you gather all the information, the solution will reveal itself. Their confidence is ideally suited to Brown's educational perspectives. Neither Brown University nor ESFP are going to get all worked up with worry. They would rather just create and have fun with discovery. So who wouldn't have fun swimming with porpoises? The concentration in **Marine Biology** at Brown offers a broad science background in biology and geology. Graduates can enter any number of career tracks from public policy to ocean research. However, the ESFP is often quite attracted to animals and a focus in animal sciences and conservancy is likely to be appealing.

ENFP will find the challenge and excitement that they enjoy in the **Commerce, Organizations and Entrepreneurship** concentration at Brown University. It includes a really innovative combination of three fields: engineering, sociology and economics. The originality of interfacing these three will keep ENFP's insatiable curiosity satisfied. This concentration requires students to further focus their studies after the foundation courses. It could be the ever original ENFP who graduates Brown University to enter the world of business consulting for profit in a technical field.

ENTP is a thinking machine. Their minds don't often take a break unless they are sleeping. It takes a dynamic mix of courses with a far reaching impact to keep this type from getting restless. The concentration in **Developmental Studies** looks at regional development and its impact from a human community perspective. There is great latitude within the acceptable course choice. The laid back ENTP must set aside their procrastination as they generate original research in their chosen area. The required foreign language in this concentration is also likely to match the geographical area of expertise. Even by Brown standards this concentration is rather wide and all encompassing.

ESFJ who has a talent for numbers will want to look at the concentration in **Statistics** at Brown University. The concentration leads to a Sc. B degree within the Sociology department. Students develop much awareness and skill with statistical methods applied to research in the social sciences. Tender hearted ESFJ is going to naturally appreciate the opportunity to apply their newly learned skills to building community. At Brown there will be significant awareness and discussion of national and world service organizations. ESFJ will be so pleased to listen to those conversations in the dormitories that define the human condition. What will they apply their newly learned statistical prowess to?

ENFJ can put their ability to see all sides of an argument and communication skills to good use in the **Education Studies** concentration at Brown University. This type is quite aware of the frequent charge that our schools are underperforming. ENFJ has the extraordinary skills to bring audiences to new perspectives. ENFJ is comfortable with leadership and establishes relationships with ease. Brown's concentration in this field will give ENFJ the background to take on critical issues in education. Their typically good organizational skills will allow them to juggle several major projects at once. While at Brown, they will seek resolution in their own minds for regional and national problems surrounding the emotional health and education of American children.

BUTLER UNIVERSITY

Office of Admissions
4600 Sunset Avenue
Indianapolis, IN 46208
Website: www.butler.edu
Admissions Telephone: 888-940-8100
Undergraduates: 3,889; 1,592 Men, 2,297 Women

Physical Environment

Butler University is surrounded by the city of Indianapolis, which is the capital of this mid-western state. The Butler campus occupies 290 acres just five miles north of downtown. The campus is laid out in a triangular shape facing east, delineated by a river at the base with fraternity houses around the perimeter of the two sides. In the fall and spring, visitors are welcomed on campus with vibrant banners hanging out of the fraternity house windows. Posters and signs announcing upcoming events infuse energy into this campus where enthusiasm is often in the air. Division I sports, Butler Bowl arena, complete with **national basketball championship** and the **Greek houses** rally the student body. The president's house is prominently located on campus and reminds one of the administration's caring, hands-on guidance.

Butler University reflects the temper and culture of the city of Indianapolis, energetic and forward-looking. The university has completed several significant renovations such as the state of the art addition to the Pharmacy and Health Sciences building. Yet, the physical environment remains mindful of the student body with indoor passage from building to building during the winter months. Winters are severe and students make good use of the recreation complex, the field house and football field. Two of the three first-year residence halls are built around a square forming a courtyard in the middle. The inner square is more shielded from the winds and this lends a sense of community for most of the freshmen.

Social Environment

While students like to have fun here, they accept that they must strive for academic excellence and so they play some but also buckle down and do their work. As interested as they are in academics, students are also interested in being trained for something in the real world. They enjoy **applied learning** and the internships that come with many majors. They respect the advice, follow through with it, and are not likely to question their professors in a challenging way. Study abroad is also part of the Butler experience, and the college has a campus in Spain as well as other programs. Academically, students at Butler have freedom to explore within **a clear structure** superimposed by the college. High school students in the upper middle of their graduation class interested in practical subjects receive good training here. Students with learning disabilities will also find that they receive attention and support.

Students who are undecided about their future can remain undeclared for two years. An advisor is appointed to undeclared students so they don't fall through the cracks. It's very likely they will graduate in four years. The curriculum has something for the artsy folks as well; in fact, students are required to attend six cultural experiences over the four years at Butler. The very **competitive dance and theatre** programs attract would-be-artists who can receive excellent training at this Midwestern university along with practical advising in their artistic work. Some will go on to teach while others find performance, management and technical positions with theaters and stages.

Butler University appeals to students who want to join clubs and organizations that draw them together for traditional collegiate activities. They will attend sports events where students demonstrate school spirit, along with their official mascot, Butler Blue II, a friendly English bulldog. Many students come from the Indiana farms with about 40 percent coming from outside the state. Politically, many of these students lean on the conservative side and come from families that have worked the land hard and **value religion and tradition**.

Compatibility with Personality Types and Preferences

Butler University prepares its graduates for the professional world of work and careers through four years of carefully determined curriculum in each of the five colleges and personal attention. Students at Butler University look to their professors for state of the art information (S) within their disciplines of expertise. The administration specifically recruits professional practitioners to function as professors on campus who bring this expertise, excitement and reality to the classes. The faculty within the performing arts disciplines are typically retired talented professionals within their disciplines. The permeable boundary between Butler's campus and the national, international scene fuels a very active off campus learning that is specifically tailored to the undergraduate's major. Individualized academic mentoring is also a strong part of the planned approach to undergraduate education.

Students who are drawn to Butler readily move into the social and academic scene with ease. The spirit on campus is evident outside of the classes. Traditional collegiate social life reigns with cheering teams throughout the athletic seasons. At Butler team spirit translates into community building and community strength. Students and professors capitalize on this energy.

Butler is exceptionally fine in their support for the undecided undergraduate also. Students who want clear guidance during their decision about educational majors will really like the Butler University approach. Undergraduates will find a specialized sequence of courses and advising in each of the five colleges. These exploratory designations help students explore majors in each discipline. At the same time, the student who is unsure of the general area will also be getting help to identify careers compatible

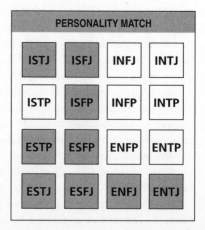

PERSONALITY MATCH

ISTJ	ISFJ	INFJ	INTJ
ISTP	ISFP	INFP	INTP
ESTP	ESFP	ENFP	ENTP
ESTJ	ESFJ	ENFJ	ENTJ

with their interests and talents. Generally, undergraduates here seek out and expect expertise in their instructors. This is exactly what the University provides.

In the following listing of college majors it is important to remember that students can fit into any college and can be successful in any major. We have found that the Personality Types below fit very well at this college. The course-of-study chosen for each Personality Type corresponds to MBTI® research and is presented as an example favorable for that type.

ISTJ often has intense concentration that is a much desired trait in the health sciences. Butler University offers the **Pre-Physician Assistant** program with undergraduate opportunities for admission into the selective College of Pharmacy and Health Sciences. This could really work well for ISTJ with their stability, perseverance and mastery of details. Butler University offers a carefully designed curriculum with considerable exposure to a large variety of medical settings that utilize physician assistants. The guidance is very realistic and focused at Butler University and ISTJs will appreciate this.

ESFP is often able to juggle several projects in the moment. The theater stage is particularly attractive to this type. The ESFP with high school experience and demonstrated talent should look to the majors in **Theater** or **Dance**. Visiting actors and professional performers take up residence at the university. ESFPs are energized by the culture associated with performing arts. The daily work environment is focused on the next performance—the immediate and daily tasks at hand. The College also offers an **Arts Administration** degree in each of these areas for ESFPs who may not prefer to continue performing in front the audience.

ESTJ has the inclination to carefully preplan for a career. The field of Pharmacy definitely requires this type of preplanning which Butler University offers in the **PrePharmacy** major. The department goes above and beyond the general idea of prepharmacy advising. The major directly pairs a clear curriculum and internships with strong academic work required by the undergraduate student. It is likely to lead to the completion of the pharmacy doctorate. There is certain admission to graduate school when milestones in the undergraduate years are passed. ESTJ can work to meet each one knowing that it ultimately leads to admission into pharmacy school.

ISFP has very desirable work characteristics such as loyalty, flexibility and practicality. In the right business environment, this type can anchor the whole organization. At Butler University, with the excellent exploratory programs and courses, ISFPs can become familiar with the corporate and nonprofit business worlds. Encouragement and careful internship selection by the faculty will smooth the way. This type typically searches for opportunities to serve customers with their warm, affirming personalities. The College of Business highlights and enhances these individual strengths in the **Exploratory Studies in Business.**

ISFJ really might enjoy the therapeutic speech and language field. At Butler University, the major in **Communication Sciences & Disorders** is designed for successful entry into graduate school. As a speech and language pathologist, ISFJs could help others directly and be a contributing member of the school system or hospital rehabilitation department. These are both important values for ISFJs. Providing language therapy at the elementary schools will take advantage of this type's expertise at sequenced routines and unerring accuracy with repetition. Butler University assertively includes these emerging therapies for mentally impaired youngsters entering school.

ESFJ could excel in the fields that require frequent communication between business and the community. The major in **Strategic Communication: PR & Advertising** at Butler University offers a strong base in experiential learning for ESFJ to excel. This type takes a personal approach to their work and their genuine, friendly ways quickly become an asset. They are also very strong in recalling and utilizing information, rarely getting their facts mixed up. With the experience afforded from the hands-on opportunities at Butler University, ESFJ could select an entry position in public relations with opportunity to work for established businesses or traditional government agencies.

ESTP is curious and quick to react. They may find a career in the criminal justice system quite desirable. The major in **Criminology** at Butler University includes a solid background in psychology and sociology. ESTPs have the interest in others and enjoy being in the middle of activities with many different types of people. This type is observant and often able to understand the needs and desires of others. At Butler, ESTPs can explore each of the work environments that require criminologists. Ultimately they can settle on the one that suits their adaptability and ability to take in a scene and quickly ascertain the pertinent information.

ENTJ might be quite impressed with the **International Business** major at Butler University. The degree requires foreign language proficiency and this hard-charging type is willing to put in the study and wants to excel. Advantages like conducting financial transactions in a native language would not be lost on ENTJs. They don't mind being a step ahead of the competition. The College of Business Administration has carefully selected international business schools for internships. These international, off campus courses will give enterprising ENTJ the global launching pad for a strategic business career.

ENFJ might find the major in **Middle and Secondary Education** ideal at Butler University. There is excellent preparation for teachers here. Undergraduates spend considerable time observing and participating in classrooms prior to actually student teaching. They are paired with master teachers located in the nearby Indianapolis schools. ENFJs like the concept of teaching the certain subjects such as history and English because of the multiple meanings and perspectives. This type could easily find the advanced classes in high school rewarding to teach because of the student's ability to think beyond the text.

CALIFORNIA INSTITUTE OF TECHNOLOGY

1200 E. California Boulevard MC 1-94
Pasadena, CA 91125
Website: www.caltech.edu
Admissions Telephone: 626-395-6341
Undergraduates: 967; 585 Men, 382 Women
Graduate Students: 1,208

Physical Environment

Cal Tech has an urban campus surrounded by the city-streets of Pasadena. The adjacent neighborhoods pose in a **small town way**, without high-rises, and with shopping and ethnic restaurants nearby. Buildings are designed along the style of Oxford University in England. There are eight residences, called Houses, for example Avery House. The students in each form **self-governing units**. Each has enclosed courtyards, corridors and alley ways, which contribute to a strong sense of privacy and identity. The interior of these residence halls is basic and looks **well-used**. Students cook their own dinners and serve themselves in the basic, utilitarian kitchens.

Many valedictorians and salutatorians get lost in the impressive laboratories. The laboratories in math, physics, astrophysics and geology really appeal to the high school student who was fond of world geography and planetary science in the eighth grade. The scientific facilities are exceptional from electron particle accelerators to the Hale telescope that supports the planetary sciences. Students at the top of their high school class are drawn to Cal Tech's off campus **research facilities** in Hawaii and Peru for astrophysics and planetary sciences. The Linde + Robinson Laboratory for Environmental Science is a stunning renovation of the 1932-era astronomy lab. The new Schlinger Laboratory is dedicated to the discipline of chemistry and the art of engineering.

The **cannon** in front of Fleming house has a history of disappearing, as other technical rival colleges steal it away. It actually made a long trip to MIT. Students here take pride in this tradition. They like prankster humor—a throwback to the 1950s—when the cannon was fired for the first time to mark the end of a semester. You won't find groomed flower beds weaving between the functional buildings. Faculty, graduate students and undergraduates are all wrapped up in their study and **discoveries**; the campus energy is devoted to knowledge with little precious energy given over to maintenance.

Social Environment

Cal Tech has a small, very select undergraduate student body highly centered on **the physical sciences**. They collaborate with the larger graduate student body so much so that in the second year of course work, undergraduate students are in some classes with graduate students. These undergraduates are expected to step up their effort and perform at graduate level.

At Cal Tech these exceptional students continue to conduct research in engineering sciences after graduation and so they don't typically intend to become working engineers in the traditional sense. Cal Tech grants only Bachelor of Science degrees at the undergraduate level. The students are brilliant, hard workers with a passion for math and science who would rather unravel a puzzling **theory** than tinker with screws, nuts and bolts. They are future-oriented students who prepare for grad school and then for working in the national labs.

They socialize around research and solving problems, eating **late night pizza** while **tackling scientific hypotheses**. Collaboration with team members who are very different from one another is the norm. Cal Tech is unusual in that approximately half of the students fall into minority categories. All students let their imaginations roam, making connections and opening floodgates of ideas from many cultures during **brainstorming** sessions. Students value truth and abide by a strong honor code whereby they can take un-proctored tests whenever they are ready. For the student who is fascinated by the uncharted areas of science and brave enough to follow their hunches, Cal Tech is perfect.

Compatibility with Personality Types and Preferences

California Institute of Technology is more than a university; rather it seems more like a national and world scientific resource. As such, Cal Tech must regularly communicate with two disparate groups: prospective high school students and world research scientists. They specifically reach out to current high school students who may be good matches for their rather unique learning environment. Analysis (T) is predominant in this campus culture. It is hard to imagine how the extreme and fundamental nature of Cal Tech research could push into scientific discovery without having almost institutionalized the tool of analysis. Of course, innovation and the pull of the unknown (N) has the next place of honor in approaching education. Cal Tech's mission clearly states that human knowledge is expanded to benefit society by combining research and education. The educational philosophy is more along the lines of a think tank that just happens to have young adults as participating members. It is an institution that prepares its graduates for the world of scientific discovery rather than careers and professions.

PERSONALITY MATCH			
ISTJ	ISFJ	INFJ	INTJ
ISTP	ISFP	INFP	INTP
ESTP	ESFP	ENFP	ENTP
ESTJ	ESFJ	ENFJ	ENTJ

In the following listing of college majors it is important to remember that students can fit into any college and can be successful in any major. We have found that the Personality Types below fit very well at this college. The course-of-study chosen for each Personality Type corresponds to MBTI® research and is presented as an example favorable for that type.

ISTJ will relate well to the factual and fundamental nature of the **Biology** option at Cal Tech. With emphasis on the basic life properties, the biology option also allows for flexibility through Cal tech research and elective courses. This type is drawn to traditional practice in medicine. ISTJ will be quite proactive at refining research skills in the undergraduate program at Cal Tech. Entrance to medical school will not be far from this undergraduates daily thoughts.

ISTP is pretty good with numbers and will enjoy the **Economics** option here at Cal Tech. Economics is approached through quantitative methods. The "Options" course within the Business Economics option is designed for both undergrads and grad students. Students apply mathematical formulas such as binomial and Black-Scholes pricing models. Using economic models such as these might enhance the freedom and autonomy that this type needs to be happy.

ESTP could like the **Business Economics and Management** option since it looks so heavily at strategy within the markets and financial networks. The course title "Game Theory" calls to this type with their flair for tackling the difficult and doing it well to boot. The department curriculum is well-grounded with courses in accounting and finance.

ESTJ who looks closely at the **Applied Physics** option discovers there will be one introductory course on energy sources followed by labs and theory courses. This major allows the ESTJ to get the immediate and useful feedback they need because fiber optics, microwaves, radiation and X-ray diffraction are all observable.

ENFP won't likely arch an eyebrow when we suggest selecting the **History and Philosophy of Science** option at Cal Tech. This broad-based observation of how science has been applied to mankind's welfare is something that would attract an ENFP. The further emphasis on writing in this major will give ENFP an advantage to pursue a career track in the policy of public health which is under such considerable scrutiny now.

INTJ is comfortable in the world of computers and the **Computer Science** option here requires an original capstone project. The INTJ has a very strong intuitive sense that is not expressed in the company of others. As powerful thinkers they will likely find it intriguing to study the limits of computing science theory in the course titled Decidability and Tractability.

INTP will find the **Physics** option at Cal Tech is designed to be a stepping stone for a career in basic research. The physics research is well complemented with the exceptional studies in planetary and geological sciences. INTP looks for patterns and is drawn to understanding the nature of the patterns they find. There will be plenty of fellow undergrad classmates who will help them with these puzzles.

ENTP will like the **Political Science** option and its emphasis on predictive methods. Cal Tech brings their powerful penchant for analysis into this social science. ENTP is well suited to find the irony in course option PS 126 which has changed its name in successive course catalogs from "Political Corruption" to "Business, Public Policy & Corruption" and now to "Business & Public Policy." Surely, these changes did not occur for lack of recent case studies in corruption.

ENTJ could like the **Chemical Engineering** degree at Cal Tech because of its broad exposure to the use of chemical reactions for energy as well as products. Within this educational survey of chemical applications, the ENTJ will find the connection to both the real and practical that they so appreciate. As this type progresses through their four years of classes and research at Cal Tech, they will be looking for potential leadership positions within business or in the graduate world of further study.

CARLETON COLLEGE

100 South College Street
Northfield, MN 55057
Website: www.carleton.edu
Admissions Telephone: 507-222-4190
Undergraduates: 2,018; 964 Men, 1,054 Women

Physical Environment

Carleton College is in a small town that is **quaint,** clean and friendly to students. The town stakes its claim that it's the "Home of cows, colleges, and contentment." Northfield has almost no crime and the college students are two to four blocks from all of "downtown." This setting appeals to students who are looking for a safe, **trendy,** artsy environment in which to express their individuality. The commercial part of town is really just one street wide along the river, with lovely old buildings, coffee shops, artisan bakeries, bars and restaurants. A former middle school is now renovated and opened as the Weitz Center for Creativity. It houses facilities and space for the visual arts. Of note is the elevator housing comprised of the old school bleachers which honors its past. October 2011 marked the start up of the college's second wind turbine which feeds into the electrical grid. This is a windy-win for Carleton students who want to "take back the earth."

Carleton students love their new student recreation center and new dorms. They especially like the **long connected buildings** so that they can walk around in shorts and flip-flops in winter. Most buildings were built around the original chapel. They are a mixture of Collegiate Gothic, modern and some that are a throwback to the 60s. The original chapel is a prominent landmark on campus, but Carleton works hard to maintain a **non-sectarian** perspective which appeals to many Jewish and other religious students. The "themed houses" help these students develop their identity and pursue interests with like-minded people.

Social Environment

Carleton students form an eclectic group, interested in a liberal education that allows them to express their thoughts and form opinions. Students expect a platform for freedom of expression in and outside the classroom. Carleton students prefer **cause-related activities** and seek to assure all are represented in student clubs. Many of these have a multicultural perspective such as Fellowship in Christ, which seeks to bring differing national and ethnic students together to explore their faith with the New Testament. All in all, they make friends easily because of the many students similar to themselves on this campus.

Students are **self-absorbed** in their education and social life. Sometimes they feel they are overloaded with their trimester class schedule. In the classroom they ask imaginative questions, not necessarily looking for a definitive answer. Similarly, in their fourth year, students must produce a writing portfolio which requires them to focus their thoughts, but some students are not ready to wrap it up yet. The **process** is more important than the grade.

There is some extreme pushing of cultural boundaries and ideologies. The **counter-culture feel** on Carleton's campus may or may not remain with students after graduation. Since part of the college mission is to "prepare them for a professionally satisfying life" this perspective will be decided by their career choices.

Students are athletic and participate in many sports. The favorite winter pastime is the annual faculty vs. student's broomball game on the "bald spot." They release their academic tensions this way. Carleton is on trimesters and this gives all incoming students the fall freshman year to "settle in" before they start playing sports or intramurals. In fact, Carleton philosophy is to give students space and time within the schedule which plays out in the extended winter break from November to January. This long break is meant to integrate hands-on learning at study abroad locations.

Compatibility with Personality Types and Preferences

Carleton College is idealistic through and through, facilitating an imaginative learning experience (N). The mentoring relationship between student and professor seems to take on the closeness evident in family relationships. Humor is very much valued on this campus. It serves to promote a comfortable familiarity between faculty and student. In this way, the campus experience encourages the student to shed conventions and attitudes (P) they may have brought with them from high school. The educational philosophy moves toward critical observation (T) of American society. Our country's diverse talents and multicultural citizenry are highly valued by the faculty and administration. Carleton students experience an intensely individualized education that builds upon and radiates from their own intellectual energy and belief. This follows from Carleton's mandate to their graduates that they should "aspire to rewarding, satisfying lives with service to humanity." Carleton College passionately brings together the intellectual values of reason and introspection.

PERSONALITY MATCH

ISTJ	ISFJ	INFJ	INTJ
ISTP	ISFP	INFP	INTP
ESTP	ESFP	ENFP	ENTP
ESTJ	ESFJ	ENFJ	ENTJ

In the following listing of college majors it is important to remember that students can fit into any college and can be successful in any major. We have found that the Personality Types below fit very well at this college. The course-of-study chosen for each Personality Type corresponds to MBTI® research and is presented as an example favorable for that type.

ENFP is often the fun-meister on campus. With their flair for the dramatic, they could easily be interested in the **Cinema and Media Studies** major at Carleton. In fact, the course titled Contemporary Global Cinemas says it all. The breadth of this major is truly impressive. These studies should prepare the student with technical expertise and creative awareness. Cinema studies are explored by nationality within the Film History sequence of three courses. The subtle humor on campus is surely apparent within this major.

INFJ likes to work with others in small work settings solving the world's problems. This works well for a career in social science. The **Sociology and Anthropology** major is an excellent preparation for graduate studies in this field. Carleton College predictably includes course work in some of the thorniest world issues, for example, Ethnography of Reproduction. This upper level course, along with several others, helps the INFJ refine which of their perspectives on human meaning could be the focus for their graduate study.

INFP with talent in art finds a perfect home at Carleton College in the **Art** major. The studio arts department offers a rich selection of handcraft courses that INFP can pursue while expressing personal beliefs through the artistic medium. The Paper Arts course offers a definitive study of dyes, colors & fibers providing a knowledge base that is sought after in specialty shops, museums and high end artifact boutiques. When combined with this type's originality and talent, the artist will not be starving in this Carleton graduate's household.

ENTJ may bring a streak of practicality to this campus and to the studies in the **Psychology** major at Carleton College. This department emphasizes analytic skills and allows this type to pursue the intellectual challenge of understanding complex human behaviors and institutions. The course in Evolutionary and Developmental Trends in Cognition will keep ENTJ busy searching for practical application through data analysis.

INTJ and the major in **Political Science** at Carleton could lead to a professional career in justice. At Carleton College, there will be many introspective moments that support this type in, perhaps, their journey to becoming a judge. The underpinning of the American political canvass is well represented in the course offerings of this department. INTJs would not shrink from the difficult decisions and dilemmas of government service at national and regional levels.

ENTP likes to start up projects or ventures. The concentration in **South Asian Studies** will prepare them for exciting opportunities in the region comprising India, Pakistan, Nepal and Sri Lanka. This part of the world is increasing material consumption as well as manufacturing. Combined with the major in **Economics** this enterprising type might work for international business concerns looking to expand services in the region. Travels to the other side of our world will help fill up ENTP's bottomless curiosity and imagination.

INTP relates to the word 'concentration' and will likely find Carleton's concentration in **Cognitive Science** a good choice. In fact they might delight in the comparison of the computer to the human mind as one of the directions this study will point them toward. The nature of careers in the cognitive sciences suits INTP who prefers to reason with technical concepts in evolving fields. Excitement for this type is to originate the cutting edge and the sharper the better.

ISTP can handle the precision and concentration needed in the work associated with **Biochemistry**. At Carleton, students study both chemistry and biology as separate fields and then pursue integration through experience and exercises developed by the faculty. ISTP likes technical work and might easily wander into the field of applied medicine in designing, operating or maintaining sensitive medical equipment.

CASE WESTERN RESERVE UNIVERSITY

103 Tomlinson Hall
10900 Euclid Avenue
Cleveland, OH 44106-7055
Website: www.cwru.edu
Admissions Telephone: 216-368-4450
Undergraduates: 4,227; 2,412 Men,1,806 Women
Graduate Students: 5,637

Physical Environment

Case Western Reserve University is located at the cultural center of Cleveland, surrounded by museums, the Cleveland Orchestra's Severance Hall and the Institutes of art and music. Students occasionally attend the performances and the more informal arts venues since they are within walking distance. The nearby Little Italy draws students in droves for their favorite foods like the tasty pizzas. The city of Cleveland itself pulls in students who are comfortable with novelty and unusual environments as exemplified by the **Rock n Roll Hall of Fame**, designed by world famous architect I. M. Pei.

CWRU's 550 acres are separated by Euclid Avenue, which is the main throughway. The north side of campus feels younger because it has newer buildings and houses first and second year students. The architecture on north campus is ultra-modern. Village at 115 is a seven building residential complex for upperclass students with many amenities of apartment-style living. The Peter B. Lewis building for business management has rounded walls that appear as if they were melted, topped off with a huge metal bow on the roof. The metal bow gives the building a look as if it were a boxed present left out in the rain. Students study in this creative, **inspirational architecture**. It's easy to see it took guts and imagination to place it on the campus. Yet the light is plentiful inside, and it's clear that the physical space is designed to break down conventional assumptions and enhance productivity.

The south side of campus has a grander, more established feel located on the hill. It houses upperclass students and **fraternities and sororities**. The hospital, engineering and science departments have existed here for a long time and appear very solid in contrast to the north campus architecture. Students are attracted to CWRU because of these top research facilities. The hospital on campus serves the Cleveland community as well as for internships in the many health-related majors. Undergraduates here spend most of their time studying to be prepared as they use these **world class research laboratories**. Varied yet cohesive, the architecture on this campus is a metaphor for the **inter-disciplinary** connections that students make between very different subjects as they move through their undergraduate years at CWRU.

Social Environment

CWRU is great for those students who like to conduct **mega research, love technology** infused with liberal arts and willing to study like heck. CWRU is also for those who like a large university in a large, mid-western city, where there is much congeniality and less attention to subjects featured in east coast and west coast periodicals. The majority of students come from the states surrounding the Great Lakes. There is a significant number of ethnic students also, Asian and international. Nine out of ten students are in the top 20 percent of their high school class and love to spend time on the computer. In fact, many students come for the advanced technology conducted at this national research university. They could graduate with top-notch skills in aeronautical engineering but also may have read Milton's *Paradise Lost*. Students here work hard. It's a given. However, those who prefer a measured and moderate pace in which to study will find this rhythm on campus. Competition is not the prime motivator.

CWRU is pulling in students who have a **practical expectation** of making a positive difference in this world. However, they are not out to break the mold and tend to be **traditional** in their dress and political views. Students are attracted to the **exceptional openness** in the course of studies and the many possibilities for research, in all of the "ologies" and human health.

There are checks and balances in place to encourage students who lean toward being too serious and single-minded in their studies. Eventually, even they get off the internet and out of their room to socialize or go to Little Italy. Students could study all day and all night. However, there is a vibrant, lively social life on campus primarily fueled by the leadership and activities of the Greek fraternities and sororities. The Greek system has strong social leadership. It is formed by the **confident**, socially popular graduates of many mid-western rural and suburban high schools.

Compatibility with Personality Types and Preferences

Case Western Reserve University is surprising in a delightful way. This university maintains the passion of a small liberal arts college for the humanities and the facilities plus commitment to advanced research of an institute for technology. They keep both of these educational missions with great success. A major characteristic of their educational philosophy is their openness (P), with few intellectual boundaries. CWRU expects to be a transforming presence in America and the world. They are an exceptional institution that develops and maintains current scientific and cultural knowledge. Through its graduates, CWRU seeks to transform communities and organizations for the betterment of human kind (F). The university stays quite fluid when it comes to prescribed academic courses. Traditional subjects of study can lead to either a bachelor of arts or a bachelor of science. Students here choose which would be better suited to their future plans after graduation. At CWRU, the organization of traditional academic majors is typically supplemented with choice and focus within the major. The major of anthropology has four concentrations plus a fifth option. That option allows the student to follow their interest with permission from the department. CWRU

PERSONALITY MATCH			
ISTJ	ISFJ	INFJ	INTJ
ISTP	ISFP	INFP	INTP
ESTP	ESFP	ENFP	ENTP
ESTJ	ESFJ	ENFJ	ENTJ

brims with creativity (N). It is in the academic bulletin of courses, exemplified in the humorous architecture, and unique in their strong support via the Greek Life Office within the Division of Student Affairs. Students at Case Western Reserve will find it very easy to socialize and learn on this campus. The whole campus culture here is fond of connecting logic (T) and free association of ideas.

In the following listing of college majors it is important to remember that students can fit into any college and can be successful in any major. We have found that the Personality Types below fit very well at this college. The course-of-study chosen for each Personality Type corresponds to MBTI® research and is presented as an example favorable for that type.

ENFJ will find the Bachelor of Arts in **Computer Science** a most pleasant way to prepare for a career in the field. They are not often drawn to such precise fields of study without obvious connections to people. CWRU, with its characteristic openness, invites this type to consider that computer science can be shaped for the benefit of others. At CWRU, this type might want to work on seismic detection through computer programming while combining research with the exceptional geology department and its state of the art research labs. Or, since a substantial part of the degree is in electives, perhaps ENFJ will choose the premed sequence.

ISTP loves mechanical gadgets. With the return to the moon on the distant American horizon, the degree in **Aerospace Engineering** is mighty attractive to this type. CWRU has a strong predisposition for space exploration and the degree is readily focused on space vehicles and space propulsion. CWRU has the amazing technical facilities to do meaningful research at the undergraduate and graduate level. This will keep ISTP smiling while tinkering with the fancy gadgets and thrilled that there is little regimentation in this research environment.

ENTJ has to find innovation within their educational studies and careers to be well satisfied. Although **Civil Engineering** is a traditional field, CWRU threads innovation and discovery throughout the curriculum. The elective sequence within this degree concentrates on environmental engineering. This is an especially timely choice for the entrepreneurial ENTJ. CWRU really prompts its graduates and faculty to start businesses. It will be the ENTJ who takes the latest ideas and technology out to the market while tackling America's growing environmental problems.

ENTP is just fine with the unusual combination of the major in **Japanese Studies** and minor in **Entrepreneurial Studies**. The fast moving atmosphere of international business with its flair for the out-of-the-ordinary is very appealing to ENTP. Avoiding routine and structure within a career is important because they are stressed by too much status quo. There will be little of that in the Japanese written characters and CWRU starts off with elementary levels emphasizing the 50 kanji characters. At this university, the daunting is possible and this is a type who will not be scared off.

ESFP likes to have a toolbox of skills which they can utilize with expertise. As a dietitian, this type gets to help others in a most direct, beneficial way. The major in **Nutrition** allows this type to get personally involved with clients. The career fields available to nutritionists will take advantage of the type's sixth sense in handling tension and conflict in the relationship. At CWRU, there is flexibility in pointing the undergraduate studies toward all the career options from graduate programs to work in the pharmaceutical industry.

ISFP might want to take advantage of CWRU direct admission for first year students to the **Nursing** program. Here students will find policies of encouragement for entering nursing programs at the undergraduate level. The exceptional quality and breadth of this four year nursing program is another indication of the openness of CWRU educational philosophy. The field of nursing is a natural for this type who prefers to be in a harmonious and supportive climate while helping others. The world of health care and its many avenues for personal commitment and career paths is going to be well understood by graduates of this university. ISFP appreciates and seeks the professional guidance that is clearly part of the educational philosophy in the Frances Payne Bolton School of Nursing at CWRU.

ISFJ often likes to work in the health care environment. The undergraduate degree at CWRU in **Nutritional Biochemistry and Metabolism** is offered as either a bachelor of science or a bachelor of arts. Since this type is meticulous by nature, the exacting requirements in this discipline are fine with them. The choice of either the BA or BS gives ISFJ the chance to carefully think through their career options. Reflective ISFJ prefers to have time and not to be rushed or pushed into career decisions. This suits CWRU perfectly since the entire campus is devoted to opening doors for their undergraduates to peer through while deciding which path to take.

ESTP likes to pull solutions together with no notice, and being spontaneous is in their nature. A **Management** degree with a concentration in finance could seem pretty sensible to them. The reality of the organizational budget can be a springboard to the solution for this type, a masterful negotiator. This major at CWRU fits in nicely with the University's overall interest in transforming society. In this case and this degree, the transformation takes place through entrepreneurial investments. This type is comfortable with the risk and CWRU is primed to teach their graduates how to move forward in the dynamic business world.

ENFP will smile at the idea of combining two rather unusual courses of study and moving forward into a fun, rewarding career track. The double major is encouraged at this university and **Music** combined with **Gerontological Studies** is a distinct possibility for ENFP who likes to motivate others with their own sense of the possible. This type simply must have fun somewhere in their lifestyles and why not at work? Music fits in nicely with the elderly population who is not as rushed and has the time to enjoy it. Music can be entertaining, calming and therapeutic.

INFP could find the **Religious Studies** major personally and professionally rewarding. As this type needs to reach out to others in a caring, individualized way, adding the minor in **Gerontological Studies** makes good sense. It allows them to enter the market place of retired baby boomers through teaching and development of spiritual materials as they move through to their golden years. This type very much wants to help others realize their full potential with inspiration. It also allows them to put their powerful reflection toward new and creative services for the aged.

INTP can tailor their own interests into specific studies about the laws of nature at CWRU. This type who loves to ponder will probably arrive on campus with a few thoughts on what they would like to study related to physics. So the **Engineering Physics** degree takes it a step farther for this theoretical type who prefers to work with complex ideas. Since INTP tends to be ingenious on occasion, this degree is right on as it is designed to apply physics principles to the development of technology.

INFJ who decides to take the degree in **Sociology** at CWRU will be in good shape when it comes to guidance and mentoring on choosing a focus within this broad field. The department emphasizes the connection to health policy and health decline throughout the life course. This type truly wants to affect the well being of others, yet would prefer to do this through an organizational structure. Therefore, advancing programs and designing services that serve broad segments of the population are ideal for INFJ. The degree in sociology at this university seeks to make just these kinds of changes at the community level for the near and long term future.

INTJ can often have a bit of the artist in them because of their bent for original thinking. There is a nice combination of studies here that will let this creative type run profitably with their imagination. The **Art History** major combined with the **Pre-Architecture** major is a natural at CWRU. The city of Cleveland right outside the doors of the campus is a wonderful study in architecture with its Rock n Roll museum designed by I. M. Pei. One only has to look at the campus buildings recently completed to see how serious this university is about design in building and its impact on the occupants to understand how well suited this degree on this campus is to this type.

THE CLAREMONT COLLEGES

Claremont McKenna College
890 Columbia Avenue
Claremont, CA 91711-6425
Website: www.claremontmkenna.edu
Admission Telephone: 909-621-8088
Undergraduates: 1,301; 684 Men, 617 Women

Harvey Mudd College
31 Platt Boulevard
Claremont, CA 91711
Website: www.hmc.edu
Admission Telephone: 909-621-8011
Undergraduates: 773; 450 Men, 323 Women

Pitzer College
1050 North Mills Avenue
Claremont, CA 91711-6101
Website: www.pitzer.edu
Admissions Telephone: 909-621-8129
Undergraduates: 1,025; 416 Men, 609 Women

Pomona College
333 N. College Way
Claremont, CA 91711-6312
Website: www.pomona.edu
Admissions Telephone: 909-621-8134
Undergraduates: 1,586; 777 Men, 809 women

Scripps College
1030 Columbia Avenue
Claremont, CA 91711
Website: www.scrippscollege.edu
Admissions Telephone: 800-770-1333
Undergraduates: 956 Women

Physical Environment

These five premier colleges are the western version of New England's **small ivies** and live up to that reputation superbly. Within a hundred years they have replicated and branded their identities well short of the three centuries of their peers in the northeast. Each has a particular architecture that drives its own character academically and socially. However, put together, they are more than the sum of the whole.

The physical environment is driven by the warm **southern California weather**, which allows for consistent outdoor activity. Students become strong in their biking skills and skateboarding. They can be seen walking or using mopeds and unicycles to get around. Students often wear flip-flops and shorts in November as they walk from one campus to the other. Because the colleges are **adjacent to one another**, it's common to have Pitzer students interact with Harvey Mudd students who are located just across the street.

The Colleges are located an hour east of Los Angeles. The San Gabriel Mountains are immediately north of the campus. There is a healthy competition among the students to see which campus uses less water in this ecologically fragile environment. Students are attracted to the Claremont campuses where they can pick limes and grapefruit on their way to class.

Pomona College has the largest lawns, playing fields and open spaces affording the organic farm started by students concerned about sustainability. The faculty and staff are **nurturing** toward the students offering their students free 10:30 PM snacks.

Claremont McKenna has an expansive interior courtyard that promotes students mingling at the snack bar on the perimeter while others play Frisbee or lay on the grass. The Spanish-style plaza, the Parent Field, is large enough to serve as the **congregation point** for the student population of all the five colleges and is often used for socials. However the new Kravis Center, solving the parking problem underground and offering distinctive architecture above ground with glass, water and cantilevered wings, now takes center place for congregation and entry to the CMK campus interior.

Pitzer College is the most "**artsy**" campus with many cartoon panels/vignettes painted on the walls. The huge "Dali-style" mural on the outside of the dining hall is impressive. The new **residential life project** has completed and opened the first phase of dormitories. They were designed by committee and seem to reflect the input of many perspectives, reminiscent of 1950s and 60's motels constructed along the highways of that era. Comfy they have to be!!

Scripps College is located in the center, surrounded by Harvey Mudd, Pitzer, Claremont McKenna and the graduate university. Scripps boasts a beautiful courtyard surrounded by the dance studio, art museum and theatre arts center lending a **cultural** feeling to this campus. The dorms are furnished with antiques and rugs. All dorms are living-and-learning units, so that classes are held entirely in the same building where students live.

Harvey Mudd takes up a narrow rectangular area on the northern perimeter of the Claremont campuses. The residence halls are located at one end of Mudd campus and students **skateboard** down to the dining hall and library at the other end. The campus celebrated the demolition of the Thomas-Garrett hall in 2011 with nostalgia and pneumatic drills in making way for a 70,000 square foot reconstitution of same in 2013.

Social Environment

Each of the Claremont Colleges can be viewed with their individual social style and unique values of the student body.

At Pomona approximately a quarter of its students are valedictorians, and the rest rank in the top 10 percent of the class. They are **high-achieving** students who like to talk, have fun and **relax**. They are **clean-cut** and happy to be at Pomona. They have interests in non-academic activities as well, such as ballroom dancing. What they wear is not important as long as it is comfortable, so there are many jeans and T-shirts, knapsacks, soccer gear and of course, lots of cell phones. The student body consists of a mix of liberals and conservatives. They are interested in discovering various perspectives ranging from the realistic to the imaginative to the outrageous.

Harvey Mudd is the engineering college for the Claremont campus. Those who select the engineering major are comfortable and confident with the broad-based engineering studies. Their team-based approach starts in first the year and it pulls in students who like to **collaborate** and socialize. Ultimate Frisbee is a favorite on this campus. High school students who may have spent their last four years behind a keyboard will grow in their ability to converse and express complex ideas.

Claremont McKenna has a reputation for being the most social of the colleges and hosting the most popular and well-attended parties. Typically, these students are **polished** and sure of themselves. Approximately 95 percent are in the top five percent of their high school class, so it's no surprise that from Sunday through Friday they are in their room studying intensely. The college motto is "Leaders in the Making." The 1,000 or so CMK students tend to be politically conservative. There seems to be a strong bond among these students who are studying to be future movers and shakers in business and industry. Although it's ok to be undecided, many students arrive with specific career goals in mind.

Pitzer students are the most counter-culture and **quirky** of the five campuses. They are the most likely to hold demonstrations and march for peace. As witnessed by their manner of dress and behavior, they like to communicate their uniqueness. There is a sense that a student can kick back here and explore their individuality and that of others.

Scripps attracts contemporary, **composed** girls who like to express themselves through the dramatic arts, reading and writing. This is a group comfortable with traditional, humanistic values focusing on caring for others. Campus social life is richly supplemented by programs and activities in the Scripps residence halls.

Compatibility with Personality Types and Preferences

The five Claremont Colleges, collectively known as the Consortium, operate in five different environments with five separate admission offices. Their cultural environments seem to stem from the time period each was founded. They physically sit across the street from each other, sharing the same compact campus space. It is a great combination and it is not surprising that they have an educational fit for all sixteen of the Personality Types. Pomona College with its claim to being first, 1887, and the sponsor to the rest is also the wise granddaddy. Their founders embraced a leadership role and looked far into the future (N). Pomona has an intellectually peaceful environment that stimulates the connection between student and knowledge. In this way, Pomona encourages passion with reason. Scripps College, the women's college of the Consortium, was founded next in the roaring 20s with the liberated ideals of the times. Since then it has developed an educational philosophy that graduates competent (S) women who take their place in society without fanfare. Claremont McKenna is a WWII baby,

PERSONALITY MATCH

ISTJ	ISFJ	INFJ	INTJ
ISTP	ISFP	INFP	INTP
ESTP	ESFP	ENFP	ENTP
ESTJ	ESFJ	ENFJ	ENTJ

founded in 1946. While winning is not their motto, the triumph that came with winning that war has seeped into CMC's culture. Leadership is a strong characteristic (T) within this student body which catapults them into dynamic professions. Harvey Mudd, the very unique engineering college, moved into a cultural open space at the Claremont institution. Their administration brought in the extraordinary emphasis on humanity (F) and put it together with technological disciplines. In 1955, America was struggling with ever increasing weaponry and technical progress that threatened to spin out of man's control; this is the turbulent vortex that Harvey Mudd competently jumped into. The youngest in the Consortium, Pitzer College, grew up in the 1960s counter culture and lovingly embraced those ideals. Here it is more than OK to be uncertain (P); in fact, it helps Pitzer students dig deep into the meaning of our souls.

In the following listing of college majors it is important to remember that students can fit into any college and can be successful in any major. We have found that the Personality Types below fit very well at this college. The course-of-study chosen for each Personality Type corresponds to MBTI® research and is presented as an example favorable for that type.

ISTJ can follow their desire to go into civil service positions through the Pomona's **Public Policy Analysis** major. It can combine with a major that further allows this type to take advantage of their comfort level with numbers. The **Economics** concentration is designed to combine with this major and, together, could easily attract this type to apply to Pomona. At the same time, Scripps College offers an approach to economics that could work for the lady ISTJ. "Intermediate Microeconomic Theory" looks at the role of government and this type often appreciates well delineated roles and responsibilities.

ISTP works well at Pomona College, Scripps and Harvey Mudd because all offer compatible learning environments for this objective type. **Computer Science** at Harvey Mudd mixes experiment, theory and design. The ISTP will be pleased with this degree which blends logic and philosophy in its attempt to harness the dynamic discipline. For example, the course in "Artificial Intelligence" will include searching, learning and representation within the environment of uncertainty. The **Art** major at Pomona has a strong technological influence and what artistic ISTP could resist "Electron Wrangling for Beginners." At Scripps, the **Psychology** major garners knowledge through observation, participation and experimental investigation. This approach leans toward utility in the field of psychology that could lead to a career in forensic psychology.

ESTP at Claremont McKenna might dive into economics through the **Financial Economic** Sequence. This concentration examines the cultural environment of high finance and allows this type to see how their instinctual problem solving can be applied in this discipline. Harvey Mudd supports a dynamic and exciting trial-and-error approach to learning about the physical world. For this type who would rather leave the books on the shelf, Harvey Mudd offers a dream come true education.

ESTJ at Pomona College could look to the **Molecular Biology** major that offers an interdisciplinary approach. That makes sense to this very practical type because it draws from the chemistry and biology disciplines. The major would provide excellent access to research and all the needed prep for moving toward medical school. The

History major at Scripps is of sufficient breadth and offers depth through the senior thesis. ESTJ's often honor history and tradition plus they have the internal focus to prepare themselves for interesting and rewarding careers in the field of history. Claremont McKenna offers an **Ethics** Sequence that requires three interesting courses in natural law, ethical theory, and morality. This is paired with any major at the college and ESTJ's objective personality will help this type learn to successfully engage in abstract ethical discussions in college, grad school and beyond.

ISFJ who is interested in **Dance** will find an outstanding program at Scripps. The major assumes that dance is an expressive art form and prepares graduates for a variety of career options such as arts administration, dance therapy and studies in kinesiology. The growing field of linguistics could draw this type in as well. At Pitzer, the **Linguistics** major is especially rich in its coursework such as Mathematical and Computational Foundations of Linguistics. Who would have guessed these two go together? Unless you know that math is another language.

ISFP who is inclined toward arts and crafts will be a good match for Pitzer College. At Pitzer, this type will be able to pursue a love of the arts while exploring and defining a successful career path. Perhaps the student will design a **Special Major** with coursework like Mexican Visual Cultures, Sculptural Objects Functional Art and Tropical Ecology with Biostatistics and Natural Resource Management. This student might wander into the national park service, arts administration or nonprofit organizations that promote the art/nature connection.

ESFP will find a very unique major that could suit them at Pitzer within the science field. The major in **Human Biology** connects the pure sciences with the social sciences. This human interface makes the objective study of science palatable for this type who is so friendly and practical. The program initiative titled Cross Cultural Health and Healing offers study that fits in with alternative medicine; both offer the right balance and focus for this type. The **Biology** major at Harvey Mudd offers the semester in environmental sciences at Woods Hole Marine Biological Laboratory in Massachusetts. Here this type can find a wonderful, creative, can do, hands-on laboratory research world that would support many graduate study options.

ESFJ at Pitzer College will find the **Religious Studies** field is viewed through the interface between political science and economic filters. The meaning of human life weaves throughout the courses in this major and campus activities. The ESFJ can also pair it with the practical discipline found in the **Organizational Studies** major at Pitzer. In the five Claremont Colleges environment, this unusual major/minor combination would make for a fun conversation at the coffee house.

INFJ interested in psychology at Pitzer will be able to feed their soul and develop that vision with courses like "Applied Community Psychology" and the compelling course "Study of Lives." At Pomona, the **Environmental Analysis** Program will let this type indulge with satisfaction in the art of problem solving as applied to the fields of law, medicine, conservation, global climate, urban planning and resource management. At Harvey Mudd, creativity rules, and the major in **Mathematical Biology** crosses over into evolutionary biology. With a sufficient background and the investigative bent of Mudders, this type could make a real contribution in research graduate studies that support practices in occupational and physical therapies, not to mention kinesiology. At Claremont McKenna, the goal driven INFJ can get prepared to find solutions to our most difficult societal problems such as terrorism and abusive governments with the **Human Rights, Genocide and Holocaust** studies.

INFP at Harvey Mudd can put their dreaming and conceptual skills to good use by majoring in **Physics.** The major is heavily dependent on experimental or theoretical research and encourages students to follow their hearts while advancing humankind. **Theater and Dance**, for the coordinated INFP at Pitzer, encourages exploration of the purpose behind entertainment and form. This is particularly true with dramaturgy and mime. Studying "Language and the Mind" will prove to be rewarding for this type at Pomona College in the **Linguistics and Cognitive Science** major. The course, "Topics in Metaphysics," allows this type to explore philosophy and perception through language.

ENFP at Pomona College can comfortably look for the big picture in the major **Philosophy, Politics and Economics**. This course of study allows a student to ponder on right and wrong as well as focus on reality. Surely the problem-analyses in this major will get the ideas flowing freely. The **American Studies** major at Pitzer College offers a strong perspective of our country which addresses the multiple ethnic influences that have shaped American culture, with one seeming exception, that of the European immigrations via Ellis Island. However, this is typically a missing thread in most American studies. This type will enjoy the wiggle room that is afforded by the department. At Harvey Mudd, this type will want to take up the interdisciplinary major, **Biological Chemistry**. It is an emerging discipline with amazing new discoveries and will fascinate the ENFP.

ENFJ could study the **Environmental Studies** major at Pitzer College and look for the human potential in varied ecology practices. One of the courses that move in this direction is the "Nature and Society in Amazonia." At Pitzer College, the human impact on nature will be studied in depth. At Claremont McKenna, the student majoring in **Government** would become astute in reference to the connection between power and governing. This type will select from concentrations dictated by their personal values. Harvey Mudd is a place where the **Chemistry** major could focus on Chemical Education coursework and receive a certificate on completion of a teaching internship in K-12. At Scripps College, this type could pursue the major in **Art Conservation**. Careers in consulting can appeal to this type who can also be passionate and must be passionate to marshal the necessary financial resources to conserve historic art.

INTJ might look closely at the **Neuroscience major** offered at Pomona College. It includes emerging concepts about the brain with courses like "Biological Basis of Psychopathology" and "Neuroethology: Mechanisms of Behavior." At Claremont McKenna, this type would look at the **Economics and Engineering** program, a dual degree with Harvey Mudd. This five-year degree would offer the intensity and the access to a career that would push the edges of building science for human needs. At Scripps, the resources are rich and available 24 hours to their student majoring in **Art** and this helps the INTJ meet their intense need for depth and analysis for meaning.

INTP who is interested in **Psychology** will like the strong emphasis on the scientific method/theory which is interlaced with the psychology major at Pomona. The nature of this psychology degree program offers an excellent stepping stone to professional schools for many fields. The **Philosophy** major at Pitzer College should keep this type's desire for deep thinking fairly satisfied with courses like "Introduction to Knowledge, Mind and Existence." At Harvey Mudd, the degree in **Mathematics** will be fun because of great math software programs like Mathematica and Matlab which allow this type to stay up late solving problems.

ENTP often attracted to politics could pursue the **Russian and Eastern European Studies** at Pomona College. Those knowledgeable of the history and ways of the Slavic peoples are in demand. Comfortable in powerful organizations, this type will offer up original interpretations should they enter a career in international politics. Whatever major ENTP might select at Claremont McKenna, it can be complimented with the **Computer Science** Sequence, a strong set of courses designed to give a graduate excellent data analysis skills. The utility of bringing software analysis to a field will definitely make good sense to this type. Harvey Mudd will resonate with the ENTP because optimism in technology and its role in solving human problems are prevalent throughout all the studies on this campus.

ENTJ should see value in the **Science, Technology and Society** major at Pomona. This type loves the large ideas and global reach of this major. At the same time, this type will be looking to put it to practical use for the future in business, politics or law. Claremont McKenna offers course electives in **Legal Studies**. Among other perspectives, this program option looks at the law as a collection of societal values. This will appeal to the ENTJ who works very hard. Forceful in a court of law, this type would try to instill positive social values in the legal verdict. The major in **Italian** is offered only at Scripps College and the Italian corridor in the dormitory has a visiting Italian resident who enriches this major. For the ENTJ, the major could lead to a number of artistic enterprises that combine creativity and consulting in the Italian culture.

COLBY COLLEGE

4800 Mayflower Hill
Waterville, ME 04091
Website: www.colby.edu
Admissions Telephone: 800-723-3032
Undergraduates: 1,615; 854 Men, 961 Women

Physical Environment

Colby College is built on a hill that **overlooks the town** of Waterville, (population: 15,000), which grew on the banks of the Kennebec River during the industrial revolution. Many students at Colby College like to ski and to snowboard at the nearby resorts in the mountains. This is an **athletic**, energetic crowd, comfortable in the outdoors. In the wintertime, they walk or cross-country ski from one side of the quad to the other on their way to class. Students love these natural surroundings and become **conscientious** about protecting natural environments. They love this quintessential New England setting.

Colby's campus architecture is uniform in red brick buildings lined up neatly around the rectangular campus green. It is punctuated by the Miller Library at the very top of Mayflower Hill. Students here are **traditional** and accept a puritan work ethic that embraces hard work and mirrors this traditional **Norman Rockwell** setting. They develop thick blood and accept the winter season, very much looking forward to the spring. The dance majors like to practice on the lawn after the snow has melted and the greens reveal its color. This re-energizes students from the long winter. The entire quad is covered with students looking to catch the beginning of their summer tan.

Looking out from the library is not only a vantage point, but anchors the campus and one can see the well-used sports fields below. Students get a good workout going up and down the hill on their way to and from practices. The downtown area feels like a small city, but students essentially remain on campus for the most part. Colby College appeals to these **environmentally respectful** students with its 714 acre campus that includes the Perkins Arboretum, Marston Bog and a bird sanctuary with many walking trails. The new BioMass electrical plant is near completion and complements the academic philosophy of Colby: reduce the college's ecological footprint and conserve all manner of energy and reuse it.

Social Environment

Colby College students are a smart bunch. More than half of these students rank in the top 10 percent of their high school class. They are smartly dressed and are **high achievers**. While mindful of how they present themselves they manage to study, study, study and play at least one club or varsity sport. Some have skied competitively in the Junior Olympics. Others may even join Colby's competitive Cycling Club that is gaining position on the national scene. Athletically, a fair number of these Colby students juggle many things successfully.

More than half of these students come from outside New England although a sizeable group says they are from "just outside of Boston." There is distinct **city-**

sophisticate flair to this rural campus. At the same time, students here are more than accepting of their professors' mentorship and support. They come to expect and appreciate this **extra attention**. The intellectual experience is **guided and structured** under the tutelage of professors. Study abroad is encouraged as a community service. What about politics? Similar to many colleges, students at Colby tend to be left of center, and question the status quo as a common rite of passage. However, these students are comfortable with traditional values as they eagerly explore cultural and social perspectives. The graduates believe that their multi-cultural studies will positively impact the communities in which they will work and live.

Compatibility with Personality Types and Preferences

Colby College presents a steady educational journey through four years of exacting undergraduate collegiate studies. The administration and faculty expect that students will gain "a broad acquaintance with human knowledge." The Colby College approach to learning seems sequential (S), orderly and often project-based or discovery based and is known as the Colby Plan. The administration highly integrates the concepts of tolerance and inclusion into campus cultural events as well as course offerings. Colby undergraduates utilize numerous avenues to learn about the beliefs and values of cultures other than their own. Students, for the most part, expect and appreciate the sensitive, empathic views (F) toward world cultures and national ethnicities. There is a broad and critical review of American history and culture as presented in the American Studies major for students who are interested in keeping their focus closer to home. Along these lines, the administration and faculty place much emphasis on campus activities that are earth friendly and highlight national and world conservation issues. In many ways, stewardship drives this campus culture. Colby students arrive as freshmen and graduate with this consistent value which permeates their careers and personal beliefs.

PERSONALITY MATCH

ISTJ	ISFJ	INFJ	INTJ
ISTP	ISFP	INFP	INTP
ESTP	ESFP	ENFP	ENTP
ESTJ	ESFJ	ENFJ	ENTJ

In the following listing of college majors it is important to remember that students can fit into any college and can be successful in any major. We have found that the Personality Types below fit very well at this college. The course-of-study chosen for each Personality Type corresponds to MBTI® research and is presented as an example favorable for that type.

ISFJ with fine organizational and recall abilities is the perfect type for careers in research and could excel as a curator in any number of natural history or science museums. The major in **Science, Technology and Society** at Colby is an excellent preparation for this work and it lets ISFJ make important contributions, yet remain independent in doing so.

ESFP often loves animals and can prepare for entry into the veterinary sciences with a concentration in **Cell and Molecular Biology/Biochemistry.** The options after graduation would include veterinarian, vet techs and numerous positions with animal reserves and zoos. As more species seem to be moving toward endangered status, there will be increasing efforts to reestablish them and the ESFP who has this coursework on their resume will be find it has much applicability.

ESTP will like the **Administrative Science** minor at Colby College. Of course, it combines nicely with a broad number of majors. The minor's survey of American organizations, public and private, is a good foundation for the risk taking ESTP considering going into small business, franchising or consulting after graduation. The course Intro to Financial Decision Making gives this type the basic tools for success in one of their favorite pastimes—negotiation.

ISFP often times likes to help others, offering services that are delivered through professional groups or organizations. The concentration in **Neuroscience** at Colby College is an excellent preparation for addiction counselors or therapists. The course Biological Basis of Behavior will be a good start for ISFP to explore the helping professions for future career options, especially in substance abuse services.

ENFJ will identify with a minor in **Human Development** since it will provide a good preparation for careers attractive to this type in child welfare services. The required courses include looking at the presence of risk and resilience in American teen cultures. ENFJ is attracted to improving the quality of life for others and will enjoy the flexibility that this minor offers for future and concurrent educational studies. Colby offers a number of educational studies which are not offered at other institutions. In this particular minor, the course titled Boys to Men addresses an area of contemporary American society about which academia is silent for the most part.

ESTJ who is attracted to numbers will benefit from a minor in **Mathematics** at Colby. It would not be unusual for this type to find themselves drawn to leadership positions on campus and after graduation. With a minor in mathematics, the ESTJ will likely rise to increasing levels of management over the course of a career. This minor with its strong offerings in both pure and applied math allows the ESTJ to gather enough solid experience with numbers to move confidently within national research institutions at the executive levels, especially if paired with any of the strong science majors at Colby.

ESFJ is often interested in the community, and this type's natural ability to reduce tension in conflicted situations suggests moving into careers that serve the public. The **Economics** minor at Colby College offers a good deal of flexibility to direct studies toward a student's interest. This minor can offer the foundational courses for an independent major that centers on **Health Studies** and draws courses from biology, anthropology and global studies.

COLGATE UNIVERSITY

13 Oak Drive
Hamilton, NY 13346
Website: www.colgate.edu
Admission Telephone: 315-228-7401
Undergraduates: 2,884; 1,349 Men, 1,535 Women

Physical Environment

Colgate University is located in **rural,** central New York, in the small town of Hamilton. After students exit from I- 90, they see expanses of farmlands, silos, cows and even a llama farm. The Colgate campus is built on a hill and the library gives the impression of a castle surrounded by water and well-tended fields. It brings out the romantic side in the students. It's not surprising that rumor has it they are fans of Harry Potter and read the volumes in Spanish while decked out in Potter attire.

At the O'Conner Campus Center, the COOP, there hangs a globe fashioned by an architect to remind students of globalization. Students here develop **international perspectives** because over half of them study abroad and learn to live and communicate with other cultures.

The lower level cafeteria with its food for take-out is popular with students, who study a lot here and often eat on the run. Weather-hardened students love to sit and warm up around the huge, round fireplace. Residences for first-year students are at the top of the hill while dorms for older students occupy the lower levels. In this way the upper class students take the first-years under their wing. Within walking distance of the campus there are frat houses and townhomes owned by the college. This campus community is **tight-knit.**

Although the college is isolated, there is a natural back-and-forth with the folks living in the village. The college bookstore was moved there and a Colgate bus takes students to and from town The new Trudy Fitness Center has all the bells, pumps and whistles; but better yet, it has a fab video previewing the facility that brings smiles to a viewer's face and humor to physical fitness routines.

Social Environment

Clubs, clubs, clubs define the highly extroverted nature of students on this campus. Leadership, community service and cultural explorations are high on the list of after class activities for all Colgate students. These undergraduates use Colgate as a lab in which to try out their skills. Essentially all of the students were in the top 20 percent of their high school graduating class. They are able to juggle many activities while getting good grades. They are attracted by the high level of **nurturing and advising** they receive from the faculty. On occasion professors will accompany the students abroad.

Many students love it here because they have a deep affection for the liberal arts. They find it easy to satisfy the core curriculum requirements and enjoy the many inter-disciplinary courses. **Imaginative** students are attracted by these classes. Logically-minded students are equally attracted to the new science complex.

Nearly half of the students join a fraternity or sorority after their first year, providing more options to develop leadership and planning abilities. Football games are both athletic and social events where many friends cross paths. The college is proud to have a substantial number of African American students on campus. Jewish students are also a strong presence and have access to kosher foods and weekly Kabbalat Shabbat worship services.

Compatibility with Personality Types and Preferences

At Colgate University there is an exceptional learning relationship between the student and professor. It is exceptional (F) in the sense of the support provided to the student. It takes the form of faculty prompting student leadership, discovery and invention characteristics of independence, rather than mentoring relationships. At Colgate support seems to translate into academic courage, so one finds less emphasis than typical on learning centers and tutoring. You find academic support after a good number of clicks into the website as you come across the writing center. The Colgate education is characterized by an intense process of student professor advising, albeit leading to independent thinkers. It pushes each student to reach within and outside of Colgate, to build knowledge in their chosen major. In this way, the Colgate experience supports exploration (P) followed by analysis (T).

In the following listing of college majors it is important to remember that students can fit into any college and can be successful in any major. We have found that the Personality Types below fit very well at this college. The course-of-study chosen for each Personality Type corresponds to MBTI® research and is presented as an example favorable for that type.

PERSONALITY MATCH

ISTJ	ISFJ	INFJ	INTJ
ISTP	ISFP	INFP	INTP
ESTP	ESFP	ENFP	ENTP
ESTJ	ESFJ	ENFJ	ENTJ

ISFJ and the **Educational Studies** major at Colgate are compatible because of this type's thoroughness and perseverance. ISFJ is likely to provide a steady, stable class environment for children. This major provides an extensive look at the difficult issues surfacing in our schools. Colgate asks their graduates to critically observe today's problems and take leadership by implementing solutions. This type will be more comfortable than others in accepting this awesome responsibility in today's classrooms across our communities.

INFJ could quickly justify the **Peace and Conflict Studies** major at Colgate as a great preparation for a graduate degree. The INFJ really resonates with this topic and also is always ready for a challenge. This research based major offers three areas of concentration: collective violence, human security and international social justice. Working with others in harmony and yet persuading them toward a common good is a true skill of this type.

INFP often wants to contribute to a cause that they believe in passionately. If they have a scientific bent and toleration for math, the **Environmental Economics** major at Colgate could be a happy find. The study of the environment easily lends itself to passion and the answers are complex and varied. Combined with economics, this major can keep INFP intensely busy reflecting on their values while preparing to sally forth and save the planet after graduation.

ESFP is a warm type of personality and well matched to the **Caribbean Studies** emphasis within Africana and Latin American Studies. As an emphasis it is unusual and it draws the undergraduate to visit Caribbean nations where untraditional and simple health care systems still have a presence in the culture. This type's curiosity about people might prompt them to carve out a career in providing practical health services to nations within the north and south American continents.

ENFP is drawn to the abstract and the major in **Philosophy and Religion**. The coursework in this major is very expansive in its review of human thought and meaning. In addition to the extraordinary Political Science Department, this type can flutter from one intriguing course to the next. Colgate's Center for Conservative Political Thought, now renamed in politically current phraseology as the Center for Freedom and Western Civilization was originally a refreshing dose of political perspective. The last update for this Center is of the 2005-2006 era. ENFP, always independent, might elect to develop human perspective with a thorough, complete study of political history and theory, but it will have to be fun!

ENTP in the **Natural Science** major will find a strong data-based curriculum with freedom to focus in an area of their scientific curiosity. Surely the emerging discipline of neuroscience which combines biology, chemistry and psychology is sufficiently wide enough to capture and retain the wide ranging observations of this type.

ESFJ who likes math is going to heartily approve of the **Applied Mathematics** minor at Colgate. This type lives well in orderly environments and what can be more orderly than math. As a minor, Colgate allows the interested student to bypass some of the abstraction of theoretical numbers. Instead, the ESFJ is going to like using the numbers to bring reason into disorderly data dumps they may find upon graduating into the world of work.

ENFJ who is ordinarily drawn to the field of communication is going to like the **Writing and Rhetoric** minor at Colgate University. Their gift of intuition will be in the spotlight during discussion in the unique course titled Visual Rhetorics. Our society is moving away from the written communications, while at the same time relying more on visuals and sound bites and ENFJ is good at the interface of all of these three.

ENTJ might decide to concentrate in **Astrophysics** if they spent a lot of time star gazing as a child. Drawn to the sciences and new ideas, this type will also appreciate the high use of logic in math, physics, geology and chemistry required by this major. ENTJ has the willingness to long-range plan and is comfortable with complexity. That is perfect for the upcoming scientific exploration as the Ares rocket or its follow on is likely to take America back to the moon in the first half of this century.

COLLEGE OF CHARLESTON

66 George Street
Charleston, SC 29424-0001
Website: www.cofc.edu
Admissions Telephone: 843-953-5670
Undergraduates: 10,121; 3,803 Men, 6,318 Women
Graduate Students: 270 Men, 1,234 Women

Physical Environment

The College of Charleston is located in the historic district of downtown Charleston. It's within walking distance of palatial southern homes such as the well-known historic row of houses called "the Battery," which overlooks the sea and Fort Sumter in the distance, the site of the start of the Civil War. The College of Charleston is the oldest institution of higher education in South Carolina; formerly a private institution, it is now a public college with all the **charm** of an era gone by. The physical center of campus is Randolph Hall and the grass-covered cistern in front of it. The new Cato Center for the Arts is an expansive facility by any standard with floors devoted individually to dance/theater, photography, visual art, music and exhibiting space. The new School of Sciences and Mathematics building wraps around a courtyard, so typical of historic Charleston. This urban campus is intertwined with city streets with many buildings being located between King and Pitt streets. Yet 17 miles south of the campus is the Dixie Plantation, a sustainable experimental enterprise that garners much grant support for its important research.

The College of Charleston has enjoyed a period of substantial growth resulting in a much improved campus. The housing situation is ideal with many more students getting into a residence hall instead of having to rent in town. Extracurricular programming in the halls helps students develop leadership as they learn and grow. The Honors College is located on campus and houses 650 honors students in some exceptionally beautiful buildings. Fraternities and sororities have houses on Wentworth and Coming Street. A **state of the art library** offers many areas in which to study quietly or with others. The nearby Medical University of South Carolina attracts many students who are thinking of graduate school and are interested in science and research or medical school.

Even though admission requirements are higher for out-of-state students, students flock to College of Charleston, charmed by the physical environment and attracted to the **strong sciences, business and performing arts**. The nearby open air market has basket weavers and ethnic Gullah stringing sweet-grass into pleasing patterns. Students enjoy this historic cultural environment that still speaks of the 1860s post-revolutionary period. As they stroll through the city, they take in the beautiful views of the sea, sometimes interrupted by undergraduates from the nearby military college, huffing and puffing along for their daily exercise in the typically fine weather.

Social Environment

What's highly valued at College of Charleston is getting along with people of various cultures and religions. There is an intense respect for the **historic past and cultural richness** of society here. There is a diverse pool of students with nearly one out of five hailing from African American or Hispanic backgrounds. There are legacy students from families with long historical lines and an aura of sophisticated society can permeate the social scene.

There are many more women than men at College of Charleston. The romance of traditional values of appearance and dress prevail in the student body, along with social mannerisms punctuating speech and manner. Students are well groomed even if they sport dreadlocks. Social activities are also traditional, from going out to bars and restaurants to attending frat parties and basketball games. The social life is light-hearted and leans toward the arts. **Service and volunteer efforts** mirror student hometown extracurricular activities. Habitat for Humanity and fundraising for medically at-risk children in nearby Medical University of South Carolina are well supported by undergraduates. The college has over 100 extracurricular clubs. They range from the campus democrats and republicans to ballroom dancing, crew and fencing. Students who like to socialize and study with others are well-suited to this campus. Successful students summon the discipline to minimize the call of Charleston's historic and social attractions.

The college serves mostly South Carolinians and its mission is to educate people of South Carolina. It has a strong adult division and graduate school. Secondarily, the college recruits students from all over the U.S. and the world with the international port lending credibility to their interdisciplinary programs and international logistics programs.

Well-prepared students for this college ranked in the top quarter of their class in high school. Students will enter a learning environment where they are required to think abstractly under the direction of professors who are innovatively teaching. **Imaginative** students who are future-oriented will be able to invent and re-invent themselves here. Undergraduates who like to socialize and study with others are well-suited to this campus. Students here are very welcomed by the city's artistic and professional leaders who utilize the students' talents in the several city-wide performing arts venues.

Compatibility with Personality Types and Preferences

College of Charleston is remarkable and admired for its preservation of historically accurate American culture. The emphasis on the performing arts and the sense of America's place in the world community is strong. The impact of the port and the city's historic origination in the 1600s has seeped into the philosophy of the administration and faculty. The curriculum offers an element of practicality (S) that reflects the needs of today's specialized careers and the college's location on the Atlantic seaboard. Students also want to attend courses taught by faculty that is knowledgeable of the American economic environment. The performing arts curriculum is solid and mirrors the city's international reputation for beauty, charm and entertainments. The Arts department predictably connects the educational studies in the arts with the city's own strong artistic legacy. At College of Charleston undergraduate students in the arts access the city's well known festivals through internships as performers and with stage management. Undergraduate student support for the annual Spoleto festival is well integrated by the College and the city. It provides that realistic thread that undergraduates here prefer. The port of Charleston is the background for the unusual and very practical study in global logistics. Incoming freighters, offloading goods that must travel to America's heartland, bring the subject of logistics alive. The international port has also influenced the solid business school that has been teaching upperclass business courses in Spanish, French and German for many years. The college archives proudly possess invaluable Jewish documents from the pre-colonial period which serve to

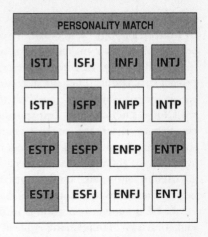

enliven cultural studies on campus. It all makes for a collegiate environment that wisely reaches into its location for academic and cultural identity.

In the following listing of college majors it is important to remember that students can fit into any college and can be successful in any major. We have found that the Personality Types below fit very well at this college. The course-of-study chosen for each Personality Type corresponds to MBTI® research and is presented as an example favorable for that type.

INFJ will be at the top of their game in the business field when it involves serving the public directly. The **Arts Management** major at College of Charleston really offers this possibility. INFJs who are often artistically sensitive souls will enjoy indulging their need for personal expression through the medium of organizing and presenting arts for the community. Their independent innovative thinking will be an asset in this field that demands flexible planning. COC offers a practical thread of required financial coursework within this major.

INTJ enjoys the responsibility and demands that come with leadership. As a result, this type often gravitates to professional positions of authority. The major in **Geology and Environmental Geosciences** at College of Charleston is representative of a discipline that is becoming critical to our country and the world community. The opportunities for specialization within this field are surprising. The department has a large array of research projects that undergraduate students support through field experiences literally around the globe and especially in the field of oceanography. Now that makes sense.

ISTJ will approve of the specific curriculum in the business school for undergraduates in the **Accounting** major. Graduates in this major often pursue further training and certifications. Undergraduate students at the College of Charleston will be in a good position to enter the advanced training because of the diligence the school follows in shaping the curriculum in this precise discipline. ISTJs love it all: accuracy, precision and diligence.

ISFP is caring all of the time and cautious some of the time. This type prefers to be out and about, performing work that requires attention to detail. ISFPs will thrive in technical professions with a cause such as ecological work that leans in green directions. The major in biology at College of Charleston has an excellent program in **Marine Biology.** The proximity of the ocean and the inland waters in the low sections of the coast makes for ideal laboratory field trips.

ESTP is often excellent at seeing what needs to get done in order to finish a project that is due. They are also pretty realistic about what resources are needed to get the job done on time. With these characteristics, ESTPs are a good bet for the **Global Logistics and Transportation** program at College of Charleston. ESTPs can elect to declare this concentration or a minor within the business degree. High stakes decisions involving movement of company products around the globe are agreeable for this type who prefers a little action to spice up their day. The port of Charleston lends a fine opportunity to gain knowledge about intermodal transport, where commodities must transfer from ship to rail or ship to truck.

ESFP is good at occupations in the service industry. The major in **Hospitality and Tourism Management** is particularly appropriate in Charleston and for the ESFPs. This major is rather uncommon at liberal arts colleges and universities. It is also in growing demand with societies' increasing emphasis on leisure and entertainment. This type is a natural at hosting events, often making others feel appreciated and welcome. ESFP's good communication skills will come in handy as they work with municipalities and corporate leaders to win approval of their novel and fun recreational proposals.

ENTP must have the opportunity to think about the future during the day. This creative type will like the futuristic work involved with restoration in the major **Historic Preservation and Community Planning.** The College of Charleston is unique in combining these two specializations in such a strong, credible curriculum. ENTPs are adept at strategic planning as they utilize their vision and their willingness to take risks. This type is also pretty good at persuasion which will be needed to secure funds for cultural projects while competing with nuts and bolts budgets. The downtown historic district of Charleston serves as a dream-come-true internship location for this type and this major. The city and the college have a unique synergy.

ESTJ is an ideal personality to pursue the concentration in **Discovery Infomatics**. This unusual combination of courses is oriented toward ecommerce and data mining. ESTJs are just the type to focus on the details and organization needed to master this rather abstract field. It harkens toward a skill set which can be applied to all academic fields from insects and their critical link to the biosphere on our planet to...simply e-commerce.

ENFP could find it hard to declare a major because of their wide-ranging and sincere interest in so many subjects. The field of **Geology** for that very reason is a good one for this type. From physics to policy, ENFPs can decide where they want to work—in the field collecting dirt samples or in the halls of Congress advocating for the environment. The major at Wooster is wonderfully open and laid back in that students are given great freedom to find their passion within the discipline. Once found however, it is time to step up their game and Wooster has the mechanisms in place to reign in freewheeling ENFPs. On the academic move, graduates might end up on the Brooks McCall gathering samples at the epicenter of the Gulf oil spill or coring mud tubes in the Bering Sea.

ISFP is another freewheeling type and their desire to be autonomous is honored in the **Theatre and Dance** track at College of Wooster. At this creative college, communication quickly translates to the written text in playwriting and performance. Since the department is organized around examining the human experience through art, ISFP can indulge in their favorite activity—defining living by their personal values. It's also not surprising that Wooster took regional honors in 2007 and was selected to perform "Nocturne" by Adam Rapp at the Kennedy Center in DC. The physical nature of this major is perfect and keeps ISFPs' need for action deeply satisfied.

ESFP loves to entertain and the major in **Music** at College of Wooster is right for this type with prior musical experience. The department is very well resourced and committed to providing an array of viable careers within the field. The Bachelor of Music offers concentrations in performance, theory/composition or history/literature for those interested in graduate study. The music therapy and music education majors offer career tracks for ESFPs who want to bring lighthearted fun into their world of work. For the ESFP who needs music for their soul, the minor will be a wonderful experience while interacting with the passionate music majors.

ISFJ wants to directly support, one on one, others in a caring way. This inclination definitely fits in with a demanding career in medicine as a primary physician. The **Biology** major at College of Wooster has the extra benefit of teaching time management and personal balance through the independent study requirement which forewarns the burnout often associated with medical training. The biology department promotes creativity by expecting students to conduct early and frequent investigations. This teaches ISFJ, not always comfortable with the unknown, to be confident in their creative endeavors.

ESFJ has an ease and way with people, especially if the people are in traditional settings like a hospital or school. The degree in **Music Therapy** is a bit unusual but nicely suited for this caring type. ESFJ will especially appreciate the Cleveland Music Therapy Consortium and American Music Therapy Association. These national organizations provide the guidelines for service delivery that ESFJ will want and need to be comfortable in providing therapeutic services.

ISTJ will fit into College of Wooster's **Business Economics** major quite nicely because of the department's thorough read on complex financial environments. Wooster's economics curriculum is steeped in the international perspectives that are common on this campus. The major is designed for direct entry into the workforce and this makes good sense to ISTJ. The coursework leads to a foundation in business decision making through quantitative analysis, a particular strength of this type.

INTP who is enamored with computers in high school will surely be attracted to the **Computer Science** major or minor. This type loves to analyze problems and apply solutions from a distance. Software applications that embed planning and development for business or government organizations are right up their alley. At Wooster, the department is located within the math department which makes it a particularly robust academic environment for this powerhouse concentrator—INTP.

ENTP can utilize the minor in **Film Studies** to support their chosen major in another discipline. At Wooster there is a wide range of film study across international cultures and subjects. The curriculum seeks to connect the dots between the visual and auditory output of films. ENTP excels at ingeniously analyzing information with an eye toward original synthesis. You can bet their independent study will draw the major and minor uniquely together because ENTP thrives on originality.

INFP has ideal personal traits for a College of Wooster degree in **English.** At this college, the purpose of studying texts is viewed from the vantage point of both readers and writers. Students explore the human issues raised in written works. This type will happily jump into sorting through their beliefs, assumptions and values. They typically make relevant observations on those perspectives found within the texts. In this way, they are expected to develop their own voice as a writer.

ENFJ is likely to be comfortable moving into the world of speech and language pathology. The degree in **Communication Sciences and Disorders** at College of Wooster prepares students for the graduate level study needed to practice in the field. The department emphasizes the linguistic evolution, human development, the cause of disorders and the options for service in the community. This type will naturally look to the psychological and emotional causes of speech disorders since ENFJ is quite good at diagnostics.

INFJ likes to develop new approaches to help people out. The field of alternative health practitioner may have appeal to the INFJ. College of Wooster offers an exceptionally strong grounding for careers in the health field with its degree in **Chemistry.** The curriculum supports follow on degrees in research disciplines and direct entry into the work force. In whatever field the INFJ wanders into with the major in chemistry, whether the physical sciences, medicine or business, this type is likely to want their work to promote and benefit society.

COLUMBIA UNIVERSITY

212 Hamilton Hall MC 2807
1130 Amsterdam Avenue
New York, NY 10027
Website: www.columbia.edu
Admission Telephone: 212-854-2521
Undergraduates: 7,934: 4,091 Men, 3,843 Women
Graduate Students: 13,496

Physical Environment

Founded in 1754, Columbia University is located in **Upper Manhattan**, a very lively and desirable area of this world class city. Despite the dynamic energy and heavy traffic just on the other side of their classroom windows, students tend to acclimate to the pace and drumbeat of the "Big Apple." They develop **city-smarts** while walking the streets with a buddy at night. They enjoy the outdoor cafés, the ethnic restaurants, the bookshops and the art that blankets the city neighborhoods. The students who come to Colombia usually appreciate theater and can't wait to visit Broadway productions.

Columbia College is the undergraduate division for the study of liberal arts at Columbia University. The University includes the Fu Engineering and Applied Science School for undergraduates. Also on the campus, reflecting the cosmopolitan nature of the city, is the School for General Studies. It is for older or non-traditional students. Barnard College for women is across the street from the main Columbia entrance. The close proximity of Barnard College gives access through cross-registering classes to a single-sex educational perspective. The Northwest Corner building added substantial scientific laboratories and research facilities with its seven floors. Prospective students may hear of the Manhattanville Project which is the future development of 17 acres recently secured and projected for mixed academic and residential use in the west Harlem neighborhood.

Housing is guaranteed all four years here, which is a huge upside, given the high cost of rents in NYC. Approximately 95 percent of students live in school-sponsored housing. The Morning Side brownstones with copper roofs and interesting architectural details have cozy rooms for students who may live in dorms mixed in with upper-level students. Some of the living and learning communities include residence for faculty families giving students accessibility to their professors for after-hours discussion and late evening imagination.

At night students may take a ride to the Met on their bike, thus supporting Sinatra's song "New York is the city that never sleeps." Undergraduates who like the **relentless intensity** of the city thrive on this campus.

Social Environment

New York City attracts people from all over the world and Columbia College has an incredibly multi-cultural and international undergraduate student population.

Undergraduates learn to socialize with **international** students very different from themselves. Many hail from far away corners of the world. All must be able to gain from experiencing the amazing cultural array of the city and on this campus.

Students here want to competently influence environments across the global economy and the world of emerging ideas. The Center for Student Advising assists with general educational curriculum planning. An advisor is assigned to the undergraduate for all four years. The advisor is a primary source of assistance when the student is selecting internships, struggling with a class or writing a resume.

Columbia's core requirements are demanding but well appreciated by students who want to write and think critically for the purposes of their own knowledge and that of others. The engineering school has majors and programs that are enhanced by emerging research within each discipline. Undergraduate students are expected to immerse themselves in these research designs.

One of the best ways to characterize the student body at Columbia is that they are very busy. These undergraduates are quite motivated and already have their next goal lined up. They tend to be **incredibly focused and ambitious**, which is to be expected because it is an Ivy League school. However, despite the competition, students here are still friendly and willing to collaborate which enhances the educational process. Each student brings some interesting aspect of their personality which generates searching conversations. Many of these conversations happen on the steps in front of Low Library. Despite the differences, the unifying quality that the students have here is a dedication to learn.

Social life is active during freshmen first days because each of the extracurricular clubs, fraternities and sororities are trying to encourage awareness and gain new members. After these initial weeks, many students socialize off campus in the city. The city can be exciting, but because of its **vastness** undergrads seem to form a tight group of a few friends that they hang out with on the weekends. This core group remains pretty much unchanged through to graduation for most undergraduate students. This requires active planning for those who want to branch out socially. Social life here hits the sweet spot among **intellectual endeavors** and cultural activities: museums, museums, museums and some typical college activities.

Columbia students are creative, **idea-driven** and able to explore possibilities. They tend to come from very well-educated families with successful backgrounds. Many undergraduate students are curious with few intellectual boundaries. They have **high expectations**. All, including the want-to-be engineers, receive an exceptionally fine liberal arts exposure in the Core curriculum. Students work with non-profit centers, design intranets for inner city public schools, learn about playground engineering and come to know some of the ethnic population needs of the city. Varsity show is a Columbia tradition that makes fun of the administration in a campus satire. The student body here has a strong sense of community and social consciousness with a will to promote change.

Compatibility with Personality Types and Preferences

Columbia University is the place for educational study (P) without limits. Undergraduate students are expected to conduct research in the exceptional labs.

This approach to education goes hand in hand with teaching laboratories where students are privileged to observe (S) and learn in an environment rarely constrained by budgets. Yet Columbia adds another element to this learning paradigm. The university expects and confidently predicts that during their four years on campus the undergraduates will be generating discovery in their respective fields. It is a tall order and students are carefully and precisely (J) taught to develop their reasoning (T) patterns of analysis.

The faculty and administration is equally concerned with developing the moral standard (F) and aggressively inserts that

PERSONALITY MATCH			
ISTJ	ISFJ	INFJ	INTJ
ISTP	ISFP	INFP	INTP
ESTP	ESFP	ENFP	ENTP
ESTJ	ESFJ	ENFJ	ENTJ

perspective within their curriculum. The Core is a series of required studies for entering students that delves into the great books and texts of western civilization as well as fundamental scientific laws. There is an expectation that students will develop a coherent belief system on the human condition and carry that forward in their educational studies and future careers (N). Columbia's remarkable storehouse of knowledge and resources is awaiting the undergraduate freshman. Together with the intensive academic mentoring, undergraduates are submerged in a culture that bears slight resemblance to the hometowns and metropolitan areas from which they came. Columbia University actively defines and completes part of the puzzle that is New York City.

In the following listing of college majors it is important to remember that students can fit into any college and can be successful in any major. We have found that the Personality Types below fit very well at this college. The course-of-study chosen for each Personality Type corresponds to MBTI® research and is presented as an example favorable for that type.

INFP will find the **Drama and Theater Arts** at Columbia sufficiently abstract and analytic. NYC Theaters mirror many of the complexities of American culture. Students in this major will reach to explore the American currents and seek to perfect their skills as they supplement their work with other departmental offerings. It is the INFP who appreciates the interface of theater with other disciplines and will seek to weave each into their own view of dramatic purpose. Impressions of the city's canvas and historical theater combine well to offer that additional layer to their foundation studies. INFPs would agree that it adds uncommon richness to the undergraduate education.

INFJ and imagination go together. The program in **Linguistics** is well resourced with the multiple language offerings and New York City itself. City internships, service learning and social entertainment all brim with exposure to the 300+

foreign languages spoken in the city. The course in Language Documentation and Field Methods certainly has unequalled access to native speakers and languages for undergraduates to study. Three study components comprise the major: spoken word, cognitive processing, and cultural medium.

INTJ is going to find much that suits their learning style at Columbia. This type is very energized by flexible ideas, far out concepts and the freedom to mix and match with intensity. The rather unusual discipline of **Financial Engineering** is a good example of this kind of innovation. INTJ's originality will be enthusiastically encouraged in this discipline. New quantitative methodologies are emerging in this field that requires courses in calculus, differential equations, probability and statistics. INTJs who are private and skeptical by nature may benefit from the four year advising system at Columbia.

ISTP will find plenty of facts to noodle with the **Chemical Engineering** degree. This type loves to observe and develop their own conceptual understanding of factual data. The technologies and research subjects under study in the Columbia labs will intrigue ISTPs. They must find the practical purpose in their coursework and then become an unrelenting in study. From chemical sensors to agricultural products, they will be all eyes and ears while mastering their technical skills.

ISTJ relates well to the direct nature of electricity, it is either on or off! The degree in **Electrical Engineering** at Columbia encompasses the alpha and omega of electrical transmission and this suits ISTJ just fine. This type prefers to live in the world of predictability and practicality. Nevertheless, this engineering degree has its twists and surprises that would be found the research labs. The sustained mentoring through four years at Columbia will help ISTJ to settle on their focus within the degree. They will approach and complete the Core liberal arts curriculum at Columbia with caution, yet likely approve when it is completed. This type takes time to synthesize knowledge coming in from all disciplines and it will always be available for recall.

ISFJ likes to learn with a little bit of instruction and a few encouraging suggestions. After this, they prefer the professor to step back so they can immerse themselves in the facts and master the subject at hand. This type is inclined to ponder overall meaning by comparing what they observe with other sources of information. The major in **Ecology, Evolution and Environmental Biology** offers this opportunity. This type will reach for competency, step by step, and their accuracy and thoroughness may require cross town trips to other labs of New York City's five consortium research institutions.

INTP will likely have their interest alerted by reading about the **Jazz** concentration. The nature of jazz music has enough random structure within its lilting sound to appeal to INTP who actually is attracted to random data. This power thinker would delight in homework that required analysis of jazz sounds at the clubs in NYC. Leave it to the INTP to find some patterns in the freewheeling instrumental play. The study of jazz is interdisciplinary and happily interfaces with all majors. It mirrors the musicians of this art form—intellectual, original, marching to their own drummer. This is the INTP.

ESTP will find the lively action they seek in New York City and the **Urban Studies** program. This type is a master at collaboration and they will scavenge the city for data supporting their research inquiries. It will be the ESTP who can establish near immediate rapport with the shopkeepers, finance gurus and ethnic personalities of the city. It will be the ESTP who pulls fellow students together to get a project off dead center. ESTPs like the survey nature of this major, jumping from one filter such as economics to another like architecture with ease.

ENFP is such a creative soul. Of course, the **Creative Writing** major is likely to attract simply because it has one of their favorite words in it. This well-developed major draws on literary masterpieces as well as the New York City experience. ENFPs will gladly incorporate human emotions on display in the city throughout their essays. The advisor will be important for this type. Personal relationships are highly valued by ENFPs. They look to their advisor to be an anchor for the chaotic energy of the city, as well as their own.

ENTP will like the **Information Science** major since it allows students to select a focus for the upper division courses. With the focus determined, students then learn and perfect information modeling systems. Hmmm... What will ENTP select for the focus, contemporary society, science/economy, health sciences, computer science or another discipline? This adaptable, creative type searches for value and meaning in many disciplines. Sampling the variety, ENTP will finally be willing to make that choice.

ESFJ will recognize and accept the lure of Columbia's **Education** program. The problems of urban schools and public education await ESFJ's patient commitment and sincere attention to daily life events. ESFJs will carefully prepare for student teaching in New York City's urban schools. With the support of an experienced teacher, their warmth will shine through in the city's charged classrooms filled with emotion, expectation, optimism and anxiety. It will be ESFJs who can confidently and credibly point the way into the future for their young charges. This education program combines with the undergraduate student's declared major.

ENFJ is exceptionally compelling when armed with knowledge while speaking to audiences. The major in **Business** is definitely resourced to arm ENFJ with considerable acumen in the field of business through undergraduate interface with the professional graduate school of business at Columbia. The abstract principles found in psychology and sociology are regularly studied in this curriculum for their interface with business concepts in finance, marketing and management. This approach will appeal to fine tuned ENFJs. This type also wants their advisor to help with the tough work of defining career goals.

ENTJ is a leader. They simply can't avoid providing direction to others. ENTJs are likely to be quite active in student-directed organizations prompting accomplishments, goals and service work. The degree in **Engineering Management Systems** also lends itself to this type of demanding leadership. The curriculum exposes the budding engineer to many methodologies that assess risk. As such, the graduates are armed with a foundation to make tough decisions in chaotic environments. The

ENTJ who likes math could immediately jump on board for this major that leads to action-filled careers.

CONNECTICUT COLLEGE

270 Mohegan Avenue
New London, CT 06320-4196
Website: www.conncoll.edu
Admissions Telephone: 860-439-2200
Undergraduates: 1,880; 749 Men, 1,131 Women

Physical Environment

Connecticut College, referred to as "Conn College," is located on a hill that overlooks the Thames River in Connecticut, near **the ocean**. The college is accessible by car from Route 95, the main north-south artery along the east coast. The same highway keeps students from walking to nearby downtown New London; many students bring cars to campus. Occasionally they venture west, where two of New England's largest casinos are located, to see variety shows or play rounds of golf. The nearby beaches in Connecticut and Rhode Island are real attractions in the spring and fall but also must be reached by car. For the most part, students remain focused on their studies at this enclosed campus.

The architecture on campus is classic with formal **gray-stone buildings**, which appeals to the **traditional studious types** who are drawn to this campus. The large expanse of lawn atop this hill forms the traditional landscaped quad, punctuated by stately trees. There is an arboretum on the upper side of the campus with a cottage that students use to relax and take a break from their studies.

Conn College's campus is for the most part self-sufficient but seeks to bring the outside world within the learning environment. It will enhance research activity, already considerable, with the 2012 opening of the New Science Building. This state of the art facility complements the surrounding marine ecology well used as natural laboratories for the biological sciences. The **"Study Away"** program specifically interfaces with the undergraduates major because the locations are carefully-chosen with faculty input. Students seek to integrate these off campus experiences in the most meaningful way. Upon return they enliven campus discussions while incorporating the new knowledge for their own future careers.

Social Environment

Conn College has many students that come from "just outside Boston," and if not that, then from Fairfield County, Manhattan or New Jersey. They are smart and sassy, come from similar backgrounds and for the most part, sport regular college attire. Art students, on the other hand, dress in imaginative styles and stand out in this socially active student body.

Students who make it through the stringent admission process here have **excelled** in high school and expect to do the same in college. They aspire to become **accomplished** writers, composers and mathematicians in the best liberal arts sense. In addition, many have experience in athletics, music, dance or acting. The majority of students are interested in ethnic cultures. Some get involved in CELLS, which is a study-abroad program for honor students who are fluent in another language. These high-performing students immerse themselves in deep, goal-oriented learning and conduct research projects on their own.

Student athletes think of themselves as jocks although they are not super-competitive as their mascot, "the camel" may aptly suggest. However, games are well attended by alumni, fellow students and faculty. This college is a good fit for those who can plan ahead, succeed in **demanding classes** and follow through from studying in the classroom to what they want to do in the real world.

Compatibility with Personality Types and Preferences

Connecticut College very much delivers an atmosphere that appreciates and utilizes a student's logical thinking (T). On this campus, high academic success is encouraged and appreciated. By exploring the use of emerging technologies, the college honors those who bring a futuristic, intuitive (N) approach to their learning. Anticipation and application combine well here and, together, they pull students toward problem solving perspectives. Four Interdisciplinary Centers offer certificates that expand and enrich students' knowledge of their major discipline. These certificates are an extension of the educational philosophy that promotes specialized, focused, (J) in-depth learning. Connecticut College nicely interfaces and supports research addressing social issues that students and faculty find compelling. Graduates find themselves quite prepared to enter society's institutions that are utilizing advanced technological applications.

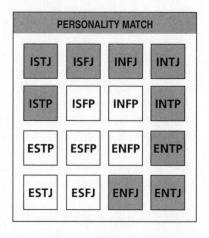

In the following listing of college majors it is important to remember that students can fit into any college and can be successful in any major. We have found that the Personality Types below fit very well at this college. The course-of-study chosen for each Personality Type corresponds to MBTI® research and is presented as an example favorable for that type.

INTJ will thrive on this campus and could select the **Conservation Biology and Environmental Studies** certificate. This certificate, one of four at the college, could reward their drive to find a larger purpose in life. It could become the underlying principal with which to pull their college studies together. Among the several requirements, INTJs inner vision will come to the forefront in the senior integrative project that presents research, findings and plans for sustainability.

ENTP can transcend boundaries here in wide-ranging dynamic discussions, but they better be prepared to logically defend their intuitive leaps. The clubs reflect the political and issues orientation of much of the student body. Club meetings that revolve around layers of issues will offer the intellectual stimulation for this restless type. The major in **International Relations** sponsors many lectures and discussion groups that would be ideal for ENTP and their nonstop speculation.

INFJ can dwell on their development of personal values here at Conn College. The **Religious Studies** department broadly opens the doors of the world's spiritual practices. The educational emphasis on awareness of the many ways humans form and practice spiritually brings analysis, problem solving and intercultural views to the forefront. The department includes undergraduates who are preparing for ordination in their own faiths through the considerable exposure to alternate spiritual and moral codes of human experience.

INTP has a skeptical nature that is careful about making premature commitments. They might find the study of **Economics** at Conn College nicely accommodates their need to reserve judgment. This type can usually manipulate several conceptual theories at once. The impossible-sounding mathematical formulas such as heteroskedasticity and stochastic trends in economics don't necessarily scare them off.

ISTP will love Conn College's extensive research equipment and commitment to undergraduate research that is complemented with a full machine shop staffed by professionals. What a dream for this tinkering type to observe and demonstrate mechanical force while exploring freshmen level general physics. ISTPs might also tinker with the visualization of sound while pursuing the interdisciplinary certificate in **Arts and Technology** at the Ammerman Center.

ENFJ with their strong communication, empathy and idealistic vision for others could easily be attracted to the certificate in **Community Action and Public Policy**. Within the crowded metropolis in and near Hartford, there are many homeless and helpless individuals within the population that receive support and encouragement from undergraduate students in this program.

ISTJ brings a mastery of the facts and complete recall that will anchor many a free-roving classroom discussion at Connecticut College. The ISTJ would probably have the perseverance to uncover many of the complex layers in Russian society. The major in **Slavic Studies**, not frequently offered, could be a good preparation for graduate law studies should ISTJ secure an international career track. This small department encourages close mentoring between student and faculty that extends to personalized study abroad semesters.

ISFJ is a natural for appreciating aesthetically pleasing living spaces. Their commitment and sensitivity toward others will naturally complement the **Architectural Studies** program at Connecticut College. This major will take advantage of their rich personalized memories in applying and connecting people with their physical environments. It is a foundational stepping stone into graduate studies in design.

ENTJ can be direct, challenging and decisive, just the characteristics needed to pursue the unusual major in **Botany**. The science research on campus is bolstered by extensive natural laboratories in the coastal estuaries. ENTJ would likely enjoy crafting a major in the pure sciences because it would be rooted in reality, and yet have potential for research study in medicinal pharmacy. However, the graduate study of insects and world agricultural crops is calling out for young scientists to step into the numerous vacancies in this much-needed discipline.

DARTMOUTH COLLEGE

7 Lebanon Street # 35
Hanover, NH 03755
Website: www.dartmouth.edu
Admission Telephone: 603-646-2875
Undergraduates: 4,194; 2,147 Men, 2,047 Women
Graduate Students: 1,100

Physical Environment

This 265-acre campus in Hanover is tailor-made for students who can tolerate cold weather and enjoy the outdoors. A member of the Ivy League, Dartmouth is located far away from any city, which tends to keep students focused on what's happening on campus. They may step outside campus for a Sunday breakfast at Lou's or Molly's but many have not crossed the nearby bridge to Lebanon, Vermont. In winter time the campus is like a cocoon, an intimate and safe world for the undergrads. The new Life Sciences Center appears fortress-like, minus the expanse of glass and open spaces of current day collegiate architecture. The Arts Center opening in 2012 serves up much needed space for the studio arts on the Dartmouth campus.

The "D" Plan: Dartmouth is on a quarter system which means that classes start four times a year (fall, winter, spring, summer). Each quarter lasts ten weeks so the content is intense and fast-moving. There is no time to procrastinate and digest at leisure, though students read, write and comprehend at **lightning speed** here and take only three classes per quarter, as opposed to five as at other colleges. The D-plan requires that every student who has completed sophomore year remain on campus for sophomore summer. An advantage is that **off-campus** internships are filled throughout the year lending flexibility to scheduling. If it seems that students are always coming and going it's because of the D-plan. It can be disruptive for some students to be leaving one quarter and returning when their friends are leaving. Yet **sophomore summer** on campus turns out to be a bonding experience for the students.

Dartmouth College was founded during the colonial period by Reverend Eleazar Wheelock who wanted to educate the Native Americans and bring Christianity to them. For over 200 years Dartmouth was a college for males. Many of the historic buildings continue to provide housing for students.

Room assignments are mixed and matched, so first year students may live next to seniors on a co-ed floor. While it's the luck of the draw where a student may end up living, the philosophy here is that better learning takes place in a co-ed, multi-age environment.

Fraternity houses provide additional housing and students take charge of organizing house activities. Greek houses are located on the same street as the President's house. Much social life revolves with the Greek system. There are myriad activities students can choose and many combine socializing with them. There are special weekends every quarter, such as homecoming, winter carnival, green-key weekend in the spring and summer-fest. These are well attended and enjoyed since there are no nearby large metropolitan venues.

Social Environment

Students tend to embrace tradition at this college with a strong history of scholarship. While students appreciate the benefits that an **ivy-league education** can give them throughout life, many are understated and not overly impressed with themselves. It's the out of the class connections with current students and alumni that adds value to the Dartmouth experience.

Dartmouth students are "**athletic intellectuals**" with a common denominator: they work hard and play hard. Greek life is alive and well here. Students visit each Greek house to socialize and catch up with their friends, Greek and non-Greek. Two-thirds of eligible students are involved in fraternities and sororities.

This campus attracts students who like to take many **challenging courses** in the liberal arts and humanities. They appreciate the opportunity to pick and choose classes around a number of distribution requirements. Engineering is also taught within the context of the liberal arts with an orientation to benefiting humanity. Students love the exciting array of liberal arts classes and caring professors who challenge them.

Commonly students do not flock to hear political speeches even though the campus has a history of **presidential campaign kickoff** speeches. While Dartmouth is not a hotbed of politics, there's lots of "Big Green" pride, a clear interest in protecting the natural environment and understanding **sustainability** global issues. There is increasing political participation because of this topic. The location in rural New Hampshire doesn't lend itself to fruitful rallies and demonstrations.

The Dartmouth student population is quite diverse in its cultural, socio-economic and ethnic origin, including the Jewish faith, African Americans, Native American Indians and international students. The enrollment of these students is well supported by Dartmouth's academic majors in African and African American Studies and Native American Studies. In the 80s Dartmouth students tended to the conservative, but now the pendulum seems to have swung and it is more equally balanced on the political spectrum and there are many social activities and interesting clubs to pursue. Dartmouth students are energetic, enthusiastic and highly social.

Compatibility with Personality Types and Preferences

Dartmouth College graduates are exquisitely educated in world awareness. They are bright citizens quite savvy in the nature of human society and its numerous conflicting currents. They are mobile, adept and accustomed to working with others (E) and successfully move in academic, political and business environments. This personal prowess likely grows out of the Dartmouth educational philosophy of encouraging many types of off-campus study. The Dartmouth Plan course scheduling process prompts learning away from campus during the four quarter school calendar. Students are leaving and returning throughout the year while accommodating their individual interests with internships, service learning and courses at international universities. It is a calculated (J) learning strategy that allows for acquisition of information and internalizing that knowledge in a very practical and accessible way. The administration expects their graduates to quickly and aptly transition to graduate schools and national and global organizations. Variety, change and new information (P) are good words for the typical Dartmouth student. Many of the academic departments clearly outline and encourage options for their students to take courses in other disciplines. Undergraduates arrive usually comfortable and confident with their ability to acquire knowledge and judiciously use that knowledge (T). The typical Dartmouth student will sign up for five courses in another discipline, identified as a modified major, just to explore for curiosity's sake. These students seek to become effective and productive citizens in the public square. Their goal and Dartmouth's educational philosophy fit together quite nicely.

In the following listing of college majors it is important to remember that students can fit into any college and can be successful in any major. We have found that the Personality Types below fit very well at this college. The course-of-study chosen for each Personality Type corresponds to MBTI® research and is presented as an example favorable for that type.

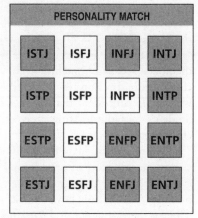

INFJ will find Dartmouth's degree in **Geography** just right for their interest in planning and emerging patterns or possibilities. Few colleges offer this degree with its interface between the social sciences and hard sciences. It is practiced at pretty abstract levels, and graduates can consult at international and national organizations on complex resource decisions. Which crop to plant, when? How will the ruling governments support or not support successful crop growth? How much acreage to plant? These are just queries about agriculture. There are many more questions posed by professional geographers in relation to space, scale, location and culture. INFJ has the imagination and insight to tackle these complexities.

INTJ will find the **Material Science** minor to be an ideal option. It is offered as an option in chemistry, physics and engineering. This type likes to quietly arrive at their positions and often with a singular idea, a seed starter, for their ultimately large vision. The material science minor could easily provide that starter concept. Dartmouth flexibility then allows for this type to follow with further studies in any of the three departments best supporting INTJ's original plan.

ISTP is a natural at learning in the labs with equipment and properties that can be seen or handled. They move at their own pace with what interests them. They are likely to choose a research project if they elect the **Biophysical Chemistry** major at Dartmouth College. This type will be comfortable with facts and logic in the required chemistry, math, physics and biology courses for this major. They will seek out research that takes advantage of their technical acumen. Regardless of the direction their studies move toward, they will gravitate to orderly, sequenced physical properties which can be observed and documented for practical application. Very little will go unnoticed by their penetrating approach to seeing what is there.

ISTJ could find the **Linguistics Modified Major** nicely interfaces with their elected major. The five courses required will creatively complement the major elected by ISTJ. This type prefers the road ahead to be clearly mapped out and they excel at majors which avoid social speculation or social theory. However, the combination of the modified major with the departments of math and linguistics could be quite appealing to ISTJs. They will master both disciplines by memory and specific detail.

INTP will find the abstractions in the **Earth Sciences** calling out to them from the course description. Should there be a hint of mystery in the course summary, INTP is likely to sign right up for it. Give them an enigma to solve and they are happy. Dartmouth's Department of Earth Science is quite active in geological research and the undergraduate INTP is likely to find the range of disciplines fascinating. This type commonly pursues the graduate study in one of the abstract sciences such as geophysics, earth magnetics, planetary sciences or geochemistry. There will be a few problems to keep them busy in each of these.

ESTP heartily will approve of the fast, productive learning pace at Dartmouth College. Off-campus programs will appeal to this type who prefers action when learning. The interdisciplinary degree in **Asian and Middle Eastern Studies** is quite flexible for service learning. Highly social ESTP may easily move into American neighborhoods that host Asian ethnic minorities to offer an amiable ear while documenting oral history. Also the study of film and video portraying Asian cultures over the past century will be favorite learning tools for this type in researching American views of this critical geographic crossroads of the world. ESTP often brings natural networking skills and will likely acquire a multicultural network throughout their four years of study in this program.

ENFP is highly curious and motivated by new experiences, especially those involving other people. The film and video industry could offer ENFP a moving platform of projects in which to explore many fresh subjects with the production of each new film. The major in **Film and Media Studies** at Dartmouth College includes a course in documentary films. This is likely to delight ENFP because most work in this category includes perspectives on humanity and the impact of humans on the planet. It will be easy for this type to become inspired and the action required in film production keeps antsy ENFP on the move.

ENTP wants new experiences plus intellectual freedom, and **Classical Archeology** at Dartmouth has a little of both. Absorbed in the learning of the moment, time spent looking at artifacts in labs will necessarily generate a few of their original questions. Intuition serves this type well as they speculate about the past with appropriate information. The department's ancient holdings will push ENTP into the future with graduate studies in archeology that will allow this type to visit the source of artifacts examined at Dartmouth as an undergrad.

ESTJ will find that Dartmouth College is one of the few educational institutions that readily combines an honors program in **Mathematics and the Social Sciences**. This no nonsense type would see quite a bit of value in bringing some quantitative order to the social science of their interest. As such, ESTJ will make a carefully considered choice among the options: Economics, Education, Geography, History, Political Science or Sociology. Although math can be quietly exciting, the social science selected will bring the action and opportunity for leadership and management that ESTJ wants in their careers.

ENFJ could appreciate the study of **Psychology.** The department approaches this discipline with an eye to present day issues and strong foundation in research and research methodologies. ENFJ will bring their penchant for harmony and cooperation to the discipline possibly moving toward a career in health well being. The course in Health Psychology might be the entry point for graduate studies and a career in health administration. This type often excels in leadership through personal passion and rhetorical ability.

ENTJ might start out with a minor in **Russian Area Studies** and decide to make it into a major if the study abroad term in Russia morphed into an opportunity to return and be productive in business or politics. This type makes rational and very logical decisions in league with their drive for leadership. They are indeed going to envision and move toward their goal whether it is a new branch office in Moscow for an international business or a staff position with an international diplomatic mission. These would be typical first steps for this hard charger just out of college.

DAVIDSON COLLEGE

Office of Admission
209 Ridge Road
Davidson, NC 28035
Website: www.davidson.edu
Admission Telephone: 800-768-0380
Undergraduates: 1,756; 887 Men, 869 Women

Physical Environment

Davidson College is located in the small village of Davidson, about 20 minutes northwest of Charlotte. The campus is in the center of this town and it's self-enclosed. It feels cozy and protected. It provides an ideal setting for the development of a **close-knit college community** that is growing alongside this town.

The 450-acre, park-like campus has impressive academic buildings, sports facilities such as a golf course, stadium and tennis courts and a choice of residence halls. The year-round temperate weather makes it possible to play outdoors throughout the academic year. The Knoblock Campus Center is a popular meeting place for students here. Also Patterson Court, with small residential homes for fraternities and eating houses, is a social magnet for all on campus. Fraternity houses are owned by the college and rented to students. They are popular and even encouraged here with 40 percent participation. Women don't live in sororities but rather in 'eating houses' which also are rented from the college. Some houses are open and accept all who would like to join; others operate in the traditional rush. Almost all students live on campus, whether in a house or residence hall.

Social Environment

Most Davidson students were overachievers in high school and continue this pattern as undergraduates. Three-quarters of these students were in the top 10 percent of their class. At Davidson they stretch their minds by putting forth their best **analytical thinking and academic effort**. There is a solid structure in place for working hard with quiet relaxation. They study and do homework, join clubs and play sports, socialize and have fun.

This college has a distinct Christian orientation with an **international presence** even though the majority of students come from outside North Carolina. This stems from the **Presbyterian founders** who strongly envisioned a religious and ethical education. Some students form an alternate perspective and would prefer a more secular approach at Davidson. This sometimes makes for **lively discussions** on campus. Students who value service and leadership appreciate a Davidson preparation for life.

The **honor code** is a strong value within the student body and incoming students are quickly oriented to code policies. Undergraduate students complete tests and exams without a proctor. Volunteer service is prominent here, and students find ways to invite underprivileged children to campus or travel with their professor to an inner city area. Undergraduates really appreciate Davidson's practice of admitting many international students to the college. The **exchange of social customs** and traditions between international students and traditional American students provides an exposure to alternative perspectives similar to off-campus study.

Students who were shy about risk taking in high school will enjoy the personal attention they receive and the **family atmosphere** on this campus. Every freshman is introduced to a senior student through Cat Connect, an organization that assigns these upper class mentors. Students enjoy chatting with the President of the college often on campus. They like the fact that professors are very approachable and available for academic discussions. When life gets too quiet here, students may drive to Charlotte for a shopping spree or go sailing on the nearby lake. Athletics are popular at this NCAA Division I college, as is their basketball team.

Compatibility with Personality Types and Preferences

Davidson is an intensely academic college with bright students who really want their studies to be the primary focus of their undergraduate years. There is less emphasis on learning through social avenues. However, they make good use of innocent pranks and jokes using this lighthearted approach to relieve the academic pressures. Students here are very fond of introspection (I) as a way to acquire knowledge. Individually or in small focus groups, they ponder concepts and information gained in class and from their readings. Their personal observations and thoughts instigate dialogues across campus and in non-class settings. Moral reasoning (F) underlies pretty much all of their conjecture and purpose in learning. Undergraduates here view the ideals of service and leadership through the lens of faith and also through non-spiritual humanistic philosophies. This willingness to explore the sources of ethical behavior attracts students who are tolerant, yet strong in their spiritual beliefs. Refining order and structure (J) in personal belief systems is the common thread that most successful student at Davidson possesses. For the most part, they each desire and work to maintain an ethical direction in campus academic and social activities. Graduates set the bar high to achieve their individual ideals of competence and expect to bring this into their careers for a lifetime of rewarding work and caring for the larger social community.

In the following listing of college majors it is important to remember that students can fit into any college and can be successful in any major. We have found that the Personality Types below fit very well at this college. The course-of-study chosen for each Personality Type corresponds to MBTI® research and is presented as an example favorable for that type.

INFP will appreciate the frontiers opening up because of the **Neuroscience** field. At Davidson, this concentration would likely be very appealing to INFP whose personal mandate is to keep life's work in synchronization with their values. Davidson funds

PERSONALITY MATCH			
ISTJ	ISFJ	INFJ	INTJ
ISTP	ISFP	INFP	INTP
ESTP	ESFP	ENFP	ENTP
ESTJ	ESFJ	ENFJ	ENTJ

a considerable amount of its own research proposed by faculty and students. INFP is very comfortable in this territory.

INFJ is a natural for the major in **Art** at Davidson because of their inclination for person-centered leadership. They are persuasive folks and move successfully into professional positions that interface with the public. At Davidson, the department is well-resourced with a substantial studio facility and a curriculum that emphasizes conceptualization, collection, curatorship as well as the obvious studies in art production and theory. This intellectual approach helps quietly passionate INFJ prepare for graduate studies or immediate employment.

ISTP could pair the analytical tools of the **Applied Mathematics** concentration with the natural sciences. This type is curious and objective. They don't mind a puzzle and are drawn to figuring things out. More often than not, they also prefer to tinker with hands-on instrumentation or with subject matter that involves researching with high-powered equipment. They are a natural for physics because of the elements and the observable reactions. With the Davidson Research Institute, ISTP is likely to be stretching the frontiers of space exploration, medical instrumentation or environmental modeling.

ISTJ is exactly the type of educator many students admire and respect. This type is very knowledgeable, controlled and prefers a clear set of rules. They can be excellent classroom managers. The program options in **Education** at Davidson offer preparation for licensure in North Carolina or options for graduate study in psychology, education and other social sciences. Although ISTJ is not drawn to one-on-one relationships, they are very inclined to management and administrative positions in the social science. Their strong memory for faces can assure a comforting steady presence in the crowded hallways of American high schools.

ISFJ will find the perspectives of the **Economics** department in tune with their own idea of gathering information that can be used in a practical way. The Comparative Advantage mentor program develops cooperative interaction between professor, student and off-campus internships in Charlotte. The Davidson Research Institute provides funds for off-campus student trips that can enliven and personalize this major with visits to stock exchanges and other financial institutions. ISFJ is intensely practical, yet also reflective. It so nicely fits in with the study of Economics here.

ISFP likes wiggle room to find their direction in life. They want freedom and thereby tolerance to examine the information and issues. The study in **Religion** as a major or minor at Davidson is to their liking because it offers a close examination of the many facets of spiritual beliefs. At the core of these studies is the existential question about the meaning of human life. Although ISFP is not one to tarry with abstract questions, this one is rather familiar to them. Personal values are critical for this type and the overall emphasis on moral and ethical behavior at Davidson is in tandem with their own wish for a life guided by inner values.

INTP will be impressed with the facilities and the research in the Davidson **Physics** department, recognized nationally. This very abstract type does not need a course of study that is directly connected to reality. Even better is a challenge that they can work on for a couple decades starting right in the Davidson physics labs. How about generating oxygen on Mars if microbes are ultimately discovered within the soil? Keep the lab open late if you pose this question, INTP is already tuning up the instruments.

ESFJ can find themselves moving toward the health fields because of their friendly nature. They are excellent at taking in facts and pretty darn good at utilizing those facts in real terms. The study of **Chemistry** at Davidson allows students to comprehend the abstract and practical applications of this discipline. This type will prefer the research that most directly connects the chemical world with the real world. ESFJ will appreciate the ability to study chemistry for the purpose of moving into a helping career like nursing or teaching. Not one to delve into Davidson's explorations of moral reasoning, ESFJ finds comfort and clarity in traditional values as found in the U.S. Constitution.

ESTJ will like the idea of combining the **Medical Humanities** concentration with their intended major. Whether they intend to move toward the health administration with a major in economics or toward medical school this concentration has much to impress efficient ESTJ. It pulls together legal, economic and political factors that explain the patterns and practice of medicine in our society. Davidson offers this concentration within the background of its own ongoing examination of moral purpose in life and society. It is an ideal academic atmosphere and helps ESTJ, sometimes impersonal, sort out emotional perspectives.

ENFJ can be quite objective and analytical. They also possess charisma and the ability to engage immediately with a group of people. Their desire to be of service for others makes good use of their characteristics. The major in **Sociology** at Davidson is a comprehensive analytical exercise in defining social life. This type is ready to sign up for the research and field work that can support change and offer solutions to various underserved populations. They are excellent at painting their vision and creative in applying solutions. At Davidson, they will find the faculty very open to their projects which involve service learning especially if they gather data that can then be examined to explain social movements.

DENISON UNIVERSITY

Office of Admission
Granville, OH 43023
Website: www.denison.edu
Admissions Telephone: 740-587-6276
Undergraduates: 2,162; 951 Men, 1,211 Women

Physical Environment

Denison University is built on a **steep hill**, like a castle, above the town of Granville. The town itself has the feel of a New England village, with its attractive colonial houses, a quaint downtown, specialty shops and golf courses nearby. The airport is a half-hour away in Columbus and makes for an easy trip for nearly half of the students who will need to this transportation option.

Denison is located on a hilltop surrounded by peaks and forests within the 1,000-acre campus. Students find that they have to walk a good deal, up and down, to get to and from class. At the same time, Denison has taken great care to create many spaces that are conducive to learning. The ergonomics of these spaces on campus are used by the students and faculty and purposely appeal to students with an appreciation of a well designed environment.

There are places for the student who gets distracted occasionally or those who prefer to study alone in complete silence, such as in the Doane Library. There are spaces for the highly social students who learn best through discussion with peers, such as in the computer center. Residential life is geared to promote learning. The expansive renovation of Ebaugh Science Center echoes the academic philosophy consistently in place across the campus environment. In this renovation, undergraduates benefit with six teaching laboratories. The hands-on method of learning is highest priority at Denison and their graduates are well-grounded in practical skills needed for those entering our workforce.

The **Slayter Union student center** is designed for students to socialize on campus during the evenings and weekends with its dance and DJ spot. Lots of planning and effort went into designing the physical campus and forming this **community**. Students who choose to spend their four undergraduate years at Denison appreciate the beauty of the campus and the nice classrooms, the dorms and these study spaces.

Social Environment

Denison students handle a pretty demanding work load and half of them rank in the top 10 percent of their high school class. Students appreciate the help that professors offer. Should students struggle here, the faculty and administration encourage use of the Academic Support Center.

A good number of students come from suburban areas and the **North East**, both from independent and academically strong public schools. Denison's campus is a familiar and **smooth transition** for them. It can be described as a safe, **supportive environment** in which undergrads stretch their perspectives and mature. Here students develop their views about the emerging issues through their educational studies and discussions. There are students who lean toward nontraditional perspectives and exercise their elbow room in the demanding academics. In the classroom, they can assert their original thoughts with professors who are exceptionally receptive.

At Denison students often dress casually but fashionably well. Some are very artsy, a bit quirky and dress in tie-died apparel. About 1/3 of the students join fraternities and sororities. Denison residential staff forms a strong community with all of these types since all students must live on campus. The **Greek organizations** tend to anchor social activities on campus.

While liberal ideology is commonplace in college, undergraduates here tend to be a bit more traditional. Some will travel the political spectrum to the right, finding a tolerant reception at this Midwestern campus, similar to Ohio's reputation as a swing state in presidential politics. Denison University, a campus with excellent **professors sharing their expertise** with their students, is a solid choice for students at the top of their graduating class.

Compatibility with Personality Types and Preferences

Denison University is dedicated, in the purest sense, to educating the youth who arrive on their campus each year. This commitment directly infuses the curriculum and residential life. The proverbial phrase, No Stone is Left Unturned, applies here. The campus is carefully planned for undergraduate learning. In a similar sense, Denison also hovers over their students with exceptional care (F) that is instilled throughout the academic programs and courses of study. The mission of the university calls administration and faculty to inspire the students who come to them. In fact, the professional educators on this campus are well able to role model inspiration. The faculty seem to have a single-minded optimism for the immediate utility of education. It fosters several one-of-a-kind learning environments and academic programs. Taken as a whole, this philosophy forms a campus community that reaches out to many types of learners. Denison provides learning options for the open ended, wondering student (N) and the one expecting to find the knowledge in an observable, structured format (S). Denison undergraduate students are likely to be smart and savvy about higher education, graduating with a strong academic foundation and clear direction.

In the following listing of college majors it is important to remember that students can fit into any college and can be successful in any major. We have found that the Personality Types below fit very well at this college. The course-of-study chosen for each Personality Type corresponds to MBTI® research and is presented as an example favorable for that type.

PERSONALITY MATCH			
ISTJ	ISFJ	INFJ	INTJ
ISTP	ISFP	INFP	INTP
ESTP	ESFP	ENFP	ENTP
ESTJ	ESFJ	ENFJ	ENTJ

ESFJ will appreciate the concentration in **Organizational Studies** not often found at small liberal arts colleges. This type is good at communication and has a strong propensity for follow through with attention to detail. They are at home in traditional organizations that serve the public. The ESFJ might enter the worlds of banking or real estate because of the exacting nature of the financial exchange and the need for personal relationships. The Denison administration appreciates both of these traits which are honored throughout the campus environment.

ISFJ is very likely to think about the health services field as they head off to college. This reflective type is very much at home helping others. The degree in **Psychology** at Denison University has a nice range of options within the coursework of this developing field. Courses in Adult Development & Aging, Cultural Psychology and Social Psychology offer much to ISFJ who is considering careers in health. Combined with courses in the **Organizational Studies** concentration, this type will be well-suited to provide personal support to patients dealing with hospital financial systems and the insurance systems, not to mention the floodgate of regulation coming with the recent health care mandates passed by Congress.

ESTP often has a strong sense of spatial awareness and personal awareness in physical space. They often are attracted to and excel at sports and other movement activities. **Dance** at Denison University is available as a minor or major. The department approaches dance through three constructs: mind, spirit and body. This type could move easily into the entertainment field with their gregarious personality. Think Disney World, Las Vegas and a host of concert tours that use choreographed performances. ESTP thrives on pressure and can pull rabbits out of hats when needed.

ESFP has a lot of energy and enthusiasm that mixes nicely in working with patients who would look to the ESFP for guidance in physical rehabilitation or recovery from injury in professional sports. The major in **Athletic Training** is offered at Denison University. To receive the needed certification for practicing as an athletic trainer, the physical education department offers strong advising during the freshman year in addition to requiring three exploratory courses in the first year. In this way, Denison practices its attentive care by realistically guiding students successfully toward certification or toward another major of interest prior to the sophomore year in college.

ISFP can excel at hands-on activities and the major in **Chemistry** offers plenty of them. ISFP is also fond of teaching young children and Denison offers advising on completing the teacher licensure immediately upon graduation with the BA in Chemistry. For the student who may be unsure of their commitment to education, the chemistry major qualifies graduates for immediate employment in many industries. This too may appeal to ISFP who might enter the health care industry in sales or technical positions.

ISTJ has the discipline to tackle a complex language. Denison University offers basic courses in Arabic. The close attention to the details of this visually challenging set of written characters is something that ISTJ could have the patience to conquer. If combined with economics or political science majors, the **Arabic Language** would likely open doors for business or government careers that focus on the Middle East. The need for this expertise is ongoing within Western governments and businesses. ISTJ can provide the glue that holds a consulting project together in this dynamic environment.

INFJ likes to pull things together from start to finish. The major in **Theater** at Denison University takes advantage of this type's ability to understand complex viewpoints presented in contemporary theater usually offered with little resemblance to the everyday world. This type can interpret those abstract themes in theater for the audience to more easily understand. Through considerable depth dramatic theory curriculum, Denison University promotes the undergraduates appreciation of the judgment and imagination found in stellar theatre. In this way, INFJ can further hone their creative visions of how things should be.

ENFJ should find the rich resources in Denison's Department of **Modern Language** pretty appealing. The ears, eyes and rhetorical skills are integral to the educational methods here. ENFJ will like the modern language virtual lounge in Fellows 103. Large flatscreen TVs receive direct programming from around the world and students are immersed in the sounds and culture of the language by contemporary native speakers. The modern language association map, utilized within the curriculum, identifies locations of native-speaking neighborhoods within the United States. It encourages an interdisciplinary thread as undergrads can search out land use and social ways of ethnic pockets across our geographic regions.

ENFP will find the level of abstraction they need to remain interested within the **Communication** major at Denison University. Unlike many colleges, Denison moves away from the persuasion and marketing aspect of this major. Denison also does not pursue the disorders of communication. Rather it focuses on the assignment of meaning between the speaker and the listener. It is quite abstract and a fine preparation for professional careers in many fields since communication carries and generates knowledge in the current day redefinitions of science, law and public policy.

INFP can be an insightful personality. The field of education is attractive to them since they enjoy both teaching and learning where insight comes in pretty handy. At Denison University, the major in **Educational Studies** can lead to a teaching license with an additional year of study after graduation. The department advises students about the practical steps needed for the licensure. For those INFPs who might prefer to teach in higher education, this major would be very desirable in combination with the masters and PhD in a specific discipline or social science.

DUKE UNIVERSITY

Office of Admission
2138 Campus Drive
Durham, NC 27708
Website: www.duke.edu
Admissions Telephone: 919-684-3214
Undergraduates: 6,578; 3,362 Men, 3,216 Women
Graduate Students: 7,772

Physical Environment

Duke University's impressive campus grew from a large endowment gained from the sale of tobacco. The Duke family was Methodist and infused funds from their industry into this college. As a result, the Gothic tower and Duke Chapel were completed in the 1930s. The **residential quad** and the **academic quad** on the West campus are separate. There is also a quad on the East side which houses all first-year students. This is about a mile away from West campus and first-year students take a bus to get to their classes.

There is much needed ongoing construction of residential units on campus and new buildings are designed to match the older, more established ones. Duke can do this because it has its own stone quarry so it can use the same stones. The overall effect is one of pleasing cohesiveness without jarring, distracting architecture. Students who come here tend to like **clean lines and functional** style.

The residence halls for upper classmen on West campus are arranged like peas in a pod with each pod overlooking its own courtyard. It's cozy and private inside the pod, so students run into their friends often. Fraternities and sororities post banners on the public side of the pods—as do other political or environmental clubs. It would be very easy to study together in groups in these living quarters.

Social Environment

Duke students are very bright and **precise.** Their **inquisitiveness** and **reasoning** power are to the point, as is their focus on solutions rather than complaints. Students come with impressive grades, test scores and extra-curricular experiences. Nearly half of the entering students want to major in medicine. However, far fewer enter med school upon graduation. Often, organic chemistry can be the obstacle. These students, rational and goal-driven, naturally move on to other career fields to meet their personal goals.

Many are **competitive** and fondly remember being on the top rung in high school, hoping to repeat that achievement at Duke. Some students are exceptionally creative, **curious** and enterprising. The typical Duke student, a top performer in high school, is likely to continue working quite hard here.

Social life at Duke is often curtailed by the amount of study involved during weekends. If there's not a sports game to attend, many students like to go to Chapel Hill to have fun. Much social life at Duke revolves around the **Greek system.** One-third of male students join a fraternity whereas a larger number of women join a sorority. All are invited to their parties, and in addition, students often form their own type of social club by getting together with other like-minded friends. It is possible that the renovations to the central residential complex may be completed marking an end to a lengthy schedule.

Students who are attracted to this campus tend to have respect and love for conventional traditions, as well as a yearning for the innovative academics, even if risk is involved. They will find fertile soil here where **research possibilities** for undergraduates abound.

Team projects and understanding connections between dissimilar problems are big here. In effect, students examine situations that often occur in business and industry. As Duke continues to forge more initiatives in research, it attracts investigative types who rely on facts, logic and analysis while at the same time learn to see the connectivity between seemingly unrelated situations. This approach to learning tends to fall in line with the Germanic university model that emphasizes undergraduate research over the more traditional lecture and writing formats.

Duke students like their **sports** and really come out for their Blue Devils. Starting in December, a favorite and fun tradition is to camp outside the Krzyzewski Athletic Complex for tickets to the February games. Students take turns keeping their place in line while studying and socializing around the clock. Living in Krzyzewskiville village has become a bonding experience for many Duke students. These experiences and memories build loyalty to the university and to each other.

Compatibility with Personality Types and Preferences

Duke University replicates a thinking pattern akin to an aircraft circling to land. In this case, the plane doesn't land–Duke undergraduates always circle in a thinking pattern. The philosophy of Duke University is to engage rigorous logical thought throughout the curriculum. Free inquiry, deductive reasoning and interdisciplinary thinking pop up as the foundation in this educational environment. Students here are perpetually reasoning (T). They seek purpose in their educational studies. They apply knowledge upon graduation to benefit mankind in a determined, impactful way. For most Duke undergraduates, science and research is the chosen vehicle to ride into a future (N) of productive accomplishment (J) and discovery. The university devotedly supports this expectation of their graduates. Both collaboration and competition are valued as learning tools on campus. Duke lore, history and traditions often serve to soften the logical edges of reason. The residential life programs are designed to promote maturation and spiritual growth. The typical Duke graduate is well connected to the world and very able to both socially network and generate major contributions for the advancement of the larger community.

In the following listing of college majors it is important to remember that students can fit into any college and can be successful in any major.

PERSONALITY MATCH			
ISTJ	ISFJ	INFJ	INTJ
ISTP	ISFP	INFP	INTP
ESTP	ESFP	ENFP	ENTP
ESTJ	ESFJ	ENFJ	ENTJ

We have found that the Personality Types below fit very well at this college. The course-of-study chosen for each Personality Type corresponds to MBTI® research and is presented as an example favorable for that type.

ENFJ prefers to learn and study with creative peers in fields where helping others is a high priority. The health sciences are quite attractive for this reason. Duke University offers the major in **Plant Biology** that easily leads to advanced study. The extraordinary research labs will provide ample opportunities for this type. ENFJs will be attracted to the healing properties found in the botanical world. Foundational work at Duke in plant physiology is the spring board for passionate ENFJs to move into an exciting, rewarding research career.

INTJ likes to be original and how about **Linguistics** for originality. The major in linguistics requires the willingness to discern pattern and system in languages. It is both an abstract and precise science. As archeologists unearth manuscripts of ancient language, it is the forensic linguist who comes to the forefront with translation help. Duke's limitless access to journals includes the intriguing Journal of Linguistic Anthropology. INTJs will uncover all available sources for their study of linguistics and in the process develop the competence that is their Number One priority.

INFJ takes pride and ownership in their expressive work. For this type, it is an expression of their inner soul and must be authentic. The rich degree in **Visual Arts** at Duke University is remarkably inclusive of several artistic threads. The photographic curriculum is particularly interesting with a course devoted to photographs from 1839 to present. The department is streamlined and focused on technique and presentation without attempting to influence the undergraduate curriculum with trendy social perspectives. INFJ will enjoy the freedom and find creative release without excessive infusion of other perspectives.

INTP will find the nature of the **Evolutionary Biology** concentration suits their personality well. This major requires quiet contemplation of biological modeling and systems mechanics within the discipline. This rather unusual major connects the INTP with a small group of likeminded classmates. Although titles of the concentrations change from year to year, the underlying nature of the biological disciplines of genetics, cell and molecular, organismal and ecology remain distinct categories from which concentrations are drawn. If you add in a can of Coke with a few bags of microwave popcorn, this type is set for hours of power studying and socializing INTP style.

ISTJ who is handy with numbers probably couldn't go wrong with Duke's major in **Statistical Sciences**. This degree will be in demand at financial institutions. ISTJ naturally brings fierce attention to the exacting nature of the statistical discipline. Since this type prefers the real world, they will be in demand to predict and explain trends in the marketplace or complex social research.

INFP brings compassion and insight to the helping professions. In order to be content, they must select majors and coursework that allow them to develop their own values, so the field of **Psychology** calls out to this type. In guiding others through personal difficulty, this type simultaneously defines their own life expectations and meaning. The department is committed to undergraduate development of broad-based analytic skills and foundational knowledge in the discipline. It prepares students to pursue graduate studies as well as entry level positions in research institutions. INFPs are likely to opt for the first and only stay for a few years in a direct entry research job.

ESTJ is often an efficient personality who could be attracted to the degree in **Computer Science** at Duke University. The very powerful computing resources here allow for levels of programming that can be applied to gynormous data problems. Here ESTJ can be productive, take charge and reason their way into advanced computing with Duke encouragement all the way.

ENTJ could easily adapt to a favored role in consulting as a **Biomedical Engineer**. The work environment needed for development of advanced medical devices is just right for this type. They enjoy perfecting operating systems. Once envisioned, the system is brought to the market by the ambitious ENTJ. Throw in Duke's competitive, motivating educational environment and this type will likely be quite content with their undergraduate experience.

ENTP is willing to tackle the tough problems. No shrinking violet, this type has the determination to succeed at any major that piques their interest. The advantage of a certificate in **Information Sciences & Information Studies** is that it is specifically designed to be applicable to a variety of academic disciplines for research purposes. Original ENTPs don't mind studying technology as long as it can lead to creating new information technology.

ELON UNIVERSITY

Office of Admissions and Financial Planning
2700 Campus Box
400 N. O'Kelly Avenue
Elon, NC 27244-2010
Website: www.elon.edu
Admissions Telephone: 800-334-8448
Undergraduates: 5,225; 2,139 Men, 3,086 Women

Physical Environment

Elon University is located in the very small and quiet town of Elon near the "triangle," within a 30 minutes drive of Greensborough, Raleigh-Durham and Chapel Hill. With fewer than 10,000 people, the city fathers and Elon together constructed the new Elon Town Center across the street from the campus which will house the Elon Bookstore and specialty foods. The campus is very attractive with many new red-brick buildings amidst two lakes, many trees, flower beds and circular open areas.

First year students live in new residence halls that accommodate the increasing enrollment and students are required to live on campus for the first two years. The university is in the midst of a decade-long revisioning of residential space on campus, called the Global Neighborhood. With the feeling of a village in part, it will feature newer, smaller housing units with live-in faculty and international cafes. Some units will be heated with geothermal energy. Language learning communities, themed houses, all female and all male dorms, singles and apartments represent just some of the residential services on this campus. **Fraternity or sorority** houses are available on campus. Many new academic buildings dot this active campus, the latest of which is the Francis Center, housing the facilities for the physical therapy and exercise science programs.

Mosley's student center is popular on this **social campus**. Fonville Fountain is another meeting place, especially on Tuesday morning when students and faculty connect over coffee to chat and visit. No classes are held during this time. On Thursdays there is an optional interfaith service in the historic Whitley Auditorium, another way for this community to come together.

Social Environment

Elon students come from all over the United States and especially New England. About one-quarter of students are residents of North Carolina. Elon bolsters the ethnic diversity on campus by bringing in many international students from all corners of the world. Fraternities and sororities play a large role here. Students are active in their club memberships, many of which are oriented toward career fields. The Greek organizations organize many of the parties and informal social events. When students want to leave the "Elon bubble," they drive nearby to Chapel Hill or Greensboro. The overall tone of the campus is **upbeat** and vibrant.

As high school students they demonstrated considerable academic and **extra-curricular skills**. They are intellectually curious and prefer experiential learning with a practical application of knowledge. Students are required to complete an **internship** before they graduate, so they are **well prepared** for the workplace. They graduate with an **experience resume** that describes their extra-curricular accomplishments as well as academic study in college. They engage in initiatives to help society at large, such as raising funds or organizing food drives to stock the local food pantries. Elon is a great fit for academically strong students who enjoy an active social life and like to learn skills that will prepare them for a career.

Compatibility with Personality Types and Preferences

Elon University is future-oriented and prepares its graduates through a strong understanding of today's best practices and technologies. The university is committed to community, the familiar traditional Christian value. Elon is a very supportive and affirming campus (F). The professor-student relationship takes on a personal nature while advising graduates for careers to come after graduation. Much administration thought and effort is devoted to programs and activities that encourage leadership acumen throughout the campus community.

Undergraduates are happy at Elon who want to be active doing important work in the world (E) and on the campus during their four year sojourn. They could be active in service learning, participation in research labs, contributing to theater productions, participating in social recreation or selecting internships that offer double the value for the student and the community. There is also a international componant which is supported by the assertive and nontraditional study abroad options. At Elon University, study abroad tends to move in the direction of well planned, substantial works for the benefit of those who need help. Study abroad locations require students to be open and OK with the unknown (P) as well as physical discomfort. Elon graduates comfortably continue their involvement and do-it-well attitude toward life upon graduation.

In the following listing of college majors it is important to remember that students can fit into any college and can be successful in any major. We have found that the Personality Types below fit very well at this college. The course-of-study chosen for each Personality Type corresponds to MBTI® research and is presented as an example favorable for that type.

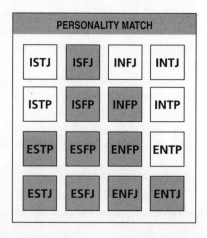

PERSONALITY MATCH

ISTJ	ISFJ	INFJ	INTJ
ISTP	ISFP	INFP	INTP
ESTP	ESFP	ENFP	ENTP
ESTJ	ESFJ	ENFJ	ENTJ

INFP is definitely motivated by working for causes that meet their approval. The major in **Human Services** at Elon University is ideal for INFPs. This type naturally settles into the health, education and counseling fields. INFPs are just fine with complexity and they enjoy the opportunity to develop well thought out responses to those challenges. Once their career choice is identified, this major will give excellent access to immediate employment. The experiential approach in this major provides a solid background for application to immediate employment in the helping professions.

ISFJ is inclined to be reflective without much fanfare or publicity about their thoughts. At the same time, they are outstanding with the details and minutiae. It is an unusual combination of skills. ISFJ is somewhere between the proverbial ivory tower and monitoring the moat filled with water below. The major in **Computer Information Systems** with a minor in **Geography** at Elon University fits nicely into this paradigm. The minor in geography looks closely at how space is used through human impact. With computing skills and knowledge of human land use patterns, ISFJs will be at the ready to provide valuable data and modeling systems for corporations and research institutions.

ISFP excels at attention to detail that helps real people in need. Elon University has a well planned major in **Biology** that allows a further specialization in **Medical Technology.** This specialization can lead to two different paths—the technical side of health services with diagnostic systems and medical equipment software systems. The other is to move toward the ecological side and pursue work/research in environmental sciences. Elon is well positioned to support environmental studies with their curriculum and coursework in the fields of geography and geographical information systems. ISFPs could select either direction.

ESTP has the smooth moves to calm down ruffled feathers with a plan that works. In the fast paced field of media production, it helps to be spontaneous and capable of solving a problematic feature story line. The concentration in **Broadcast & New Media** pretty much falls into this description of career fields that require folks who think on their feet. Elon's courses in the journalism and strategic communications within the very strong School of Communication really add the beef to the program.

ESFP goes for the active, hands-on learning and Elon University will not disappoint them. The **Exercise and Sport Science** major is a strong understudy for professional graduate study in occupational or physical therapy or possibly more specialized training in cardiac rehabilitation or nutrition. ESFPs are realistic and can handle change with ease. They enjoy solving problems by combining their typical common sense with the known information at hand. Their friendly, easy-going personality is an asset in this field.

ENFP is a creative type and loves to collaborate with others in the process. The major in **Journalism** is excellent for these reasons. ENFP gathers new information while expertly collaborating with those who have that information. It is all on behalf of the reader who they want to involve in their own excitement about the subject with news articles, or radio/TV broadcasts. Elon University has very robust programs in the School of Communications and the minor in **Multimedia Authoring** would be a natural course of study for ENFPs who intend to move toward the visual arts and marketing.

ESFJ can be counted on to cooperate and give a personal touch to their work. The major in **Physical Education and Health** fits this personality type quite well. ESFJs direction with students in the classroom and gymnasium can be counted on to be pleasant and productive. The major leads to qualification for positions in K-12th grades. However, a good number of undergraduates pursue advanced training for specific fields such as Athletic Trainer. ESFJs enjoy solid advising and encouragement within the **Department of Health and Human performance.**

ESTJ is all about organizing themselves and other people and they like to have fun too. The major in **Sport & Event Management** at Elon University is not commonly available at undergraduate liberal arts institutions and is indicative of this campus' commitment to rewarding follow on careers and work. This major develops planning and management skills across several venues, tourism, cultural arts, sports stadiums, national parks plus more. The no-nonsense list of courses will definitely meet with ESTJ approval.

ENFJ likes think analytically while in conversation. They will enjoy the typically close professor/student relationships on the Elon campus. Research projects, service learning projects and internships are frequent options at Elon that really speak to ENFJs. The **Public Administration** major is ideal in many ways for this type. It is common for careerists in this field to speak often and with a need to persuade. ENFJs excel at both. They are also very focused on improving the common good and, again, this major is all about understanding the function and operations of government services provided to its citizens.

ENTJ likes variety and independence in their educational studies. The major in **Economics** at Elon University offers both through their focus on undergraduate research. It suits ENTJs especially because they typically are opportunists ready to move forward into individualized study within the economics discipline. Their desire to long range plan is also usually pretty strong and they look after their own career track as well as their employer's business objectives with ingenuity. The major in economics at Elon requires an original research project that ENTJs will view as an opportunity to learn, network and develop their business acumen.

EMORY UNIVERSITY

1380 Oxford Road
Atlanta, GA 30322
Website: www.emory.edu
Admissions Telephone: 404-727-6036, 800-727-6036
Undergraduates: 7,231; 3,249 Men, 3,982 Women
Graduate Students: 6,150

Physical Environment

Emory University is located in the city of vibrant, thriving Atlanta, Georgia. Atlanta's Hartsfield International Airport and the public subway and bus system make it easy to reach this campus. An important physical feature is the new pink granite buildings. They stand out with their modern, striking architecture. One of these buildings is the Cannon Chapel Worship Center that supports students who seek continuing contact with their spirituality. Adjacent to the campus is the CDC (Center for Disease Control and Prevention) and Emory Hospital that calls to students who are focused on pursuing careers in the **health sciences**. Students here are likely to engage this unique location and many actively use the large park on the far side of the campus for concerts and walkathons. Emory University is **deceptively large**. There are well-developed cycling routes and shuttle buses to bring students from one side of the campus to the other.

Buildings on campus are large and designed in several styles as newer buildings grow up among the established ones. The campus itself gives one the feel of the large city that surrounds it. The students here are often **independent** and can function in a demanding environment. The contemporary library with much light promotes study. The Roberto Goizueta Business School, named after the former CEO of Coca-Cola, is located on the Emory campus and pulls in students who have an interest in entrepreneurship. Efficiency is a strong undercurrent on this campus surrounded by the city. As such, an extensive facilities upgrade in 2012 will reduce water usage and demands on the electrical grid.

For those who prefer a gentler touch, **Oxford College—a satellite campus** 45 minutes east of Atlanta—draws students who want a more relaxed setting socially and in the classroom. It is open to first and second year undergraduate students who prefer a quieter and more intimate setting. This alternative campus is a unique and distinguishing feature of Emory. It allows the university to enroll students who otherwise may become intimidated as freshmen on the Emory campus in the faster lane within the heart of thriving Atlanta. The Oxford campus reflects the administration's careful communication and outreach with its undergraduate student body.

Located in Atlanta with its moderate southern weather, Emory University attracts **cosmopolitan students** from all over the U.S. and the world. The numerous Fortune 1,000 companies headquartered in Atlanta add to the superb choices for internships and off-campus learning. The Whitehead Biomedical Research building, among several health-oriented research centers near or on campus, is an award winning, environmentally sustainable laboratory that offers numerous research directions.

Social Environment

At times reflective and reserved, many students expect their activities and connections will lead to power and success in their future careers and personal goals. Emory is a **rigorous** and **structured academic powerhouse**. Students here meet high academic and intellectual requirements. They are **driven**, hard-working and inclined to set and meet their expectations. Many value tradition, honesty and being responsible in their academic work. Here, the students started and maintain the honor code and its functions. This environment is also supported by the **spiritual programs** and the college's relationship with Candler School of Theology on campus which reaffirms the ethical value system.

Socializing occurs around structured academic group projects, service learning and sports. Emory's motto is "Athletic for All." As a Division III University, more than half of the students are active in intramurals. There is also traditional socializing within the many Greek organizations. The Greek life is well supported and approved by the University in part because they are providing connections and service with the surrounding neighborhoods. The leadership and friendships within the Greek houses also help to unify the overall campus environment. **Service initiatives** organized by students are common. Since bustling Atlanta is right outside the campus, they often go to a new restaurant, a baseball game at the Brave's stadium, shopping in eclectic stores or to volunteer in the community. The substantial northeastern student population is right at home in the big city.

Emory works for the independent, strong individuals willing to tackle issues that cut across regional and national borders. They can assign fun to second place in order to reach a larger purpose.

Compatibility with Personality Types and Preferences

"Students who explore and expand upon the current body of knowledge with world class professors" is a good way to think of Emory's broad educational philosophy. Emory students are obliged to learn and to apply that knowledge while improving the world during college and after graduation. Independent, self-sufficient students thrive here. A healthy appreciation and comfort level (S) with the facts is a necessity and a given. At the same time, Emory demands more than just learning and reciting data. Logical, sequential thought (T) is expected to lead somewhere—be it an end point or a beginning point. At a minimum, one's study would travel the route of previous brilliant minds in their endeavors. Intuitive leaps (N) are routinely accepted and expected in the classroom, although not as the primary learning tool. The administration and faculty at Emory are exceptionally open to creative students who may want to propose a new line of study or a new location for an off-campus experience.

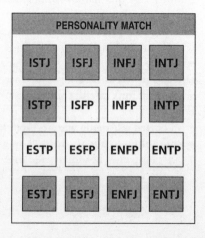

PERSONALITY MATCH			
ISTJ	ISFJ	INFJ	INTJ
ISTP	ISFP	INFP	INTP
ESTP	ESFP	ENFP	ENTP
ESTJ	ESFJ	ENFJ	ENTJ

The energy here is purposeful and directed toward accomplishment as well as accrual of knowledge. The business school, mirroring preeminently successful Coca-Cola, has an overall influence toward administration of the university. The School of Theology has an equal if not greater influence with the university in that ethical standards and ethical practices must stand up to critical review. In its own way, Emory is a very affirming environment for undergraduate students. At graduation, students are well-positioned for continuing professional studies and are likely to serve as ethical anchors in their communities.

In the following listing of college majors it is important to remember that students can fit into any college and can be successful in any major. We have found that the Personality Types below fit very well at this college. The course-of-study chosen for each Personality Type corresponds to MBTI® research and is presented as an example favorable for that type.

ISTJ will find the campus environment to their liking since it focuses on learning first and residential life activities after that. Learning makes sense when the very best mastery of the subject is the goal. The minor in **Computer Informatics** is a great choice for this type who wants to bring utility to uncorrelated data. Undergraduate students elect either the bioinformatics or business computing track. In either case, ISTJs will be data mining and completing a practicum in software engineering. The Emory campus has the clean lines and functional organization that ISTJs approve of.

INTP is the curious, global type who understands quickly and gets intensely absorbed in their studies. They are an excellent fit for intellectual Emory. The joint major in **Economics/Math** allows this type to solve equations and/or puzzles, favorite pastimes. At the same time they can be quite successful in management positions within complex environments. Leadership is an unknown quantity to the young INTP, but the Goizueta School of Business provides the exposure and introduces INTP to executive level careers in business.

ENTJ will appreciate Emory's joint degree in **Psychology & Linguistics**. This latter field is becoming well entwined with brain development. The ENTJ who has a passion for this field will also gain much from Emory's comprehensive graduate programs in psychology. In fact, undergrads will often conduct research in Emory's exceptional medical laboratories for the physical sciences. ENTJ is all about energy and enthusiasm, just like Emory.

ESTJ likes the familiar educational model i.e. the teacher as the giver of knowledge and students as the eager recipient. With the BA in **Physics,** this type can be ready to enter medicine, law, teaching or business. ESTJs, however, will want to narrow down the focus early in the freshman or sophomore year to make sure they satisfy their requirements for a planned degree. They will look to the faculty for input in reaching this decision and faculty builds strong relationships with undergraduates here through the research studies.

INTJ, ever the original, independent and skeptical student, will find that Emory applauds their style. There is enough wiggle room in the curriculum to explore emerging interests. INTJs penchant to directly challenge the wisdom presented in class may not get an eager welcome in Emory's model of education. However, the depth in curriculum offerings overcomes any self doubts and this type's internal vision will develop and mature in four years. The minor in **Science, Culture and Society** is just the ticket to stretch that vision with its self proclaimed 'intense discussion of research issues.'

ISTP who is detached and seemingly "laid back" could draw some arched eyebrows from their hard-charging peers. Fortunately ISTPs pay close attention to the process and will be appreciated in the **Biology** major. If field work with the Yerkes Regional Primate Research Center is available, all the better. Observing primates and drawing conclusions through facts comes naturally for ISTP.

ISFJ is the careful individual who wants to serve mankind and absorb facts delivered in a stable environment. The department of **Nursing** at Emory's Woodruff School of Nursing considers it a privilege to care the ill. ISFJ would agree. With attention to the details, Emory efficiently offers graduation with this professional degree after completion of four calendar, academic years. This type might find extracurricular programs offered by the school of theology for undergraduate students definitely worth exploring.

INFJ might relate quite well to the **Religion** major at Emory which is exceptional for its academic and moral foundation thanks to the Chandler School of Theology. The School, while remaining solid with its historical Christian heritage, offers a plethora of extraordinary courses to the undergraduate. The curriculum addresses religious questions that we are familiar with, minus contemporary political agendas. INFJs will salute the complex nuances this department is willing to take on. Emory University has multiple foundations of strength, to counter contemporary political agendas, such as the prestigious Transforming Community Project, funded by the Ford Foundation.

ENFJ likes to start with the people approach before acknowledging the hard facts. The interesting joint major in **Classics/History** gives this determined type flexibility to sort out a career track. Emory undergrads wrestle regularly with abstract thought, infused by moral reasoning. At the same time, the campus environment is covered up with reality through the School of Nursing and the Goizueta Business School. Within the dorms, the extracurriculars and the social scene, ENFJs will interface their abstractions with peers who prefer employment on graduation. This type can handle the juxtaposition and move forward confidently after graduation to employment or grad school.

ESFJ could easily be attracted to the hands-on **Business** undergraduate degree at Goizueta School of Emory University. The undergraduate degree calls for courage, knowledge and an ability to spontaneously make informed decisions. With a favorable view toward entrepreneurship, this type is resourceful and motivated in salesmanship. They can be invaluable, loyal business partners, especially when the enterprise is offering services to the public.

FLORIDA SOUTHERN COLLEGE

111 Lake Hollingsworth Drive
Lakeland, FL 33801-5689
Website: www.flsouthern.edu
Admissions Telephone: 863-680-4131
Undergraduates: 2,185; 895 Men, 1,290 Women

Physical Environment

Located half-way between Orlando and Tampa, the town of Lakeland does have a lake that flanks the college on one side. The most striking features are the many buildings designed by the American architect, Frank Lloyd Wright. The chapel has long rectangular windows that shoot rays of light throughout the day, creating a mood and feel that moves **spiritual individuals.** Newer buildings such as the library blend in with **Wright's classic architecture** and call to students proud of America's architectural heritage. The Rinker Technology Center includes a cyber lounge and the latest technology for seminars and work spaces. The modern Christoverson Humanities building features the deep red colors of the college and compliments the Wright architectural perspectives. The college is true to the Wright legacy with ongoing renovation and maintenance of those historic structures.

The performing arts facility does an outstanding job by drawing in students who are serious about **music and dramatic performance**. The planetarium offers students and the community a way to come together as they explore the heavens and appeals to prospective students who like a **family feel**. A wellness building and athletic center provide students with many activities that foster fitness and health. The religious center accommodates students who want to continue their worship experience in college.

The pool and lake offer a **fun-in-the-sun** lifestyle and competitive water sports. Students who want more diversion drive to Orlando or Tampa and the gulf coast beaches. Orange trees are part of the campus landscape, a practical reminder and laboratory for students interested in studying citrus **horticulture** and turf grass management. These niche degrees are well supported by the Florida climate and this particular campus.

This college draws students who want that residential, private college feel. It appeals to many students who respect and are proud of **American architectural heritage**.

Social Environment

The majority of students come from Florida and prefer a **reliable, predictable** college environment. Undergraduates at Florida Southern are **cooperative** and collegial with one another. Students are also inclined to follow a clear-cut preparation for professional and **applied careers**.

The successful Florida Southern student graduated high school and ranked in the top half of the class. Professors are attuned to students with differing learning levels, interests and abilities. The academic environment requires that students step up to the plate and work hard with the assistance of faculty. This campus is drawing students who are drawn to traditional liberal arts studies in **reading and writing** even though there are many applied studies in the curriculum.

Traditional **fraternities and sororities** are alive and are well supported here by the majority of the student body. Rules and regulations are established by the college such as **visiting hours** in the Greek houses. This college has a strong and lengthy relationship with the town of Lakeland. Since the 1970s, students and community leaders have pooled their efforts through a non-profit organization in order to benefit their community. Students participate in the many **service projects** for Lakeland families and seniors who are representative of solid **Middle America**. Students here focus on their studies with considerable responsibility. They are proud of their academic and artistic work and expect to be successful and productive throughout their careers.

Compatibility with Personality Types and Preferences

Florida Southern College has a solid tradition of easily recognizable American social values which evolved on this campus community through decades of membership and affiliation with the Methodist Church. Florida Southern's ethical belief system is easily understood in the Cornerstone Concept that outlines the standard of behavior expected of all students who enroll at the college. The honor code is considered a personal obligation of each student and care is taken by the administration to communicate it to prospective students. At this university, the standards identified in procedures and policy are written to apply equally to faculty, staff and students. Academic philosophy leans heavily toward practical knowledge and skills. Much of the faculty in business has had entrepreneurial experience in the private sector.

The helpful website is loaded with considerable detail (S) that is designed to be supportive of the students. Care is taken to spell out any impact college policies may have on the students. The Second Year Experience focuses attention on returning sophomores akin to that given to first years on campus. It is typical of the inreach to students. The entire community honors friendliness and contribution to others through service learning (F). From this foundation of strong values and helping others, the college promotes educational excellence. At Florida Southern, there is much to be appreciated in traditional American perspectives.

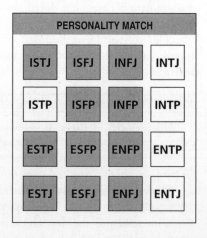

PERSONALITY MATCH

ISTJ	ISFJ	INFJ	INTJ
ISTP	ISFP	INFP	INTP
ESTP	ESFP	ENFP	ENTP
ESTJ	ESFJ	ENFJ	ENTJ

In the following listing of college majors it is important to remember that students can fit into any college and can be successful in any major. We have found that the Personality Types below fit very well at this college. The course-of-study chosen for each Personality Type corresponds to MBTI® research and is presented as an example favorable for that type.

ISTJ will get both the core coursework with the **Business** degree and **Finance** concentration emphasizing skills and management tools. The latter offers an emphasis on planning and risk management which familiarizes ISTJs with a valuable skill set. Often meticulous in their approach, ISTJ will respect and well utilize the excellent student professor collaboration at Florida Southern.

ISFJ would rally to the call for help from the juvenile delinquent population in our youth detention facilities. On this campus, the degree in **Criminology** is well supported by the overall educational philosophy of service to others. Whether this type pursues the major or minor, their reflective nature and ability to clearly see reality will be an asset in the career field. There is also an option for a double major, **Sociology & Criminology**, that would position this type to serve both the individual and the community at large.

INFJ has a mind full of impressions best understood by non-INFJs as "artistic impressions" which could be straight out of the art history books cataloging calm landscapes of nature. The major in **Youth Ministry** here is traditional in spiritual foundation. The curriculum includes leadership options and direct internship experience. INFJs will find commitment to bring relevant and supportive programming into our teen communities. This passionate type will naturally help adolescents sort through social media influences.

ISFP and art is a natural. Artistic expression on this warm campus is also a natural. This type might look into the **Studio Art** major with flexibility for concentration in sculpture, painting, ceramics, printing or photography. The department has a robust curriculum and seeks to explore the relationship between art and emotion. This type, both sensitive and astute, will appreciate the wide variety of options.

INFP seeks to find meaning in human existence and it's a tall order, even for them. The **Religion** major at Florida Southern is a good starting point for their inquiry. The department has a well developed Judeo-Christian course of study. The culture and history of this campus brings an ideal foundation for studying theological critiques. Historic collegiate traditions, dating back decades, help students assimilate current cultural perspectives with spiritual studies.

ESTP is lucky to have the unusual **Landscape Horticulture Production and Design** major at Florida Southern. The courses emphasize the high risks in the horticultural business and this suits the action-oriented and trouble-shooting ESTP. Dare we say, it is a 'hands-on' discipline? This department has other desirable options in citrus farming and turf grass management which also allows this type to be outside and on the go.

ESFP has the willingness to craft together two separate majors that are both offered at Florida Southern College: **Marketing** and **Sports Management**. For this type, the state of Florida with its strong spring training camps in baseball and college football teams has good options for sports reporting and internships. This solid combination of courses will likely form a successful preparation for the wide world of athletics.

ENFP is going to find that the **Graphic Design** studies here offer a wide scope within the discipline. First there is a print emphasis or web emphasis to choose from within the minors. This choice in minor is available to pair with the advertising major in communications. Or maybe ENFP will turn it around and major in graphic design with just a few advertising courses thrown in along with a few public relations courses. On this campus there is no shortage of coursework that ENFP is likely to want to take.

ESTJ will smooth into the **Accounting** major or minor with comparative ease. This very exacting discipline allows the student with this type to bring their impersonal powers of judgment into the arena of objective numbers. Combine this activity with the need for taking charge while auditing a client's firm and it's awfully enticing major for take-charge ESTJs.

ESFJ is a natural conversationalist as well as news reporter. Their innate interest in the well-being of others is a distinct advantage when interviewing eye witnesses to traumatic events in our communities for the nightly news. The News Media I, II, III coursework provide the primer for both anchor and news reporter positions. The major in **Broadcast, Print & Online Media** takes advantage of their memory for details and steady approach in critical situations.

ENFJ will find a warm, personal faculty in the department of **Psychology**. The curriculum emphasizes human behavior and interpersonal relationships which suits this type just fine. ENFJs will thrive on the personal mentoring with this department. Their extraordinary communication skills will be amplified with new insights secured in this degree.

FURMAN UNIVERSITY

Office of Admissions
Greenville, SC 29613
Website: www.furman.edu
Admissions Telephone: 864-294-2034
Undergraduates: 2,761; 1,168 Men, 1,593 Women

Physical Environment

Located on 750 acres at the base of the Blue Ridge Mountains, this academically rigorous liberal arts university moved to this location in 1958. The architecture is a mix of colonial Williamsburg style and red-brick walkways that crisscross in a Jeffersonian way. The **landscape** with the trees, flowers, fountains, lake, softball fields and an 18-hole golf course is nothing less than breathtaking. The classroom buildings are modern and house their most popular majors. The University also includes a music conservatory.

Many of these buildings are environmentally certified and designed with recycled materials for energy efficiency. The technology classrooms are designed to pipe in fresh air and oxygen. The geothermal project is in full swing with 11 buildings scheduled or completed. The student center, hub for many student activities, the huge, multi-level dining hall, the renovated library and other buildings are either brand-new or have undergone renovation recently. The Bell Tower, a **60-bell carillon**, overlooks the pond, flanked by an amphitheatre used for **outdoor concerts**. New apartment-style residence halls and conference center take full advantage of the views. There are running trails around this pond and lots of woods on the far side. The architecture here appeals to students who are lively, active and caring of the environment.

Social Environment

Furman students reflect familiar trends of American society. They value their family and hometown traditions that reflect Christian values, being well-groomed and proud of their daily appearance. About one-third of the students are actively involved in a religious organization with the university becoming independent of its formal Baptist association in 1992. Orientation takes place during the first week of classes when students and parents meet with academic advisors. Parents get **extra preparation** for dropping off their kids and dealing with the empty nest syndrome. During family weekend, everyone is invited, including cousins, uncles and grandparents. A Furman education is a family affair!

Furman University has a strong community spirit and civic minded students. The local area is the prime beneficiary of undergraduate volunteer hours and all are involved. Furman students are also environmentally conscious and politically interested. Well known speakers are often on campus, scheduled by the university's non-partisan political think-tank which also funds student research. Greek organizations initiate many volunteer and **philanthropic projects** for organizations such as the Society for the Deaf and Blind and Habitat for Humanity. Furman University reflects conservative tradition that focuses on moral, prosocial behavior.

Students like the liberal arts and like to dig deeply into a major. They gain depth while participating in internships, study abroad and other experiential education. The Furman academic **calendar is nontraditional** and it adds length and **rigor** to the collegiate workload. The great majority of students come from out of the state. There are 168 student associations, which include a Pan-Hellenic council representing Greek fraternities and sororities. The **social scene** is lively at Furman. Paladin Night is an all-night event with movies, music and cultural life programs. Students must guard against becoming over-involved with so many activities from which to choose. Overall, this generation of Furman students wants to positively contribute and support their community, the nation and the world.

Compatibility with Personality Types and Preferences

Furman University purposely combines traditional religious values of the 20th Century with a trendy educational outlook. Faculty and administration set a vibrant foundation of social and academic experiences for undergrads. There is a strong attraction to technology in use by today's generation. Furman embraces and uses it. Students are familiar with class collaborative projects that are supplemented by text messaging. This experiential learning is a hallmark of the university's attraction to the future. Students who have mastered the scientific method are encouraged to join faculty in research where they are closely mentored during research activities.

Furman actively encourages students to bring their new-found knowledge gained through this research off campus with the "traveling class" offered in the curriculum by disciplines. Service to others (F) is a common theme and most students participate in volunteer events that are organized and developed by national collegiate service organizations. There is also a strong ethic for productivity. The pathways (J) are in place for undergraduates to double major and take additional coursework. Furman provides a creative environment through hands-on research and direct learning. Students who appreciate getting the facts and details (S) in place first and then moving toward a general understanding of their subject will do well here.

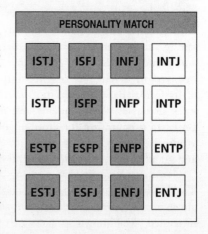

In the following listing of college majors it is important to remember that students can fit into any college and can be successful in any major. We have found that the Personality Types below fit very well at this college. The course-of-study chosen for each Personality Type corresponds to MBTI® research and is presented as an example favorable for that type.

INFJ will find the **Theater Arts** curriculum at Furman University really quite thorough. Each undergraduate will be practiced in all the positions of theater performance including stage management, technical crew, publicists and actors. As introspective INFJ rotates through each of the responsibilities in performing art, they will bring imagery and symbolism to enhance the dramatic presentations. This department generates strong professor-student relationships, ideal for INFJs, through its smaller size and three annual performances.

ISTJ might take a close look at the **Economics** degree at Furman University. It has much that appeals to ISFJs, specifically, the step-by-step survey of the economic discipline. This sequential approach is their preferred way to master the abstract discipline. The required capstone course in senior year has several prerequisites that include the course Empirical Methods in Economics. This type of direct observational study leads to the best understanding for ISTJs.

ISFJ with a good ear for music will want to take advantage of the impressive music department at Furman. The major in **Music Theory and Composition** rotates emphasizing performance in the choral, vocal, solo, ensembles and string quartet. The ISFJ is a sensitive person and quite aware of how others are feeling during any given activity. This type will bring a personal meaning to their musical composition and performance along with a precise, possibly understated performance.

ISFP just might move toward a career in pharmaceuticals. The **Chemistry** major at Furman offers further specialization. The track in biochemistry has the action and practicality that they want. ISFP appreciates the utility of hands-on research in the labs along with the detailed observations of chemical reactions. This major prepares ISFPs for pharmacy school or fundamental research for industrial applications. ISFPs prefer to see a light at the end of the tunnel. The department shines forth through student faculty collaboration in research and numerous other learning experiences.

ESTP could sign right up after scanning the courses at Furman for the **Information Technology** interdisciplinary major. It is their practice to quickly jump in with a practical, expeditious goal in mind. This major offers graduates a broad and solid understanding of business practice and application of software and programming. ESTP will benefit from the nuts and bolts in the course titled Project Management. With this practical collection of skills ESTP is quite ready for technology-intensive business environments.

ESFP is a natural at public relations. The major in **Communication Studies** will prepare this type for several dynamic, fast-paced career options. Above all, ESFP needs to be with other people in an environment charged with purpose and preferably fun. Their ease in social situations is ideal when combined with a solid foundation in communication theory. At Furman, students learn to formulate their message via analysis of the topic and its social and moral implications. This type often seeks to give others a helping hand. ESFP's infomercials, produced at WFTV, would be chocked with useful, factual information.

ENFP will start off the freshmen year at Furman sampling most if not all of the fun cultural events and activities. This campus is ideal for ENFP since Furman enthusiasm and optimism runs high. The major in **Business Administration** gives good exposure to the wide entrepreneurial field. This works well for ENFP who likes to take in all the possibilities before selecting a career track. The investment club is pretty successful and active on campus and another good bet for ENFP.

ESFJ should find the friendly, harmonious environment they prefer within the Department of **Biology** at Furman University. Academic work tends to comprise two avenues of learning favorable to the ESFJs. First there is the read-study-memorize of most first-year courses. This is followed by the application of those principles in the laboratories and exceptional field experiences in upper level courses such as the African Ecology. It is also one of the traveling courses in the **Biology** curriculum.

ESTJ is often a go-getter. This type sees their goal and efficiently pursues it. The major in **Accounting** prepares graduates for the gate-keeping function in fast-paced financial economies. It will be the ESTJ who can guide organizations with firmness while identifying errors with resolve. The department offers a broad education that could lead to graduate study or employment on graduation. This practical approach, tied to the reality of facts and numbers, is desired by ESTJ.

ENFJ is going to be fine with the major in **Health Sciences.** The curriculum essentially requires graduates to become strong advocates for a healthy life style. ENFJ is interested in the individual as a whole person—their emotional health, spiritual health and physical health. The department functions almost as a center that advocates for well-being. There is a well-equipped laboratory for studying performance in running and body composition. Since this type is exceptionally talented at speaking to large audiences, the message of well-being could easily become their prime career focus.

GEORGE WASHINGTON UNIVERSITY

212 I Street, NW
Washington, DC 20052
Website: www.gwu.edu
Admissions Telephone: 202-994-6040
Undergraduates: 10,358; 4,223 Men, 5,375 Women
Graduate Students: 14,777

Physical Environment

Which university is closest to the White House? Which university broadcasts famous programs such as CNN Cross Fire? It's George Washington University's downtown campus. Visitors may walk the city streets E to J or 20th to 24th and admire the **tall buildings and Federal style houses** without immediately realizing they are on the campus of GW. The architecture lends credibility to the university image of being well connected to the power circles in the district. Most of the campus buildings occupy the area formed by Avenues of Pennsylvania, New Hampshire and Virginia. Students walk to **DC museums** and monuments, from the Smithsonian to the Vietnam Veterans Memorial and the Korean War Veterans Memorial. Prospective visiting high schoolers are also wowed by the 'real' history here. The latest addition, Square 54, offers residential and commercial services, functioning as a town center for students, faculty and DC residents.

The Potomac River offers walkways for joggers and bikers who choose to walk instead of taking the METRO, the DC subway. The **city hustle and bustle** is amplified by a multitude of ethnic shops and restaurants. Students who are attracted to power and important venues find this university very appealing. Here the physical environment combines the nation's capital with classroom education and recreational city experiences.

The housing options at GW are many, ranging from living and learning to residences for fraternities and sororities and recreational space for sports and fitness. The university tries to keep students busy on campus, although the city itself remains a huge draw. The goal of the school is to keep students in school-sponsored housing by offering a wide variety of residence halls. GW also offers a quieter location at its Mount Vernon Campus, formerly a college for women. This campus is fenced in and has many mature trees and red-brick buildings and offers classes in liberal arts. Students can take classes at either campus.

Social Environment

Students come from a considerable **variety of socio-economic** backgrounds. Some have parents in the diplomatic core. Others may be referred to GW by their country's embassy in Washington DC. Home-grown U.S. students from across the nation regularly enroll for this unique collegiate experience. The worldly international students provide an open door to other cultures for the American undergraduates. American students expect to secure **internships in federal offices**, national lobbies, corporate business headquarters and nonprofits. **International students** expect to enlarge their knowledge of American society and practices.

GW is a large university and students gain bureaucratic skills simply by negotiating their own educational study and presence on campus within the first year. They learn to expertly navigate the somewhat tight rules of the university. To counter the impersonal impact of the city and largeness of the student body, the residential life is bolstered with **homey, fun activities** that remind undergraduates of the calmer lives in their hometowns. **Volunteer initiatives**, very familiar with the millennial generation, are well supported. Collegiate activities help to bolster and resupply student energy reserves to deal with the city and remain positive, self-directed. Students who want more personal connections will find their niche on the Mount Vernon campus. The year-round celebratory atmosphere in DC rises to a new zenith around the holiday season. The Thanksgiving preparations, lighting of the tree at the White House, the presidential inauguration and such political occasions create a privileged setting that helps students understand that they might be an important part of what's happening in the nation in the future.

Compatibility with Personality Types and Preferences

George Washington University takes much of its persona from DC, the nation's Capitol. GW echoes the pragmatic nature of DC. The nation's Capitol must function for the district citizens, the nation, and always be cognizant of its impact on the global population. Perhaps more than any other characteristic, GW emulates this practicality. On this campus questions within all academic disciplines are: What works? What is real? What is of value that we all agree on? (T) Not surprisingly, facts and actual experience weigh heavily in daily educational studies and internship experiences in the district.

Students drawn to George Washington University want to experience it all, so their friends on campus and the student body in general must serve as a stable anchor. Prospective students appreciate that the campus offers a secure, predictable collegiate atmosphere within its buildings. The environment is fast-paced energy outside of campus and students want a safe place at the end of the day. They are expecting to build and advance their academic skills. They want to learn how to negotiate the dynamic administrative environments of lobbies, regulatory bodies, executive offices and departments. GW's curriculum is magnified several times over through its faculty and access to prominent speakers. Collaboration between the university and other influential partners, such as Ford Motor Company, add to the allure of real time problems and solutions. Professors can be careerists who function as high level civil service employees, policy makers, party officials, lobbyists and think tankers among the legions of administrative types who work in DC. Above all else, students who are successful at GW are drawn outside of themselves, outside of their dormitory and outside of their campus (E), drawn into the

PERSONALITY MATCH			
ISTJ	ISFJ	INFJ	INTJ
ISTP	ISFP	INFP	INTP
ESTP	ESFP	ENFP	ENTP
ESTJ	ESFJ	ENFJ	ENTJ

GEORGETOWN UNIVERSITY

Office of Admission
37th and P Streets, NW
Washington, DC 20057
Website: www.georgetown.edu
Admissions Telephone: 202-687-5084
Undergraduates: 7,553; 3,385 Men, 4,168 Women
Graduate Students: 5,832

Physical Environment

The two tall steeples of Georgetown University soar above the Potomac River as they did in much earlier times, before **Washington, DC** became the capital of the United States. In the early 1800s the nation's capital moved from Philadelphia to Washington, to a strip of land between Maryland and Virginia, and established an independent district named after Columbus. Today Georgetown University occupies 110 acres of this very busy city with a population of over half a million. The city subway and buses make transportation to and from the airport and into town a streamlined trip. The university is intrinsically part and parcel of the nation's capital that offers many resources and opportunities.

The historic architecture portrays the original religious philosophy of Georgetown founders, the **Jesuits**. Dahlgren Chapel of the Sacred Heart, located right in the center of campus, offers daily religious services. The campus buildings have many inclusive spaces for celebrating the spiritual life of students, regardless of their religion. The new science center has removed undergraduate science courses out of the old blackboard classrooms. The dramatic new, current technological facility bears a resemblance to historic architecture prevalent on the campus. The university has developed a strong security presence on the campus to help undergraduates negotiate the unpredictable nature of the city.

Today's residence halls have all manner of conveniences. Dormitory floors are air conditioned and are designed to foster a supportive community. Each dormitory has a chaplain in addition to RAs. This is particularly important since students must live on campus for the first two years. These residence halls form the meeting places where students from various departments can form tight knit communities. Each individual school and college provides "educational study" in its campus buildings. Undergraduates from the School of **Foreign Service** take many courses in their seven-floor tower while nursing students and pre-med students take classes at the Georgetown hospital. The undergraduate educational studies tend to be compartmentalized. It is usually difficult to take courses outside of your major in other schools and departments on this campus.

The Georgetown campus is not only a stone's throw from the **White House** but also a stone's throw from the nation's most important monuments and museums. When students need a diversion from the intense academics, Washington is a power-charged capital that offers many options.

Social Environment

Georgetown students graduate at the top of their high school class. They are particularly adept at **abstract reasoning**. They enjoy ethical and religious discussion on the human condition and what it means to be Catholic in 21st Century America. Georgetown students tend to come from worldly, influential families. It also has a multi-ethnic student body that comes from around the globe. True to its Jesuit tradition, GU embraces people of other religions and respects their ideas and customs. Many students speak more than one **language.** The student body is as diverse and vibrant as the city itself. GU School of Foreign Service attracts students who are near-proficient in a foreign language resulting from sufficient study in high school or from speaking another language at home.

A number of majors in the undergraduate curriculum, such as in the School of Foreign Service, cover **unique disciplines** that are offered as graduate study in other universities. Spirituality and **moral reasoning** remain the philosophical glue that holds this academically wide-ranging university together. Students who fit in here enjoy building a framework of knowledge that includes ethics, religion, civilization, peace and justice. It's for those who want to serve in the time-honored medical professions or policy positions within government, diplomatic corps or international organizations. At Georgetown and in the capital, students observe power and policy at work. They see the government up close and feel the power in action in our nation's capital.

Georgetown students work hard and play hard. This demanding academic environment finds students partying on the weekends. Other stress busters include rooting for the Hoyas, often nationally ranked in several sports, especially basketball. Students also join religious and other ethnic fellowship clubs.

Compatibility with Personality Types and Preferences

Georgetown University could be thought of as a successful experiment in power and engagement. This influential university is in a privileged position from which it develops educational content, now through international, global perspectives. This university, predating the Revolutionary period, has an exceptional history of its own in reference to a time when America struggled to become a viable nation. Looking over to the Capitol, two blocks from undergraduate housing lofts, provides a visual cue as to the university's familiar coexistence (E) with power and leadership in our national government.

Much like the government itself, this university is organized by departments and colleges similar to a wiring diagram (J). The undergraduate schools and colleges are quite separate from each other. One can imagine the State Department with its own culture and mission as quite separate from the Treasury Department. In this way, Georgetown's School of Foreign Policy and the School of Business can be envisioned as existing quite independently of each other, yet part of the same university. Students drawn to this campus are attracted to the power, influence and potential for leadership in the nation's seat of government. They are students who see decision and policy making very clearly in their career path. They are students who can visualize the fast and impersonal pace of the city and its opportunities while taking a tour on a campus visit. Undergraduates are exposed to a full academic fire hosing of abstraction (N) and factual knowledge (S) in the four undergraduate years.

In the following listing of college majors it is important to remember that students can fit into any college and can be successful in any major. We have found that the Personality Types below fit very well at this college. The course-of-study chosen for each Personality Type corresponds to MBTI® research and is presented as an example favorable for that type.

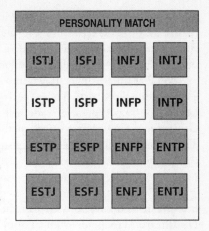

INFJ desires an understanding of other peoples and their cultural values. They apply their insight to ethnic cultures with ease because of their natural empathy. In the School of Foreign Service the major in **Culture and Politics** looks to understand how societal outlooks, perceptions and beliefs are translated in power and action. It is pretty abstract and the INFJ is particularly suited for it. With this degree, INFJs will be valuable consultants for many international and national organizations.

INTJ often has a strategic plan after sufficient study of a particular problem. However, they are not inclined to speak up about that plan since it usually contains a few unorthodox ideas. This type typically wants to work in an environment that allows them the freedom to try out their ideas. They analyze rapidly and with ease. A field with fast moving factors and data points is attractive to INTJs. The study of **Finance** at Georgetown University would seem to provide this. The department focuses on global financial mechanisms and organizations like the World Bank headquarters in DC. Disciplined and objective, INTJ happily would don a suit for a day at that office.

ISTJ likes to correct infractions of rules that we all should have followed in the first place. This type is dedicated to accuracy and doesn't mind studying the fine details for total understanding. The major in **Operations and Information Management** could appeal to ISTJ for these reasons. It explores the nature of systems that 'run smoothly.' ISTJs are surely approving of that since they find common sense in procedures that were developed for good reason.

ISFJ often has a technical side or at least an affinity with technology. Drawn to the fields of health and medicine, the major in **Human Science** at Georgetown holds out good options for ISFJ. Undergraduates get a firm grounding in biological and chemical principles in the state of the art teaching laboratory. Faculty regularly focus on current research and its applicability to current problems in health. ISFJs equipped with analytical skills are just the type to introduce new concepts in established organizations such as government bureaucracies.

INTP can find the right amount of complexity in the **International Health** major at the School of Nursing and Health Studies on the Georgetown campus. The course descriptions and overview by the department call attention to the nature of disease as it travels across regional and political boundaries. The issues in this field are truly sobering. INTPs, with their objective analysis, can develop potential solutions for discussion. This type can see through emotional misinterpretation of reality when confronting global hunger and illness. INTP is happiest bringing order and purpose out of seeming intellectual chaos. Global Health will offer them many opportunities.

ESTP at times will be drawn into the field of trade, especially if there is dynamic action and a little risk. This type is skilled at identifying the unspoken goals in negotiation between buyers and sellers. The major in **International Business** at Georgetown University focuses on the international business trends and practices. This foundational knowledge supports ESTP managers as they smoothly enter the environments of negotiation. The international qualifications can be gained in several ways. It meets the plug-and-play personal style of ESTPs.

ESFP has the common sense to go into tough management environments like health care and survive with flair, helping others to cheer up also. The major in **Healthcare Management and Policy** in the School of Nursing and Health Studies can prepare ESFP for the demands in this much-needed field. At Georgetown, the undergraduates will focus on management competencies as well as the various bureaucratic environments within hospitals and nursing facilities. ESFP will warm to the demand of establishing friendly relations and using their persuasive skills with other members of the upper management team. It will make their day, week and month to improve treatment for those who enter the hospital environs.

ENFP likes to be around a group of self-directed peers who are enthusiastically tuned to the task at hand, preferably several tasks at once. This type has a way with persuasion. The concentration in **Marketing** at Georgetown explores several marketing focuses. One of them, brand management, includes the life cycle of products studying the alpha to omega that represents the big picture so favored by ENFPs.

ENTP may not immediately jump at the concept of getting a degree in **International History.** However, it could make sense to this typically confident type because it draws coursework from several disciplines and roams across national and cultural boundaries. Following the thread of a topic, like labor relations through the centuries and across continents, could easily attract ENTP. Students in this major will develop a theme and develop it in just such a fashion. This is ideal for ENTP who can lose interest in assignments that are too familiar or do not hold out a tantalizing discovery.

ESFJ will be in synch with the people side of work environments. The degree in **Sociology** at Georgetown offers much that could appeal to this type. There will be a strong use of methodology identifying tough social issues. The faculty is not shy about asking undergraduates to dream up idealistic perspectives and solutions. However, conscientious, traditional ESFJs will prefer across the board studies without narrowing the focus to one arena. Their strong organizational skills will be valuable in personalizing the broad nature of this complex discipline.

ESTJ marches down the road of life as a very determined and practical traveler. The department providing curriculum in **Government** takes an interdisciplinary, pluralistic approach to the subject. As such, undergraduates will study through the lens of current trends in international views centered on justice. This type has the personal determination to push through to their goals, securing a foundational understanding of the nature of governance. The advantage of studying this subject in the nation's capital will not be lost on this results-oriented, practical type.

ENFJ will take leadership positions in the right circumstances. Supportive, harmonious relationships with an organization would likely draw them forward to those positions. The degree at Georgetown University in **American Musical Culture** is unusual yet prepares graduates for careers in journalism, arts management and/or entertainment law. In each field, ENFJs would bring their creativity to the workplace along with their distinct desire to include all players in the decision making. This major requires a senior capstone project. The options for musical internships in the nation's capital are considerable and varied. Poised ENFJ will find fascinating internships in DC museums, the Library of Congress and other national sites that are housing musical treasures.

ENTJ is happy to step out and conduct the orchestra. Educational studies which stretch the imagination with large ideas and complex concepts really do appeal to this type, yet most ENTJs carefully avoid ivory towers. They will not waste their time working on projects grounded in fantasy and maybes. The comparative studies in politics at Georgetown attempts to make sense of what is. The **African Studies Program** in the School of Foreign Service is helping the millennial generation understand the role of power and politics that is ever present on this continent. The ENTJ will find that it travels nicely with several of the majors available in the field of foreign service.

GEORGIA INSTITUTE OF TECHNOLOGY

22 North Avenue, NW
Atlanta, GA 30332-0320
Website: www.gatech.edu
Admissions Telephone: 404-894-4154
Undergraduates: 13,948; 9,458 Men, 4,490 Women
Graduate Students: 6,993

Physical Environment

Georgia Tech is located near **downtown Atlanta** where I-75 and I-85 merge. Residence halls built for the 1996 Olympic athletes overlook this connector, nevertheless the campus is bordered by residential neighborhoods on other sides. Students retreat from the hectic city pace on the tree-lined campus. Many students walk to Ponce de Leon Avenue over the connector to well known local restaurants, clubs, galleries and shops. The city of Atlanta calls out to many rural and suburban students who come to campus excited about a smorgasbord of opportunities. Professional sports teams, the Braves and Falcons, as well as the Atlanta Symphony attract a cross section of students.

The Georgia Tech campus has an **enclosed, tight and angular** appeal with its new buildings and architecturally bold design. The sports complex and natatorium also built for the summer Olympics attract athletes loath to give up their track records and winning team statistics. These sports-minded students like to exercise, swim and play on the intramural teams. Creative techies are right at home in the state of the art **laboratories** inside the dramatic modern architecture. The **concrete and aluminum** structures on this campus are similar to the manufacturing and technical environments that most will enter as they start their careers. Students attracted to innovative solutions come to study environmental science and technology at the top research complex donated by the Ford Motor Company. Water conservation in manufacturing is the most recent initiative in this successful collaboration.

Social Environment

Successful students typically rank at the top of their high school graduating class and have outstanding standardized test scores, especially in math and science. The majority of students come from the state of Georgia. Many come from familiar towns and countryside across the state, lending a cohesive feel to the social life. They are not turned away by the **study and work demands** of this unique, public institution. Students try to keep balance between **fun** and the books, yet academic study is intense. Many join Greek life because of their sponsored social activities on campus. Some form networks through friends at the nearby colleges for other social outlets. They enjoy their mascot, the Yellow Jacket, which reflects a social nature of this campus. Archrival the University of Georgia brings out the fans at games and maybe the yellow jacket stinging defense! This campus draws those who like **traditional school spirit** and strong competitive teams to cheer.

Many students expand out from the focused engineering track of studies to include subjects in other disciplines. Initiative and creativity are typical of these undergraduates and they bring these strong skills to their different technical fields. On this campus, students approve of the clear expectations within the science majors.

There is concern on campus over the issues that affect humankind: economic upheavals, new diseases, hazards in the environment, the cleanliness of the air we breathe and the cost of gas. Students and faculty seek to build upon innovative research to **solve mankind's problems**. These students form a strong can-do attitude and academic network in this training ground for 21st century technical careers. Those who like practical, hands-on research are thriving.

Compatibility with Personality Types and Preferences

On many Saturday mornings, a surprising number of students are out and exuberant in the morning. Students are likely to go through their day actively, with physical vigor and a twinkle of humor. This campus is for the folks who like to see, touch, feel or listen to materials (S). They seek to understand the environment and its properties; they are comfortable with themselves, metal, the circuits, the temperature, the physicality which is always present on this campus. At the same time they are fairly logical (T) folks who analyze and put stuff together for a purpose. The GA Techie likes to dissect the step-by-step presentation of what actually exists: whether it exists in a theorem or in a piece of metal. The learning experience expects to move undergraduates into the future through combining the foundations in each discipline with experimentation.

Educational philosophy is strongly centered on benefiting the overall society. These emerging sustainability concepts have long been featured at Georgia Tech. The impact of society's manufacturing and production have been a central theme on campus for decades. Faculty and students support living in an environment that shepherds natural resources while being efficient but yet comfortable. Graduates have a strong grounding in the benefits and reality of technology. Academic philosophy well incorporates multidisciplinary approaches in separate degrees among its several schools. Foundational and advanced knowledge within the individual disciplines is solid, practical and reflective of reality. They are alert to societal costs of these same technologies, capable of making the tough calls between reality and ideals during the application of new technologies.

In the following listing of college majors it is important to remember that students can fit into any college and can be successful in any major. We have found that the Personality Types below fit very well at this college. The course-of-study chosen for each Personality Type corresponds to MBTI® research and is presented as an example favorable for that type.

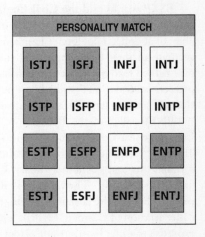

PERSONALITY MATCH

ISTJ	ISFJ	INFJ	INTJ
ISTP	ISFP	INFP	INTP
ESTP	ESFP	ENFP	ENTP
ESTJ	ESFJ	ENFJ	ENTJ

ESTJ is an outstanding fit at Georgia Tech. The Georgia Tech course catalog is exceptionally clear in setting out information about what a student will need to graduate. Course credit is awarded at Georgia Tech for top scores on the SAT Subject Tests taken in high school. The degree in **Building Construction** is a good choice here for this type. The department emphasizes the management skills needed to monitor large construction sites. ESTJ is a natural administrator and has the no-nonsense personality to reason profitably with the construction trades, also no-nonsense folks!

ENTJ wants to take the practical material that abounds on this campus and reshape it into something new, futuristic and maybe just a little beyond the truly practical. ENTJ has the driving force to open their vision up in the classroom discussions and in the labs. Aeroelasticity should appeal to a person of this preference who has a penchant for math and calculated risk. It's possible that the Navy or Air Force will need engineers with courses like this in the **Aerospace Engineering** degree, to repair and monitor the aging American aircraft fleets.

ENTP could easily be attracted to the Bachelor of Science in **History, Technology and Society**. The breadth of this curriculum appeals to the type's desire for the big picture and originality. Inclined to be avid readers, albeit later in life, the ENTPs like the variety and survey approach of this degree. The courses offered are compelling to the ENTP and offer a break from the exacting nature of the engineering studies. The graduates in this major have excellent analytical skills that are applicable to developing countries planning to upgrade their industrial capacities.

ISTP is quite observant but likely to be one of the less vocal students at outgoing Georgia Tech. Outside of the classroom however, ISTP will be on a mission if it comes to collegiate robotics competitions. This type would know if the robot will work before other team members can push the start button. This type is a good partner on collaborative student teams making friends along with the metallic parts. The degree in **Materials Science and Engineering** is an excellent choice here for ISTP. Upperclassman work in teams to design, build and operate a process, component or material studied in the first years on campus.

ESTP would find the **Civil Engineering** degree at Georgia Tech a good bet for their inclinations. The course work includes projects which require students to lead and collaborate. They prefer hands-on experimentation since they are typically very accurate in their observations. At the same time, their natural skills in smoothing over ruffled feathers between the skills and trades that come together on construction projects is ideal. ESTP will be first in line when it comes to fun at Georgia Tech and this will serve to let off academic steam built up throughout the week.

ENFJ will find the Bachelor of Science in **Global Economics and Modern Language** searches for creative solutions to big, really big problems in society. Georgia Tech interfaces the many human issues confronting world populations with financial mechanisms and economic theory. Courses like Health Economics will warm the heart of the ENFJ. Their desire is to care for others. This type is comfortable in courses that require sustained reading like economic theory. The choice of language concentration of German, French, Japanese or Spanish allows them to take economic expertise to other locations on planet earth.

ESFP can often have a good eye for design. This type is naturally curious and prefers to learn with others in study groups or with people in collaboration. ESFPs

because they bring practical experience to the table. At Guilford, the liberal arts curriculum is moving toward **applied and practical knowledge**; adult students support this approach. This is an ideal place for those who would like to learn in a community quite conscious of traditional Quaker values.

Compatibility with Personality Types and Preferences

Guilford College fits uniquely among small liberal arts colleges with its Quaker vision of education that incorporates equality. Surrounded by southern cultural roots, it is a meeting place for varied perspectives. The administration and faculty bring a profound sense of tolerance that translates into caring (F). The curriculum and the many activities outside of the classroom capture the quality of life students here hope to generate in their work and living environments. Service and volunteer initiatives are considerable and support the nearby community in creative and long-lasting programs. Undergraduates have the full support of the campus resources and administration when they improve or initiate projects and practices for the benefit of underserved citizens. Students here are going to be comfortable expressing multiple views (P). You could say that there is a common theme in questioning the status quo in a manner that accepts both quiet indifference and steady demand for change. The undercurrents of Quaker philosophies promote sustained inquiry. It is the sensitive, individualistic student who is likely to find his way to and remain at the Guildford campus. The college educational philosophy strongly encourages experiential learning in off-campus experiences, internships, field studies and research, often in the local area. Graduates, regardless of their major, will be acutely knowledgeable of diverse perspectives within society and the impact each has in shaping and forming the larger community.

In the following listing of college majors it is important to remember that students can fit into any college and can be successful in any major. We have found that the Personality Types below fit very well at this college. The course-of-study chosen for each Personality Type corresponds to MBTI® research and is presented as an example favorable for that type.

PERSONALITY MATCH			
ISTJ	ISFJ	INFJ	INTJ
ISTP	ISFP	INFP	INTP
ESTP	ESFP	ENFP	ENTP
ESTJ	ESFJ	ENFJ	ENTJ

ENTP is just the type to cope well with rapid change. The dynamic **Computing and Information Technology** Degree at Guildford might attract this type. Operating systems, networking systems and computer software provide the foundational coursework. Students here will also explore how technology is changing human behavior, including hacking and the security threats presented. Further, students will be expected to take a position on the utility of these changes, and ENTP is more than willing to take a position.

ENFJ might find value in the **Health and Fitness** track within the Sport Studies major at Guilford. Improving health through diligence in exercise and activity makes good sense to ENFJs who prefer diagnostics and therapies that holistically support the clients. The overall cultural environment at Guilford is likely to be exceptionally satisfying and energizing for this type who diligently seeks harmony.

ISFP would rather show you with action rather than tell you in the classic college tests, essays and discussions. The solid Theater Arts Department offers this type an alternate expressive form in theater stage productions. At the Guilford campus, **Theater** is especially oriented to serving others. This type is adept at creating pleasing visual interiors and will enjoy expressing their deeply held values in stage art. The course Filmmaking Capstone will let them shine forth.

ENFP likes the complexity that is found in the unique **Peace and Conflict Studies** major at Guilford College. The subject is directly supported by the Quaker philosophy of nonviolence. ENFP has the ability to inspire and finds the creativity required for conflict resolution. The interrelation between individual, local and global levels of conflict is a focus of the major. As protest movements grow within our nation and the world, this background gives ENFPs access to positions in institutions unaccustomed to dealing with violence.

ISFJ is one to prize accuracy, notice the details and stick with a demanding job. These characteristics match up quite well with the strong **Forensic Biology** major at Guilford College. The course in Forensic Chemistry is focused strictly on examining physical evidence at a crime scene. This makes good sense to ISFJ who seeks to partner productively with others in the community. This type, occasionally in need of a little cheerleading, is inclined to underestimate their contributions. At Guilford, faculty and student reflection is likely to bolster the ISFJ's confidence.

ESFP will like taking several introductory science courses in the **Earth Studies** minor here. It is very suitable for this curious type because it relies on considerable hands-on field work—a preferred way of learning for ESFP. This degree is complimentary to majors in physics, chemistry and biology. At the same time, the optional course in Images of the Earth: GIS and Remote Sensing can be invaluable for professions in law, science and journalism. ESFPs will find firm agreement on campus for their disinclination to form critical judgments about others.

ESFJ has what it takes to be an excellent translator and the **German** major at Guilford has much to commend it. As the European debt crisis develops and lingers, the linchpin strong economy of Germany has much influence within the governmental bodies seeking resolution. ESFJ with elective courses in conflict studies and a solid knowledge of this language will be well-situated as an international translator within these power circles.

INFJ tackles studies with a passion and the **Biology** major at Guilford College could be just the right ticket. This type prefers to ruminate on their possibilities, relationships and values, refining and defining each of these with their precise thinking. Guilford is an ideal environment to encourage this rather private type to bring some of that rumination out into the public square for others to benefit from their insight as well.

INFP has a good helping of insight and ability for self-direction. In fact, they are excellent researchers. The major in **Forensic Accounting** might be attractive since this type likes complex systems. The white collar crime and accounting fraud is often deeply layered. Along with their strong penchant for communication through the written word, INFPs could become crackerjack investigators. Their humanistic vision would necessarily drive an interest in cleaning up financial enterprises preying upon the unsuspecting public.

HAMILTON COLLEGE

198 College Hill Road
Clinton, NY 13323
www.Hamilton.edu
Admissions Telephone: 315-859-4421
Undergraduates: 1,864; 874 Men, 990 Women

Physical Environment

Celebrating its bicentennial in 2012, Hamilton College is a bright, educational laser light. Namesake and Founding Father, Alexander Hamilton, would approve of its legacy and stable relevance in undergraduate education today. Looking at the way the buildings are huddled together on a hill, the college may seem like a farming community or an Indian settlement. It overlooks the village of Clinton and owns 1,300 acres near the Adirondacks. Of different historical periods and assembled like a hamlet, the campus well accommodates the life and activities of the student body. Founded by Samuel Kirkland, a missionary to the Oneida Indians in the 1700s, this frontier school educated the children of white settlers and Indians. In 1965 a new campus was dedicated to the education of women. The new Sadove Student Center has the fun architecture expected of this campus. It pulls together Southern Appalachian extended porches, with New England Salt Box design and multiple gables for shedding ice dams. It is all so inviting for upcoming Quidditch event planning.

Much of the Hamilton design permits students to remain indoors and walk from one end of the campus to the other in 15 minutes. The fitness and dance center opened in 2006, softening the harsh winter weather. On the other side of the main road, there is the remarkable architecture of the Beinecke Student-Activities-Village, a **yellow rambling structure** which includes the Filius Barn. Here many events such as concerts, lectures and parties take place. The connecting bridge, Martin's Way, brings students to McEwen dining hall and other impressive residential and academic buildings on the south side of campus. Other features are a ropes course, a climbing wall and an **outdoor education center**, which satisfies many students who want to leave behind their urban residences and experience life without red lights and traffic jams. Among the many **athletic** facilities, Hamilton also boasts a golf course.

The rural location of this campus limits opportunities for immediate volunteer activities. Yet, students join HAVOC, an outreach coalition for service to the local area. Throughout the campus many blue bins are used to separate and recycle glass, metal and paper by the environmentally-friendly student body. Ahead of the curve, the college built a glass, ultra-modern and "**ultra-green**" science building, heated through geothermal methods, in 2005. Students are actively drawn to the science majors which coincide with a strong **environmental stewardship** perspective and ongoing Anarctic and Artic research.

Social Environment

Students desiring complete **academic freedom** will appreciate being able to take classes they select, without having to satisfy a set core of requirements. In 2002 the decision do without a core curriculum was made. With the help of **close advising**, students sign up for challenging classes. The college provides a strong safety net via the academic advisors and the professors who become mentors. The academic advising is very strong and in sophomore year **students defend** their course selections to satisfy their academic plan which is similar to an independent study. The only required courses are three **writing-intensive** classes reminiscent of this college's past emphasis on rhetoric and elocution. Writing and public speaking are at the core of a Hamilton experience. Many choose an internship in Washington, DC and complete a thesis in senior year. Every year the college has nearly 50 graduates in the government major. Other popular majors are psychology, mathematics, public policy and world politics.

These students are **bright, ambitious**, motivated and intellectually curious enough to risk getting a lower grade to learn outside of their major course of studies. A dance major may take a computer science or economics course and end up majoring in those subjects with a view to working in management. These persuasive individuals care about the environment. The dining halls have special foods for vegan and vegetarian diets, along with foods for those who have allergies. The food is fresh and much hails from the Farm to Fork initiative which supports local farmers and their products.

Compatibility with Personality Types and Preferences

This college is quite interesting because of its long history and evolution into an educational environment for students who like analysis (T) but thrive in an atmosphere that relentlessly seeks answers for problems. At Hamilton, these students can run with their ideas and innovations (N) and are not likely to experience much interference. The Hamilton undergraduate would not be satisfied with a midterm and final exam approach to grades. Speaking and writing, which allow for eloquence and intellectual rigor, are king on this campus. The intellectual exercise is designed to lead to order and productivity. Alexander Hamilton, revolutionary proponent of the national banking system, is both the namesake of this college and the guiding philosophical light for educational studies.

Not particularly doting or focused on their personal feelings, the Hamilton student is committed to intellectual exercise. Departmental philosophies typically exhibit and approve of intellectual rigor and intellectual courage among the students. Learning often centers on solving problems and collaborating with peers for the solutions. It can be a humbling experience with the bright undergraduate student body on this campus. In this way, students move forward with their personal development, refining their ability to analyze and honor accountability. Tender-hearted sensibilities are reserved for socializing at Hamilton. Collaboration and cooperation in the curriculum enhance budding interpersonal skills. Yet primarily,

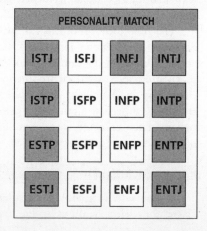

PERSONALITY MATCH

ISTJ	ISFJ	INFJ	INTJ
ISTP	ISFP	INFP	INTP
ESTP	ESFP	ENFP	ENTP
ESTJ	ESFJ	ENFJ	ENTJ

undergrads yearn to develop strong professional skills and frequently move into powerful positions in government and industry.

In the following listing of college majors it is important to remember that students can fit into any college and can be successful in any major. We have found that the Personality Types below fit very well at this college. The course-of-study chosen for each Personality Type corresponds to MBTI® research and is presented as an example favorable for that type.

ISTJ will use their intellectual storehouse to collect, maintain and retrieve all the geologic formations that are spelled with 10+ letters. In the unusual **Geoarcheology** studies on this campus, they will also be able to work quietly as they hone their skills with this exacting science. Their specialty of noticing all the small details and sticking with a project till they master it will be very applicable to this major. This type will also like pushing the educational frontier in the field to advance human awareness of our distant past.

ISTP at Hamilton College is going to have a ball in the **Computer Science** department. This type will relish the independence of developing their own course of study and it may easily be connected to technical applications. Once the student gets the basics of this discipline, Hamilton's intellectual rigor will encourage this type to push into new network applications. ISTPs with their wry sense of humor will sign right up for the course, Secrets, Lies and Digital Threats.

ESTP's fast-paced trouble-shooting skills in land development will be well used and grounded through the **Environmental Studies** concentration at Hamilton. There is natural science track that captures undergrads and signs them up for the geoscience field trips. The senior project gives ESTP a chance to employ newfound research skills with their natural bent for bringing competitors together. For example, this type would get a productive dialog going between Save the Guppies and the employees of Bulldoze Construction Company. Don't you wish you could sit in on this meeting. This is an educational activity that makes sense to this type who isn't all that impressed with traditional approaches to learning.

ESTJ will like the concentration **Economics** with its overview of financial mechanisms in advanced economies. This is followed by the requirement of a flexible Senior Project. This type is a strong administrator who understands rules in the discipline is likely to choose a senior project that shows foundational understanding of advanced accounting methods rather than an issues-oriented paper. It's about accountably for ESTJ, explanations and policy-laden practices will be given an arched eye by this natural leader.

INFJ who likes literature should be drawn to the **Creative Writing** concentration at Hamilton. It offers workshops and study in poetry, fiction and novels. The course curriculum is truly enticing, an INFJ who can turn a word is glued to the course catalog. The concentration is housed in the Department of English which boldly includes traditional literatures as found within Victorian society and the American south.

INTJ will not be daunted by the string of impossible sounding coursework in the **Biochemistry/Molecular Biology** major. Their incise, intense reasoning will come in handy as they plow their way through organic chemistry, vertebrate physiology, cellular neurobiology and perhaps, geomicrobiology. This last is a newly emerging discipline and this type wants to be at the head of these emergent knowledge boundaries.

INTP enjoys working individually. The **Philosophy** department at Hamilton College pushes undergrads to develop original inquiries into fairly common human experience, like telling lies, agreeing that zebras are gray. These are human behaviors that are becoming too familiar on the American scene. INTPs are curious and dispassionate enough to understand gullability in America today. Here at Hamilton, there will be an opportunity to explore this phenomena, as long as INTP brings their powerful thinking to the table.

ENTP has to try everything, more or less. Shakespeare's quote "all the world is a stage" is one that this type can live by. At Hamilton, the **Theatre** student has several options for their Senior Program: research paper, writing a play, performing an acting showcase, directing a play or designing a production. This variety gives ENTP the elbow room to freewheel their way into the Senior Program decision.

ENTJ on this campus is going to relate to the power and accomplishments that seem to flow in around the exceptional Hamilton graduates. Perhaps this type might like to reach for influential positions addressing American society and governance. ENTJ will be very well served in the **Government** major at Hamilton College. This department boldly carries within its curriculum coursework on conservative political thought, not often found in today's liberal arts institutions. Similarly, there is a course on congress and legislative politics. At Hamilton, ENTJ will study the political realism, as well as idealistic governance.

HAMPSHIRE COLLEGE

893 West Street
Amherst, MA 01002
www.hampshire.edu
Admissions Telephone: 413-559-5471
Undergraduates: 1,529; 612 Men, 917 Women

Physical Environment

The idea for Hampshire College was put into practice with the purchase of 800 acres of orchard and farm land in the 1960s. Prospective students get a close look at the Red Barn and sense first hand that this isn't your typical college. The wide-open farm land and country setting creates a sense that students can experiment with new ideas. The unique dormitories that are environmentally-friendly draw **eco-minded** students. The Longsworth Arts Center hosts a Solar Canopy of photovoltaic panels used for both research and generating electricity. A large yurt, of Native American heritage, blends nicely with the collegiate environment and functions as a media center.

Hampshire dormitories mimic neighborhoods of the countryside, suburbs and city. Referred to as the **"mod" architectural style**, their purpose is to bring together students who share similar tastes and interest in living style. For example, those who prefer city dwelling can elect the Prescott House, one of the smaller residential complexes with tall buildings connected by catwalks and stairways. First year students, however, start out in Dakin and Merrill Hall which are traditional dormitories, with many single rooms, closer to the dining facility.

There are **eclectic students** on this campus, possibly former wallflowers, who want to experiment with new activities. For some, practiced kayaking skills in the pool naturally translate into white-water rafting in the nearby hills. The Hampshire setting becomes a working farm and a living laboratory for some students who want to test out their **"earth and animal friendly"** philosophies. Students often use their bikes on the many dirt trails around the campus. Vegan and vegetarian students plant organic gardens, and some conduct research on the campus farm. Other students like quiet, private living arrangements and find the campus is well-suited for this also.

Social Environment

Hampshire students are creative and quirky. Their curiosity plumbs the depths as they study the past, seek out the new and follow their intuition. More than half the entering students say they are going to study in a particular area but end up changing. It's part of the **Hampshire experience** to share ideas and be open to many perspectives. They evaluate and re-evaluate their point of view. Students become very good at connecting seemingly unrelated information to their course work.

Hampshire students rank in the top quarter of their high school class with standard scores in the top 20 percent. The academic system is most striking. Students don't receive grades, rather they receive **personalized narrative evaluations** from their professors. This qualitative grading system encourages generation of ideas and refinement of those ideas in discussion and papers. Students who thought of themselves as "**alternative**" will likely feel in their element here. There are no general education requirements so students can satisfy their academic curiosities in the first year.

Activism is an element of the social activity on campus. Frequently, it is directly connected to their educational coursework and social life. The faculty and administration support curious, alternative undergraduates; however, there are clear guidelines for community responsibility and community standards. Random ideas are channeled into safe, acceptable activities such as the "outstallations" which are mini exhibits permitted in public spaces with permission. There are no Greek fraternities and sororities and traditional athletics are virtually non-existent. As a result of intense attention supporting the individuality of students, there is less community-wide loyalty developing, leaving energies for the upcoming transition into the real world upon graduation.

Compatibility with Personality Types and Preferences

Always looking out to the world, past the campus boundaries of the college, Hampshire students are drawn to the optimism of improving what they see (N). Their focus is not on the student body or the college town of Amherst. They are oriented toward the globe and they see potential with a capital P. Students are aware of the dire issues in today's world societies and seek to keep up with twists and turns affecting their chosen interests. Course work at Hampshire College also leans toward developing practical solutions. Policy protests are not first choice solutions for this student body well-grounded in reality. Most students here expect to impact the current and future society with innovation that improves the state of the art within their chosen disciplines. As a group, the students and faculty readily share insights while studying unusual subjects together, creating a synergy for improvements. At this rather unorthodox campus, research springs up from reality and is designed for current practice. Hampshire is all for analysis of the real world. Ideas, thoughts, meanings and passions fly on this campus. They willingly acknowledge the status quo and conventional institutions along with counterculture concepts as long as the ideas have good utility.

The student body pushes for space and freedom in the individual student activities and within the curriculum. Nontraditional projects and coursework can take a giant step out of the conventional box. This gives Hampshire the appearance of being radical at times. It keeps them exploring (P) and open to solutions of their own devise. The faculty acknowledges this approach to learning by offering areas of study, rather than majors or minors. In fact, students spend the first year in Division I, exploring four of five content areas. The middle two years are oriented to defining and securing knowledge in the chosen concentration. Division II, The last

PERSONALITY MATCH			
ISTJ	ISFJ	INFJ	INTJ
ISTP	ISFP	INFP	INTP
ESTP	ESFP	ENFP	ENTP
ESTJ	ESFJ	ENFJ	ENTJ

stage is reserved for a two semester project and internships. With this approach, undergraduates hold a trust in emerging knowledge and they strive to transfer those benefits into their chosen career paths. The ongoing practice of observation and analysis drives the faith in human kind (F) that lies at the core of Hampshire College.

In the following listing of college majors it is important to remember that students can fit into any college and can be successful in any major. We have found that the Personality Types below fit very well at this college. The course-of-study chosen for each Personality Type corresponds to MBTI® research and is presented as an example favorable for that type.

ENFP can be quite flexible, therefore **Legal Mediation** might call out as a worthy activity. ENFPs could explore this through the course in Conflict Resolution & Historical Analysis at Hampshire College. This type can understand the abstract connection between culture and power in conflict negotiation. This college is an ideal environment for the interdisciplinary perspective needed for successful negotiators. Not only is Hampshire's philosophy open and acknowledging of competing views, but it is also very much based in what is practical.

ENTP is going to sample much of what Hampshire offers. As a natural for the analysis of complex political trends, the course in Corruption and the Composition of Government Expenditure could grab their attention. As one would expect at Hampshire College, the current role of the U.S. government will spark debate. On this campus, articulate ENTPs will find plenty of other outspoken peers in the area of study titled **Social Change**, or they might lean toward **Economics** depending on where intuition pulls. Fortunately, this college would happily combine these two areas and approve an original ENTP self designed area of study -- hmmm... Social Economics?

ENFJ enjoys suggesting change and often does so with compelling communications. Here at Hampshire, ENFJs will practice their inclination to change the status quo. The faculty would encourage studying the unintended effects of do-good improvement projects. ENFJs would get a realistic grounding in what is actually possible vs. what seems to be possible. **Architecture and Environmental Design** might be the intellectual foundation for an ENFJ passion filled career, especially if you add a course titled Urban Space and Nature.

ISFP will love studying nutrition the Hampshire College way. Agriculture, Food and Human Health, a freshman course, will be a pleasure for this type because students distribute produce to a nearby inner city school. The type's ongoing quest to define inner values will be honored here. The area of study in **Agriculture** defines the discipline as reflecting American cultural values. The department focuses on the challenges of small farmers operating in the market agricultural conglomerates. Optimism and reality infuse the studies.

INFP is often searching for meaning behind reality. They are likely to be quite curious about the nontraditional medical therapies reviewed in the course Healing, Western and Alternative Medicine. Hampshire curriculum examines successes and failures of both traditional and nontraditional medicine. The **Health PreMedical Studies** would satisfy INFP's curiosity and requirement for passionate belief in their undergraduate experience.

INFJ will likely be mildly amused by the course Consumption and Happiness. This type is drawn to the complexity of human behavior. As new counseling therapies are developed in the field of psychology, INFPs will enthusiastically welcome the evolution. Hampshire College offers a program of study titled **Culture, Brain and Development**. It requires novel thinking about individual human development. It is a disciplinary area that is marked by abstraction and insight and INFJs are likely to excel.

INTJ with a scientific interest will like the intellectual wrestling with dilemmas in the health sciences. This type will take part in the discussion and research with original perspectives. The **Biological/Life Sciences** will be ideal for graduate school or med school and this type is likely to bring along that same originality to the first years in med school.

INTP could be inspired by the Digital Photography & New Media course. The course work is highly individualistic through the use of technical practices that express and create art. Sometimes retiring in social conversation, INTPs explore their inner perspectives through the camera lens. As an introductory course, it could open the door to the world of **Applied Design**. At Hampshire College this area of study is focused on designing universal industrial products and alternative transportation.

ESFP arrives on campus with impulsive energy and a willingness to try alternatives. So the course Domination, Resistance & Meaning-Making would spark their curiosity. The **Communications/Media Studies** area of study takes advantage of their social ease with change and variety. The department aptly identifies the reality that a product is created by the media generating a message. ESFPs will come to understand the media as a creator of materialistic society. The department also prepares students to understand 'ownership' within the production process. It is a key foundation for working in the fast-moving, competitive new media industry – always realistic at Hampshire College.

HARVARD COLLEGE

5 James Street
Cambridge, MA 02138
Website: www.fas.harvard.edu
Admissions Telephone: 617-495-1551
Undergraduates: 6,641; 3,318 Men, 3,323 Women
Graduate Students: 9,960

Physical Environment

First-year students arriving at Harvard College live in 17 residential dormitories reserved for their class. These buildings are located on Harvard's campus and in the residential area around the university and near the Charles River. Some Georgian-style residences were built in the 1700s while others are more contemporary, built in the 70s. Each building has a distinct floor-plan and feel, which exerts a certain influence on the students who room there. Imagine living in the same residence as Ralph Waldo Emerson and David Henry Thoreau. The **historic significance** permeates the academic experience. First-year students stick together and eat at Annenberg dining hall. These common experiences bind incoming undergrads together and help them comprehend this **complex university**. The new Campus Service Center, opened in 2011, houses many services needed by undergraduates previously scattered across the campus landscape.

In this setting, first-years meet with people very different than themselves. They become accustomed to the city just outside their dorm room. They can guess whether the people they run into on campus are prospective students or individuals observing the passing scene for the afternoon. Upon completion of **their first year,** students know one another well and have formed solid relationships. Freshmen quickly realize that Harvard assigns the upper class dormitories, identified as houses, to students so as to form **well-balanced student communities**. They are ready to be placed into one of the 12 upper-class houses, where they will likely stay for the following three years. Some students may form groups and put in a request to live together in the same house, but the remainder go through the lottery system as individuals.

Each house forms a small community with its own flavor and identity. The housemaster, proctors and tutors come from a variety of backgrounds. House masters often are professors who live on a floor with their family, lending guidance to students in a **family-like setting**. They mingle with students and help them evaluate their academic selections and possible areas of concentration. In some departments, sophomores taking tutorials are assigned to course sections based loosely on the houses they live in (e.g. Psychology 971). Thus houses become an extended classroom as well as a playground for fine turning artistic talents, from music to dance to sports. With so much to do and learn there is no uncommitted down time. The house system fosters student social and emotional development while at the same time sharpening talents across a broad spectrum. Students learn firsthand of new cultures, divergent political views, **international perspectives, talents and skills** from those in their house. All an incredibly enriching and transformative experience, the house system is currently under study for enhanced design and construction options in the coming years.

Typically students become extremely **loyal to their house** and Harvard guarantees housing for all four years. This tends to be more economical since rents in Cambridge, a suburb of Boston, are quite expensive. Accessibility to Boston city life is by subway, the T, and students travel into the city as their time permits.

Social Environment

Students who are admitted to Harvard College have the **intellectual curiosity** and emotional resilience to pursue much of what Harvard has to offer. Students have achieved well beyond that expected of their 18 years of age. Not only have they completed high school with top honors, but they have honed out a particular skill or two in music or dance or sports. Some **artists and well known professionals** compose another category of student, taking a break from their career to complete an undergraduate education. Regardless of their achievements, they all arrive at Harvard ready to soak up the knowledge that both the professors and other students bring to the table.

Students can pursue whatever they like at Harvard College, and it's cliché to say that they will find the time to involve themselves in whatever they enjoy doing. Some will pursue the parties either in residential houses or at the nearby colleges. Others will embrace the academics and extra-curricular activities with full speed ahead. A student concentrating in pre-med could also play in a band, contribute to the Crimson Newspaper and be a member of the equestrian club.

Intellectual intensity in the classroom is expected, as students set extraordinarily high standards for themselves. They rarely power down—rather each waking moment is interfaced with intellectual inquiry. By sharing experiences and thoughts, they begin to see the **relativity** of their own ideas. This campus has hosted **developmental** theorists researching moral development and developing a framework for collegiate student development policies. College students reap the rewards of this work since Harvard's administration and faculty apply their findings. Thus the campus environment promotes students who soak up knowledge and search for moral and political clarity.

During Harvard's "shopping week" students test-drive classes by attending any they might like. Some are interested in so many areas that they enroll in courses outside of their favorite departments or create their own major. Academic curiosity outweighs **academic risk**.

Passion for knowledge is strong among first year students. This translates into highly-focused individuals who intend to become masters at their craft, thereby improving the world around them. Students form values that accommodate their career goals and intend to benefit society. Graduates may enter Harvard with conventional success in mind, but many leave with the intention of making this universe a better place.

At Harvard, **Social Clubs** are officially recognized. There are also unofficial organizations that students seek to join as a popular forum for social interaction. Some social clubs are more exclusive than others and leave their gate more or less open. In a way, these clubs can be compared to **Greek life** which requires that students rush to get in. Harvard administrators and residential faculty actively advise as well as oversee all of the social organizations to ensure activities and goals are compatible with Harvard's residential life perspectives. Some of these social organizations form individual **social networks** spanning the decades of graduating classes with their loyal alumni.

Compatibility with Personality Types and Preferences

Harvard is all things to bright students. Simply put, there is not a personality preference that cannot be accommodated quite well at Harvard College. The educational philosophy is both deep and wide in scope. The structured students (J) who like to plan with defined objectives, practical rules and clear regulations will find them in Harvard's concentrations, tutorials and general exams. The curriculum reflects faculty belief that knowledge is approached from a variety of avenues. A concentration in biology includes courses in all the physical sciences as well as anthropology and psychology.

The core course requirement at Harvard is fulfilled by choosing from among hundreds of entry level courses in the 40 available concentrations. These 40 are further expanded by options within each. This all really suits the flexible, free-flowing (P) students who will want, and maybe try, to sample most of the disciplines Harvard has to offer. For folks who like their facts and details straight up (S), observable, verifiable knowledge rules over the world class research venues in the physical and applied sciences. The faculty and student body are constantly reasoning with logical analyses (T). Harvard University expects to expand the universal body of knowledge through exploration, discovery and novel investigation.

Students preferring other ways of knowing, often intuitive or instinctual (N), will really enjoy the residential house system where Harvard College expects students to learn from each other. In fact, this house system is ideal for the undergraduates who want frequent, close communication with others (F). Those students who are outgoing and expressive (E) will find the social contact they want outside of the classroom with club participation and house participation that is expected and extensive. Those folks who are quieter (I) will actually find some anonymity in the academic world which is very individualized and can be tailored as to feel like a solo educational experience. Upon graduation, students hold a world view that prompts them to move aggressively and competently through their career work that should, indeed, increase the body of knowledge.

In the following listing of college majors it is important to remember that students can fit into any college and can be successful in any major. We have found that the Personality Types below fit very well at this college. The course-of-study chosen for each Personality Type corresponds to MBTI® research and is presented as an example favorable for that type.

INTP is a good bet for the concentration in **Earth and Planetary Sciences**. This field is developing as fast as the NASA exploration of Mars is sending back new images. The

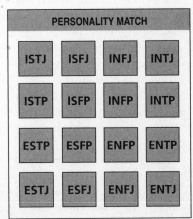

PERSONALITY MATCH

ISTJ	ISFJ	INFJ	INTJ
ISTP	ISFP	INFP	INTP
ESTP	ESFP	ENFP	ENTP
ESTJ	ESFJ	ENFJ	ENTJ

department has purposely fashioned the studies across physics/chemistry/biology and engineering. The INTP will love to find patterns and solve riddles about earth's oceans, atmosphere and solid core. Intellectual order is paramount for this type and seeking order in the solar system is a suitable lifetime career for these powerful thinkers. Back on earth at Harvard's house, they are likely to be easy and casual on the social scene when they appear. In fact, they may miss more than a few events hanging back, trying to solve the latest complex riddle in physical space. Activities and intramurals may serve to bring reality into their week and give their minds a much needed time out.

ESTP is quick to sum up a problem and gifted with the ability to offer a workable solution. The concentration in **Environmental Science and Public Policy** offers the possibility of indefinite troubleshooting within the public arena after graduation. They excel at what can be done with efficiency. They have less enthusiasm for theory and abstraction, it interferes with real action. Students may specialize in natural or social science within the concentration. However, the foundational courses are clearly in the hard sciences. In the house, ESTP will be first in line for the party, the fun and the social learning. They are likely to initiate house social activities. This type is often well coordinated, physically athletic and may lead and participate in sports activities. This type may also be attracted to seeking entrance into one of the selective social clubs.

ISTJ is very accepting with the high academic structure in the first two years of engineering sciences at Harvard. In fact, this type will be just fine with signing up for the suggested basic course Math 1. Their need for accuracy requires a step-by-step, comprehensive mathematical understanding. The **Engineering Sciences** curriculum allows new concentrators to take the four introductory courses that preview the five types of engineering degrees. This allows ISTJ to judiciously sample the disciplines of engineering and ultimately select the one right for them. This synchs with their motto—"Do it right the first time." Most often humor is one of their underlying traits. It is a wry humor reserved for their close friends. In the House system they will likely find and add humor in the social programs. In the social activities they can express their penchant for accuracy. This could give them satisfaction as they set and reach their personal goals.

INTJ will find the **Mind, Brain and Behavior** initiative just original enough for their liking. They will not shrink away from seeking and gaining permission to be admitted to this initiative. They have the confidence to enter the process. This type has powerful inner vision and the ability to transfer those original thoughts into the real world. The interdisciplinary work of tying together cognition, neuroscience and computers is ideal for this type. They can look for patterns in the data bits to their mind's content. Then they can follow a hunch to search out similar patterns in the brain's chemical pathways. In the house they will review and pass judgment on the various social offerings. They are likely to more fully participate if it exposes them to novel activities.

ENFJ absolutely enjoys an audience. They can beguile and guide listeners to a different viewpoint or novel interpretation. They are masters of the use of language. The **Romance Languages and Literatures** program allows ENFJ to double their fun and charm audiences with a second or third language. A personal connection between student and professor works well for ENFJ. The mentor/advisor relationship is defined in tutorials and is a feature of this concentration. ENFJ is likely to find ways to please their advisor in the process. Department curriculum supports undergraduates going into education and this type can be a dynamic teacher. They could easily gain the admiration of their K-12 students while promoting the study of a foreign language. They will join in house social learning and activities with ease. They may be prompted into leadership of the house because of their genuine interest in others and great communication skills.

INFP absolutely must have time and emotional space to search out their personal understanding of life and its meaning. Once this is completed they extend the vision to the larger community expecting to make a worthy contribution. This type sees value in the **Comparative Study of Religion.** INFP is just fine with abstract speculation like the moral development of civilization. Even the study of differing methods used to understand religions is up their alley. This area of study could quickly lead to a joint concentration in religion and another field. In the residential house, this type is likely to be a quiet participant who carefully considers their options before joining in with the faculty and other students. Their perfectionist tendencies might easily come out when participating in social activities where they would strive to be the best.

ESFP is often quite entertaining and a career in the entertainment field brings spontaneity and emphasis on enjoyment. ESFP could look favorably at the **Visual and Environmental Studies** which embrace film, photography, video art and environmental studies. At Harvard, the student productions are at a near professional level. The ESFP is likely to go for the filmmaking because film, of all the arts, can contain and express enthusiasm, enjoyment and be visually appealing. It might also bring out the performer in their personality. The actual production of film and the study of theory behind it suffice for ESFP who may elect not to write a thesis. In the House system this type will be front and center with most if not all of the social programs and social activities. ESFP lives to socialize and socializes in order to live. They would join any of the activities involving participation with others and would likely show interest in joining one of the selective clubs.

ENTP can take advantage of their intuition in any of the disciplines studying human behavior. It is a complex arena since it attempts to understand the basis of the human personality. As a concentrator in **Psychology**, ENTP would excel at impersonal analysis while researching perception, memory or motivation. These basic processes are likely to be of more interest to the ENTP than counseling or rehabilitation. ENTP may be drawn to personality theories and research more than to the individual counseling of clinical psychology. Harvard's Psychology Department can accommodate the wide and evolving nature of this discipline. Without a required thesis, ENTP has more time to participate in undergrad research. This type will likely try a succession of activities at Harvard; their curiosity draws them into many possibilities and ENTP might be bored with the repetition. ENTP will try to sample all of the social activities in their house. They must be careful to avoid burn out on this campus.

ISTP will be in high heaven in Harvard's **Mechanical and Material Science Engineering** concentration. State of the art equipment will entice them as they build robots and design experimental parts. In these labs, the ISTP will absorb the theories and engineering knowledge with much enjoyment while observing the physical properties with accuracy. This concentration also suits ISTP because a written thesis is not required in the engineering sciences. They will likely select an activity or club to join that allows a lot of room for spontaneity and being laid back. In the house system, they will scout out a few good friends who they respect. Once they have that small circle of similar-minded friends they will pick and choose social opportunities that suit their interests and are less gregarious in nature.

ISFP devotes much thinking time to clarifying their personal values. They are likely to want to focus in an area that is contributing to the welfare of the community. The concentration in **Chemical and Physical Biology** has the right stuff for ISFP if they have a tolerance or liking for math. Although not necessarily an innovator, this type will be extremely happy with the action of dissecting and reconstructing cellular networks. Their penchant for careful observation and meticulous accuracy is ideal for this discipline. Their sometimes fragile sense of self will get much recognition and approval from others in this pioneering field that is advancing knowledge through genetic research and discovery. This type will thrive and develop in conjunction with the spontaneous and planned social learning within their house. They are joiners. To ISFP the house could become as intimate as a home environment. Their quick adaptability to change will find ISFP always present and ready from day one of the sophomore year.

INFJ will thrive with Harvard's philosophy of clubs and activities. The level of resources available assures that activities can be accomplished at a professional level. INFJ only has to decide which of the student activities to join. This type should find it meets their exacting standards and relish their participation with personal pride. INFJ is very good at comprehending complex subjects such as liberty. Surely in America, there will be awareness of this basic human right and its trampling currently and through the ages, often under the guise of intellectual philosophers. Harvard's **Social Studies** brings the basic philosophical texts on this subject into the curriculum. INFJ has the resolve and grounding to analyze texts in this chimeric discipline. The required senior thesis in this concentration is started only after the one-on-one tutorial where a topic is mutually selected with the faculty advisor who shares similar interests. This mutual process is important to INFJ because they must be passionate about their work to do it well. It will give them a notch up in the petition and application required to be selected for this concentration.

ISFJ will like the detailed and sequential nature of **Human Evolutionary Biology**. Students may choose either focus in lab studies or field studies. ISFJs excellent memory and love for facts nicely combines with their inclination for reflection. If you add in their typical thoroughness you see how the learning style of ISFJ fits this concentration so well. On graduation this type could pursue graduate study in researching disease through individual medical trials. Since ISFJ really values improving the health and life style of individuals they might go to the work force directly to apply their knowledge through wellness programs. They will enjoy Harvard's exceptional attention to student programming. Within their house they will be loyal contributors to the learning and living experience.

ENFP will gladly consider all the options and possibilities on the Harvard campus. With 40 available concentrations and 300 clubs to consider for participation, this type is all smiles during freshman year. The hard part for ENFP will be making choices among the many enticing options. Fortunately, should ENFP generate one of their very original ideas, Harvard will follow through and put together a specialized concentration. Within the **Sanskrit and Indian Studies** concentration, the ENFP might consider the South Asian Studies option. It focuses on the complexity and the unity of ethnic speaking Sanskrit or Hindu Urdu peoples. The goal of these studies is to gain an overview and understanding of the cultures. This suits ENFP who can be indifferent to what they consider mundane details. The optional thesis, if they decide to write one, will be a first class read.

ESFJ will be very comfortable in their house at Harvard which will quickly become their home. They will really like the academic and social programs that promote friendships within the house. In fact, they will be encouraging others to participate. They value loyalty and it allows them to really benefit from Harvard's residential living. As dependable members, they are likely to accept leadership positions on occasion. The **Physics** concentration with a teaching option could be a good choice for this type. Their strong need for order and sense of responsibility are very desirable traits for K-12 teachers. ESFJ's persuasive skills adapted for the classroom will be well-appreciated by school administrators. ESFJ will also like the department's practical approach to this concentration. Down to earth ESFJ sees that the general exam, tutorial or thesis would take away time and effort they would rather use in developing classroom skills and gaining experience.

ENTJ is usually attracted to complex, very large systems. The Harvard concentration in **Neurobiology** definitely fits this description. ENTJs are goal-oriented, but capable of opening up their visual lenses to catch otherwise unnoticed patterns in volumes of data. The human nervous system, as the focus of this concentration, presents this type of gigantic perspective from molecule to human body. It may be overwhelming and unappealing to some other personality types but certainly not to this type. Ambitious ENTJ might just join the scientists who are emulating the nervous system via software. Imagine the diagnostics and profit. Socializing and social choices are likely to revolve around ideas, action and projects. Harvard will not fail in providing near endless opportunities that meet this demand by the ENTJ.

ESTJ will very likely approve of the **Applied Mathematics** concentration at Harvard College. The department has excellent flexibility within the first two years for undergraduates to explore areas of interest while getting good exposure to the interdisciplinary nature of the discipline via neighboring concentrations. ESTJs will like tailoring of their own curriculum and degree in consultation with an advisor. This rather intensive effort is required to sift through all the fields that rely on math, physical, biological, social, engineering and management sciences. ESTJs are definitely up to this challenge, however, they will be anxious during it and quite relieved when their educational focus is settled upon with the advisor. Within their house and during the first year on campus, this type is likely to enjoy and interact with the many different types of students on this campus. The endless action at Harvard College, only slowing down while most are asleep in the wee hours, calls out to ESTJs to participate and take on administrative and organizational roles within the clubs they choose to join.

HAVERFORD COLLEGE

370 Lancaster Avenue
Haverford, PA 19041-1392
Website: www.haverford.edu
Admissions Telephone: 610-896-1350
Undergraduates: 1,177; 548 Men, 629 Women

Physical Environment

Located 10 miles outside of Philadelphia, Haverford College has a suburban campus with all the charm and mystery of a Thomas Kinkaid painting. The campus reveals itself slowly, allowing the visitor to enjoy the paths through the woods with reflection. Students who feel comfortable here probably looked for smaller, less active environments. Centuries-old trees surround these Quaker buildings and add to a feeling of safety, both physical and emotional, lending a special aura to the campus. Students who are attracted by this campus love **nature**, like to run track and participate in field events.

The architecture of the buildings speaks to the love for simplicity and spirituality of the **Quakers**. This 19th century campus is one that encourages students to look to the past for human meaning that can be explored by thoughtful discussion. The Magill Library has a comprehensive collection of original Quaker books and students have access to rich historical documents. The oldest section was built in 1863 and has a spiritual feel with arched windows, cathedral ceilings and wooden support beams. The Koshland Science Center includes advanced research options such as nanofabrication which acts as a modern counterpoint to the historical presence on this campus. Students who like the sciences and wish for strong pre-med advising are attracted by this exceptional science center. The new Kim Tritton dormitories open in August 2012.

The Center for **Peace and Justice** arranges for field trips throughout the world, such as Africa and Guatemala, for these students who are typically focused on social justice in the world. The Gardner Athletic Center offers everything a student athlete or non-athlete would desire in order to keep in shape during college. The favorite walking trail is called the "Trust Trail" which is part of the first year orientation experience. The town of Haverford is near other fine liberal arts colleges that offer cross-registration of classes, expanding the variety of courses available with other educational perspectives.

Social Environment

Students come from New England and the Mid-Atlantic regions; they are typically organized, well-groomed and thoughtful. The essence of this college community is to understand what **tolerance and non–sectarianism** mean. Freshmen are assigned to Customs Groups and live together during the first year. As part of the first year experience, upperclass mentors discuss and explore the nature of diverse backgrounds and tolerance. This flavor of the historic Quaker meetings is welcomed by students who want to become aware of racial, cultural and ethnic identities. Formerly quiet students in high school will appreciate the non-competitive experience in the classroom.

Accepting others and living an honest life means becoming a precise **observer** of the world. Students here almost hold a paternal world view as they incorporate and examine the many evils evident around the globe. Professors focus on the moral, ethical education of the individual student. This **value-driven education** attracts students who may have attended a Quaker high school who add depth to the discussions about social justice. Students without a Society of Friends background are likely to have heard similar discussion at the family dinner table centering on community, politics and education. Some students expect to leave behind the homogeneity of their suburban high school. Undergraduates here are excited about meeting people from different social environments. They purposely select study abroad and internships that will accomplish this goal. Their intention is to help others through empathy and understanding.

Students who like the arts and social sciences find the peacefulness of this campus conducive to intense pondering. Competition is not present in the classroom and students let go on the playing fields for stress relief. They let their creativity emerge within the very safe confines of this campus that honors reflection. Graduates will move forward into their careers with great openness and considerable awareness of the positive and negative inclinations of society. They are resilient through their knowledge because of this **talk-discuss-argue education**. The Haverford education might be thought of as active listening whose purpose is to build a literate community ensuring peace and prosperity.

Compatibility with Personality Types and Preferences

Haverford College offers an education that intensely seeks to understand other peoples (F) of the world. It is a high purpose and very true to the founding Quaker principles of the college. Undergrads are typically analytical with a human perspective. They come to the campus eager to learn and expect to debate and master written expression with articulate, commanding thought. They study humankind looking for positive qualities (N). Their internships take them to areas in the world where much of the population is destitute. They are courageous in their choices since their

idealistic observations of human nature must be accommodated with the reality of poverty and cruelty. They commonly bring knowledge or plans for improved living conditions and a fair number remain in touch with their study abroad locations, expecting to return.

Students at Haverford ask very difficult questions and quickly discern the endemic nature of misery in large segments of the earth's population. Undergraduates look within themselves and to the faculty for explanations and solutions. Yet the educational philosophy is to mentor students in examining their own roots and personal experiences for answers.

PERSONALITY MATCH			
ISTJ	ISFJ	INFJ	INTJ
ISTP	ISFP	INFP	INTP
ESTP	ESFP	ENFP	ENTP
ESTJ	ESFJ	ENFJ	ENTJ

Overall, resignation is not an answer and the campus culture defiantly stands up to the ills and errors in human society. In partial answer, there is an ever-present overlay of values and ideals for the human condition expressed in the curriculum through conventional courses and majors. Also in answer to the dilemma of societal ills, the campus itself models a community populated by rational people. During four years of undergraduate education at Haverford College, students are going to discuss, search for, argue and practice living a life congruent with their well-defined ideals.

In the following listing of college majors it is important to remember that students can fit into any college and can be successful in any major. We have found that the Personality Types below fit very well at this college. The course-of-study chosen for each Personality Type corresponds to MBTI® research and is presented as an example favorable for that type.

INFJ is persistent and penetrating, just the qualities needed to study and practice **Economics.** This type is caring and yet very private. The field of economics offers them a complex and intriguing subject of study. INFJ will be very interested in theories of economic practice that contradict each other. As graduates, this type will bring passionate energy to analyses of production, distribution and consumption of goods in society. Haverford will refine their ability to develop a penetrating approach to this discipline that will also provide them access to jobs and grad studies after commencement.

ISFJ has a memory that won't quit. This type can take in facts and store them for retrieval like a researcher in the congressional library. The major in **Computer Science** at Haverford College asks this intriguing question: Are there algorithms not presently known that can solve intractable problems? In reality, the coursework also is somewhat straightforward compared to the other highly abstract curriculum offerings. After all, computers are simply tools and ISFJ is comfortable mastering skills and bringing them to the community. ISFJ studying at Haverford College gets the ideal preparation to design and operate data systems utilized by nonprofits and international aid organizations.

ISFP and **Classical and Near Eastern Archeology** are a bit of a natural fit. The study falls into the Bi-Co category which essentially means Bi-college. Bryn Mawr and Haverford campuses are within a mile of each other and students can cross-register for courses and majors. ISFP's sense of design and proportion will be an advantage on digs of ancient city states around the Mediterranean Sea. The focus of this degree is to collect wisdom from the classical age and bring those positive social constructs into the light of modern day. This type is ideal for learning by sight, sound and touch, basically being active. It is a direct, real, here and now activity that offers freedom to reflect – a favorite ISFP pass time.

INTP will like the **Chemistry** major at Haverford College because there is an opportunity to complete required core chemistry courses at foreign universities. This type is always looking for clarity in their thoughts and is quite curious. The field of chemistry offers the complexity they seek and the ability to cross-check their intuition by predicting outcomes of lab experiments. This is just swell stuff for an INTP. Haverford takes an interdisciplinary approach to this discipline and INTP can quickly synthesize seemingly unrelated topics. This independent type will take advantage of both overseas study and interdisciplinary courses for the freedom and rewards gained via their logical analysis.

INFP might find personal meaning in something simple like an ice cream cone on a hot day. Indeed they are searchers of meaning. The major in **Fine Arts** has courses in the third year identified as "experimental." The faculty expects undergraduates to take artistic risks and bring forth ideas cussed and discussed during their first years on campus. The fine arts majors must develop personal themes and communicate those ideas through their art. Studio work produced by INFP might reflect the dilemmas of the human psyche. INFP will be up to the challenge and has loads of peers across campus ready, willing and able to imagine.

ENFP will find a welcome place for their enthusiasm and persuasive skills in **Education**, a Bi-college major located on the Bryn Mawr campus. This philosophy of teaching encourages awareness and use of multiple intelligences. It resonates well with ENFP who is often a cheerleader supporting improvement in others. This major also has the level of complexity needed by ENFP to keep them engaged and fulfill their own creative instincts.

ENTP at Haverford College might like the major in **Growth and Structure of Cities.** It is unusual because planning for urban communities is studied as a process that travels through other disciplines, such as law, communications, the arts, medicine and social justice. ENTP will find there is plenty of novel discussion surrounding the courses in this major as desirable community is explored, defined, and examined. The course Analysis of Geospatial Data Using GIS could fascinate this type. It presents opportunities galore to make sense of geographic and social constructs as viewed by the satellites with software interface. It might just be the ENTP who decides to look for evidence of peace and serenity in communities around the globe via satellite data feeds. Let's hope they find it.

ESFJ is all about the community and the people in it. They want their studies to directly benefit humankind. They also have a fine ability to collect, remember and use facts. The Haverford Biology department offers a core program in **Biology— Molecular, Cellular and Developmental**. It is an extraordinary curriculum that offers a taste of over the top cellular research at the introductory level. Traditional ESFJ may find it a bit too large, but the warm nature of this campus, with its calming Quaker heritage, will help tame the impersonal nature of the discipline and maintain the personal, human perspective.

ENFJ will find that the **Peace, Conflict & Social Justice Studies** echoes back to the founding principles of the Quakers who were practicing nonconflict when the founding fathers were meeting to declare the Revolutionary War! Two centuries later, liberal arts colleges across America have the freedom to strongly endorse this concept. At Haverford College, there is no shrinking from the ills of collective human society. Students here are intellectually prepared to travel and return from geographic locations with little human hope. ENFJs who take these journeys will have the perspective to compare the American neighborhood with personal knowledge of conditions across the globe. Graduate studies for this type might then focus on American Studies. Perhaps their dissertation topic would be: Why People from Across the Globe Seek Entry to the United States of America.

HENDRIX COLLEGE

Office of Admissions
1600 Washington Avenue
Conway, AR 72032-3080
Website: www.hendrix.edu
Admissions Telephone: 800-277-9017
Undergraduates: 1,426; 641 Men; 785 Females

Physical Environment

Hendrix College is located in central Arkansas, about a half hour from Little Rock. The campus is in a **park-like setting** and has a mix of traditional and modern buildings, such as the library with its semi-circular entrance and bright skylight. Hendrix has a theatre with a rotating stage and a larger stage where students put on five annual productions. The environment has a cozy, "well used" feel. In 2010, the college and city of Conway opened a mixed use residential and business setting on campus. Containing the new Hendrix Bookstore, the area also houses 130 upperclass students in multistory apartment units. The new Student Life and Technology Center is described as the "living room" of the campus and well deserves that name for its function and comfort on this forward-thinking campus.

In good weather students watch movies or have fun at night by **the brick pit** with themed parties for all holidays. All are invited or drawn in by the music and dancing. In this park-like setting there are other interesting nooks and crannies. "Pecan Court" is another location to chill out. There are a variety of residence halls including one coed-dorm, a language house and a house where students live and study issues of sustainability and ecology. Students hold **poetry slams** and listen to other students jam on the piano most Wednesdays.

Social Environment

Hendrix undergraduates were **studious** in high school and achieved positions at the top of their class. At Hendrix they gain clarity through similar attention to study. They appreciate studying the classics. They are imaginative thinkers, often with a good sense of humor that combines with **self-drive**. First year classes are comprehensive, demanding and require the undergraduates' attention and ability to synthesize large amounts of information. Academic expectations remain high and progress in intensity as graduates are expected to synthesize and form personal perspectives in reference to the global nature of learning at Hendrix. Students here are quite interested in **cultural activities** and discussions are richly supplemented by their interest in visiting speakers and foreign documentaries.

The award-winning Odyssey program requires this very expectation within the undergraduate student body. Hendrix College engages their energetic students through Odyssey and generates personal learning, academic **travel** to foreign cultures and other options for active learning. All undergraduates develop their Odyssey plan with a faculty member. It is individually tailored and much approved on the campus by students and professors who view it as one of several culminating experiences during the four year education.

Compatibility with Personality Types and Preferences

Hendrix College and studying other cultures is almost synonymous. Faculty and administration see huge value in learning through the perspective of other world nationalities. This education follows several paths and most definitely includes development of personal character, ethical inquiry and sensitivity to contemporary issues involving other cultures as well as service (F) travel to foreign countries. Students are encouraged to submit detailed plans for individual learning that encompass service learning in other parts of the world. Their planning and development of the proposal is quite sophisticated. Undergraduates are mentored by professors who often guide students in devising research projects. The overriding purpose of student research on this campus harkens back to student learning and imaginative plans (N) are common. Research projects as options are common within the curriculum and also mirror the college's value for learning through other cultures. Some of the projects are service-oriented, involve indigenous populations and include the potential of returning after graduation to gauge success.

The frequent and encompassing nature of these projects prompt campus-wide attention and enhance undergraduate anticipation (P) of contributing toward the greater community after graduation. There is regular attention and deep interest in current world problems and defining the needs of the greater global community.

In the following listing of college majors it is important to remember that students can fit into any college and can be successful in any major. We have found that the Personality Types below fit very well at this college. The course-of-study chosen for each Personality Type corresponds to MBTI® research and is presented as an example favorable for that type.

PERSONALITY MATCH

ISTJ	ISFJ	INFJ	INTJ
ISTP	ISFP	INFP	INTP
ESTP	ESFP	ENFP	ENTP
ESTJ	ESFJ	ENFJ	ENTJ

INFP approaches learning by gleaning large intuitive hunches as they survey text or subject. The discipline of **Psychology** nicely lends itself to this initial approach. INFPs live in the larger world of idealism and psychological research holds out the potential to benefit mankind. The department nicely introduces the undergraduates to the major subfields in psychology and focuses on the methods of scientific research that advance those specialties. The discovery of DNA has generated hundreds of genetic studies associated with human behavior and the human nervous system. It all fits for INFP who is likely to move on to graduate school.

INFJ likes variety in the work place and the major in **Allied Health** at Hendrix College is created for entry into several career paths. Courses are designed to give a thorough understanding of the human body. Students select a concentration from physical/occupational therapy, physician assistant or nursing. INFJ refines their personal belief system with precision and will select one of these and assertively prepare for admission to the graduate schools.

INTJ is focused on turning insight into reality. Their career interests typically center on the sciences, technology, arts, health, business or the professions. The minor in **International Business** at Hendrix College would nicely complement any one of these fields. INTJ likes complexity with plenty of challenges thrown in. Their inclination for original thinking could lead to declaring a major in **American Studies** that offers plenty options with international organizations such as the World Bank.

ISFP really enjoys working with their hands while creating useful products. Among many occupations, two jump out for career satisfaction in the sciences. Marine biology and plant biology within the department of **Biology** at Hendrix might lead into landscape or entertainment industries. The department is focused on advising students with practical options on graduation. The Odyssey program, so amenable to research proposals, would well deliver an enterprising perspective in either marine ecology or botany.

INTP will like the flexibility of the **Computer Science** major at Hendrix College. It is quite possible that a few select friends will team up with INTP and generate novel computer applications in one of the social or natural sciences. In many of the courses, projects allow INTPs to apply their innovative concepts in software programs. INTPs are always ready to learn in depth and will appreciate the final phase of study as each student selects a focus for specialization.

ENFP should really check out the **American Studies** major at Hendrix College. It is one of few American studies programs offered with balance and breadth of scope. The major offers an extraordinary number of courses that focus on cultural understanding, minus the trendy cultural filters prevalent in society today. ENFP will appreciate the interdisciplinary nature through coursework in journalism, regional government, international politics, southern studies and other departments.

ENTP is going to like the idea of studying political science at Hendrix College. The major in **Politics** starts out with the basic freshman course in Issues in Politics. This course directs students to study a single, topical issue through the lens of political theory, comparative politics, American politics and international relations. With a strong leaning toward impersonal analysis, ENTPs will be introduced to multiple approaches and the advantage of dispassionate inquiry. Hendrix College will expect confident ENTPs to reach their positions utilizing scientific inquiry first and passion second. ENTP could not agree more.

ENFJ who enters the business world often prefers a small enterprise. They enjoy the personal relationships that come with single product financial organizations. The degree in **Economics and Business** at Hendrix College is a good bet for ENFJ. It includes the complex subjects of fiscal policy, trade and interest rates plus others, yet it also includes the reality-based subjects of accounting and business law. This type of preparation lets ENFJ discover financial institutions that thrive on connections between employees, consumers and the product such as that found in fair trade markets.

JOHNS HOPKINS UNIVERSITY

3400 North Charles Street/140 Garland
Baltimore, MD 21218
Website: www.jhu.edu
Admissions Telephone: 410-516-8171
Undergraduates: 4,997; 2,403 Men, 2,594 Women
Graduate Students: 6,400 Men, 6,750 Women

Physical Environment

Johns Hopkins University is located in northern Baltimore on 140 acres of land with lots of trees and handsome brick buildings. The university and hospital bearing his name were founded by Johns Hopkins in early 1800s. Johns Hopkins University adopted the German educational model around 1880-1910s, similarly building large physics and science laboratories to anchor undergraduate and graduate learning. American universities, emulating the **Germanic model**, pursued this organizational structure which ultimately led to the award of Doctoral degrees. Thus, the long-established emphasis on medical research and graduate education at Johns Hopkins University.

The flagship building on campus is Gilman Hall, easily recognizable by its **huge ionic columns, stained glass windows** and indoor circular staircases. Named after Daniel Coit Gilman, the first Hopkins president, it's a 24-hour student-study area. It reopened after a major renovation in 2010, sporting an atrium that houses the archeological collection. Those artifacts are reimagined by an artistic rendering by objects suspended mid air above in the multistoried space. Alumni Memorial Residence, "AMR," has single rooms and is coed by floor. The majority of first year students live in the freshmen quad. The campus also expanded on the other side of North Charles Street, where newer residences and a bookstore offer upperclass students more amenities right in the city. Although it's farther from the classes on campus, the most coveted dorm for freshmen is Wolman, because of the suite-style rooms with kitchenettes. Many new construction projects are active on the JHU campus, with Brody Learning Commons, opened in summer 2012, enhancing the library study experience where undergraduate students especially spend considerable time.

Social Environment

Students themselves shape the essence of the Hopkins undergraduate experience. They create a peer culture that values intellect and collaboration. It's the highly **self-directed** and self-motivated student who takes well to JHU. The millennium tshirt reading : *academics... social life... sleep* on the front is followed by *pick any two* on the back. Undoubtedly, life at Hopkins is about prioritizing and finding time for all that there is to do, without sacrificing some part of college life.

Undergraduates learn in the lecture halls and after hours by exchanging their views, discussing the **challenging material** presented in the curriculum. Research is quite competitive and students must independently petition for grants. The enterprising undergraduate, given the nod for research, will join professors in **cutting**

edge research within the prestigious Johns Hopkins labs. Many who come to this university for pre-med quickly realize they can take fascinating classes in other subjects that they want to explore. Hopkins has a strong reputation for pre-medical studies, yet many in the student body do not go on to major in the sciences. In fact, less than half go on to medical school. Undergraduates here secure **competency** in other fields, such as creative writing or international politics. Students say their professors are simply amazing since they combine state of the art research with teaching responsibilities.

Successful students at Johns Hopkins developed leadership skills and were committed to a select few extracurriculars while in high school. Maybe they enjoyed tutoring or volunteered at their local hospital. At Hopkins they put these skills into practice. Is there a social life on campus? Yes and no. It depends upon the student. Those who seek it out will find it through participation in organized sports and other campus groups such as the fraternities, sororities and social traditions on campus like the **Spring Fair** which is the largest event on the social activities calendar. Undergraduates students enjoy face-painting the little kids who attend with their parents, often professors at Hopkins. The concert draws thousands of people into the recreation center, including the President. There is no football team and the most intense sport on campus is lacrosse, played at Division1 level. The other sports are Division-III and tend to be lower key.

Orientation for freshmen is a week-long affair that packs in **light-hearted activities** like the a cappella and drama groups showcasing their talent. A Hopkins alumnus turned comedian comes on campus to entertain.

Undergraduates who attend Hopkins are as passionate about academics as they are about a select few outside pursuits. Their **depth of commitment** and collaborative spirit works well within the student body of this intensely academic university. Graduates will make their mark through advanced studies and the formidable analytic skills and competencies they gain at Johns Hopkins.

Compatibility with Personality Types and Preferences

Johns Hopkins University is a research center in scope and application that impacts our national economy. The administration and faculty consistently pursue research that is centered on invention and innovation (N) in the classic sense. Activity in the research labs is driven to pursue, invent or discover new applications through current scientific (S) properties. This university aggressively pursues generating knowledge. The academic philosophy is nicely understood as JHU finds learning and research are codependent as well as all-inclusive when it comes to teaching undergraduate students.

Faculty builds research designs that are reflective of current problems in our society. The head of NASA at the turn of the century was a former Johns Hopkins faculty member. He exemplified the very real and extraordinary research interests of Johns Hopkins University as applied to national space exploration goals.

Undergraduates spend the first years coming up to speed in the highly technical scientific and behavioral science disciplines (J). Social science and the humanities degrees take a similar approach in that students undertake a study that helps them focus on foundational knowledge in their chosen major. Upper-class coursework draws widely from expansive (P) current day societal problems in need of realistic solutions. JHU graduates are steeled in the art of 'what is and what could you make of it' (T).

In the following listing of college majors it is important to remember that students can fit into any college and can be successful in any major. We have found that the Personality Types below fit very well at this college. The course-of-study chosen for each Personality Type corresponds to MBTI® research and is presented as an example favorable for that type.

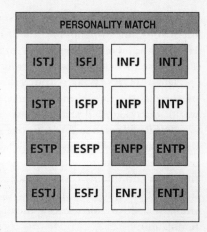

PERSONALITY MATCH

ISTJ	ISFJ	INFJ	INTJ
ISTP	ISFP	INFP	INTP
ESTP	ESFP	ENFP	ENTP
ESTJ	ESFJ	ENFJ	ENTJ

INTJ will find the major in **Earth and Planetary Sciences** is well-designed for turning their ideas into research inquiry. Dealing with outer space will be a tough assignment, but INTJs are not likely to step back. Johns Hopkins' department presents basic concepts in the undergraduate years, specifically geared toward further research at graduate levels. This wide-ranging discipline includes the entire planet as well as those planets in our solar system and beyond. The labs on campus and strong scientific orientation of faculty will allow INTJ to dream of designing research projects for the moon landing, hopefully in the first half of this century.

ISTP will want to look into the **Materials Science and Engineering** degree at John Hopkins. Without a doubt this type will appreciate Johns Hopkins' focus on utilization and practical application. In fact, ISTPs can specialize with advanced courses in their last two undergraduate years. Energy research is currently looking at phase transformations during self-propagating reactions in multilayer foils. How about that! ISTPs heartily approve of the self-propagating words since they are all about efficiency. This type of advanced study can lead to industrial positions in research or application to graduate engineering programs. ISTP prefers to see the light at the end of the proverbial tunnel; they are not inclined to study without an end in mind.

ISTJ is one for knowing the rules and keeping track of the reasons behind the rules. A BA degree at John Hopkins in **General Engineering** could be the perfect preparation for law school and a career in intellectual property or patent law. The several JHU programs and centers focused on the social sciences and humanities will offer appropriate elective courses in combination with solid grounding in the engineering sciences. ISTJ is up for courses in engineering technology as a comprehensive foundation for intellectual property law.

ISFJ has a wonderful ability to revisit the day from an hour-to-hour perspective. They do not miss much as the passing scene unfolds before them. As a result, they are particularly good at understanding and preserving the meaning of cultural practices. The minor in **Museum and Society** at Johns Hopkins supports practicum options in working with museum artifacts and archival collections. This type is thorough and values much about the traditions of society which are both excellent characteristics for a museum curator.

ESTP often has a personality with pizzazz and, combined with their skill at negotiating, they might enter the health policy career field. The major in **Public Health Studies** offers preparation for the masters program in Public Health at JHU. The coursework crosses many other disciplines and offers numerous opportunities for specialization. ESTP prefers the real world and all of its messy, problem-generating practices rather than theories. Human health policy contains a heavy dose of real world issues that need practical, real solutions. ESTP is ready for this type of action.

ENFP will get to study the field of **Anthropology** through the practice of directed research at Johns Hopkins University. The department also focuses on the methods used to bring forth meaning from geographic regions and ethnic populations. With these two educational perspectives and the skill sets that each nurtures, ENFP will have multiple options for graduate study. Cause-related and passion-prone, this type will have little trouble selecting the discipline in which to apply their undergraduate foundation.

ENTP will likely enjoy the degree in **Geography** at Johns Hopkins. It focuses on the human impact and use of land as determined by geologic formations and social factors. The department encourages further specialization with Human Geography or Physical Geography. In both cases, the coursework is interdisciplinary and demands abstract thinking and creativity. ENTPs pretty well spend their waking hours dreaming up possibilities, or another way to put it: abstract thinking + creativity. This unusual major is an ideal option for ENTP.

ESTJ often moves toward professions which require administration or other functions of leadership. The major in **History of Science, Medicine and Technology** sounds a bit unusual on first look. However, orderly, well-planned and executed ESTJs know this major is an excellent background for graduate studies in policy, government, medicine or law. The Johns Hopkins dynamic environment, so closely related to advanced research, will also help tradition bound ESTJ learn to appreciate the future.

ENTJ is not likely to regret signing up for the **Entrepreneurship and Management** minor in combination with any of the engineering degrees at Johns Hopkins University. JHU even allows students to take just three basic courses in this area or complete the seven courses for the minor. The three course option is ideal for enterprising ENTJs in the engineering curriculum that is already packed with research and requirements.

KALAMAZOO COLLEGE

1200 Academy Street
Kalamazoo, MI 49006
Website: www.kzoo.edu
Admissions Telephone: 269-337-7166
Undergraduates: 1,356; 587 Men, 769 Women

Physical Environment

There really *is* a Kalamazoo College in Michigan! It's been in existence for 175 years, making it one of the oldest liberal arts colleges in the country. Kzoo College, as it is often referred to, is close to the downtown district. Students walk together in **small groups** down the college hill to get to the shops in town. The college takes advantage of its location in this working community by focusing on service within the campus's immediate neighborhoods. Yet, it also has one of the highest participation rates in **study abroad and internships**. The energy often flows in and out of the campus by semesters as many are coming or going. Kzoo excels in learning by doing, experience (S) and integration.

The campus buildings hug a steep hill with red brick walls encircling a cozy quad forming the campus center. The quad projects a **calm**, smallish space where students gather on steps in twos and threes. Weather permitting, it is the student center for this **reflective student body** The Hicks Student Center offers a strong place of identity and meeting for the travel intensive undergraduates. Renovations are smartly completed with equal care for historical context and attention given over to study spaces. A classic reminder of this ethos is the commanding mural above the dining room which reminds one of the magnificent Diego Rivera murals at the Detroit Institute of Art. Diners relax and ponder the scene above. It acknowledges the human relationship (F) between rural Michigan farmers, industrial workers, their leaders in the manufacturing era, and wisdom as represented by Kzoo students, faculty and academic philosophy.

Very typically, students took a keen interest in the construction costs of the Hicks center. Some objected to the extra cost of certification as a "green" building. True to the colleges' reflective philosophies, undergraduates here discerned there are extra costs in government-directed mandates which necessarily represent politics far removed. Undergrads tend to bring an **ethos** of not being wasteful, reminiscent of the Dutch Reformists who settled along the southern Lake Michigan region. This **efficient,** (J) few-frills approach characterizes the students who, for the most part, respect authority and appreciate the guidance they receive from their professors at this college.

Social Environment

Students who enroll at Kalamazoo formerly approached their high school studies stoically. At Kalamazoo, they branch out with confidence and **intellectual exploration**. Most of them rank in the top 15 percent of their class and may have been accepted by more selective universities. However, they enroll at KZoo because they want to build strong relationships with their professors and pursue their education with dedication. Students have **free reign** to explore what they want to study before they commit to the college's signature piece, the experience-based plan of education well presented in the Kalamazoo College admission materials. The **K-Plan** is an educational tool that outlines the four-year course of studies clearly and prompts a resume that catalogs the graduate's skill set. They will work on developing a plan for their **career** and complete an extensive thesis-like research. They will study abroad for the most part in third-world countries in conjunction with objectives of their K-Plan. Kzoo is ideal for rational, hard-working students who care about exploring and getting to know the world. They visit India or Botswana to learn the local dialects, live with a family and integrate with that particular culture. Perhaps upon their return they continue with individualized instruction in that dialect as part of the Neglected Languages Program offered on this campus.

Kalamazoo College students often go beyond the required study in order to earn an above average grade. Students are **down-to-earth** and dress for comfort more than style. Many of the quieter students really get animated when they engage in a conversation about their beliefs or observations from out-of-country studies. They return with a strong **cultural knowledge** base which they meld with their K Plan resume. These students follow an intellectual approach to their careers and their future.

Compatibility with Personality Types and Preferences

Kalamazoo College adopted experiential ways of learning decades ago when few other colleges pursued this type of education. The concept of learning by doing (S) forms the foundation of the academic curriculum here. Kzoo very much encourages students to select a variety of off-campus experiences. These real world environments in profit and nonprofit research laboratories, businesses and countries within and outside of America are honored as primary avenues of knowledge. The next level of learning is the hallmark of Kzoo faculty, foundational knowledge. Here, interdisciplinary study does not preclude analytic understanding of the undergraduate major field. Professors guide undergraduates to supplement this foundational knowledge with experiential learning. As a result, undergraduates encounter vibrant classroom discussion and considerable written requirements that forge individual passion with analytic skill. Structure and order (J) is critical to this process as well as intensity. The experiential activities purposely reach for the outer edges of the familiar world as well as the practical, everyday world. Kzoo students mix it up as they define their cause-related perspectives. They are returning from studying abroad in unusual locations or within the U.S. that are less traveled or overlooked. Those attracted to Kzoo come seeking a precisely intellectual and utilitarian education. Kalamazoo College delivers exactly this.

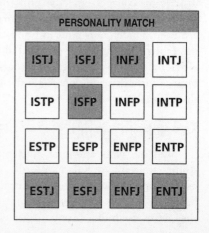

PERSONALITY MATCH

ISTJ	ISFJ	INFJ	INTJ
ISTP	ISFP	INFP	INTP
ESTP	ESFP	ENFP	ENTP
ESTJ	ESFJ	ENFJ	ENTJ

In the following listing of college majors it is important to remember that students can fit into any college and can be successful in any major. We have found that the Personality Types below fit very well at this college. The course-of-study chosen for each Personality Type corresponds to MBTI® research and is presented as an example favorable for that type.

ISTJ will probably like the Kzoo approach to **Computer Science**. Not surprisingly, the department approaches this evolving science with a practical bent. Students will learn about emerging trends in computing technology that seem to be serving, or is it shaping, humankind. Software modeling, think hurricane predictions, and algorithms, think your flight cancelled without seeming reason, are the current content of this discipline. Here at this college, ISTJ will get a good dose of the practical applications that help them accept and incorporate new ideas in this rapidly evolving field.

ESFJ could select a concentration in **African Studies** to accompany their major in the social sciences. This type is a strong cheerleader for organizations. Much of the service work in Africa is delivered through international agencies with currently functioning programs. This avenue is appealing to ESFJs who like to work within traditional organizations. However, to stay content with a career path ESFJ must provide services or products to needy populations. Kzoo has extensive study abroad options on the continent.

ISFJ might go into the major of **Psychology** through the field of education. This type is responsible, loyal and supportive of fellow workers. Combined with a strong foundation in human personality theory, ISFJ could become a dynamite educational administrator or school psychologist. The department prepares undergraduate students to select from three broad options for graduate school as scientists in research, practitioners in counseling or consultants in professions such as business and law.

ISFP fits in nicely on this campus with their enjoyment of active, supportive environments. The degree in **Math** at Kzoo lends itself to practical applications and ISFP can look forward to good internships whereby this abstract discipline can be put to hands-on use. ISFP could easily seek internships in industry and government. Kzoo is actively building discipline area Guilds with alumni through Linkedin. ISFP, quite adaptable to change, may start the math guild. Future employment guaranteed!

ESTJ may just like the **Health Studies** concentration here at Kalamazoo College. This predetermined set of courses prepares students for these options: veterinary medicine, dentistry, optometry, pharmacy, physical therapy, chiropractic, nursing, physician assistant, medicine, etc. The field is growing as the population ages in our country. This type might just choose to become a pharmacist fairly early on since they want to have things settled and order is valued in pharmacies and by ESTJ too.

INFJ finds the lack of 100 percent accurate answers acceptable in the **Environmental Studies** concentration. In fact, this type likes to come up with new ideas in which they take pride. At Kalamazoo College, the concentration is interdisciplinary and the senior individualized project is advised from INFJs major department This type is especially adept at initiating their ideas within traditional organization such as a nonprofit, commercial business or governmental office. They understand the mechanisms of power within and expertly plan to set about their goals.

ENTJ was in the thoughts of Kalamazoo College faculty when they designed the **Human Development and Social Relations** major. The core courses focus on the stages of human development over the lifetime. Inclined to consulting, ENTJ might offer advising in child developmental stages to educational enterprises such as textbook publishers. As increasing numbers of middle income neighborhoods are experiencing struggling schools, this hard charger might recognize the needs in this presently forgotten foundational building block of American culture.

ENFJ is excellent at training professionals in business and corporate environments because of their persuasive and polished personality. The Kalamazoo major in **Business** with foundational courses like Theory of the Firm and National Income & Business Cycles is both overarching and real. The studies give ENFJ needed exposure to the tough problems in this sector. The practical, signature approach to education at Kalamazoo prepares this creative, compassionate type to confidently enter professional enterprises such as Apple, Verizon, Citibank, Macy's, etc. They bring harmony and cooperation to the team as they take on tough managerial issues.

KENYON COLLEGE

Gambier, OH 43022-9623
Website: www.kenyon.edu
Admissions Telephone: 800-848-2468
Undergraduates: 1,648; 763 Men, 885 Women

Physical Environment

Gambier and Kenyon College are very much intertwined in this rural Ohio landscape. The campus essentially sits on a very large park reminiscent of an **English landscape**. Kenyon's Quarry Chapel is on the National Register of Historic Places. The mature oak trees cast shadows on the heavily **Gothic** stone buildings, creating a surreal feel, especially under an overcast sky. Ascension Hall was built in 1859 and casts a mysterious visual impression with a time-worn front door and original leaded glass windows. Students really identify with haunting tales and **ghostly traditions**. The fall colors and temperatures keep students outside in the evenings speculating about old campus rumors. The centuries-old cemetery on one corner of campus is fodder for Kenyon legends. It's not surprising that Halloween is a favorite holiday at a favorite time of year.

The new Gund Art Gallery and athletic center stand in stark contrast to Gothic architecture. The Kenyon Athletic Center is attractive to avid athletes who come from all over the U.S. and international locations. Kenyon students support their teams. The natatorium has 20 lanes and resides in this recreation complex, replete with indoor track, many ball courts and a theatre.

Students attracted to Kenyon often have a full resume of extracurriculars. Kenyon undergraduates are comfortable with the broad educational perspectives. They typically are interested in drama and musical productions. An old bank building adjacent to the campus now houses a black box theatre where undergrads hone their acting and directing skills.

The former haunting tale associated with an old pool of yesteryears still hangs on. The modernization of this campus has not taken away the **renaissance fair** feel that one might have when visiting a medieval village. It definitely draws students who find historical periods fascinating.

Social Environment

Nowadays, Kenyon College recruits predominantly suburban students from the right and left coasts, as well as the major cities of the middle states. Out-of-state students far outnumber those who come from Ohio. These "coasties," familiar with a more active pace of life, more amenities, more competition athletically and more variety, come to slow down at this intellectual campus. However, they look to the faculty for academic structure and guidance as they expand their foundational knowledge.

At Kenyon, students learn to understand what they read and practice their writing skills so that they graduate with the ability to achieve **clarity of thinking** and clarity of **written expression**. The underlying philosophy holds little value in acquired knowledge if one can't express it clearly in writing and preferably in speaking too. These skills are required to delve into Kenyon's curriculum in the liberal arts and sciences. Students may sign up to do an independent study or blend several majors and finish up with an interdisciplinary degree.

The social scene is diverse and **eclectic**. It comprises very athletic students, groups who oppose the status quo and common culture, those who join a fraternity or sorority and those who are conservative. You can tell who they are by the way they dress: some wear vintage clothing from second-hand stores while others frequent Macy's.

The lack of a big town nearby encourages students to rely on one another for social engagement and stimulation, especially since students must live on campus all four years. They form a **close-knit** community together with the professors who live nearby. Some students find their marriage partner here and return to get married on campus.

Compatibility with Personality Types and Preferences

Kenyon College is very straight forward (S) in its dedication to teaching students. The faculty and staff provide an environment that is totally centered on individual student progress during their four years of undergraduate studies. Kenyon students, in turn, passionately connect with the social and learning atmosphere at Kenyon and Gambier—the small town that is intimately tied with Kenyon College. Gambier brims with rural Ohio lore and is immediately familiar and comfortable to families and students who travel from considerable distances to attend this college. Undergraduates here enjoy and actively participate in building and maintaining the intellectual community. There is agreement between student and professor to acquire and solidify personal knowledge (T). Learning at Kenyon College is greatly characterized by specifics, analyses and principles - in that order. There is a guided curriculum for each major which assures graduates enter professional studies or the world of work with broad skills. Students who find Kenyon attractive also very much appreciate the numerous programs supplementing residential life. Faculty and students devote much energy to the advising and learning process and collaboration is a byword, whether its faculty/student or student/student.

In the following listing of college majors it is important to remember that students can fit into any college and can be successful in any major. We have found that the Personality Types below fit very well at this college. The course-of-study chosen for each Personality Type corresponds to MBTI® research and is presented as an example favorable for that type.

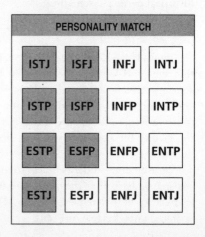

PERSONALITY MATCH

ISTJ	ISFJ	INFJ	INTJ
ISTP	ISFP	INFP	INTP
ESTP	ESFP	ENFP	ENTP
ESTJ	ESFJ	ENFJ	ENTJ

ISTP will find **Biology** at Kenyon College ideal. The department focuses on observations of recent research and examines those findings in respect to basic principles. It starts with the specifics and builds up to the generalities.

This type will also approve of the utility of this approach. Research findings tend to be focused and purposeful in biology and this allows ISTPs to see where their studies are leading. With amazing research findings in this century alone, Kenyon College has a wealth of material to analyze and fit into larger biological systems.

ISFJ has a terrific, almost sponge-like memory for people and places. It works well for the **Asian Studies** concentration at Kenyon College. This reflective type will find a well-planned series of courses and study abroad options. The year of foreign language in Japanese, Chinese or Sanskrit can be fulfilled in the traditional semesters of language on campus or by an approved immersion summer program. Asian Studies becomes a very attractive addition to any other major that ISFJs might choose, perhaps art history or anthropology.

ISTJ will not shrink from the senior integrating exercise in Kenyon's **Economics** degree. It is just right for this type. Kenyon emphasizes economic models as a way of understanding the behavior of society. So ISTJs who are people-oriented, yet not all that touchy feely, can participate in building community with economic models that analyze and predict behavior. This type is very much attracted to facts and data, so the precise nature of the course work will be fine with them.

ISFP needs openness and flexibility to sort out what will be their life's work. This type prefers to be doing things that are related to helping other folks. The interdisciplinary program in **Neuroscience** at Kenyon College offers a track in biopsychological courses that will take advantage of ISFP's astuteness in observing people. With a few years of additional training, ISFPs with this degree can move into any of the specialized health services like physical therapy. It would also be ideal preparation for technical positions whereby kind-hearted ISFPs could interface the medical procedures with the patient.

ESTP is quick to size up a social environment. Gregarious and socially smooth, ESTPs will be in and out of the action at Kenyon with ease. The concentration in **Public Policy** is easily paired with a major in economics or political science. ESTPs like variety so taking courses in several areas is fine. They will be drawn to off-campus experiences to supplement the Gambier experience. The efficiency and one-stop shopping of Kenyon's Center for Global Engagement makes it more likely that ESTP can find that experience that is packed with active learning and perhaps a little risk taking.

ESFP loves to socialize and Kenyon College offers multiple ways to become attached in the college community. This campus will work very well for ESFPs. The major in **Studio Art** will also provide a fine foundation for careers which involve offering pleasing design services to clients. With disposable income, young people are looking to improve their living spaces more so than past generations. Enticing courses like Installation Art and Painting Redefined have a large component of fun and interest within. Since these art forms draw the viewer into sensory experience through sound, sight and smell, ESFP will be delighted to create it

ESTJ will be very approving of the concentration in **Law and Society**. It seeks to provide a wide, solid study of legal institutions and laws. As a foundational body of knowledge, this allows graduates to competently frame the tough legal issues of our day. Whether ESTJs go on to medicine, law or government, this concentration prepares them to deal with the conundrums that seem to regularly pop up in these fields. ESTJ is just the impersonal, practical leader to become a fine administrator, rarely allowing confusion to overcome the day.

LAWRENCE UNIVERSITY

Office of Admissions
115 S. Drew Street
Appleton, WI 54911
Website: www.lawrence.edu
Admissions Telephone: 920-832-6500
Undergraduates: 1,443; 656 Men, 787 Women

Physical Environment

Lawrence University is a liberal arts college located in downtown Appleton, Wisconsin. It overlooks the bank of the **Fox River**, before it empties into Lake Winnebago. Built during the Industrial Revolution by the mill owners, opulent mansions that now form "millionaire's row" line the banks of this river. Undergraduate Lawrence students like to shop or walk **together in groups** to downtown Appleton, adjacent to the campus center.

Lawrence University is the major attraction in Appleton, with its beautiful art galleries and theaters that bring in students and citizens for **musical and theatrical performances**. The **Wriston Art Center** on campus hosts permanent collections of paintings and exhibits the art work of graduating students. Often, students gather together and sit on the steps of Wriston to chat or play an instrument, except in the winter when everything is snowed under. The campus architecture is a medley of modern and traditional buildings laid out with pleasing regularity on **horizontal and perpendicular streets**, like a Monopoly game, especially the residence halls which are all of the same color. Most students live on campus, and the residence halls are arranged according to specific themes, such as "opera appreciation house" or "swing dancing club." The Warch Campus Center generates much energy with its multiple use spaces and amazing glass portals to view the sky and landscape. It was made possible by an anonymous donation. Undergraduate students suggested the room arrangement, furnishings and use prior to its completion.

Social Environment

Students are very creative here and **artistically inclined**, whether or not they are part of the **music conservatory.** They sing and play the many pianos found throughout the campus, and enjoy the blend of liberal arts with the performing arts. Students appreciate the **values-laden curriculum** that includes **original texts** of authors quite varied, Plato to Shakespeare to Einstein. In the well-designed **Freshman Studies** program, they discuss the nature of mankind, and are likely to debate difficult concepts like the limits of knowledge. Students are encouraged to use their judgment and freely bring their suggestions up to the administration. The president is very much accessible for the students and invites them to her house for ice-cream socials and other events.

The coffee bar in the student center stays open every night. A professor might play guitar, while the next night a student might read from a classic play. Most students here are liberal in terms of their thinking, expression and political beliefs. Ironically, although republican-leaning students are in the minority, Appleton is reputedly a conservative town that promotes a peaceful environment and upholds a traditional way of life. Some pockets of Lawrence students look a bit like the 1960s groupies, yet they fit in within current alternative norms. This is in contrast to students who are in the music conservatory comfortable in formal wear and dress attire. Half the student population comes from the state of Wisconsin, followed by Minnesota and then Illinois. Greek life comprises about a fifth of the students. Together, these groups form a cohesive population of **thoughtful** young adults and yet each student has a definite individuality.

Although the weather is brutally cold here it is mitigated by the genuine warmth of people. Students say people here are "real" and are not interested in trends. Perhaps it's the study of human nature in ancient texts or it's something in the water that develops the internal compass of students at Lawrence University.

Compatibility with Personality Types and Preferences

Lawrence University pretty much defines educational cohesion. Intellectual ideas come to the campus and freely float around for students to snag and incorporate for their own use. Conversation is continuous and debate, argument and agreement (T) is a regular extracurricular activity. Those concepts that are retained by students, faculty or administration find their way into the curriculum and the independent learning projects of the students. Lawrence University offers students the option of tutorials in many majors which further expands the vehicles by which ideas are generated. This regular conceptual review seeps into everything else for the purpose of forming future knowledge (N).

The residential life, extracurricular programs, the study abroad and the service learning all support the academic goals of the administration and the student population over the decades. All the aspects of residential life come together and form an intellectual spirit on campus, yet it is not a sober or quiet place. On the contrary, it is quite an active, chatty campus (E). Undergraduates enjoy and expect to be in dialog with each other. Their academic interests can become political passions over the course of the four undergraduate years. Their focus is on the future and contributing to their disciplines. Students who want to become competent through the vehicle of precise thinking will find the campus ideal. Most look to graduate studies as an extension of the undergraduate studies. All this, to position themselves as unobtrusive decision makers and leaders in society.

In the following listing of college majors it is important to remember that students can fit into any college and can be successful in any major. We have found that the Personality Types below fit very well at this college. The course-of-study chosen for each Personality Type corresponds to MBTI® research and is presented as an example favorable for that type.

PERSONALITY MATCH			
ISTJ	ISFJ	INFJ	INTJ
ISTP	ISFP	INFP	INTP
ESTP	ESFP	ENFP	ENTP
ESTJ	ESFJ	ENFJ	ENTJ

INFP wants to find their studies in agreement with their values. They prefer to study a topic in depth and to keep it organized, preferably by themselves. The interdisciplinary minor in **Cognitive Science** requires pulling information from the three specific fields of psychology, philosophy and computer science. Individualized work with a professor, in the form of tutorials, will suit INTPs as they develop their hunches assemble supporting research and theory to a design a small scale research study, possibly turning the hunch into reality. That would be cognitive science in action!!

INFJ might like the **Anthropology** minor at Lawrence University The academic philosophy of the department is to develop reliable skills and perspectives within the undergraduate student to accurately understand the culture of others. Coursework includes foundational theory, methods and analyses. INFJ is the thinker who can take it all in and then recombine that within a research study. This minor will nicely supplement the majors in the social sciences.

INTJ with their bent for originality and an interest in computers will like the **Mathematics-Computer Science** interdisciplinary major specifically designed for post-baccalaureate study. It allows the viewing of large data constructs through methodological manipulation. once INTJ defines the problem in a quantitative sense, any number of algorithms will be researched for the solution. This challenging type of work is very much desired by INTJ who naturally jumps between these two disciplines for the methods and solutions.

INTP can indulge their curiosity in the study of the nervous system at Lawrence University. This field is a frontier with lots of challenges and discoveries yet to be made. INTP is attracted to fields with challenges and the major in **Neuroscience** is just such a one. It lends itself to research at the undergraduate level through collaboration with faculty. This is a favored way of learning for this type. They like to see how one factor or piece of data fits into a larger system. They enjoy speculating about potential outcomes. They like the What-If Game. This much focused discipline with its numerous unknowns is right up their proverbial alley.

ENFP is drawn to speculating about improving the lives of others. The minor in **Ethnic Studies** at Lawrence University is ideal for this purpose. It requires coursework across departments which will keep boredom at bay for restless ENFPs. It also offers a curriculum and learning style that uses speculation. Department faculty pose observational questions like: What are the politics of their ethnic practices? ENFP is not daunted by this type of highly abstract question. In fact, they prefer them. It is very much like Lawrence University to rely heavily on the intuition and academic courage of their undergraduate students.

ENTP could enjoy studying **Government** by making the most of the tutorials at Lawrence University. The department interfaces recent political crises into the curriculum. ENTPs like this broad-based education. It gives them a foundation to enter into a variety of political arenas armed with knowledge and propose change-centered solutions. The major centers on political analysis in the first two years. This is followed by the more familiar courses such as constitutional law in the junior year of study. ENTP will fare well with this sequence. Their ingenuity in searching for patterns and solutions will be immediately rewarded in the freshmen and sophomore years. Their potential impatience in studying the functions of government can be lessened by reference back to the dynamic social issues studied earlier.

ESFJ will find that the interdisciplinary major in **Natural Sciences** with an **Education** certificate really meets their career inclinations. The natural science majors at Lawrence University include course work in biology, chemistry, physics and geology. This is ideal for the ESFJ interested in becoming a science teacher in high school. Their expertise with these disciplines will be desired in the secondary schools by the students who sign up for AP Chemistry or Physics. ESFJ will be very much appreciated by these 'show me' AP high school students. Lawrence University has a solid program of internships in the local schools. This meets practical ESFJ's expectations and desire to be supporting community.

ENFJ will make good use of the **Biomedical Ethics** minor. This type's interest in resolution and harmony often pushes them into consulting careers. ENFJs like the independence but want to be connected with others. Their inclination to make improvements while remaining open is an ideal set of characteristics for mediation and negotiation. They are competent public speakers and will wade into thorny social situations utilizing this vehicle to establish their credibility. The major nicely combines with public policy and all health fields.

ENTJ would find an interdisciplinary major to their liking in the **Mathematics-Economics** major at Lawrence University. The Senior Experience is a great exercise in guided creativity and demonstration of mathematical prowess. ENTJs will take the option to shine here, stepping out into an assertive, logical, orderly research design. Lawrence University administration expects that graduates will become influential in large policy venues. The option to combine economics with math bolsters ENTJ's application for prestigious graduate study in economics. This type is also very practical and just may move straight into the world of business which delivers the action and leadership opportunities which they seek.

LYNCHBURG COLLEGE

1501 Lakeside Drive
Lynchburg, VA 24501
Website: www.lynchburg.edu
Admissions Telephone: 804-544-8300, 800-426-8101
Undergraduates: 2,142; 871 Men, 1,271 Women

Physical Environment

Lynchburg College is located in the center of Virginia, in a town of 220,000 inhabitants, nestled on a hill with views of the surrounding Blue Ridge Mountains. The collegiate administration and faculty strongly interface their educational mission with the economic needs of central and western Virginia in the Blue Ridge Mountains. The campus architecture is made up of many red-brick buildings with white columns in the Georgian style. The original buildings date back to 1903, when the college was established as a **non-sectarian, Christian**, liberal arts college. Hopwood Hall is where students take most academic classes. It is named after the founder, Josephus Hopwood. The college seal is engraved in several places such as the Chapel and the Spiritual Life Center where often students engage in volunteer initiatives. This seal symbolizes the college's commitment to **faith and reason**.

The Hobbs Science Center provides special labs for health science majors such as nursing students, who get to identify body parts on cheerfully colored plastic cadavers. These labs are designed for **pre-professional** students interested in physical and occupational therapy, pre-dentistry, pre-optometry, pharmacy and veterinary science. The Claytor Nature Study Center provides an environmental laboratory of upland forests and wetlands. It is well used by the education majors focusing on lesson development for K-12. Heated with geothermal energy, it is proof positive of the Lynchburg commitment to economy and common sense. Projected enlargement of this facility will encourage undergrads to extend biological research and observation with short term overnight accommodations.

The heart of campus is Shellenberger field and it is surrounded by residence halls. It is named in honor of Professor William Shellenberger (1952-1989) who taught movement science, recreation, health and fitness and coached sports. Recently, refurbished, its rededication ceremony was much appreciated and welcomed by current students and alumni who supported the project. This field gets a lot of use by students who play soccer or throw Frisbees. It's where they hold the annual Thanksgiving flag football game.

Social Environment

Students who like sports and the outdoors will enjoy this college where physical fitness is clearly well supported. For a liberal arts college, it is unusual that there are more males enrolled than females. Women here are athletic and feminine. Some will find their life partner here within the group of like-minded undergraduates. Most students find a place on a sports team of their choice and get to play often. The academic majors in athletic training and physical therapy support this lifestyle. Lynchburg College boasts a prestigious plaque for best overall athletic program.

Academic classes are taught in an **interactive,** discussion-style manner. Students become active learners as they engage in their major with **supportive professors** and **apply** what they learn. While many students come here for the pre-professional programs in the health sciences, the college also appeals to the **fitness enthusiasts** who want to major in business, communications, theatre and fine arts. Primary source readings are interfaced throughout the curriculum to develop students' speaking, writing and reasoning skills.

Students who are looking for that classic college experience will enjoy the Greek **fraternities and sororities** that are an accepted and well-established part of social life at this college with opportunities for leadership and service. The college requires new special interest groups to petition for approval. Greek and non-Greek groups socialize well together. Greeks live in the same residence halls as other students. Approximately 50 percent of the students come from outside Virginia. Scholarships are available based on academic merit.

Compatibility with Personality Types and Preferences

Lynchburg College has a solid understanding of the American landscape, both social and business in orientation, located along the Atlantic seaboard. Founded on religious and ethical perspectives, the administration reached out to these communities and established an historical and ongoing appreciation from its founding in 1909 to the present. This inclusive perspective, many decades later, provides the student body with a optimistic educational environment that is based on realism. As such, the curriculum is a cross between humanistic principles (F) and today's careers and occupations (S). The college is focused on helping students learn skills and develop talents that are useful in today's society. Complementing this appreciation for traditional American community, the college has always turned to experiential learning. Collaboration with local public and private enterprises plus regional organizations has a significant presence in the undergraduate degrees. Off-campus (E) study is comfortably incorporated into the curriculum by Lynchburg's faculty, most with experience in their field of expertise outside of academia. In fact, the educational philosophy seems to embrace whole person, integrated learning concepts like the strongly amplified program in physical and spiritual wellness. Undergraduates who appreciate a warm, yet realistic approach in the classroom will find success here. Prospective students who seek entry into career tracks after graduation will find their preparation to be above and beyond. Lynchburg College is connected in many senses.

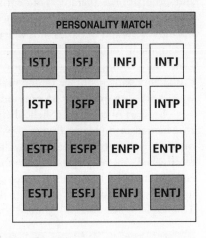

PERSONALITY MATCH

ISTJ	ISFJ	INFJ	INTJ
ISTP	ISFP	INFP	INTP
ESTP	ESFP	ENFP	ENTP
ESTJ	ESFJ	ENFJ	ENTJ

In the following listing of college majors it is important to remember that students can fit into any college and can be successful in any major. We have found that the Personality

Types below fit very well at this college. The course-of-study chosen for each Personality Type corresponds to MBTI® research and is presented as an example favorable for that type.

ISTJ might find the **Exercise Physiology** major at Lynchburg College falls in line with meticulous procedures that they prefer for their own lifestyle. ISTJs are superb, dependable workers in these precise workplaces. The department maintains a strong network of area facilities that offer internships for the students. With this major ISTJs will be helping folks experiencing difficulty in fitness, health or performance, It is also a strong background for graduate study in many of the health-related careers. This type's appreciation of common sense nicely combines with physiology theory and its application to physical fitness.

ISFJ will find the **Business Administration** degree is focused on competency with a capital C. The faculty in the School of Business emphasizes this attribute through a solid curriculum heavy on foundational knowledge. It equips this hard-working type with the skill set to pursue the accuracy they favor. ISFJs very much enjoy one-on-one time with their customers and the department requires undergrads to select a second major. At Lynchburg College it will be easy to select the second major in the helping professions. This personal approach to the business workplace, combined with their desired competence, comes naturally.

ISFP will find that Lynchburg College honors practicality in educational studies. The business school faculty hails from the ranks of professional entrepreneurs. As a result, the major in **Accounting** offers the realism that ISFPs crave. The department also outlines doable options to secure the CPA certification upon graduation. This type is quietly bound to their internal value system and applauds the careful consideration given to student resources, both time and budget, as well as upfront 'revelations' on personality characteristics suitable for accounting careers. Faculty inundates undergrads with internship experiences and competently address ethical considerations that exist in today's mid-size and large corporations.

ESTP likes to operate by the proverbial 'seat of their pants', yet their exceptionally fine observational skills and memory are skillfully applied and ready throughout the work day. The major in **Economic Crime Prevention and Investigation** at Lynchburg College is unusual and requires knowledge from several traditional academic disciplines. ESTPs are likely to relish the thought of investigating white collar fraud and corruption. This type also likes the survey approach to building a body of knowledge. The major and the career field of investigation is ideal for the type. Faculty in this department have law enforcement and fraud investigative experience. Their credentials are the sad result of today's cultural, relativistic, legalistic reasoning. Without unyielding moral conviction, the slope gets slippery.

ESFP very often likes to be with other people and in the middle of the action, oftentimes outdoors. The minor available at Lynchburg College in **Outdoor Recreation** will be an excellent companion to the other careers which appeal to this type: Education, Health Care, Entertainment, Social Services and business. A second minor, and another appealing choice for this type would be **Coaching**, especially if ESFP intends to go into education. It is unusual for a liberal arts institution to offer these two minors. Both of these minors add very desirable skill sets for the graduates.

ESFJ typically has the inclination to be of service and support to others. In the world of business, this can translate to sales representative. ESFJs with their pleasant, affirming personality, can bring this asset to the **Sport Management** major or minor at Lynchburg College. Organization and dependability are bywords for this type and well interface with the highly scheduled, seasonal world of sports. Lynchburg College actively updates this curriculum to reflect the increasing presence of sports entertainment, sports leisure and sports commerce in today's society. Internship offerings are exceptional from the Baltimore Orioles to Special Olympics Virginia to U.S. Marine Corps – Quantico. Wow.

ESTJ hangs on to their no-nonsense approach in emotionally charged environments. This type is often pulled toward the traditional professions such as law, medicine and engineering. The investment in additional graduate school training comes naturally to ESTJs. This type is masterful at putting together cause and effect lines of reason which allow them to excel in high stakes careers. Lynchburg College developed a system of advising for its **Pre Professional Program** that provides direct, timely advice in each of the dental, medical, optometry, pharmacy, physical therapy and veterinary fields. Advisors are selected to mirror the professional interests of the undergraduate ESTJ. Advising takes on the dual role of foundational undergraduate studies and admission to professional school

ENFJ often wants to be personally productive for the benefit of others. ENFJs also love to be mentored and advised in a one-on-one relationship with their advisor. This type interfaces passion/cause with their education and seeks to personalize their knowledge and its application to the community. Lynchburg's minor in **Museum Studies** carried this quote in October 2011: "Curators piece together the puzzle of times we didn't see. It's a puzzle that will never be completed." So well said. ENFJ is superb at 'well said.'

ENTJ has the inclination to compete for one of the desired openings in the **Athletic Training** major at Lynchburg College. The entry level, professional positions secured by ENTJs on graduation with this degree will lead to the stature and levels of influence sought by this type. This independent type likes the challenge and wants to be accountable for their own organizational plans. Athletic trainers are key to athletes and professional or semi-professional sports teams. ENTJ does not mind stepping into this dynamic, powerful environment.

MARQUETTE UNIVERSITY

Office of Admission
Marquette Hall, 106
Milwaukee, WI 53201-1881
Website: www.marquette.edu
Admissions Telephone: 414-288-7302, 800-222-6544
Undergraduates; 7,999, 3,839 Men, 4,160 Women
Graduate Students: 1,057

Physical Environment

The city of Milwaukee is a **vibrant** place to visit and attend college. It was settled by Eastern European immigrants who came down from Canada, probably via the Saint Lawrence Seaway and the Great Lakes. The streets are clean and not jammed with traffic. The **downtown skyline** reveals sharp new buildings alongside old-world neighborhoods built in the 1900s. The city sports excellent museums, art, lakefront walkways, ethnic festivals and much more. It's also home to Anheuser Busch Beer Company and the Harley Davidson motorcycle company. The weather can get very cold here, on the edge of Lake Michigan, "when the gales of November come hauling," to borrow the words from Canadian singer Gordon Lightfoot.

Milwaukee is particularly easy to get to from the Midwest, so it's no surprise to find many mid-westerners at Marquette. Both the tall city-skyline and the university are dramatic contrasts to the flat prairies. The residence halls are **tall rectangular towers** except for the one which echoes the shape of a beer can. Upper class students typically move off campus to university-owned apartments. These residences are adjacent to the campus and it is an easy walk to and from classes. The Discovery Learning Complex opened in 2011 is a spectacular engineering and science facility which promotes student generated research projects to explore fundamental science concepts.

Social Environment

Marquette University appeals to students who are used to working hard and producing results. This strong **work ethic** binds the city together as it does the university. The **Jesuit ideals** fit in well with that. In addition to a very **rigorous course of study**, students get involved in serving the community. This campus is most remarkable for the intensity of service and leadership activity within the undergraduate student body. The city with many nearby neighborhoods offers students additional options to serve.

Students at Marquette come from traditional Catholic families for the most part. It would be a bit difficult to be an out and out atheist here, when the drum-beat is all about faith and fellowship. Students respect rules and have a deep respect for **social convention**. They are ok with traditional roles. They don't have to be leaders when they arrive on campus but they will almost certainly develop **leadership** here because of the many prompts to generate new energy into common ideas.

Fraternities and sororities have been an institution at Marquette for more than 100 years. They offer multiple ways to engage in **volunteer activities** and leadership. Members of fraternities and sororities are often members of other clubs. **Sports** are also very popular and games are well attended in the Bradley Center, especially their Division I basketball team. No matter which tower students choose or which organizations to join, they will develop a **wide circle of friends** from all over campus. Social life and parties are always at the ready here. Marquette graduates do indeed have a wide network of peers and the student body greatly benefits from strong **alumni support.** Pride in the city and the university is very evident.

Compatibility with Personality Types and Preferences

Marquette University is quite orderly (J) and reasoned (T) in its educational philosophy stemming from the Jesuit principles. The mission of the university infuses values of truth, excellence and faith throughout the collegiate environment. Analysis of ethical responsibility is pervasive and for the benefit of the undergraduate student body. Along with development of strong personal character, students are offered a series of programs and opportunities that build leadership skills. All this is to encourage harmonious (F) values of community, the community within the city of Milwaukee and the American community. The Jesuit ideals are oriented toward productive citizenship and the university carefully and assertively supports this.

The undergraduates here are discouraged from remaining in a small, familiar circle of friends found during the freshman year. Many programmatic and informal mechanisms are in effect to encourage undergraduates to enlarge their circle of acquaintances (E) on this campus. The underlying advantage of this social prompting allows students to become familiar with and identify with organizations and enterprises of the university, city and nation. Within this framework, the university with its realistically (S) oriented curriculum ensures that graduates can secure immediate employment in career tracks that are needed by society. Students who are drawn to this university, beyond comfort with religious spirituality, are conventional in the sense of their expectations. They intend to have one heck of a good time in college and then settle down after graduation or post-graduate study, raise a family and make lifelong contributions within their selected discipline while actively supporting America, their state and city of residence.

In the following listing of college majors it is important to remember that students can fit into any college and can be successful in any major. We have found that the Personality Types below fit very well at this college. The course-of-study chosen for each Personality Type corresponds to MBTI® research and is presented as an example favorable for that type.

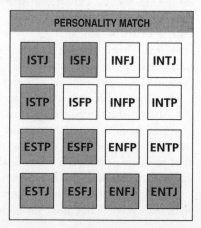

PERSONALITY MATCH

ISTJ	ISFJ	INFJ	INTJ
ISTP	ISFP	INFP	INTP
ESTP	ESFP	ENFP	ENTP
ESTJ	ESFJ	ENFJ	ENTJ

ISTP is a maverick on occasion but in a quiet way, often with a wry smile. The major in **Business Economics** with a minor in **Air Force and Aerospace Studies** just might suit their sense of the efficiency. The very realistic education with faculty active in business consulting and real-time publishing passes the ISTP reality test. The hands-on orientation for selecting internships and the mentor program junior year will open up options for multiple career tracks. The minor in Air Force and Aerospace will certainly move ISTPs toward the large military industrial complex for a career. That career is likely to be satisfying for this very mechanical type that enjoys being around metal and moving parts.

ISTJ is excellent at covering all the bases as does the natural science major in **Biochemistry and Molecular Biology** at Marquette University. It allows ISTJs to acquire, explore and analyze life-regulating mechanisms from the traditional world of biology and chemistry. This persevering type will not become discouraged with the precise and intense studies or the effort needed to retain and apply it. Naturally, these qualifications will be well received at research institutes across the nation. Yet, common sense ISTJs like having both of the options: work and/or advanced degrees in the field.

ISFJ with their strong work ethic fits in perfectly at Marquette University. The major in **Biomedical Sciences** will serve this type well. The hands-on nature of health care specialties, such as dental hygienist and respiratory therapist, are very rewarding for ISFJs. This type is intensely private, but also gentle with people and very sincere while helping others. This major provides an excellent foundation for entry, with additional graduate training, to many of the medical professions or research institutions in the health sciences. The department is well resourced and quite up to date with advising for career options in this dynamic field.

ESTP is brilliant at pulling a team together with workable, impromptu redirection. This skill will come in handy as they manage construction projects, nationally and internationally. The school of engineering at Marquette University has this much needed degree in **Construction Engineering and Management** for this restless, action-oriented type. Smooth ESTPs won't pause for reflection, but maybe lunch, as they work with electricians and plumbers. The required co-op helps this type recognize the best way to leverage their skills and knowledge. Dinner with the investors at the end of the day, no problem. At Marquette, graduates will have the financial acumen as well as the engineering credentials.

ESFP will find that Marquette University is one of a small handful of colleges offering the major in **Advertising.** This type is excellent at conveying messages. ESFPs with an artistic talent will enjoy this productive opportunistic curriculum. Marquette University networks generate extensive listings of internships. Students may well arrive at the office ready to go having generated ad copy in the Mac labs on campus. Milwaukee's fine urban design and visual spaces sitting on the western edge of clear, turquoise Lake Michigan provide plenty of visually-pleasing inspiration.

ESFJ occasionally will consider a career in business. To keep ESFJ's interest it must combine profit with the interests of customers or employees within the entrepreneurial organization. The major in **Human Resource Management** is an excellent choice for solicitous, supportive ESFJs. Their strong loyalty and appreciation of organizational structure will be advantageous in this position at large corporations. At Marquette University, there is a solid integration of human values, community responsibility and the business school is assertively pro profit.

ESTJ is a solid bet for a career in **Real Estate** with their predisposition for standard operating procedure. At Marquette, students will gain skills and ability in the transaction of current properties, but equally important the development of future properties. Commercial real estate transactions are well understood on this campus with the College of Engineering and its construction management studies. The College of Business also expertly interfaces the studies with ethical frames of reference for graduates who will necessarily be involved in community changes and development. It's very close to an interdisciplinary degree.

ENFJ is frequently caring and sensitive of others, quite capable of promoting the well-being of those they meet on the job or in the community. The major in **Social Welfare and Justice** at Marquette University is a natural course of study for this type. The curriculum at Marquette University offers a concentration in **Victim Services.** There is clearly a growing need for this expertise as ethical behavior is often snarled, and devalued in legalistic renderings by bureaucracies and courts.

ENTJ is cool under pressure more often than not. This characteristic is ideal for a career in **Public Relations.** Not particularly well known among the millennial generation, this degree gives entry to powerful positions within large business enterprises. First years study public relations principles, sophomores study media writing and advertising. Upper-class students take electives with an interdisciplinary infusion of perspectives. All of this prepares dynamic ENTJs to refine their analytic skills and move confidently to front and center on the public stage.

MASSACHUSETTES INSTITUTE OF TECHNOLOGY

77 Massachusetts Avenue
Cambridge. MA 02139-4307
Website: www.mit.edu
Admissions Telephone: 617-253-4791
Undergraduates: 4,252; 2,323 Men, 1,929 Women
Graduate Students: 6,108

Physical Environment

Massachusetts Institute of Technology is located on the bank of the **Charles River** in Cambridge. The river is like a window to the most happening parts of crowded Boston that include museums, Beacon Hill and many other colleges and universities. The river provides a mental break for MIT students who like to jog along the banks or set sail on the waters. Sailing and crew are well-developed sports here since they tend to rest the mind while floating the river, watching the Boston traffic jams on Storrow Drive. The **Division III** designation of athletics encourages MIT students to be athletes and go out for the teams, as they play at a less demanding level.

This 155-acre **urban** campus has an eclectic mix of buildings, from neoclassic to I.M. Pei design to slab and limestone. Some were put together like a Lego construction, giving the campus a **utilitarian feel**. These buildings don't have names and are referred to by numbers. The "infinite corridor" connects buildings 7, 3, 10, 4 and 8, so that students don't have to walk outside. The "infinite corridor" has lots of student traffic and it's a metaphor for the pursuit of knowledge which is **endless** here.

These underground tunnels are additional meeting places that students use during inclement weather to get to and from class. Dormitories are unadorned and simple as are the lawns and grounds. The front lawn of the "dome" is where students traditionally hold their **"infinite buffet,"** which consists of long lines of tables filled with yummy food. All in all, bright students who like MIT also favor clean cut, angular design and practical spaces.

Social Environment

Students enjoy themselves here if they can balance the intense study schedule with a social life. Students must get used to taking in knowledge as if drinking water from a fire hose. They rank at the top of their high school class and the top ranges of standardized tests. Competitive students are the exception rather than the rule. Some perfectionists strive for all A's. Most students like to **collaborate** and work well in research teams. With high intelligence as the common denominator, the student body has multiple racial, ethnic and economic representation.

MIT students are creative in many ways. They are over the top with their conversations full of far-out, theoretical ideas. They are the musicians who played instruments in and out of school. They are **innovative** in math and science and appreciate delving into the liberal arts and humanities. Most were the acknowledged math and science wizards of their high schools. Some have more difficulty letting go of their Big Cheese, Bright Bulb reputation. Their questions are perceptive and logical. MIT students create a **dynamic learning environment** where it's fascinating to compare iPod programming features with one another. They are likely to linger over lunch and get wrapped up in a discussion about the chemical composition of copper. The majority had at least one out of three perfect SAT subscores. About one-half of the students were valedictorians, yet each student must come to a personal reckoning about the grade point average they will pursue. As former hometown wizards, will they now reach for A's, accept mostly B's or tolerate an occasional or frequent C?

Undergraduates here learn by doing research. The work ethic at MIT is intense and students are set in two frames of mind: **work hard and work harder**. The students understand that there is a lot they don't know. This causes them to behave academically **like grad students**, jumping right into research when the opportunity regularly presents itself.

With such academic rigor, students find **humor** to be paramount in relieving stress. They enjoy clever practical jokes and love pranks. Who can forget about the Boston police car that was hoisted on top of the Dome? MIT undergraduate students bond over their love for the sciences and possibly other things, like food. **Food** is nurturing for undergraduates who are learning to socialize across many diverse cultures and ways of thinking. Parties at MIT form around food often times with the students striving to become chef-like. **Eating together** also includes socializing at some of the finest restaurants in Boston. Most MIT students are down to earth and easy to please in social venues.

MIT students dress for comfort and not trends. Undergrads fit socializing into their schedule when it makes sense with their academic goals. Friendships often start out as a common interest in an academic subject or class. Conversation may roam over to the realm of politics but it is not a dominant topic on this campus. MIT is a unique university, dedicated to advancing technology but very much immersed in humor and the social sciences for balance. Alumni are powerful and tend to observe with a critical eye and doubting mind many of the expansive humanist philosophies of MIT's peer intellectual institutions.

Compatibility with Personality Types and Preferences

Massachusetts Institute of Technology is a powerhouse of technical invention. No surprise there. There are few universities of this caliber in the world. MIT remains true to their technical roots, decade after decade. That being said, MIT's School of Humanities, Arts and Soc Sciences has expansive courses of instruction. An undergraduate can declare a social science major and still be immersed in technology simply by living on this campus. The student body is powerful in intellect, commitment and energy. Both social science and science degrees lean toward objective, technical applications. On graduation students are likely to promote this technology at regional or national levels

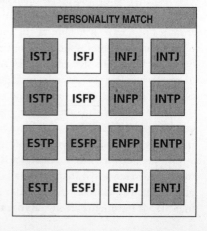

PERSONALITY MATCH

ISTJ	ISFJ	INFJ	INTJ
ISTP	ISFP	INFP	INTP
ESTP	ESFP	ENFP	ENTP
ESTJ	ESFJ	ENFJ	ENTJ

and, of course, use innovation (N) in their work places. There are few universities that educate well in the humanities and provide their graduates interface to the most advanced technical applications available for their discipline. MIT is one of them. Here there is little that goes unnoticed (S) in independent research or student collaboration. Those admitted are competent, objective observers (T) of their environment. Students come with a strong inclination to improve life's experience for themselves and society (F). They are only constrained by the physical laws of nature. All technical discoveries get a thumb's up (P); the new knowledge will be quickly interfaced.

In the following listing of college majors it is important to remember that students can fit into any college and can be successful in any major. We have found that the Personality Types below fit very well at this college. The course-of-study chosen for each Personality Type corresponds to MBTI® research and is presented as an example favorable for that type.

INTJ reigns supreme when it comes to original thinking. It is often difficult for them to clearly express their never-before-heard-of ideas, yet given time, this type will conceptualize plans that will be awesome when revealed. In the **History** major at MIT, their opportunity will come with the two required theses, the subjects of which infuse value into the undergraduates specific education since the department's scope is necessarily broad. INTJ will bring coherent perspective to theme, geographic area or historical period.

ISTP will be surprised and impressed with a look at the **Middle Eastern Studies** at MIT. This interdisciplinary minor is designed to familiarize the student with ancient, secular and fundamentalist Islamic nations. Quite naturally, it is an introductory level of knowledge but highly valuable given the extraordinary conflicts that have erupted in this region since America's withdrawal from southeast Asia. ISTP will search through the electives for courses with an applied perspective such as Issues in Islamic Urbanism.

ISTJ is just the type you would want to manage our national nuclear infrastructure. Their penchant for accuracy and perseverance meets up nicely with this precise science. The national demand for expanding energy sources puts MIT's **Nuclear Science and Engineering** major in the spotlight. Although ISTJs don't seek the political spotlight that accompanies this field, they are drawn to the detail of operating nuclear reactions. The graduate studies department, providing research and solutions for after effects of nuclear accidents, offers an optimistic framework for risk-averse ISTJ in this curriculum.

INTP would be studying the past and the future with the **Earth, Atmosphere and Planetary Sciences** at MIT. This curious type will delight in formulaic rabbit holes sloping into global climate, tectonics and deformation and the solar system. INTP is intrigued by the impossible. In fact they are not sure it is impossible. They will devote all their energy to the solution. Sign them up for planetary missions. They have the patience to work decades toward that sought after human Mars landing in the latter part of this century.

INFP could find their ideal course of studies at the ideal location with the double major in **Science, Technology and Society** at MIT. The purpose of this study is likely to warm the heart of idealistic INFP. It addresses questions many have asked: what is technology doing to help humanity? How and why has society used it in the current practices of journalistic media? It will be INFP who cannot walk away from these difficult and threatening queries. The curriculum is complimentary, i.e. abstract/technical, to most MIT majors. It offers the newly minted MIT graduate an uncharacteristic depth of knowledge in the professional world.

ESTP is a great troubleshooter when it comes to stalled projects involving people and processes. The MIT **Civil and Environmental Engineering** degree also emphasizes another of this type's talents, getting the most bang for the buck. Satisfaction for ESTP means carefully using resources, working with folks in a pleasant manner and solving problems. The Department's direction is applied technology and avoiding resource depletion. This type's gifts synch perfectly with the unstable environment, both political and geographic. Their easygoing personality and passion for a solution find a home at MIT in this degree.

ESFP will elect to perform in the arts on occasion. Their unerring sense of beauty comes in handy in this very visual medium of communication. The flexible major in **Theater Arts** at MIT is the result of student/advisor collaboration. The coursework mirrors the student's interest in theater. Two theses are required and add depth in their area of interest. Other courses can be taken from outside the department. ESFP, always up for novelty and fun, will likely take elective courses in MIT's media and arts lab. The entire engineering acumen is at the disposal of this creative laboratory focused on the visual and moving image.

ENFP might at first think the **Urban Studies and Planning** degree nice for other people, but generally dry and potentially a bit boring. At MIT, however, the department has infused plenty of abstraction. The curriculum cuts across subjects in sociology, business, geography, engineering, education and transportation. Of course technology enhancement is readily apparent in the daily undergrad experience at MIT. Enthusiastic, inventive ENFP will love the idea of enhancing any or many parts of urban living with technology. ENFPs have the empathy and innovation to short circuit development sprawl with solid alternatives in city planning.

ENTP may find the details in the foundation courses for the **Economics** degree at MIT to be less than exciting. In fact, their enthusiasm may peak before they reap the rewards of putting their instinctive hunches into action. For those who stay on, the dynamic financial markets will be theirs to observe and learn about during the independent research phase of the curriculum. ENTP will then step forward to solidify their foundational knowledge in preparation for an MBA or off to work after four undergraduate years.

ESTJ will be able to put their precise ways to good use in the **Aeronautics and Astronautics** degree. ESTJs require prove-it-to-me logic that is ideal for space exploration. Their penchant for thinking and learning in steps is also very desirable in the unforgiving space environments. ESTJ understands the goal: get it right. This degree has numerous departure points within it. The process of getting man into space involves application of the most advanced knowledge across many systems. ESTJ must decide which system to focus on: will it be propulsion or computing in the spacecraft? This degree has MIT written all over it.

ENTJ will not shy away from the **Management Science** degree at MIT's Sloan School of Management. Faculty inundates this undergraduate curriculum with studies in optimization, math modeling and other formulaic approaches to efficiency.

The productive, quick ENTJ sees the reasoning behind this approach and will stay on top of the daily inundation of systems science. They are motivated by competition and move toward taking charge. Upon graduation, this type will confidently enter the risk and reward side of enterprise armed with quantitative skills of the MIT cadre.

INFJ will find that the degree in **Biology** at MIT heavily interfaces mathematical formulas. There is great research interface between the live organisms and the chemical codes dictated through DNA. The major has considerable flexibility and undergrads can find themselves in courses with grad students if the topic interests them. The variety of research is difficult to surmise, but the 70 major research groups throughout the campus gives on a good hint. INFJs are self-directed for sure and can shuttle between the test tubes and electronic data banks with ease. During the go-betweens, this type is looking to push out of the amorphous box.

MIDDLEBURY COLLEGE

Office of Admissions
Middlebury, VT 05753
Website: www.middlebury.edu
Admissions Telephone: 802-443-3000
Undergraduates: 2,480; 1,217 Men, 1,263 Women

Physical Environment

Middlebury College is located in the north-central part of Vermont, about an hour from Burlington and three hours from Montreal, Canada. The average winter temperatures range below the **freezing mark**. Ross Commons dining hall and dormitories are connected so students can walk the interior hallways. Students who make friends with ice and snow head for the skating ponds, hockey rink and nearby **ski** slopes. Those from southern climates who are not skiers tend to be surprised by the weather here.

Although the location is isolated, the town has about 8,000 people. The campus, established in the 1800s, is separated in quarters by four streets, Weybridge, College, South Main and South Street. It is a large campus to travel. The **academic quad** is surrounded by the Mead Memorial Chapel, the McCullough student center, the main library and multiple academic halls. On the other side of College Street there are important buildings such as the Freeman International Center and Atwater dining hall, which are busy places, especially in the summer when students are focused on one single task: learning a foreign language.

Middlebury's residence halls are referred to as **'The Commons'** and this is where first-year seminars are held. There is an ongoing refurbishment of these older buildings converting or adding new residence spaces. There are five buildings in the Commons and freshmen identify with the community of their particular residence. Taking seminars in the building where they live, with the same group of students, makes it easy to make friends in the first year. It encourages **academic conversation** between students, while they eat lunch or dinner or study in dorm lounges. This physical housing arrangement also facilitates interaction with professors and deans who live on the same floor with their families. These faculty members are often responsible to coordinate social events such as field trips and socials for students.

All juniors and seniors on campus are required to rotate out of their Commons to other housing options across campus. However, students, often elect to move with their Commons hallmates in small groups to other residences. With this 4/2 plan, Middlebury students will also get a new infusion of friends from the other Commons.

Social Environment

Middlebury College attracts **super-achiever** students, usually clean-cut, **serious** and determined to study and get the most out of college. They abide by rules, respect convention and ranked in the top five percent of their high school graduating class. Middlebury College tends to mirror their hometown secondary educational experience, orderly, intense and productive. Risk taking within the undergraduate student population tends to be of two types: intellectual exploration and **pushing the edge athletically** with winter sports like snowboarding.

Sports are a way for students to get out of their heads. They take a break from incessant academic speculations. With assistance and support from the college, several recent graduates developed Muggle Quidditch international competitions held at Middlebury College during good weather. For those unfamiliar with Harry Potter, two teams compete on a soccer field by running around with a cape and riding a broom. This game is not for those students who care about what others think, because they certainly look funny in these outfits. At Middlebury this game takes on a life of its own, regardless of how Harry Potter played it. 'Silly' works when undergraduates want to take a break here. So successful, the competitions and administration of the International Quidditch Association had to move to New York City in 2011.

Did we mention Middlebury students are **cerebral**? Undergraduates gain an exposure to foreign cultures and civilizations through the exceptionally strong emphasis on **foreign language study**. Through off-campus study in other countries, they synthesize multicultural perspectives with their academic disciplines. Many become aware of social issues, such as poverty and immigrant laborers, that are present in northern Vermont. Blessed with high intellectual ability, these students combine careers with research and service to the community. They take their place in quiet leadership positions after graduation.

Compatibility with Personality Types and Preferences

Middlebury College is rooted in historical literature. The academic environment honors the works of the early American poets with a philosophical thread. The developing American psyche of the 1800s combined with the poetic observations on life's meaning painted an ethical and responsible citizen in this literature. That ethic is studied at Middlebury College. It prompts the undergraduate to let go of self-oriented perspectives that could be considered intellectually inhibiting. Individual goals of the undergraduate student are likely to be interfaced with responsibility toward the world. This is a strong overarching theme at Middlebury College.

By using multiple viewpoints, questions are posed and faculty asks students to find shades of meaning (N) within the several answers offered by students. The academic studies are all about anticipation and inspiration. Students must be comfortable with ambiguity at some level. However, there is optimism in the student body that ambiguity will retreat and clear purpose will emerge. Middlebury students are inwardly (I) confident. They are expectant of serious and even tedious study to achieve their goals. Their resultant expertise is not comprised of facts or skills, but it is an overall intellectual view of the world through the lens of their academic discipline. That viewpoint is abstract and graduates are often cause- and passion-related upon graduation (J).

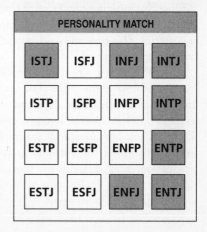

PERSONALITY MATCH

ISTJ	ISFJ	INFJ	INTJ
ISTP	ISFP	INFP	INTP
ESTP	ESFP	ENFP	ENTP
ESTJ	ESFJ	ENFJ	ENTJ

In the following listing of college majors it is important to remember that students can fit into any college and can be successful in any major. We have found that the Personality Types below fit very well at this college. The course-of-study chosen for each Personality Type corresponds to MBTI® research and is presented as an example favorable for that type.

INFJ absolutely must look at the **Biology** major at Middlebury College. The department has state of the art technical equipment and imagination to keep vision-prone INFJs happy. These individuals are always dreaming about what could be—given the current state of things. They do not live in an ivory tower. Rather this type starts with reality and typically develops a darned good grounding. This completed, INFJs strap on all kinds of wonderful goals that could improve the current state of things. Independent research is a strong thread within this curriculum. Students are expected/encouraged to develop their own strands of investigation. Additionally, Middlebury's extraordinary programs in the language can give this type access to research in their choice of geographic areas around the globe. How about a minor in **Chinese**?

INTJ will find that the **Geography** major at Middlebury explores the abstraction of space coming together with human utilization. The department website elegantly describes the nature of this long-standing discipline. It is an excellent choice for INTJ who is original and digs deeply into all subjects to which they are attracted. INTJ can be assured that this major will open a lifetime of extraordinary, novel thought as paired with exacting measurements in scale and units of human utility. The discipline is applied to square inches and to continental land forms plus all the inbetweens. You go for it INTJ, society needs a lot of bright young adults to enter this field. Fairly resistant to current political trends, this discipline has the long legs for applicability to intractable problems.

ISTJ is one for knowing the facts and keeping them quite straight. This type could easily become an archivist or librarian cataloging and retrieving precious documents and everyday useful knowledge. The major in **Literary Studies** would provide this type with an uncommonly fine understanding of literary works. Thorough ISTJ will precisely capture the author's literary meaning by use of an outlined method, finding the building blocks of perspective within each of the world's masterpieces. The breadth of world authors included in this major will not deter ISTJ, rather it will attract. This type will easily select a specific period or culture to study as required by the department.

INTP wants to create and develop complicated plans. The goal is important, yet the process is the prize. The major in **Theater** at Middlebury offers much in the way of process. The department approaches theater through analysis. INTPs excel at analysis. Drama interpretation through rich study of literature will absorb INTPs. There are multiple major tracks and specializations within this major. INTPs are likely to look for dilemma as an inherent part of the arts they pursue. After graduation, they might move toward performance or administration of the arts. Clever, ingenious INTPs may also secure the business acumen through appropriate internships to act as an agent.

ENTP might get intrigued by the major in **International Politics and Economics** at Middlebury College because of the complexity. This curious and restless type must have complexity in their world. Second majors and minors are not approved because of the sheer volume of content in this major. ENTPs may overcome hesitation though because they are attracted to the exercise of power, typically optimistic and confident. This interdisciplinary major is well-supported by the several departments. ENTP will enjoy jumping from one perspective to another through the variety in study abroad, foreign language and regional specialization.

ENFJ could be ideal in a career associated with higher education. The major in **American Studies** at Middlebury College offers a smorgasbord of subjects on the list of courses approved for the curriculum. The department approaches the discipline in slices of perspective securing much from current trends in the American social climate as created by the media.

ENTJ likes complexity with a little competition added for pizzazz. The major in **Environmental Studies** at Middlebury College is a pizza with everything on it. This interdisciplinary curriculum offers 13 specializations. ENTJ is required to order a slice with half anchovies, but will still need to select other toppings from the list of 12.

MUHLENBERG COLLEGE

2400 Crew Street
Allentown, PA 18104-5586
Website: www.muhlenberg.edu
Admissions Telephone: 484-664-3200
Undergraduates: 2,370; 1,034 Men, 1,336 Women

Physical Environment

Located in the Lehigh Valley, Muhlenberg College feels like the geographical and philosophical middle ground between **Pennsylvania Dutch** country and the city of **Philadelphia.** General Muhlenberg's brass statue stands in front of the Gothic chapel, the first building on this campus. Students' input was essential in the recent construction of residence halls which fosters student involvement and a sense of community. Completion of phase II at Seegers Union has added more inviting spaces for student collaboration. The science building with its superb facilities draws in students who can see themselves using the sophisticated equipment and are interested in pre-med and pre-vet programs. Another distinct building, the newer **Trexler Theatre,** encourages some to cross over and participate in the Broadway-quality productions offered by the drama department. Their exceptional black box theater tempts some students from other majors to try out writing and acting. Moyer Hall Forum is an exceptionally interesting lecture series, open to the public, and draws in undergraduates who are interested in culture and religion. The combination of the newer glass addition to the "homey," older gym supports the widespread **athleticism** on campus. The campus has a landscape that entrances a viewer with its picturesque rolling countryside and doors painted in Amish red. It speaks to the purposeful perspective maintained within the Muhlenberg study body.

Social Environment

Muhlenberg students are **very active** and vocal in the classroom and socially. They thrive on academic assignment, friendly competition and a challenge. They have a conventional sense of risk-taking, like pulling harmless pranks. The majority of students played sports in high school and enjoyed it, so they continue in college. They like taking the one semester of required physical education. Through these activities many become confident and find their academic niche which fits in with Muhlenberg.

Since 95 percent of students live on campus, they form a loyal, tight-knit community. They are **high-achieving** and rank at or near the top quarter of their class. Many Jewish students and ethnic minorities feel quite comfortable here because there is a sizeable number of each at Muhlenberg. The Institute for Jewish-Christian understanding brings the perspective of multiple religious beliefs and attracts students who are spiritually inclined. **Music** is a medium on the campus to support reflective extracurriculars. They value work that helps humanity, whether through research or active volunteerism in the Lehigh Valley or abroad. They appreciate their surroundings and understand quality when they see it which reflects their hometown values. They often enjoy getting to know their professors and are usually confident in those **mentoring relationships**. Students graduate with a solid moral perspective of responsibility and citizenship. While mindful of the recession and the extra time it will take to land that first step on the career ladder, graduates have the resilience to attain personal and career success.

Compatibility with Personality Types and Preferences

A Muhlenberg education is sanely traditional, solid and moral. A student will find academic guidance very clear and spelled out with detail in the course catalog. Here, friendly and frequent (E) conversation is welcome and one would likely find students conversing around the campus pretty much anytime. This carries over to the classroom where discussion is guided and amplified by faculty. In this manner, students acquire the content and knowledge. The educational philosophy prompts the individual student to accept responsibility, become productive and offer humane service (F) to others. The Lutheran religious tradition comes forward in this way. You can also find a simple efficiency in the academic course of studies and the campus recreation options. Excess or wastefulness of human energy and earth's bounty is dimly viewed. Departments are well interfaced with the economy and job markets that graduates will enter. Academic experience outside of the classroom is highlighted throughout the curriculum. Students expecting to transfer to professional schools find the same care and advising for this next step as those starting employment on graduation. At Muhlenberg, undergraduates seek balance and use of personal talents as a moral imperative.

PERSONALITY MATCH

ISTJ	ISFJ	INFJ	INTJ
ISTP	ISFP	INFP	INTP
ESTP	ESFP	ENFP	ENTP
ESTJ	ESFJ	ENFJ	ENTJ

In the following listing of college majors it is important to remember that students can fit into any college and can be successful in any major. We have found that the Personality Types below fit very well at this college. The course-of-study chosen for each Personality Type corresponds to MBTI® research and is presented as an example favorable for that type.

ENFJ will find one of the eight **Foreign Languages** offered at Muhlenberg College a desirable course of study with any choice of major. Typically astute with languages, a second or third language magnifies the power of this articulate type. The faculty has the Language Learning Center at their disposal to develop and create lessons for undergraduate students. ENFJs will be well positioned with this major to pursue graduate work in disciplines that typically interest them: communication, education and counseling.

ENTJ is going to like the practical idea of combining the **Asian Traditions** minor with their declared major. Both courses in Modern China and Modern Japan will position this student for 21st century careers in emerging markets. The five required courses are interdisciplinary and chosen from these departments: philosophy, history, political science, sociology and religion. It all makes sense for this type who wants to make things happen. ENTJs are likely to appreciate the sound practicality that is found at Muhlenberg.

ESFJ will readily approve of lifetime fitness through physical exercise and activity. Muhlenberg requires all students to take the **Principles of Fitness and Wellness**. It connects the dots between exercise and achieving "the highest potential of personal well being." The excellent athletic facilities are equally matched by students' enthusiasm for their athletes, club sports and NCAA competitive teams. Travel and service are preferred activities for ESFJs. The major in **Italian Language and Literature** could be ideal for career tracks in international tourism, language translation and the arts. Being sound and fit, ESFJs can handle the rigors of air travel.

ESTJ with a mind for numbers will totally like the Accounting Department at Muhlenberg. With an eye to the international nature of finances, the department encourages a study abroad at University of Maastricht in the Netherlands in approved business courses. **Accounting** majors at Muhlenberg can seek the certified public accounting credential by completing 30 extra credits in the department on campus or transfer into a Master of Science in Accounting degree at a nearby university. ESTJs naturally want to complete the degree in the most efficient way possible. The Muhlenberg program is excellent for this type.

ENFP will be able to take advantage of their warm persona in the **Media and Communication** major. This major introduces students to the pervasive presence of media messaging in our culture today. Media theories and application compose the second focus in the major with courses like Audience Analysis. Students will also produce media in film, radio, television and/or advertising.

ESFP finds the **Dance** major on this campus congruent with the college's philosophy that athletics and wellness are foundational building blocks in life. This type's energy and enthusiasm would be welcome in the strong dance and theater programs on campus. ESFPs are natural entertainers and will find it easy to connect dance and drama. Double majors are an option, and ESFP may elect **Dance Therapy** for a second major.

ISFJ will be comfortable pairing the minor in **Public Health** with a major in **Social Sciences**. The coursework in the minor prepares ISFJs to enter the helping professions with administrative acumen. This skill set can give conscientious ISFJ a leg up on securing a rewarding career track in bureaucratic American health systems. It will be very helpful as they advocate for their patients.

ESTP is going to take advantage of the Investment Society club and the **Finance** major at Muhlenberg. ESTPs like to acquire skills through experience. The department provides undergraduates with a sound understanding of complex financial mechanisms. The department seems to avoid the common practice of linking foundational courses with trendy cultural paradigms. ESTP will be more comfortable with this approach since it is absent electives and mandates that can dilute skills and understanding in this discipline – a discipline which can be punishing in cyclical and bear markets.

NEW YORK UNIVERSITY

22 Washington Square North
New York, NY 10011
Website: www.nyu.edu
Admissions Telephone: 212-998-4500
Undergraduates: 20,281; 7,929 Men, 12,352 Women
Graduates: 12,960

Physical Environment

The physical environment of New York City is part and parcel of the NYU experience. On the way to class students walk in, through and around tall skyscrapers, **negotiating the jamboree** of streets and traffic outside the various NYU buildings. Washington Square offers some respite within its park near the Washington Arc. The arc at Fifth Avenue is a city landmark and a meeting place for students. Nearby Greenwich Village attracts students to its coffee shops. Many visiting high school students react to the university as they do to the city: they either love it or hate it, with nothing in-between. Some fall in love with it at first sight while others, realizing that NYU and the city are intricately woven, are not sure whether they could manage the university *and* the city. However, those who enroll at this **very selective** university settle in and take advantage of the myriad activities in and around NYU.

Students like to mill around Washington Park, watching singers, performers and chess players. Some even like to take in operas at the Met and legendary plays and musicals on Broadway. Students who are already "citified" become even smarter at navigating the "city that never sleeps." Reserved students about to explore the immenseness of this city for the first time may like the anonymity of being in a wave of people entering the subway. Even the livelier NYU student can find that needed quiet nook in one of the numerous NYU libraries. The city is a research laboratory for the social science majors with its **over-the-top internship** opportunities. Successful students have an inclination and desire to engage the city.

There is no traditional, self-enclosed campus and with **14 schools in six different buildings**, students negotiate a **complex physical landscape**. The renovated Center for Genomics and Systems Biology left the outside façade while completely gutting the interior to provide the technical support systems one can imagine the research studies will utilize. Perhaps in deference to politically correct trends, the NYU Catholic Center is scheduled for a 2012 renovation into a 'spiritual life center.' The city's constant stimulation of the five senses draws a physically and emotionally resilient student. For those who can manage themselves and their time, NYU and the Big Apple are exceptionally rewarding.

Social Environment

The name recognition and **excellence** of the programs attract many students with many different personalities. Each incoming student searches out like-minded friends to form a stable place from which to explore the city. For some people it can be a month's long task to find that close-knit sense of community. Very often the social life and emotional connection to NYU is through the particular department or school a student attends. This is supported by the fact that about a quarter of the students do not live in university housing and disappear into their city apartments after classes. Students in the College of Arts and Sciences come across the greatest variety of individuals in their courses. Tisch School of Art has a very cohesive social scene with the fewest traditional-minded students. Stern School of Business students are likely to take more conservative views.

Those students who sift through the several hundred extracurricular and interest groups find their niche. The extensive physical fitness facility is a magnet and meeting place for all. For some students the social scene revolves around intramural and club sports, for others private parties and the local club scene keeps them so busy that they may need an extra semester to graduate.

NYU is distinguished by its enrollment of undergraduate students from many ethnicities and **cultural backgrounds**. The campus environment is much like the novel nearby eateries with a Chinese restaurant that also serves Puerto Rican dishes. The NYU student is exposed to an extraordinary number of views and perspectives. They are fairly **assertive** individuals able to take advantage of the university's extensive academic offerings and enjoy physical and social interface between the university and the city. NYU students form a student body of very bright, preppy, funky, funny, actively involved individuals. Yet, the university is subject to the troubling national trend of significant male under-representation in its student body.

Compatibility with Personality Types and Preferences

New York University may seem like a graceful enigma. On a first visit the university can seem cold, distant and indifferent. The next visit changes your mind as you see the careful wrap-around services and attention given to the students by the administration and faculty. It is indicative of how the university grew as the city's namesake and was always tuned to the city population and city needs. As expected, the resources of this world-class city extend into and throughout the university which offers 2,500 courses of instruction. NYU accommodates most personality preferences with an exceptional selection of learning options and degrees. The student who comes to NYU already is, or wants to become, swanky in the current and classic sense. Potential students are attracted to the intellectual environment as well as the social life of the city.

The required list of core courses, as outlined in the Morse Academic Plan, guides students in the classics during the first two years. The faculty presents complicated social issues from the classics and ancient thought that can be objectively viewed by statistics. The curriculum goes to considerable length to reveal what the limits of that objective approach can be (T). The graduate of NYU is also going to explore how the written word in historical texts creates society (N). Both this study of objectivity and the creation of society are highly abstract and not often featured in required core courses at universities. Similarly, the NYU website featured a compelling video on the use of mathematics. The portrait of the

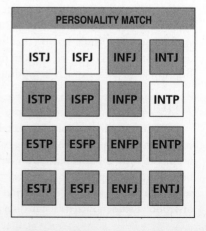

PERSONALITY MATCH

ISTJ	ISFJ	INFJ	INTJ
ISTP	ISFP	INFP	INTP
ESTP	ESFP	ENFP	ENTP
ESTJ	ESFJ	ENFJ	ENTJ

math discipline painted by the NYU faculty, as it applied to future America, could entice a student to declare the math major. The student who is successful here can cope with the demands of the city (S) and can glide across the millions of steps on city sidewalks that they will traverse with the same underlying grace of this university, so deserving of it namesake.

In the following listing of college majors it is important to remember that students can fit into any college and can be successful in any major. We have found that the Personality Types below fit very well at this college. The course-of-study chosen for each Personality Type corresponds to MBTI® research and is presented as an example favorable for that type.

INFJ can bring their insights to **Medieval and Renaissance Studies**. This major will occupy INFJs as they ponder the decades of time between these two distinct periods. Their careful expertise in the discipline will be in demand if they pursue internships in archival work places likely right in New York City.

ENTJ may pursue **European and Mediterranean Studies.** The department offers a five year BA/MA and a political science focus. High powered ENTJs can secure internships with international organizations in the city, possibly the United Nations. Diplomacy may be an area of interest because of the inherent power and need for decisive leadership in the career field. ENTJ may select the European language of greatest utility for their intended career track, or perhaps add a second.

ENFP has the big picture and abstract perspectives that it takes for the curriculum in **Metropolitan Studies** at NYU. For those who pursue this interdisciplinary major, careers materialize in the not for profit, public administration and government planning sectors. This is fortunate because ENFPs like to solve problems and consider a variety of solutions and may just pursue each of these career tracks.

ENFJ likes to be independent and yet in close empathy with others. The degree in **Sociology** at NYU so credible because of the hundreds of ethnic languages. ENFJs will combine their interests with societal needs and pursue research topics in this underappreciated discipline. Much of the curriculum is focused on American culture and its shortcomings. ENFJ pursuing an international career track may have to propose a strand of research that identifies social inequalities in other cultures or nations of interest to them.

INTJ and NYU are a delightful combination of letters. This type will jump right into questioning the historical texts and the art forms that are studied in the core courses of the Morse Plan. Questioning is this type's specialty and this level of abstraction will be welcomed by INTJs in these freshman and sophomore courses. Beyond that, the field of **Economics** offers limitless speculation with hard, factual data to power INTJ innovations. This all works for these private, power house thinkers. The department offers two tracks, the more practical policy concentration and the more abstract theory concentration which INTJs will likely explore first.

ENTP absolutely enjoys the idea of the Mind. Powerful thinkers in their own right but not particularly verbally savvy; others sometimes miss ENTPs' penetrating, original perspectives. There is a very good interdisciplinary major for this type, titled **Language of the Mind**. It crisscrosses through linguistics, philosophy and psychology. ENTPs will puzzle at night, quietly, to interface these disparate disciplines. With much practice, they will capture the dreamy ideas the next morning for class! The nature of language is precise at its basic and linguistics keep the abstract interfaces with philosophy and psychology grounded in this major.

ESTJ can bring their quick, crisp decision making to the health field with a degree in **Neural Science.** This degree focuses on one of the new frontiers: the brain. NYU has the resources and the medium to grow both ideas and biological cells as this science moves forward. Large, expansive, roaming NYU will sometimes challenge this type, but this major will provide refuge with its science base.

ESFJ will be the lucky child who studies **Psychology** at NYU. The department is exceptionally focused yet intentional in its excellent survey of this evolving field for the undergraduate students. Courses in the natural sciences, social sciences and lab research really round out the foundational studies. Research seeking to understand human personality abounds at NYU. The course Social Psychology focuses on the impact of individual behavior on the larger group. This type likes to deliver personal services in schools, hospitals or community health centers. NYU has a fine observatory for studying individuals within the larger community: New York City.

ESTP just might decide the BS in **Computer Science** at NYU offers the efficiency they like. The degree is tailor-made for the ESTPs who might meet the requirements for the degree in three undergraduate years. This would leave a couple semesters to enjoy the Morse plan academic options and have fun in the city. ESTPs with 4 or 5 on their AP language exam may opt out of the foreign language requirement.

ESFP could select a minor in **Biology** at NYU since it will allow them to explore career tracks that interface human health and preventative medicine. ESFPs might respond to the growing need for specialists in addiction research. Undergrads can count on good advising for career decisions with the major sociology, centered on American problems, or the major in psychology bolstered by exceptional research studies at the doctoral level.

ISFP could bring their special talents to the curriculum in **Urban Design Studies.** This major prompts undergraduates to use their fine-tuned senses. The course work at the elective level will delight thoughtful ISFPs who prefer to work with real services/products for real people. These titles bring smiles to the face: Parks, Plants & People, Reading the City and Architecture in New York: Field (Fun) Study. Careers that come to mind in museums, conservation, city and metropolitan planning and historical preservation would appeal to ISFPs.

ISTP understands the value of a minor in **Physics**. In fact, it probably appeals to this type so handy with physical and mechanical properties. The minor complements many other concentrations in the sciences, math and engineering. Independent and objective, ISTP can sit back for the first two years filling the core courses within the Morse Plan while picking up the physics minor. Junior and senior years can be reserved for completing the major concentration.

INFP with the love of books, fairly typical, may decide to pursue a minor in **Irish Studies** at NYU. In addition to the mythic qualities of this nation, the poetry and drama often laced throughout their history will very much appeal to this type. Perhaps INFP will move toward the career of librarian or research specialist. This potential focus will definitely take great advantage of NYU's unusual archival collection in Irish Americana. The distinguished professors on faculty, specialists in Irish studies, will come to know and warm up to the INFPs who bring creativity, caring and the need to express their vision through the arts or written word.

NORTHEASTERN UNIVERSITY

360 Huntington Avenue
Boston, MA 02115
Website: www.northeastern.edu
Admissions Telephone: 617-373-8780
Undergraduates: 15,699; 7,751 Men, 7,948 Women

Physical Environment

Northeastern University is located in that part of Boston defined by the Huntington and Mass Ave intersection. It's extremely **accessible** by both the MBTA subway trains, which stop right on campus, and the trolley that runs on a continuous loop on Huntington Avenue. Students quickly learn to navigate the city and so a car on this campus, or in Boston for that matter, is a burden rather than an amenity. Northeastern University has buildings and spaces that support African American and Latino culture. A favorite for all students is the Curry student center, which stays open late for students who like to watch television or hang out. As Northeastern grew, more residential complexes were added around its perimeter including the Marino Athletic center. Hence the campus perimeter is **asymmetrical** because it borders other colleges and is divided by a busy avenue.

The main campus looks a bit like a business park with modern buildings, cobble-stoned walkways and high rise elevations. The effect of this physical environment for undergraduate students is to subliminally remind them that they are preparing for the real **world of employment**. On Northeastern's campus they will become comfortable **navigating the crowded cityscape** and the buildings in the financial districts. The opportunities to explore the city like a tourist are numerous and fun in good weather. Students get their city legs rather quickly and the mandatory co-ops and internship programs in Boston blur the line between it and the university environment.

Social Environment

Northeastern started out as the first American branch of the YMCA in the very late 1800s. Boston was then a city of immigrants who were hard-working and looking to live out their dreams. The YMCA helped out in many ways. It offered a reading room and lectures. Young men attended these lectures and used the library. Northeastern has re-invented itself many times over since then, yet the **YMCA philosophy** of serving the community remains a strong feature of the educational philosophy. NU hosts the Volunteer Clearing House on campus and, spur of the moment as well as planned **volunteer** events in Boston are viable options for today's millennial undergrads. They also readily embrace the **urban lifestyle** of Boston. Most come from suburban areas of New England and find the expected ethnic representation within the student body that most large, international cities draw.

Students and parents are attracted by the robust co-op program. It offers **excellent job experience** and occasionally a paid position, often during the summer. These field experiences start early in the sophomore year and are frequent to the point that most Northeastern students graduate in five years, instead of four. Students must be motivated to find such work during the co-op terms. Most students secure enough real work experience to successfully enter the job market on graduation.

Parents are also attracted by the administration's encouragement of family and parent involvement in the campus life of their student. NU encourages parents to inform the college if their student is experiencing a difficult adjustment to college. The university publishes an excellent handbook for parents and families which nicely outlines the administrative in's and out's of the campus.

Socially, they get involved in clubs, activities and sports. Some really jump into student government and leadership activities, honing their skills for graduation. The college plays at the Division I level and students like to watch the Huskies basketball games. Some develop business and individual personas that match the offices of their co-op experience. Others may join in with one of the many interest groups on campus, bypassing for now the professional lifestyle. Regardless, on this campus all undergraduates will explore their personal expectations in relationship to work and career.

Compatibility with Personality Types and Preferences

Northeastern University is true to its history of preparing students for employment and careers. The modern urban setting of this campus adds credibility to the college experience. Students and faculty are in agreement that advanced skills and capabilities are desired. These skills and capabilities are acquired through a sequential learning (S) process, typically involving direct work experience.

The mentoring and advising relationship between the faculty and students (F) is carefully conducted. Students at Northeastern enroll to acquire expertise and professors have this knowledge to provide. The faculty-student advising is reciprocal and dynamic. It generates its own information set which reflects Boston's economy. The university is very much in tune with the city's financial fortunes. Energy flows between the students, faculty and city giving the student's day an outward feel (E) of productive, purposeful activity. Students are drawn to this energy and learn to manage studies, city internships, volunteer service and the persistent call of the vibrant city social scene.

Of near equal focus to productivity is the volunteer service that university students provide to the ethnic neighborhoods within a short T ride of their campus. Undergraduate student leadership is adept at sizing up the needs of these nearby communities. Volunteer service to the community is encouraged, expected and remarkable for its quantity. It is a natural extension of the university's relationship with the community. Similarly, the educational philosophy really emphasizes multiple cultural experiences, the more the better, to prepare graduates for careers of accomplishment.

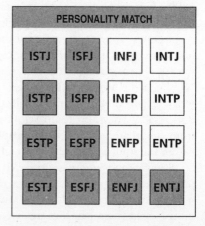

PERSONALITY MATCH

ISTJ	ISFJ	INFJ	INTJ
ISTP	ISFP	INFP	INTP
ESTP	ESFP	ENFP	ENTP
ESTJ	ESFJ	ENFJ	ENTJ

In the following listing of college majors it is important to remember that students can fit into any college and can be successful in any major. We have found that the Personality Types below fit very well at this college. The course-of-study chosen for each Personality Type corresponds to MBTI® research and is presented as an example favorable for that type.

ISTP, if musically talented, will be intrigued by the **Music Technology** major at Northeastern. It connects the aural tones of music with the logic of computers and sound equipment. ISTP takes in information through their senses and thinks with it logically. In this case, musical patterns, tones and rhythms are interfaced with software. The degree requires music composition and this type could compose a kaleidoscope of notes into a pleasing musical track.

ISTJ often has the attraction to details in the business world. The degree in Business Administration at Northeastern has seven robust concentrations. In fact, the college encourages undergraduates to select two concentrations or add a minor from other disciplines. ISTJs could declare **Finance and Insurance**. It focuses on the precise valuation and legal research of properties. It is an intensive, solo activity often. This suits masterful ISTJ. As a member of a regional properties enterprise, such as Trump properties, ISTJ is valued for accurate, comprehensive input. They bring stability in the world of merger and acquisition.

ISFJ likes research combined with structure and some level of predictability. The major in **Criminology and Public Policy** very much orients itself to prevention through structure and predictability. Students find the curriculum centering on the individuals who commit crime (criminals), and the institutions, organizations and communities that unknowingly enable crime. The major requires knowledge of current social research. Establishing personal connections with others in this humanely-oriented career track is much preferred by this type.

ISFP is an active soul that enjoys the outdoors for the most part. The combined major in **Environmental Studies** & Environmental Geology can certainly accommodate. It all appeals to ISFP's boots-on approach to learning. ISFPs are good at discerning the impact of human activity on the physical environment. They have the technical predisposition to excel in the geology courses and labs which utilize a fair amount of equipment.

ESTP has a fine memory for detail and they miss very few if it interests them. The business degree with a concentration in **Accounting** may seem a little dry on first pass. However, that is misleading, especially at Northeastern University where ongoing interface with the career field reveals the increasing responsibility and power that is conferred on accountants. This suits ESTP who also likes to be where the action level is high. As an accountant or chief operating officer, ESTPs bring commitment to getting past problems with an acute awareness of the issue at hand. There are internships available just a few T stops away on the subway in the financial district.

ESFP is a creative soul and this might easily be channeled into music. The major in **Music Industry** at Northeastern is ideal for this type. The department takes advantage of the social network between Northeastern and the city of Boston. The city offers much entertainment for the 20-something crowd and ESFPs excel at entertainment. In the process, they will gain the skills and network to secure a position within this major industry, perhaps in Nashville, Orlando or maybe with Apple iTunes.

ESFJ will really approve of Northeastern's emphasis on community service and awareness of urban needs just outside the multi-storied dormitories of this tall, compact campus. This type enjoys bringing information and coordination to the work environment. They are very social and often combine this ease with their attention to detail. The major in **Organizational Communication** is a discipline that would interest and make sense to them. The degree easily prepares ESFJs for public relations positions in large organizations, business, government, teaching, etc.

ESTJ is usually comfortable in positions of authority. They tend to be natural administrators. ESTJs could declare the business major with a concentration in Supply Chain **Management**. This type will analyze objective data with ease in relation to critical resource allocation. Advanced study and certification can lead to powerful positions within manufacturing enterprises. Northeastern University is ideal for helping ESTJs orient to multiple ethnic perspectives on productivity.

ENFJ is most enthusiastic when working on behalf of others in friendly supportive work places. This type also likes to generate creative solutions with the big picture in mind. The major in **Human Services** at Northeastern offers it all. The major is also paired in a dual degree with **American Sign Language**. Obviously this would move ENFJ into the world of hearing-impaired. At the same time, it could take advantage of the type's natural language ability and skill in communicating causes they believe in.

ENTJ will thrive in active Boston and on the Northeastern campus. This type would do well to merge the concentration in **Management Information Systems** with coursework in entrepreneurship also offered at the university. The major provides strong training for positions as systems analyst, programmer or database designer. Each of these career tracks is ideal for small businesses. The broad skills and expectations for successful small business appeal to ENTJs who can maximize their leadership and strategic planning skills. The entrepreneurial side of information technology comes naturally to ENTJ.

NORTHWESTERN UNIVERSITY

633 Clark Street
Evanston, IL 60208
Website: www.northwestern.edu
Admissions Telephone: 847-491-7271
Undergraduates: 8,413; 4,037 Men, 4,376 Women
Graduate Students: 7,938

Physical Environment

Northwestern University is located 12 miles **north of Chicago**, on the banks of Lake Michigan, and offers a distinct suburban environment despite the proximity to the city. The campus has many tall, modern buildings that offer spectacular views of the lake. The typical freezing temperatures in the winter can dip ten degrees below the nearby inland neighborhoods because the **northern winds** sweep in from the lake. Students enjoy riding their bike on campus and the hardy may still use them in winter weather, when the walkways are scrupulously snow plowed.

Northwestern houses popular majors in the Kellogg School of **Business** and Medill School of **Journalism**. Significantly expanded in fall 2012, the **Technological Institute Infill** now offers students analytic labs for biomedical research and a clean room. Located to increase awareness by all in the college community, it showcases the rich learning experience within the chemistry department curriculum. The Norris Center functions as a student union that houses offices for recognized student groups. The handbook of policies amplifying contracts and direction for various group activities is comprehensive. The **"Rock"** is near and dear to the students' hearts and gets painted pretty much every night with promotional slogans or to announce an upcoming event. This tradition of 100+ years is now enhanced with a webcam view that is refreshed each five minutes. How about that for getting the word out.

Social Environment

Students accepted to Northwestern rank in the top five percent of their high school graduation class. They are attracted to the **well-resourced schools** within the university for communication, education and social policy, music and engineering. The faculty, always pursuing leading edge research in all of the schools and liberal arts, reaches out to undergraduates through their fascinating research designs. These undergraduates come from the Midwest region and from throughout the U.S. and the world. The majority graduated from public high schools and are comfortable talking about and living with diversity. Northwestern University is for those students who want **the full college experience**. The university is one of the Big Ten schools with Division I sports and has lots of school spirit. Along with the enjoyment of athletics, the performing arts are a big part of the culture here. The **Greek life** is vibrant and Greek chapter houses are involved in scholarship, fundraising and civic initiatives. The chapters supplement the residential life experience for both Greek and non-Greek.

Northwestern University is not historically or currently affiliated with any religion yet there is significant student-led religious presence on the campus. The university attracts students who appreciate the order and structure of the physical campus and the extraordinary research facilities. Undergraduates tend to be socially adept and go in for group activities when taking a break from securing that foundation of **solid liberal arts** subjects. The dance marathon, a tradition started in 1975, raises substantial funds for Chicago area charities.

Compatibility with Personality Types and Preferences

Northwestern University has an expectant feel to it. A walk through the campus reveals a very large physical facility. The open spaces between buildings are filled with energetic, purposeful students moving toward their next destination. That might be a class, research labs, social club or internship since rest and relaxation is probably allocated to the middle of the night and weekend mornings. These students are engaged (E) and interested in connecting with each other. There is a sense of individuality, almost as a personal educational mission among each member of the student body.

Educational study, casual conversation and academic discussion with other like-minded movers and shakers is common. The purpose is to gather up and digest (T) knowledge. This is to prepare the graduate for a professional position, preferably as a leader within their career field. Political passion within the school and department faculties at Northwestern University is common. It translates into firm positions on the current cultural topics. Traditional perspectives are not noticeable, but rather there is an undercurrent of improvement for present day American society.

Students who are successful at Northwestern select their major with certainty. The schools of engineering, journalism, communication, education and music are very visible and accessible to the whole undergraduate student body through elective courses. Undergraduate academic policies within each of these specialized schools reaches out and encourages the undecided student to identify and align toward their individual interests. Students typically bring intensity to their major once identified. Northwestern University is a bold institution, mindful of their ability to inform the public square.

In the following listing of college majors it is important to remember that students can fit into any college and can be successful in any major. We have found that the Personality Types below fit very well at this college. The course-of-study chosen for each Personality Type corresponds to MBTI® research and is presented as an example favorable for that type.

INTJ would find a strong element of design in the school of engineering. One of Northwestern's uncommon engineering degrees, it is focused on product design and

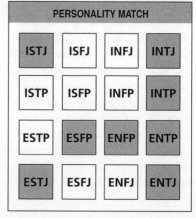

PERSONALITY MATCH

ISTJ	ISFJ	INFJ	INTJ
ISTP	ISFP	INFP	INTP
ESTP	ESFP	ENFP	ENTP
ESTJ	ESFJ	ENFJ	ENTJ

their manufacture. Design seems to interface most of the studies in engineering and has a home in the Segal Institute of Design which is available to all engineering students and others in the arts also. INTJs might especially enjoy the **Manufacturing and Design Engineering** program at Northwestern because it expects and requires innovation. Innovation, of course, is second nature for this type.

ISTJ can often find themselves with invitations to leadership positions after a few years in their profession. They typically become experts in their discipline. They don't often feature arrogance as a characteristic and garner support for leadership positions from their peers. However, these same characteristics can also become an Achilles heel. The certificate at Northwestern University in **Leadership** introduces this type to concepts of successful persuasion. It can be paired with any major and the curriculum is presented through course work, retreats and self study.

INTP will find the ideal minor at Northwestern for their personality type. It is titled **Critical Theory** and requires that the student reflect on literary and political premises, concepts and categories. This works out well since INTPs can find themselves drawn to philosophical concerns in the right circumstances. Northwestern will provide the needed research options and independent learning favored by this very abstract type.

ESFP and **Drama** go together very well. This type is such a natural at entertaining others; it must be in their genetic code. Northwestern University requires the undergraduate student craft skills across the several layers of theatrical performance. Students will often perform on the stage and complete a three-year study sequence of dramatic texts that explore human behaviors. Sociable, friendly ESFPs will naturally be attracted to elective coursework that puts them in touch with others as theater always does.

ENFP likes a big picture to ponder. In fact, they like the coffee-table-books approach—lots of them. The minor in **Global Health** offers many electives. However, ENFP may select the courses which explore national health systems and ethnic health practices. They work for ENFP who likes variety and innovation. This type might be drawn to business or nonprofit ventures in health sciences.

ENTP is attracted to power and may be comfortable moving toward executive career tracks. The major or minor in **Political Science** at Northwestern University requires students to understand political theory, comparative politics, American politics and international relations. Research requirements in this department assure the graduates have the ability to discern between propaganda and honest results. Don't be surprised if ENTP's curiosity, impersonal analysis and confidence develop a healthy skepticism in the social sciences. Along with a **Leadership** certificate, they could move right into that executive track with success.

ESTJ will like the orderly way the Department of **Biology** presents this wide-ranging as well as evolving discipline. Students are first grounded in foundational knowledge. Then the department highlights emerging knowledge through exposure to current research studies. Undergrads will next concentrate in one of five subspecialties. ESTJs, straightforward and logical, may elect the Plant Biology track. Currently, few millennials are entering Ph.D. graduate study of crop invasion by insects. With eminent boomers retiring the field is wide open.

ENTJ could select the minor in **Transportation and Logistics** at Northwestern with confidence that it is likely to come in very handy. This type is often successful in complex manufacturing environments. ENTJs would like their efforts to bring order to the disorganized world they perceive. The nature of this career field requires analytic thinking and a willingness to take calculated risks. Both of these are characteristic of ENTJs who will use this minor study profitably in the long term.

NOTRE DAME UNIVERSITY

Office of Admission
South Bend, IN 46556
Website: www.nd.edu
Admissions Telephone: 574-631-7505
Undergraduates: 8,415; 4,511 Men, 3,904 Women
Graduate Students: 3,343

Physical Environment

The Notre Dame campus opens up to velvet lawns, tall trees and a straight path to the **gold-domed** administration building that can't be missed. It's the center of campus. It's a mystical sight, flanked by the breathtaking **Basilica**, with pealing bells that ring throughout the day. The statue of the founder, Father Edward Sorin, in friar's garb, stands facing the gold dome. No wonder Notre Dame students call themselves "Domers"! Some students are attracted to the campus because of its inspirational landscape, a benefit that all can enjoy in this community. Other students are equally attracted to the grandeur of the architecture that appears to be devoted to the power of God more than the power of humanity. The grotto, a replica of the French shrine of "Our Lady of Lourdes," celebrates the spread of Catholicism in America. This campus has age and character with 1,250 acres and main entrances punctuating stone walls that define the campus perimeter.

Large numbers of influential **alumni** groups come into town for football weekends, staying in the newly developed south side of town. Prospective students take notice and appreciate this renovated section of the city. Undergraduates remain on campus for the most part because the **Notre Dame campus facilities** are over the top. The Compton Family Ice Arena follows in this over the top tradition.

Notre Dame football has a life of its own. The football stadium is another signature location that preserves tradition at this university. Its stadium, renovated in the 90s, seats 80,000 fans and showcases the Notre Dame marching band, with its bag-pipes and fiddles, featured on national TV during televised games.

Social Environment

Compared to their peers at other liberal arts universities across the nation, "Domers" here are in the middle of the road with their political views. They are traditional endorsing their Catholic faith, but there are also some liberal Catholic views on this campus. Students might find the familiar religious practices and teachings of their home parishes or might not. Regardless, these undergraduates are **confident** in their abilities and work very hard. On the weekend they play hard. The Fathers of the Holy Cross offer mass in the residence halls as well. Students are comfortable joining this proud, vibrant and **well-established community** and find fun traditions within the single sex undergraduate dormitories and the restaurants on the campus. The university is successful at countering the troubling national trend of male under-representation in college over the past 20 years.

The majority of students come from public high school and one quarter are ethnic minorities and first-generation. There are no social fraternities or sororities, so friendships are formed and grow in the 29 residence halls. Most live on campus for four years. The residences become part of a student's identity on campus which is fostered by the 'stay hall' system. If a student lives in North quad he's loyal to the North environs and activities. However, there are also hundreds of well-supported student groups, one of our favorites is the Big Yellow Taxi. Football tailgates are popular ways for students and parents to meet up and connect with one another. Whether the ND team wins or loses, the team likes to conduct itself with respect for the opponents in a classy manner.

The ethos of Notre Dame revolves around **strong academics**, mighty athletics, religious seriousness and service initiatives. There is a clear representation of the entire Notre Dame collegiate family: students, fans, parents, alumnae, the priests and the administration. Well-connected and well-known alumni in entertainment and media secure access to celebrity speakers for campus events. The clear expectation of graduates is for success and service to others, in part by leveraging the powerful Notre Dame network.

Compatibility with Personality Types and Preferences

Notre Dame is a reflection in reason (T) and community. The community takes on many layers of meaning at Notre Dame. At the most reflective level, it relates to the larger community of mankind as evolved in the Bible from Adam and Eve through Jesus Christ. That is pretty reflective. At the most obvious level, community means the present day campus environment. At its core, education at Notre Dame means service to the community, and the purpose of the service is to bring justice to the community. Social justice is approached via contemporary American political trends. President Obama spoke at the university shortly after his inauguration. His views on abortion became an immediate subject of controversy within the larger Notre Dame community as briefly reported in the press. The Orestes Brownson Council on Catholicism and American Politics, a student group, focuses on these types of turbulent political currents.

In respect to the daily educational experience at Notre Dame, faculty and departments are very much connected to the present day world of careers and vocations (S). Undergraduates find much academic depth and familiarity in the structure (J) of the curriculum. The First Year of Studies ensures comprehensive knowledge of Notre Dame's educational options as well as professional advising for all incoming freshmen. At the completion of the first year, students move into upper level programs and courses with confidence as a result of this professional advising experience. With strong expectation and strong support featured across the campus, "Domers" and are both academically and socially gregarious in the Notre Dame community (E) and beyond

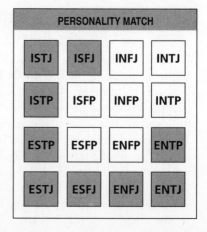

PERSONALITY MATCH

ISTJ	ISFJ	INFJ	INTJ
ISTP	ISFP	INFP	INTP
ESTP	ESFP	ENFP	ENTP
ESTJ	ESFJ	ENFJ	ENTJ

OBERLIN COLLEGE

Office of Admission
101 North Professor Street
Oberlin, OH 44074
Website: www.oberlin.edu
Admissions Telephone: 440-775-8411
Undergraduates: 2,907; 1,304 Men, 1,603 Women

Physical Environment

Oberlin's main architecture was established in the late 1800s and so the campus has a heavy sense of history. Students coming from the east and west coast have two reactions: some feel they have stopped running, others find it too isolated. They observe that this town consists of a few streets around the campus. Others are really happy to have found a haven for their **idealism**. Students clubs often hold their meetings around a fire pit in Tappan Square across from campus also where graduation ceremonies are held. There is an easy give and take atmosphere between the college and town.

Within a two year period, Oberlin celebrated the renovation and construction of three well needed facilities: the Allen Art museum, the new geology facility, the new student residence. These construction projects updated small, aging buildings and brought architectural excitement into the campus. With several rare collections in art and Greek statuary, historic treasures are in safe keeping and students enjoy classes within the renovated Art Museum. The **music conservatory** is now bolstered by the Kohl Guilding, opened in spring 2010 which houses the jazz department along with a priceless collection of jazz memorabilia. Conservatory students form a tight knit group reaching for superlative musical performance. Oberlin undergrads enjoy the conservatory's exceptional performances on campus.

The Center for Environmental Studies sports solar panels, bio-degradable materials and a natural, self-sustaining greenhouse. Students at Oberlin are highly concerned about the environment. It is a common subject among students and they are exceptionally proud of this facility. Administration and faculty pursue efficient utilization at considerable monetary costs such as newly installed geothermal wells and mechanicals operated by stringent climate controls.

Students must live on campus for three years and most study abroad for two semesters. Housing options have responded to the student body concern and passion. Upperclass students might choose the Victorian homes where undergraduates **share responsibility** for planting vegetables, planning meals, buying the food and cooking. In some houses students create a commune-like atmosphere. **Independence and practicality** are highly prized living skills among these **bright** students. The collegiate environment truly meets the expectations of the student body and the long Ohio winters do not prevent students from living their own, unique lifestyle.

Social Environment

Oberlin students arrive with an interesting list of assets, both academic and personal. These students are bright, intellectually curious and **free-spirited**. They are avant-garde types who typically remain so after graduation. They strive to be accomplished, intensely academic, yet not competitive with one another. Oberlin students tend to act on their views by forming and supporting cause-related clubs and groups. The most popular cause is that of service and the administration reciprocates with a service clearinghouse that generates much volunteerism in the surrounding communities. On today's campus, Oberlin students prefer to combine practical reality with their **alternative viewpoints**.

There are no fraternities or sororities on this campus and students gather around their interests and service initiatives. There are several groups for students interested in ecological sustainability through social change. In some ways these committed students seem the most willing to challenge the status quo for their favorite cause. Studying abroad might open eyes to the poverty in other countries. For the individual student, study abroad might be a **confirmation** of their original views or a **turning point** determined by multiple definitions of 'poor' and shades of poverty. Regardless of cause, they all thrive in this intellectually-charged atmosphere

Follow up work after graduation could center on personal discovery as refined during four years on campus. Graduates will want to affect public and institutional policy, guided by their **corporate vision** of how society should work. They expect to persuade others of the credibility of their vision. Oberlin offers a flexible and supportive environment where students emerge as passionate as on their first day freshman year.

Compatibility with Personality Types and Preferences

Oberlin College brings to mind the word alternative, but not in the sense of fashion. Educational philosophy here is about shining a bright light on organizational practice that is failing to meet the needs of mankind. Since there is no shortage of organizations that fit this definition, the range and approach to educational studies is wide open for Oberlin undergraduates. This intense intellectual environment leans heavily toward a future orientation (N). After all, significant change requires planning for the future. Productive change is not often accomplished in the present and rarely, if ever, affects the past.

Students here are very capable of dissecting a verbal argument in a precise way (T). This is certainly their inclination, and they favor learning in this manner. With access to their brightness and advanced high school courses, Oberlin undergraduates carefully study the present day body of knowledge in the field of their interests. This serves two purposes, the obvious reason being pure and simple knowledge. The second reason is for the purpose of discerning the shortcomings in that field. Once the deficiencies are known, students are then inclined to identify systems of thought and lines of research to overcome or undo those deficiencies. Four years of undergraduate study at Oberlin serves to sharpen their intellectual abilities well beyond those of otherwise well-educated citizens. Graduates of this college are quite competent, very able to perceive and respond to knowledge and very desirous of designing change to overcome shortfalls in society.

In the following listing of college majors it is important to remember that students can fit into any college and can be successful in any major. We have found that the Personality

Types below fit very well at this college. The course-of-study chosen for each Personality Type corresponds to MBTI® research and is presented as an example favorable for that type.

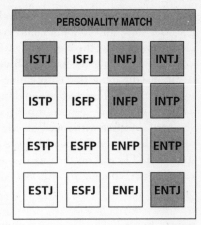

PERSONALITY MATCH

ISTJ	ISFJ	INFJ	INTJ
ISTP	ISFP	INFP	INTP
ESTP	ESFP	ENFP	ENTP
ESTJ	ESFJ	ENFJ	ENTJ

INFJ will appreciate the sophistication and desire for objectivity in Oberlin's course of instruction in **Religion**. This type is often passionate in respect to their beliefs. Integrity is also critically important for INFJs. The department credibly approaches religion in three critical areas not typical in collegiate curriculum: traditional, modern cultural and religion-based. It seems that with spirit and intellectual bravado, this department has avoided current day cultural amorphisms that dilute the nature of this discipline.

INFP could be fascinated by the turn of the 21st century emerging knowledge about the human brain. The major in **Neuroscience** at Oberlin College is a great foundation for this type who may become a pioneer pushing the science forward in 2045. INFPs like to come up with original work that is comprehensive and penetrating. Faculty are determined to help undergrads find their niche among the many disciplines it crosses.

ENTJ can study **Physics**, a fundamentally abstract subject, at Oberlin College, yet still prepare for the practical world. The major is a gateway to numerous advanced professional degrees. ENTJs prefer to have work that is acknowledged by others as being important and needed. At Oberlin, students may also find courses in astrophysics and materials physics. Leave it to the competitive ENTJ to figure out a way to generate revenue for their cause, workplace and passion.

INTJ is a perfect fit for Oberlin College in our opinion. This precise thinker is truly capable of peering into the future and crafting a vision. Powerful and single-minded with their original projects, INTJs sometime seem like a freight train on a slow, steady roll. The area of study in **Applied Mathematics** will put them in dynamic collaboration with other students and professors of a similar persuasion at Oberlin College. The department supports using math as a stepping stone to other fields of study. The power of math and the power of the INTJ personality together make for a very astute graduate.

ENTP is interested in so many subjects. What will they be when they grow up? This type will likely try several careers, so an undergraduate degree in history with a good dose of abstract thought is ideal. **Jewish Studies** at Oberlin deliver on both and ENTP will be required to concentrate in religion or history of the Jewish nation. Regardless, awareness of this rich field of knowledge will guide this type to pursue a specific strand of knowledge in graduate study. ENTPs often identify dynamic fields in the social sciences such as economics or political science.

INTP could enjoy the **East Asian Studies** at Oberlin College, a major that attracts many students. This type likes to put patterns together. Astute INTP can find a pattern in chaos or just plain confusion for that matter. They will not shrink from the economic complications of emerging China or resource-constrained Japan. With graduate study in economics, this type could successfully consult on the differing challenges faced by these two nations.

ISTJ might take the major in **Biochemistry** right into the agricultural sciences, a traditional discipline that is becoming critically important. This type has the attention to detail that will be needed to address crop production and land efficiency. ISTJs will be pleased with the department's rigor in the field. The curriculum is noticeably absent of interface with social, trendy topics that can divert energy and resources off of the difficult work in mastering this subject even at the undergraduate levels. Don't stand in ISTJ's way on the way to class in Quantum Chemistry and Kinetics unless you are sharp enough to catch some of their wry humor as they circumnavigate you.

OCCIDENTAL COLLEGE

Office of Admissions
1600 Campus Road
Los Angeles, CA 90041
Website: www.oxy.edu
Admissions Telephone: 323-259-2500
Undergraduates: 2,102; 904 Men, 1,298 Women

Physical Environment

Occidental College is located in an area called Eagle Rock which was one of the first towns to be founded around Los Angeles in the late 1800s. This area is becoming gentrified with artists and people from various cultures who have settled here. The town's architecture is a blend of Spanish mission style and art deco houses giving it an eclectic and multi-cultural feel. Occidental College, on the other hand, has a **Mediterranean feel**. It was designed by Myron Hunt, a famous architect, and is nestled between the **mountains of San Gabriel**. The campus is hilly and has many steps on its 120 acres.

Students are **relaxed and playful** in the welcoming **California weather**, yet, if the weather becomes arid because of brush fires in the mountains, the beautiful Gillman fountain at the entrance to the college is turned off, reminding all on campus of the fragile ecosystem. Students enjoy walking to the Johnson Center, a popular meeting place. Thorne Hall is the major auditorium used for the graduation ceremony and **musical** performances. Students are required to reside on campus for the first three years and are assigned to a dormitory by the first year seminar topic they select. In this way, through living-learning residence, faculty and students form familiar, comfortable relationships. There are 13 residence halls, all **governed by students**. The academic buildings and especially the extensive science labs are the settings for **experiential education**. The inter-faith chapel and cultural center reflects and appeals to the **multicultural perspectives** that are predominant on the Occidental campus. There are opportunities for working as extras on movie sets, being that Oxy is near Hollywood and the movie houses. The California Semester allows first semester students to take multiple day trips into Los Angeles to study its natural history and geography.

Social Environment

Adventuresome students enroll at Occidental College and sign up for classes that may be very challenging, novel or exciting. Oxy students value the **relationship** that they build with their professors and the intellectual stimulation of the classroom. They closely explore new concepts and trends. Certainly the city offers a regular infusion of both.

The ethos of this college is "equality for all," "valuing diversity" and "change." Oxy students wear many hats and have **many interests**, from playing Division III athletics to intellectual clubs. One strong interest on this campus is politics. Students have a reputation for leaning toward the left side of politics and align with the

Democratic Party and Independents for the most part. Perhaps the recession will realign some of these traditional patterns.

There are approximately 100 social groups on campus that **affiliate around specific interests**. Some of the most active organizations are Hillel and Inter Varsity Christian Fellowship (IVCF). The Greek life at Occidental is well supported by the student body as the chapters actively participate in athletics and other campus causes as well as hosting open social mixers for Greek and non-Greek alike. The performing arts are a staple within the campus community. The dance ensemble is very popular. With two performances annually, it always has sellout crowds. There is a weekly Friday afternoon jazz performance on the lawn by the students enrolled in the music major. It is also popular with students who want to chill out from five days of coursework and values-driven discussions. Students really come to know each other well at Occidental outside of their immediate group of social pals. The curriculum drives a search for personal beliefs and those conversations are familiar during the four-year curriculum.

Compatibility with Personality Types and Preferences

Occidental College is a passionate place with much energy devoted to integrating service learning experience in Los Angeles' ethnic neighborhoods. Undergraduate students peer through the lens of these L.A. communities seeking world cultural awareness and knowledge. Students sign up for service learning in the city as easily as signing up for a required course in their major. Occidental College and Los Angeles have a blurred boundary line in respect to where the campus stops and the city starts. The administration, faculty and student body are all equally devoted to improving society, especially L.A. society which they would view as a microcosm of other regions of the U.S.

The demanding nature of this goal requires the Occidental community to search out, discover or develop innovative (N) social practices and policy initiatives. The undergraduate student body and its individual members would hope to see their successful initiatives find a life in community practices throughout the nation. For this reason, the undergraduates at Occidental often translate their values-oriented perspectives into practical plans and initiatives of action (J). In certain ways, the administration pointedly develops regulations that rein in these passionate student innovators. With all their values-driven goals, the student body here is also comfortable and accepting of the real world.

In the following listing of college majors it is important to remember that students can fit into any college and can be successful in any major. We have found that the Personality Types below fit very well at this college. The course-of-study chosen for each Personality Type corresponds to MBTI® research and is presented as an example favorable for that type.

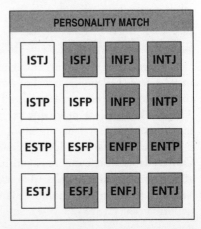

PERSONALITY MATCH			
ISTJ	ISFJ	INFJ	INTJ
ISTP	ISFP	INFP	INTP
ESTP	ESFP	ENFP	ENTP
ESTJ	ESFJ	ENFJ	ENTJ

INFP likes the time and solitude to develop their ideas. Those ideas pretty much have to be in harmony with their own belief system that incorporates helping others. The major in **Sociology** at this college is quite robust with nearby multiethnic Los Angeles to serve as a classroom. This is a stepping stone degree to careers in law, social work, journalism, public health, education and, of course, graduate studies in sociology. When their personal values synchronize with one of these avenues, this strong-minded type will firmly declare their future career specialization.

INFJ occasionally enters the field of health sciences to provide direct care, as in dietitian. The Department of Biology here offers an emphasis in **Cell and Molecular Biology.** It is an ideal foundation for advanced graduate study. INFJ will want to pursue the registered dietitian license since it is required to provide direct services to patients. For INFJs preferring the administrative side of Health service, the masters degree in nutrition gives entrée to administrative positions in hospitals and health centers.

INTJ sees far into the unknown and enjoys creating systems that might reveal new information. The major in **Physics** at Occidental College offers further options in chemistry and mathematics. INTJs are prone to scientific research and this degree opens doors in two frontiers, that of geophysics and astrophysics. Geographic features in the LA basin just might influence the decision.

ISFJ will find the study of **Music** at Occidental College ideal because of its location. A great deal of entertainment programming originates in the city, bolstered by nearby Hollywood and broadcast studios. At this college, music is also a major form of relaxation and reason to gather socially for the weekly jazz sessions offered by Oxy students. This strong department offers a breadth of music courses and the city offers the options to observe professional musicians at work. ISFJs gain energy and build resilience with the hands-on activity of the performing musical arts.

INTP will smile at the idea of a minor in **Computer Science.** This type is drawn to solving puzzles likely could not walk by a table with a Rubik's cube on it without giving it a whirl. The skills attained with this minor will bring extra power to solution finding in INTP's major. Biology, chemistry and history each are fields that call out to them and benefit from statistical analysis.

ENFP loves to be with and around a wide variety of people. They appreciate and need the various perspectives to energize plans for themselves and others. The degree in **Urban and Environmental Policy** at Occidental College is linked to public affairs and civic action. ENFPs will find this field satisfies their innate curiosity and need for an abstract challenge. Internships will abound in the city of Los Angeles. The major allows for specialization in economics, housing, health, transportation, air/water quality, etc.

ENTP is often interested in politics because of the associated high stakes and prestige. Their ingenious, quick thinking can come into play within many of the political arenas. The major in **Diplomacy and World Affairs** at Occidental College is an excellent choice for ENTPs. The college has a long-time affiliation with the United Nations and students in this major might be selected for this very desirable semester internship. The degree is suited for careers in government, international business, law and banking. ENTPs are rarely at a loss for ideas and will enjoy exploring the breadth of options connected with this major.

ESFJ is an ideal candidate for the major in **Kinesiology**. ESFJs enjoy and excel at utilizing skills they have learned. They are conscientious and naturally make those around them feel valued and comfortable. This is a science-based discipline that prepares graduates to work directly with clients needing physical therapeutic support. ESFJs are up for learning and memorizing the sequence of physical movements. They naturally take a personal approach to their work which will help them avoid costly and potentially dangerous errors in directing patients.

ENFJ often enjoys careers associated with counseling. The major in **Psychology** at Occidental College concentrates on emotions, behavior and cognition. Each of these topics are attractive to ENFJs who prefer warm, harmonious workplaces and the opportunity to be creative while supporting others.

ENTJ will take advantage of careers in the discipline of **Cognitive Science** offered here. It requires coursework in the traditional fields of linguistics, philosophy, psychology, computer science and mathematics. It is an evolving scientific field that offers much challenge and opportunity. ENTJs are naturals at long-range planning, innovative thinking and leadership. This major calls out to them.

PEPPERDINE UNIVERSITY

Seaver College
24255 Pacific Coast Highway
Malibu, CA 90263-4392
Website: www.pepperdine.edu
Admissions Telephone: 310-506-4392
Undergraduates: 3,000; 1,380 Men, 1,620 Women
Graduates: 4,700

Physical Environment

Pepperdine students enjoy breathtaking **views of the Pacific** Ocean and the sunny Malibu beaches. The call to **surf** the tall waves is strong. This location attracts lovers of water to the campus who then mix in with otherwise spiritually-oriented students. The hills on campus make for a physically active lifestyle, as long as students avoid the bus to and from their uphill dormitory! The views of the ocean from the inside of these sun-bathed, modern buildings remind the student body of the beauty of God's earth. The graduate school is set apart on the upper side of the mountain and well reflects the purpose and order of the Church of Christ. Seaver College for undergraduates also attracts students who simply want to study in sunny California and abandon colder climates.

Social Environment

Pepperdine was founded by a very successful Christian business entrepreneur. Students carry on his legacy by **serving others** through commercially profitable activities such as non-profit management and fundraising. It all mixes quite well with Pepperdine's philosophy of helping others in a contemporary way. The university attracts students who are comfortable with spiritual and academic guidance in the important areas of their life. Professors accompany their undergraduates on mission trips. A partial purpose of the trips is to help students encounter real-life experiences and **develop personal skills** and talents. Student-led ministries like the Christian Surfers of Pepperdine bring religious awareness to the surfing community.

Pepperdine is not for students who harbor doubts about religion or **Christianity**, although not everyone is necessarily intensely spiritual. Non-believers are accepted here. There is a religious thread that runs through the educational, social and intellectual life of this campus. Harmony through individual and community goals is valued and actively defined by the student body. **Community service**, mission trips and volunteering are in the forefront. In these ways students become involved on campus with lesser participation in traditional social outlets. Popular bands, nationally touring college campuses and downloaded to iPods are not a staple of Pepperdine's semester schedule. There's a strong emphasis on clean living and **healthy** eating habits. Dating is typically taken seriously and might easily lead to marriage following traditional societal values.

Most students live on campus and come from all over the U.S. and international locations for a variety of reasons that prompt them to enroll. As a result they form a geographical, spiritual and ethnically diverse group, yet they all enter with strong academic skills, stand behind **humanitarian causes** and ultimately form a tight, caring community.

Compatibility with Personality Types and Preferences

Pepperdine University and Seaver College are exceptionally clear in communicating their educational goals (J). Even the website is easy to use and well organized. A purposeful life is the outcome of education and Pepperdine students reach this goal through reflection, service to others and promoting values which are Christian-centered. The college campus environment is both consistent and caring (F). Practically all of the activities outside of the classroom are driven by humanitarian concerns. The momentum of shared beliefs and cultural campus activities builds contemporary friendships within the student body during the college years. The university predicts these relationships will be life long. Friendship and community is expected to serve as the guidepost for a turbulent American 21st century. All in all, loyal and dedicated students fit in well at the Pepperdine campus. Students who like traditions and people-centered activities in the larger community (E) are also likely to be comfortable here.

In the following listing of college majors it is important to remember that students can fit into any college and can be successful in any major. We have found that the Personality Types below fit very well at this college. The course-of-study chosen for each Personality Type corresponds to MBTI® research and is presented as an example favorable for that type.

PERSONALITY MATCH			
ISTJ	**ISFJ**	INFJ	INTJ
ISTP	**ISFP**	**INFP**	INTP
ESTP	ESFP	ENFP	ENTP
ESTJ	**ESFJ**	**ENFJ**	**ENTJ**

ISFJ, often times a reflective and thorough soul, could enjoy the degree in **Liberal Arts** at Pepperdine. This rather unusual degree is rich in the fields of history, culture, sciences and the arts. It is a fine course of study for a student who might want to become an archivist or librarian which is a desirable career for this type. The degree will allow the ISFJs to identify their subject specialty and be well prepared to select an appropriate graduate degree.

ISFP is good at remembering and using information that is practical and useful. This is the right attitude for a **Nutritional Science** Degree. The course titled Communication in Dietetics has a service learning requirement where students learn to counsel, program and evaluate for different dietary problems with those in the nearby community. This type of learning-by-doing is perfect for the ISFP.

INFP hopes to express their inner thoughts with a lot of personal distance between themselves and others. Art serves a wonderful channel for this purpose. If you combine art with words, you have a minor in the Fine Arts department called **Multimedia Design**. An option here at Pepperdine might be to pair a minor in multimedia with a communication major such as journalism or Rhetoric and Leadership, both equally appealing to INFP.

ESTJ is going to get an exceptionally fine **International Business** degree at Pepperdine University. Part of the philosophical core of this campus is to reach out and learn extensively about other cultures. The university has access to many cross-cultural currents because of its location on the coast and proximity to Los Angeles. There is a wealth of relevant courses for a prospective business person. It would be hard to pick out one from the exceptional list, however "Ethics and International Politics" would be a stand out on this campus. The ESTJ is going to appreciate the practical nature of this well-positioned course of studies.

ESFJ often enjoys people and it shows through their natural ease and curiosity about others. They typically like to support other people and help them move forward. So with these inclinations, an ESFJ with an interest in athletics is going to smooth right into the minor of **Coaching.** Not only do you study the obvious areas like training and conditioning, but this Pepperdine minor also includes social and psychological aspects of coaching. The university's strong department in teacher education would be natural for this type also.

ENFJ can jump right into the **Public Relations** degree and find an outlet for their passion and dedication. The degree at Pepperdine has both theoretical and practical courses. This works perfectly for ENFJs who can give a speech better than most. This type's desire for harmony within the community nicely fits in with the public relations curriculum. Casework presented as actual business problems require students to identify the real motive as well as the most ethical solution.

ENTJ who is usually quite extraverted functions as a go-to-person. They have both the energy and the drive. With their ability to focus on the future and gifted with artistic talent, the degree in **Advertising** could be right for this type. Located within 30 minutes of the huge Los Angeles metropolitan area with its extraordinary entertainment corporations, there are more than a few exceptional places to secure an internship in advertising. ENTJ will do all the securing necessary.

PRINCETON UNIVERSITY

Admission Office
P.O. Box 430
Princeton, NJ 08544-0430
Website: www.princeton.edu
Admissions Telephone: 609-258-3060
Undergraduates: 5,149; 2,618 Men, 2,531 Women
Graduate Students: 2,582

Physical Environment

Princeton is a town that plays host to this very prestigious **Ivy League** university. The suburb has upscale neighborhoods and the university is a mecca for intellectual activity that spills out onto the town through the arts, music and clubs. The town has impressive businesses such as the Dow Jones and Company and ETS, which must remind students of the importance of those SAT scores in getting admitted to Princeton. After office workers go home and the shoppers leave Nassau Street, this suburb becomes quieter and students head out to Prospect Avenue, which they refer to as "the street." The street has many "eating clubs," where students meet and talk with their peers over dinner. Just about all of the students reside on campus or in school-sponsored houses for all four years. It's clear to see why the campus architecture and the park-like setting are simply breathtaking with **castle-like residence halls**. There are Gothic and Georgian-style buildings, and the impressive Blair Arch. Princeton grads frequently choose to marry in the gorgeous chapel. The Princeton campus has that old world, English feel to it, notwithstanding the newer buildings designed by I.M. Pei and Robert Venturi, that round off this impressive campus.

Social Environment

It is known, without reading on these pages, that Princeton students are **bright and work hard**. They were serious students in high school as they achieved their Ivy League university admission, yet once they enroll they reveal a sense of humor and camaraderie. Although some competition in class arises from the way the grading system works, the atmosphere is one of cooperation. Academically, in first and second year, students take classes to fulfill **distribution requirements** in seven different areas of study, including **epistemology** – the study of knowledge, its limits and validity. The first two years are like a warm-up that prepares them to chart their individual academic path as upper class students. Undergraduates select their major among 34 departments and while they cannot double major, they can add an independent concentration, similar to a minor. Students are required to **conduct independent research** as part of their **junior paper** and in conjunction with their **senior thesis**. This requires the approval of an advisor with whom they work one on one. This thesis could be a basis for a post-baccalaureate study or PhD program, or perhaps might become a successful addition to our American society like the program Teach for America which started out as a Princeton thesis.

Students who want to study abroad are advised to do so during their first and second year of college, because it's too difficult to do so in junior and senior years.

Princeton now offers a gap year experience to admitted high school graduates who are selected and elect to volunteer service in third world countries for one year with most expenses covered by the program.

Princeton undergraduates typically come from independent schools or excellent public schools. They hail primarily from the eastern seaboard. Close to one half of Princeton's recent incoming classes are students of color. The university has been successful in building and **sustaining a community** that is supportive of many various races and backgrounds. Weekly and monthly dinners are designed to bring students together and foster community. Bi-monthly lunches are planned to give students and faculty a chance to communicate outside the classroom.

Other socials avenues that provide fellowship are the "**eating clubs**." There are ten eating clubs, all coed, located off campus near Olden or Prospect Streets. Each eating club has a different theme and is run according to its own goals. Some houses offer elegant dinners served on china. Other eating houses function like old-fashioned frat houses, with pool table, video games and beer nearby. Membership is open to all students, however, there are a limited number of positions open annually within each. Greek fraternities and sororities, along with the Eating Clubs, provide leadership opportunities and social activities such as formals, sponsorship of arts events and service. There are a high percentage of recruited athletes. Sports are very important, particularly football games with long time rivals.

In addition, there are an additional **200 clubs** that represent the arts, hobbies and causes. Students **look to clubs** primarily for exploring their inclinations. At Princeton University, the academic philosophies prompt intellectual exercise regardless of the noun used to describe it. Sleep may be the only real down time here. In Spring 2011, campus humor jestingly advised "get clones."

Compatibility with Personality Types and Preferences

At Princeton, students enter the freshman doorway and proceed in any of 360° directions (P). It is a precise university that can be thought of as an infinite three dimensional grid of informational cubes. During their four years, undergraduates will traverse the infinite cube, similar to the Rubik's cube that is a cerebral mind puzzle. They will recombine it with those cubes of information already assimilated and known from the previous week or semester. Princeton undergrads are always searching for the next (N) nugget of information that brings meaning to their understanding of a discipline. It is exciting, intense, rewarding and cautious labor. After all, one wouldn't want to get lost in the infinite cube of knowledge. That could be an overwhelming experience.

The Princeton undergraduates' life journey is about utilizing thought (T) through individual effort. Students approach their educational studies in a measured way; their pace is moderated by their interests and curiosity. The administration and faculty expect an independent search for knowledge. Academic courses and methods encourage students to research information (S) and occasionally present it as a formal lesson to others in preceptorials. Professors listen and become observing advisors with mildly directive mentoring. Some students reach for their understanding of a discipline through collaboration that is inclusive of peers (F). The reading courses are a type of learning experience agreed upon by professor and student. Both of these educational tools provide information and knowledge that is not going to be covered elsewhere in the curriculum. Students can put their own educational plan together (J) and propose it to the faculty. It is yet another avenue for the curious undergraduate with a desire to enter a particular cube in the infinite grid on this campus.

The junior year brings a most intense effort, known as the Independent Work. It calls to mind the nature of how these very bright students learn—independently. Graduates of Princeton are most capable of standing resolutely, moving forward into discovery and accurately crafting new knowledge into useable information cubes for society at large.

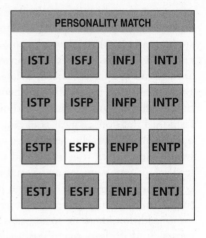

In the following listing of college majors it is important to remember that students can fit into any college and can be successful in any major. We have found that the Personality Types below fit very well at this college. The course-of-study chosen for each Personality Type corresponds to MBTI® research and is presented as an example favorable for that type.

INFP is most satisfied when they can devote their talents to the benefit of others. The certificate in **Language and Culture** at Princeton would allow INFPs to move into the international arena. This certificate is paired with any other concentration at Princeton. Perhaps this type will concentrate in a field like sociology that also leans toward benefiting others. Undergraduate INFPs can choose the languages within Princeton's robust departments. The coursework must remain different in the language certificate from the sociology concentration. Passionate, committed INFPs normally have a level of perseverance necessary for this additional academic load. It follows from their continuous search for personal meaning. What INFPs offer meets their own very high standards and addresses the needs of society. INFPs can be valuable members of any team that needs a little vision.

INFJ will really take to Princeton's infinite educational pathways of knowledge. They are always focused on thought and values which turn over and over within their minds. Princeton offers a curriculum that can respond to any of their insightful interests and they are likely to thrive here. This type prefers to pursue those insights independently, quietly and with a drive toward new concepts. They have a moving picture of ideas, like a movie theater, that shapes their thinking. The concentration in **Psychology** is well suited for INFJs. The department organizes itself as an explosion of ideas in studying the human personality. This type might find their own unconscious impressions coming into view as they eagerly complete all their assigned readings. INFJ is also the type to tackle metaphysical questions. This topic has segued into the work of psychological theorists such as Carl Jung. INFJs will take advantage of Princeton's residential houses for their social venues. They may be too busy to devote much time or energy to theme-oriented social clubs.

INTJ is most independent and private in respect to their ideas that typically take months to percolate and come to full fruition. However, when the time is right, they are propelled to share those ideas. Very intense thinking is their style, so much so that they are sometimes unsure of how they got to the position they now command. The concentration in **Astrophysical Sciences** gratefully accepts these bold thinkers. Courses such as Stars and Star Formation call out to their imagination if they are interested in the sciences. This type will appreciate the novel performing arts and join with others who also like music with an intellectual beat. Eating clubs and social clubs that feature the arts, lectures, music and theater will appeal to this type.

ISTP goes for little machines that move around on the floor. There is a child lurking within ISTPs. Therefore, the **Robotics and Intelligent Systems** certificate is likely to bring a smile to their face. In fact, ISTP wants to get their hands on the control stick. Better yet, ISTP wants to program the data commands and make this little machine do more. They want those little machines to dance. This type focuses their strong logical analysis on any product, service or technical gadget that can become useful. There are so many applications in today's world, from pacemakers to space technology to diagnosticians. The Princeton clubs are ideal for this type. They will enjoy finding that interest whether it is the billiards club or a club devoted to redheads. ISTPs will put a wry smile on their faces and show up for the meetings.

ISTJ can catalog huge numbers of facts and have them available for spontaneous recall. It is their specialty which is indispensable in many organizations. Princeton's certificate in **Finance** could easily take advantage of this desirable skill. It is common for ISTJs to master categorizing and assigning value to financial assets. This very precise discipline is a good bet if the ISTJ is inclined to math. Undergraduate ISTJs may elect to find a few friends together and follow their collective social interests in one of the Princeton clubs or residential college social activities.

ISFJ looks closely, sees what is there and commits it to memory. This is done with ease. They should look into the major in **Art and Archeology** at Princeton. This unique combination of disciplines mirrors educational philosophies at Princeton. It is also perfect for the ISFJ who fills their inner world with portraits of personal meaning. The department expects their graduates to be able to put linguistic meaning into visual art and artifacts. It's a tall order and rather painstaking detective work is required. Sign up this type who will stay on the job till it is done. ISFJs will benefit from Princeton's style of socializing. They take a unique perspective and bring their own kind of humor to a social gathering. Whatever their inclination, there will probably be a club that matches their interest. ISFJs must be gently pulled away from their studies and encouraged to drop their anxiety over taking a break.

ISFP brings to college discussions a lighthearted, practical touch which overshadows their deep-seated personal values. Many times, others are often not aware of this. Give them a problem to solve along with the space to tackle it and they are satisfied. ISFJs prefer people-oriented problems. The certificate in **Environmental Studies** offers a selection of elective coursework that allows ISFPs to study the humane perspectives in their course choices. A course titled Disease, Ecology, Economics and Policy fits the bill because it ties together the land with its inhabitants. It also doesn't hurt that their terrific memory for people-oriented information will be at their fingertips. ISFPs strive for approval in the classroom and later in the workplace. Environmental issues are detail-oriented and allow this type to shine. Princeton's social style offers a good helping of the unusual for this type who tends to march to their own drum. Here they will find others interested in the same tune and that will also be affirming to this type who can be self-conscious.

INTP will find the **Computer Science** department at Princeton University full of very interesting options like artificial intelligence, bioinformatics, digital media and computational social science. Upon meeting the major's course requirements, INTP can pursue a Certificate for Application in Computing in one of those options. That certainly works for most INTPs who are always on the lookout for the unknown, lurking within two separate disciplines. This type likes to analyze and logic is their specialty. They are most capable at putting together large conceptual schemes to generate solutions. It is an ideal characteristic for those willing to learn how to program computer software. They can also be pretty informal and messy in their work. Last minute socializers, they will temporarily stop right-clicking the mouse when a few buddies encourage them to play.

ESTP is a type that appreciates a little snazz in life. Sometimes this type will define that snazz in the form of risk-taking, so environments and ideas that include the element of risk are fine. The concentration in **Mechanical and Aerospace Engineering** will not disappoint them. The department is organized such that a student could receive an engineering degree that is one or both of these two types of engineering. ESTP will quickly determine which of these two delivers the most adventurous learning. They are likely to look for experiences that allow them to participate in something that has immediate practical use. ESTPs can survey the ten broad areas of research in the department, potentially choosing the Lasers and Applied Physics or the Vehicle Sciences and Applications. ESTP likes to socialize with an interdisciplinary approach. They are likely to find several clubs, perhaps an eating club that combines excitement and physical finesse. In these they will be lively and get things going.

ENFP might just be interested in the concentration in **Sociology** at Princeton once they understand how enthusiasm seems to drive the department's approach to problem solving. In this discipline, the focus is on society and the nature of what is not working well within society. It can be a sobering study without humor and might tax some ENFPs because they need some excitement and fun in their life. School violence and corporate behavior comes into critical focus as large negative currents in America. ENFP will want to lighten it up. Their enthusiasm will carry over to the Princeton clubs. This type will enjoy the freedom to join and unjoin any clubs that capture their interest.

ENTP finds it difficult to come across an idea or a topic in politics that isn't interesting. They risk over-committing at times trying out so many ideas. At the end of the day, this type tends to move toward sources of power and the application of power. The major in **History** at Princeton with a certificate in **Contemporary European Politics and Society** is a nice combination for ENTPs. It could give them an entrance into the world of European-based world organizations. This type will likely offer up novel perspectives in the Independent Work and Senior Thesis. The

ENTP must summon up the discipline to choose their topic earlier from among the interesting choices in western civilization. This type is likely to have fun with clubs and social activities that engage their mind which is never at rest. They are likely to be learning while socializing.

ESFJ is very interested in what makes other people tick. They are caring souls themselves and often wish that everyone else would be too. The concentration in **Religion** at Princeton moves toward the study of other cultures. Spiritual authenticity is much approved by this type who supports community and tradition. The religious practices of a culture within the historical period will humanize this abstract subject for ESFJ. This warm type will also light up rooms they enter with their affirming observations. Collaborative studies and joining in a group preceptorial suggested by fellow students is just fine. They are likely to be quite active in social activities, finding several clubs and remaining with those throughout their years on campus.

ESTJ is often excellent at officiating and becoming a source of accuracy for others who do not have time to find the right answer. ESTJ is very credible in this role because of their practicality and willingness to make a decision. The certificate in **Translation and Intercultural Communication** focuses on revealing the meaning in written documents. Such documents as foreign language, poems, cultural stories, webpages and technical writings might have meaning to the author but not necessarily to all readers. This type wants to translate that meaning for others to use. As a cultural translator, the ESTJ is likely to be accurate, observing and impersonal in providing listeners with the meaning. With this major, ESTJs might bring an intercultural perspective to socializing at Princeton by translating good stories for the membership in several of the clubs.

ENFJ could select the concentration of **Comparative Literature** and then choose to express their typical charm through the **Creative Writing** certificate. In exploring these two disciplines, the ENFJ will delight in the use of the word, the turn of the phrase and the double meanings. They are more than capable of utilizing any of these masterful techniques in oratory. They are also capable of bringing humane lessons found in substantive literature to the audiences of today. This type must be connected with others in a harmonious way. They are empathetic with diverse perspectives. Literature and language most commonly explore and satisfy their need to connect with others. They are likely to find social venues in the clubs or in the residential colleges that are empathetic in nature. Others in the clubs will welcome their cuddly natures.

ENTJ doesn't mind making a few considered judgments for improving the state of the art. They are often right up front with their interest to organize and innovate. Princeton's certificate in **Global Health and Health Policy** is likely to catch their attention as a worthy subject. This type wants to influence others and has the ability to support and craft plans that are frequently successful because of their considered judgments. The concept of disease patterns will certainly draw them into computational research, nicely tied with a major in Computer Science. Their big-picture thinking will cast a perspective large enough to gain respect from others. Their instinct to be innovative and to try something new will also gain credibility in the crucial arena of worldwide diseases. Participation in Princeton's clubs is a win-win for typically confident ENTJ. Their ability to lead and to withstand anxiety could prompt them to consider application to a selective eating clubs. They will also bring their leadership talents to several other social clubs.

ROANOKE COLLEGE

221 College Lane
Salem, VA 24153-3794
Website: www.roanoke.edu
Admissions Telephone: 540-375-2500, 800 388-2276
Undergraduates: 1,951; 857 Men, 1,094 Women

Physical Environment

Roanoke College is located in downtown Salem, a small suburb of the city of Roanoke, within 20 miles of the **Blue Ridge Mountains**. Prospective students will relate to Roanoke's strong emphasis on their location in the Blue Ridge Mountains. Prospective students see themselves as wanting to be on this campus for the next four years. Here, the campus setting is an important part of the experience. The physical landscape and buildings are very much valued for their **beauty and function** in promoting learning and social development. Older campus buildings have stately columns and six buildings are listed on the **historic register**. Newer buildings are over the top functional and so welcoming. Caldwell and Ritter Residence Halls, open in Fall 2012, bring definition to the Athletic Quad with their stately, vertical architecture.

Students appreciate this lovely campus as it often mirrors their home communities. The streets that surround the campus, except for Route 311, tend to be quiet. This setting appeals to undergraduates who are looking for a quiet campus where learning and undergraduate socializing comprise all the action. It is an environment without distraction. The superb sports facilities encourage athleticism in the student body. There are numerous intercollegiate **athletic teams** and many **intramural** and recreational programs including outdoor-adventure-type programs.

Social Environment

Roanoke College is populated by spirited students who are **socially involved** and **morally responsible**. This is not a campus where a student can be anonymous. They are fun-loving, **purposeful**, actively engaged with each other and very involved with community service. Students may spend hours **volunteering** at the local hospital. Greek life and **RC After Dark** provide plenty of social spirit while nicely balancing academic and service pursuits on this campus. Students who are politically aware find ways to express themselves on this campus. They may protest the fact that an ordinance is not environmentally-friendly. They are more likely to participate in causes that involve service such as the annual sweet potato bagging for needy distribution shelters around the state. Within two hours, the students bag a full truck load of potatoes dumped in front of the student center. No matter their major, the Roanoke student is bound to encounter academic conversation and policies that teach social **responsibility, ethics and values.**

Students graduated in the top 40 percent of their high school graduating class. The administration may be open to students who have a weak spot in their high school transcript or test scores, yet students like this who are successful at Roanoke buckle down and study hard on arrival. Roanoke's admirable academic diversity well reflects American middle class society and enhances the learning experience for all.

The academic top scholars attend the Honors program and all students benefit from the **consistent faculty attention**.

Compatibility with Personality Types and Preferences

The Roanoke College campus is for folks who are comfortable with reason and service. The faculty expects students to seek and apply that reason in their daily lives and upon graduation. Roanoke College naturally communicates the expectation of being responsible and the commendable goal of getting things done (J). This doesn't mean finishing for the sake of calling it 'done.' High energy stands out on this campus and it helps build an active community (E). Balance is the byword for emotional health. The interface between faculty and students is evident and purposeful in preparation for graduation and beyond. The educational philosophy nicely supports several highly sought-after technical and vocational degrees. This lovely campus grows out of its Lutheran roots with both human caring (F) and a solid, realistic affection for American society.

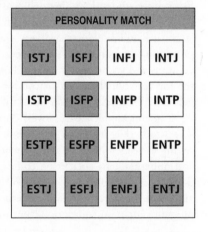

In the following listing of college majors it is important to remember that students can fit into any college and can be successful in any major. We have found that the Personality Types below fit very well at this college. The course-of-study chosen for each Personality Type corresponds to MBTI® research and is presented as an example favorable for that type.

ISTJ might take a look at Roanoke's unusual **Health Care Administration** concentration. It offers a strong perspective from which to explore career options within the industry such as medical, nursing or pharmacy degrees. Of course the concentration also offers immediate employment in hospitals, clinics and insurance companies. The course titled Health Care Economics tackles the difficult and ethical task of analyzing how public institutions, like the U.S. Congress, formulate and impact the delivery of health care. ISTJs, with this major, will gain an understanding of conflicting health data. The ISTJ won't become overwhelmed. ISTJs can patiently figure out positions on health issues.

ISFJ has the ability to collect large quantities of information from the disciplines of biology, chemistry and physics for the major in **Medical Technology**. Bravo for their precise recall of facts and perseverance. Both will come in handy as they seek a 4th year internship at nearby hospitals. Equally attracted to the world of people, their strengths are very desirable for Roanoke's major in medical technology. Their gentle, reflective ways will be welcomed by patients and staff alike in stressful medical environments.

ISFP at Roanoke College absolutely must look into the **Health and Exercise Science** major, perhaps with the additional concentration in **Health Care Delivery**, offered in the Sociology Department. This combination of courses reflects ISFP's and

Roanoke's philosophical combination of reason and service. The course Aging and Society emphasizes "an examination of the aging process, both for the individual and the nation." Roanoke is all about the belief in their graduates who will influence health perspectives in their neighborhood, community, region and nationally.

ESTP will want to consider the **Athletic Training** major. ESTPs like to get the gist of an assignment from several angles. Taking courses for the Inquiry program in chemistry, literature, statistics, physics and psychology will give them plenty of angles. The course titled Vikings and Farmers brings home the relationship of human health and the environment. It also offers a rare glimpse into northern Europe, different from the literary perspective typically found in liberal arts institutions.

ESFP is quite oriented to the here and now which makes them darn good at handling a crisis. The Roanoke major in **Criminal Justice** could lead to a position as a probation officer. This college campus, focused on practical knowledge, has what it takes to introduce both caring and correction into the criminal studies coursework. Alert, sociable ESFPs would do well to consider this major at Roanoke.

ESTJ would be interested in the **Business** degrees here. The department offers a concentration in Business Information Systems. The practical nature of courses offered within the business department, along with the Roanoke educational philosophies, promote strong analytic skills. ESTJs are masterful at practical judgment and can bulk up their less preferred inclination of spontaneity in the course titled eCommerce. Their inclination is to make an unemotional decision which will be valued in the business world.

ESFJ and the **Human Resource Management** concentration is a fairly good bet. Their curiosity about others often allows them to remember detailed information about those they meet during the course of the day. This type is fair with others while patiently explaining the law of the land. ESFJs will insist on balancing the needs of the company with the needs of the employees. Their loyalty, being a strong characteristic, will be evident at their work environment.

ENFJ who is interested in teaching will do well to look at Roanoke's wealth of coursework and experience available for want-to-be-teachers. This type is likely to relate well with children. As one would expect, Roanoke covers the multiple issues surrounding our community schools in the course titled **Principles of Education**. ENFJs possess the sociability to successfully complete a teaching internship in the Department of Defense schools overseas. This holds true for internationally accredited schools also.

ENTJ who wants to follow through with their inclination to be in charge often pursues advanced credentials in graduate school. Combine this with an inclination for business, and you have an argument for an undergraduate major in **International Relations**. Students select a geographic area of concentration in Europe, Africa, South America or Asia. The department offers simulations of international courts on campus. The undergraduates gain familiarity in this way prior to study abroad.

ROLLINS COLLEGE

1000 Holt Avenue
Winter Park, FL 32789-4499
Admissions Telephone: 407-646-2161
Website: www.rollins.edu
Undergraduates: 1,810; 740 Men, 1,070 Women

Physical Environment

Rollins College is located in tony Winter Park, Florida, within reasonable access of the Orlando International Airport. The campus is tucked away in a **quiet, residential** area, with ranch-style houses built in the 60s. Many of Rollin's buildings are soft, calming colors, pale pink and white, with terra-cotta tiled roofs. The many arched doorways and round windows remind students of Mediterranean villas. Several new buildings have brought a touch of the modern to this old world charm. Many students from the north are quickly taken by the warm climate, architecture and **lakes.** In fact, **Lakeside Path and Outdoor Classroom** is not only calming but will have pizzazz when the cement podium is connected with power outlets and T3 internet access. This speaks to the **Rollins IT infrastructure** which is over the top in all data bit categories. Students appreciate being tanned, healthy and casually dressed. The physical setting of this college invites a love for leisure, recreation activities and lifelong individual sports. Overall, the campus has a **compact, enclosed, warm feel**.

Nearby, the downtown area has many designer shops. Boutiques, stores and similar businesses stock merchandise that appeals to a number of the students. The student government has secured discounts at a number of these for the Rollins community. Historically, Rollins was founded with the support of the Congregational Church in 1885. The church on campus stands as a reminder of this historic past. The outdoor recreational lap pool is open year-round for students to swim and sun-tan. From poolside, students look out on the lake, where water-skiers and sailboats commonly are on the water. The **architectural and natural beauty** of the campus is part and parcel of the Rollins attraction and college experience.

Social Environment

Classes are small and the **faculty is dedicated and attentive** to the students. Students here like their professors who communicate **clear expectations** for class requirements. Rollins took a page out of John Dewey's progressive educational philosophy when they developed the core curriculum called a "Taxonomy of Educational Objectives." Undergraduates will find this clear, sequential method of learning used throughout the curriculum.

The college is committed to serving the **Central Florida** community as well as out-of-state students. This may explain the diverse economic backgrounds of undergraduate students. A good number of the students hail from the north and graduated from independent schools and strong suburban schools in the big cities, while other groups from Florida are often from nearby public schools sometimes with financial aid and work-study support. There are also "non-traditional" students, such as adult, graduate, part-time and evening students whose presence is felt, especially in the evenings, on this small campus.

There is a strong **Greek system** where approximately one-third of the students are members of sororities or fraternities. There are three living and learning residences. Students may elect to live in these themed residences where they will take classes with their residence hall mates and attend artistic and social events for their residence. Students also participate in a wide selection of clubs and activities, many focused on their academic interests like the Biology Club and many others oriented to dance and theater. Students dress for comfort and some for fashion, based on the outdoor seasonal temperatures. Students who are attracted to Rollins College like the extra programming in residential life. **Services for the undergraduate student body** like the Arts at Rollins College interface participation between Winter Park museums and the festivals at Rollins' own Annie Russell Theatre.

Compatibility with Personality Types and Preferences

At Rollins College students will know where they stand with the professors. A clearly outlined course of studies in the General Education Requirements, or the alternative Rollins Plan, will be appreciated by those students who like to be grounded (S) in the practical world of today. The Rollins College Conference courses are first year seminars that require students to analyze a particular topic. The RCC fulfills two purposes. First year students get to know a small group of fellow students. The topic studied in their assigned RCC is also the same topic studied in a separate course taken during the semester. In this way students can analyze (T) one subject from two different perspectives.

The administration has an attentive faculty which oversees the undergraduate student body on this campus. There are a number of programs and activities which include features of mentoring and guidance which are offered to the student. The Pre-Orientation Program is an excellent example of this commitment and gets to the heart (F) of mentoring with newly arriving under-represented students. It offers several days of transition services about information on campus and provides an opportunity for friendships in the opening days. Students attracted to this campus appreciate the clear communication, thoughtful recreational planning and emphasis on service options that the administration offers.

In the following listing of college majors it is important to remember that students can fit into any college and can be successful in any major. We have found that the Personality Types below fit very well at this college. The course-of-study chosen for each Personality Type corresponds to MBTI® research and is presented as an example favorable for that type.

ESTJ is an excellent fit on this campus. They will understand and value the accountability required to earn a Rollins degree with academic practices that are

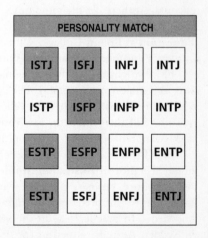

PERSONALITY MATCH

ISTJ	ISFJ	INFJ	INTJ
ISTP	ISFP	INFP	INTP
ESTP	ESFP	ENFP	ENTP
ESTJ	ESFJ	ENFJ	ENTJ

technologically aggressive in combining efficiency with learning on this campus. ESTJs are more than able to analyze information and reformulate organized patterns, similar to algorithms with Rollins' exceptional IT capacities. The software principles and capstone project in the **Computer Science** major at Rollins College are nicely organized and likely to meet with ESTJ approval throughout the four years. The Senior Audit, required of students to petition for approval of their degree, should go without any hitches for this type.

ISTJ is going to be rewarded for their sustained effort and desire to unearth a large collection of pertinent facts. The extensive and heavily used information technology systems at Rollins will be a dream tool for this type. The Olin Electronic Research and Information Center has been a step ahead of the technology curve and will have the heavy duty software and databases to manipulate data. The **Biochemistry/ Molecular Biology** major is just such a degree that will ultimately make heavy use of technology. ISTJ will appreciate the advanced approach to technical number crunching on this campus.

ESTP will get appreciation from their peers for their ability to quickly solve problems in the social scene. For example, they will jump in and work through the natural tension generated in the artistic process of playwriting within the Fred Stone Theater group. The minor in **Theater Arts and Dance** at Rollins, as well as the major, is outstanding. This type is one for the action and they enjoy performing. ESTPs could also be attracted to other Rollins clubs like the Student Alumni Association because their energetic, focused style of leadership will shine with older generations.

ISFJ is also an excellent fit on this campus that is near many of the ground water lakes in central Florida. The degree in **Marine Biology** at Rollins College is quite a good fit for this type. ISFJs will find there is a demand for precise observation and manipulation of the recorded information. They are very adept at this as long as standard procedure is followed. Rollins College faculty are quite well-structured in their approach to education and ISFJs will find that very helpful.

ISFP learns through hands-on participation. They seek to secure a personal inner meaning that is critical for satisfaction and fulfillment. They prefer to support and encourage others. At the same time, they are likely to add variety and change into their daily work. All in all, these characteristics support selection of the major in **Education** at Rollins College. With additional coursework, ISFPs can complete the Teacher Education Program that is outlined by the state of Florida.

ESFP might stretch their imagination by concentrating on the potential for fun with this major/minor combo. The courses in biology might easily lead to graduate studies in occupational therapy. Fellow grad students will smile when ESFP, taking advantage of their minor in **Environmental Studies** suggests a new concept "field and stream rehabilitation" that would be fishing of sorts!

ENTJ will like the global perspectives brought to Rollins through the culturally-oriented minor in **Australian Studies**, not typically found at liberal arts colleges. Art, literature, business, geography and botany of the land are all covered. Equally important to this preference is Rollins' comfort and even mandate which is putting knowledge to practical use in the world beyond academia. Required course work in Sydney, Australia is perfect for opportunistic ENTJ who might also survey the landscape for potential summer job offers too.

SAINT LOUIS UNIVERSITY

Office of Admission
13 Dubourg Hall
St. Louis, MO 63103-2907
Admission Telephone: 314-977-2500
Website: www.slu.edu
Undergraduates: 7,086; 3,118 Men, 3,968 Women
Graduate Students: 1,881

Physical Environment

St. Louis University, or SLU as students say, is located in mid-town St. Louis, near the art district and medical centers. The campus covers about a mile of the downtown area. This linear, inner city campus is connected by landscaped lawns, pathways and architectural spaces that create a **self-enclosed and cohesive** environment. Students walk downtown to the many restaurants and theatres. Mindful of the city streets, undergraduates also volunteer in soup kitchens and clothing distribution centers for the local homeless population. Students **readily volunteer** with Catholic Charities and other relief organizations in the true **Jesuit tradition**. The **St. Louis University Hospital** is located one-and-a-half miles from main campus on Grand Boulevard which is adding pedestrian and bicycle traffic friendly renovations in 2012. The hospital draws in students seeking **medical careers** in occupational and physical therapy, pediatric research, nursing and public health. The long-established Parks College of Engineering and Aviation is located on the other end of campus. It has a wind-tunnel and advanced technical instrumentation. The St Louis airport is only seven miles distant from the campus.

SLU offers a variety of on-campus housing options. The Griesedieck complex includes First Year Interest Groups which house freshmen together with two or three of the same classes. Marchetti East and West Towers and the village apartments appeal to upperclassmen. However, these rooms are limited and on-campus housing is not guaranteed for four years. There are other halls that form **living-and-learning communities** which make it easy for residents to study together. Members of the 18 Greek sororities and fraternities primarily live in DeMattius Hall. Students who want to get involved in **community service** can enter the MICAH program and members are housed on the same floor within the dormitory.

The brass statue of Billiken, campus mascot, is a funny-looking dwarf and a good luck charm. Undergraduate students set themselves up for success by developing spiritually, academically and socially. **Sports** have a good presence on campus. SLU is in the Atlantic 10 conference. Undergraduates support their basketball team with energy and will enjoy the new Medical Center Stadium that is the home for SLU's track and field team. Others take in a Cardinals game or watch with amusement as the city begins to love the Rams again. For fun, students enjoy visiting nearby Forest Park for picnics or long walks.

Social Environment

Catholic, hard-working and **goal-driven** describe the students here. They are comfortable with their spirituality. Students are motivated to transform society, not in words but in deeds. The Jesuit teaching philosophy is much opposed to mediocrity. Students **strive for excellence** in academics and in life, under an umbrella of ideals that presents a positive view of the world. That ethical truth permeates the classroom and the social experience.

The most popular majors are within the health sciences and undergrads will get much support in their choice of career path from the Office of Pre-Professional Health Studies. It provides exceptional courses starting with "Foundations of Medicine" through "Introduction to Medical School." Students typically have a good idea about what they want to major in. Students like courses such as "Foundations of Medicine and the Helping Profession" which have an internship component at the nearby hospitals. The university has strong health sciences in the curriculum. Students with an excellent academic record can apply in their sophomore year for admission to the University's medical school.

Regardless of major selection, undergraduates at this university receive a realistic and superior education. They graduate well-prepared for the challenges of the 21st century workforce that are sure to evolve.

Compatibility with Personality Types and Preferences

Saint Louis University calls out and welcomes prospective students on their website in the familiar text and language of high school students. The university reaches out to students in a trendy way yet the message is clearly Jesuit. Students who positively respond are comfortable at some level with searching for truth and competence in God's world. The central theme of this philosophy is serving (F) the poor and disadvantaged. It supplements the educational curriculum with distinct purpose and practical utility (S) in each major and minor.

The university projects its deep optimism in mankind's ability through supporting the American national community. The faculty and administration fine tune their course offerings to reflect today's occupational demands. This same curriculum will be adjusted when the needs of society transform and evolve. Graduates are typically in touch with and contribute to their professional career fields at many levels over a lifetime. This sensitivity also translates into personal balance and students actively seek relaxation in athletics and the latest bands coming to campus (E).

Since current majors and degrees answer the needs of America's 'help wanted,' students are pursuing some pretty demanding majors. Experiential and technical learning is common and available through the university's local, regional and national networks. The SLU campus in Madrid, Spain is strongly conversant with the nearby Spanish citizens and accesses the European sensibilities for those studying abroad in international

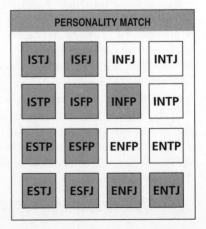

PERSONALITY MATCH

ISTJ	ISFJ	INFJ	INTJ
ISTP	ISFP	INFP	INTP
ESTP	ESFP	ENFP	ENTP
ESTJ	ESFJ	ENFJ	ENTJ

majors. Graduates of Saint Louis University typically excel in graduate schools and workplaces. They move into community service and leadership that underlies their personal career goals.

In the following listing of college majors it is important to remember that students can fit into any college and can be successful in any major. We have found that the Personality Types below fit very well at this college. The course-of-study chosen for each Personality Type corresponds to MBTI® research and is presented as an example favorable for that type.

INFP always has a couple of dreams and possibilities up their sleeve so flexibility in course studies is a prerequisite. At Saint Louis University, the degree in **Nutrition and Dietetics** exposes students to several work environments in this field and adds one more—personal nutritionist/chef. Regardless of their employer, INFP will find the freedom and autonomy they need to be creative and satisfied. Often this degree will lead to positions as a consultant. This also suits INFPs because they can pursue work that is in synch with their vision of a humane world. The educational philosophy at SLU is music to their ears.

ISTP has the intuition and patience to use sensitive diagnostic equipment. The degree in **Clinical Laboratory Science** at Saint Louis University is demanding of both of these inclinations. Much of the course work focuses on biological processes and so the ISTP is going to jump at the chance to internship in the hospitals. This type is fascinated with the options and potential use of technical equipment. On the job, they are likely to improve the state of the art in diagnosis.

ISTJ will relate to historical and spiritual perspectives at Saint Louis University because this type prefers stability and traditional organizations. This dependable type is a natural for the field of **Accounting.** At SLU, this is a concentration within the Business Administration degree. ISTJs can tote up a line of figures more accurately than just about any other type. This university, this degree and this type are exactly what American corporate business can use to bring accountability back into their world.

ISFJ likes to be directly involved, one on one, helping others. They are often found in social service and health care careers. The four year degree in **Occupational Science** at Saint Louis University is perfectly tailored to pursue licensure in Occupational Therapy with the 5th year Masters Degree. The university's hospital and the downtown medical centers in Saint Louis make access to clinical settings a breeze. ISFJ is thorough and the extra year will not likely be viewed as a burden. Rather, this type will appreciate the department's clear guidelines and expectations in a major that requires attentive advising and precise training. These are both SLU specialties!

ISFP is the perfect personality to be interacting with patients receiving medical treatment for illnesses. The program in **Radiation Therapy** within the Allied Health Sciences offers technical training that would be enjoyable for ISFPs to bring to the work place. They are naturals at affirming and supporting those around them. Their patients are likely to be grateful for their emotional support during treatment visits on those inevitable down days. ISFPs will immediately pick up on a patient feeling badly and respond with encouragement.

ESTP likes to be working with and studying 'how things really are.' The Bachelor of Science degree in **Aviation Management** fits the bill and SLU is one of the few universities offering it. ESTPs will be in the hangar at Park's College aviation facility among the aircraft. Upper level class work includes aircraft fleet management and engineering disciplines in aviation such as reliability, life cycle and project engineering. This type is a good troubleshooter and can excel at pulling together materials and people to accomplish aircraft operations.

ESFP will find that Saint Louis University offers the **Social Work** degree. This type is very comfortable helping others. The excellent internships and experiential learning are available within a quick walk to the St Louis neighborhoods which will prepare ESFPs for the demands of social work. SLU's educational philosophy and moral emphasis will also help protect against discouragement that can accompany this helping profession occasionally.

ESFJ can tailor a business degree at Saint Louis University to secure employment that meets their strong need for a harmony in the work place. The major in **Human Resource Management** with a certificate in **Service Leadership** is ideal for managers who must monitor hiring and firing, retirement and other critical services provided to employees. Typical city municipalities and large corporations all have resource managers and internships will be forthcoming for ESFJs who are curious about and supporting of others.

ESTJ is often quite good at collecting, finding and analyzing facts. What could be better for a major in **Investigative and Medical Sciences**? The degree has a flavor of intrigue since it was added several years ago into the curriculum to meet the forensic science needs of our nation's crime labs. ESTJs will also appreciate the practicality of the degree since it is a fine option for entrance to medical school or pharmaceutical research. All in all, ESTJ's penchant for organizing facts and applying logic will be ideal for this undergraduate degree.

ENFJ likes a diverse array of people and their viewpoints. At the same time, they are excellent communicators and talented at delivering messages that are in synch with their personal ideals. The certificate in **Political Journalism** will offer this type a focused practice in all of the above. It pairs up with any major and especially fits well with a degree in communication or political science. This type has a natural inclination toward leadership with internal discipline. These skills just might keep ENFJ on the job in the rapid, swirling world of political campaigns. Certainly their idealistic vision will find a home at Saint Louis University.

ENTJ has the vision to work in an emerging field like **Biomedical Engineering**. There is much on the horizon for this type to look forward to utilizing their crisp strategic planning. ENTJ is very much about business at the same time. Perhaps there will be patents in the future for this entrepreneurial type. Saint Louis University is all about applying your knowledge. The course work and department will fit this type's inclinations pretty well.

SALVE REGINA UNIVERSITY

100 Ochre Point Avenue
Newport, RI 02840
Website: www.salve.edu
Admissions Telephone: 401-467-2583
Undergraduates: 2,028; 619 Men, 1,409 Women

Physical Environment

Salve Regina University is bordered by the **opulent Victorian mansions** of Bellevue Avenue and **The Cliff Walk** towering over Easton Bay on the Atlantic Ocean. This university was sponsored by the **Catholic Order of the Sisters of Mercy** who in early years utilized the **historical buildings** in **resourceful ways** to build financial reserves.

There is a clear interrelationship between the students and geographic location. People come from all over the world to visit the mansions on Bellevue Avenue and the **coastline of Newport**. In September, students rub elbows with the last summer tourists and then enjoy the town as their own. The renovation of the historic Stanford White Casino Theatre will become available to undergraduates in the strong theater major. Students will descend the "40 steps" to the huge boulders by sea and some may ponder the scenery. Popular water sports, **sailing and surfing,** are super.

Historic Ochre Court is the first stop for visitors, the focal point of campus and the center for many ceremonies. The elegant architecture draws in students who are curious about the values and ways of the Gilded Age. Sophomores are housed in these historic buildings on campus, while first years are assigned to traditional dormitory style residences that support community building. Upperclassmen elect modern housing options adjacent to campus.

Social Environment

The unique residences described above encourage immediate friendships for first years. The well-documented sophomore slump is headed off with the excitement of returning students and their assignment to palatial residences. On this campus, students and faculty form a solid community which reflects the mission of the Sisters of Mercy. Students of all faiths are taught in the Catholic tradition of **harmony, justice and mercy**. During the 1990s, the long serving President of the University and the Order generated stability and diligence. Generations of students readily valued the campus environment and often become committed to directly serving the community. This university community standard continues with **Service Plunge,** an overnight service and leadership retreat for incoming freshmen and transfer students. The male – female student numbers above reflect the unfortunate trend of reduced participation by young men in collegiate education quite common in American universities.

Salve Regina University attracts students whose high school transcript records solid B academic work. The vast majority come from out of state. Students who may be concerned about their academic and organizational track record in high school will find **solid academic support** from the Salve faculty and staff. The curriculum from nursing to historic preservation, biomedical sciences and specialized degrees in early childhood education, is very much designed for **developing skills** to take into the workplace.

Compatibility with Personality Types and Preferences

Salve Regina University is for students who like their education to be straight forward (S) in a fun, evenly-balanced atmosphere. The entire feel of the campus has much in common with the words responsible, healthy and caring (F). Faculty is attentive and actively mentors students toward academic competency. The faculty and administration pay close attention to the needs of incoming freshmen. The Student Government Association is quite active in partnership with faculty on academic policy. The campus with its small feel is very conducive to forming friendships within the classes and in the dormitories. The comparatively safe and nearby city of Newport encourages exploration and offers undergraduates the ability to acquire city sophistication. The university has taken considerable advantage in developing certain educational programs that feature the impact of the international port and the historical presence of the Navy. Collaborating with other students in teams and projects is a common learning experience at Salve Regina. This approach to learning helps students gain leadership and social acumen as well as set realistic goals. A constant thread in the Salve Regina education is to build skills, develop a strong base of knowledge and identify personal values for the work force. Overlaying all of this is a delightful social atmosphere that supports healthy emotional growth.

PERSONALITY MATCH			
ISTJ	ISFJ	INFJ	INTJ
ISTP	ISFP	INFP	INTP
ESTP	ESFP	ENFP	ENTP
ESTJ	ESFJ	ENFJ	ENTJ

In the following listing of college majors it is important to remember that students can fit into any college and can be successful in any major. We have found that the Personality Types below fit very well at this college. The course-of-study chosen for each Personality Type corresponds to MBTI® research and is presented as an example favorable for that type.

ISFJ will really appreciate the historic and elegant architecture at Salve Regina. Aside from this however, ISFJ's inclination for personal precision will point in the direction of a **Medical Technology** degree. Their meticulous observation is well matched with serving others both of which provide this type with a sense of accomplishment and satisfaction. It is a major not often offered at liberal arts universities.

ISFP may look closely at the **Social Work** degree at Salve Regina. The department has an international perspective that is well understood in Newport that served as an international port for centuries. Social work with an international perspective looks at worldwide community development. The curriculum also explores intergenerational attitudes within cultures around the world. Interaction with young children or the elderly is naturally appealing to ISFPs. Since this campus is so attentive to human concerns, it is a perfect place to pursue a helping profession.

ESFP is quite attracted to work environments that require specialized skills. The major in **Early Childhood Education** certainly fits this description. The course in "Authentic Assessment" prepares the Salve Regina graduate in this field to recognize when a child's development is out synch with the typical growth patterns. This type likes to have fun and is very much aware of the present. Who better to play with the kids, yet notice both the strengths and weaknesses of each child entrusted to their care?

ESFJ surely understands a founding philosophy at Salve Regina University: relieve misery and address its cause. The **Nursing** degree is comprehensive and well-supported through internships in densely populated Newport. There is a strong component of coursework in mental health. ESFJs will gain sustenance and comfort from the pervasive helping nature that permeates this campus. This type builds strength from values-oriented discussion. Moral guideposts allow ESFJs to avoid becoming overwhelmed while nursing the sick and dejected.

ISTP loves action and mechanics. The **Interactive Communication Technology** major at Salve Regina University will allow ISTPs to develop computer-generated media. The curriculum looks closely at the communication process. Along similar lines, the technical aspects of theater will definitely pull this type in. Classes like Stagecraft will utilize their troubleshooting instincts. The minor or major in **Theater** is nicely paired with the close study of communication arts. The technical perspectives in both theater and computing are really pleasing to this type. It is a nice combination of study that is not offered frequently at small liberal arts institutions.

ESTP likes to work with real things. They have a good sense of space and mechanical knowledge. The major in **Cultural and Historic Preservation** will take advantage of both of these. Laboratory courses in this major are on location at preservation projects within the local community. On occasion, coursework will involve archeological digs and ESTP's fine observational skills will be brilliant at the dig. The coursework in this major is well-selected and ESTP will appreciate this rather unusual major at a small liberal arts institution.

INFJ could really enjoy the long established and unique **Administration of Justice** degree at Salve Regina. Mercy, in all its senses, is the go-by for the Salve Regina administration and faculty. Undergraduate students will examine and develop a commitment to values that serve the doctrines of fairness. The curriculum helps students explore the meaning of mercy, harmony and justice, three very different words. Practical, reality-based components are explored relating to probation, parole and juvenile justice. This educational study will keep the INFJs content as they ponder the abstract values and the necessary relationship with the practical enforcement of justice.

ENFP might be drawn into the combined major in **Anthropology and Sociology** through their preference for the big picture and change. Certainly our nation is experiencing changing social patterns. There is a need for ENFPs who can readily provide constructs to decipher social issues. It is important for this type to bring enthusiasm and creativity to their workplace. ENFPs also prefer to work with a diverse group of people. This is all consistent with Salve Regina's educational philosophy.

ENFJ and the **English** degree jump into place with a review of curriculum options in this field. Students specialize in one of three areas: English Literature, English Literature and Secondary Education or English Communications. Fine literature is woven throughout the three majors so that the student gains practice in writing and thinking precisely. Combined with the Christian ethical perspectives, this curriculum offers both the complexity and service perspectives which are attractive to ENFJs.

SARAH LAWRENCE COLLEGE

1 Mead Way
Bronxville, NY 10708-5999
Website: www.slc.edu
Admissions Telephone: 914-395-2510, 800-888-2858
Undergraduates: 1,227; 345 Men, 882 Women
Graduate Students: 255

Physical Environment

You won't find big bold signs announcing the location of Sarah Lawrence College as you exit the Hutchinson River Parkway north of New York City. The pale green signage for the college is barely noticeable as one drives onto the campus. Located 30 minutes from the Big Apple, Sarah Lawrence College is tucked away from the noisy hustle and bustle of the city and quietly welcomes the visitor with a sudden silence, tall trees, green lawns and **English Tudor-style** buildings. Modern buildings have been added to one side of the campus; they are covered by ivy. Below the tall canopies of fir trees the hard edges of the modern buildings are softened. Here students can imagine the tales of Robin Hood and the **enchanted forest**. It's an inviting place, ideal if you want to set up an easel and draw or paint and ideal if you want to relax or get down to **intellectual and creative** conversations with other students. SLC was established as a liberal arts college in 1926 and became coed in 1968.

The Tudor-style dormitories house faculty offices, classrooms and conference rooms where morning meetings with the Don (advisors) are held. The proximity of the professors' work-space to the living and sleeping space of the students fosters easy interaction and ongoing communication between the faculty and students. These dorms characterize the nature of this college where **learning and living** take place together without designation of specific dormitories or halls. Ninety percent of the students live on campus.

The external environment is conducive to personal growth and self-expression without traditional social foundations Thus there is a psychological symmetry between the park-like setting and the work of these undergraduates who prefer abstraction and SLC's free rein to explore their inclinations.

Social Environment

SLC students merge their private world with that of others on campus by actively **sharing ideologies, sentiments and beliefs**. However, they may never execute actions based of these ideas, especially if they enjoy discussing and debating for its own sake. They like to study what is meaningful to them. Those students who remain committed to their chosen area of **independent study** in the first year, under the tutelage of their Don, will secure the advantages of a Sarah Lawrence education. The hallmark student is the one who is attracted to the medium of writing and interested in the wide range of liberal arts, from the esoteric to the unknown. Written evaluations are rendered and grades recorded only for the purpose of a transcript. The vast majority are in the top one-quarter of their high school graduation class.

The curriculum and the mentoring system keep these students on track because they enroll in **three year-long courses annually**. In one of these courses there will be tutorials with one professor who is referred to as "**Don**," who will mentor the student several times a week for the entire academic year. Thus it becomes quite important for students to develop their intellectual and personal relationship with their "Don." Students with a passion delve deeply into their selected area of study and are expected to express that passion in **writing often**.

Many students are supportive of one another's personal style no matter how different. For the most part, they tend to form strong ties and become a closely-knit community of idealists. They are not over the top on athletics. Casual banter and trendy spots may be of less interest.

Compatibility with Personality Types and Preferences

Sarah Lawrence is a campus for those futuristic-oriented (N), caring folks (F) in a casual but compelling way. Since the administration and faculty expect students to take charge of their own education, it's very possible for undergraduates to choose coursework that is tailored to their interests. Sarah Lawrence faculty wants students to develop individual perspective and beliefs that can direct passion toward their studies and careers upon graduation. The student body at this university is change-oriented (P) and attracted to novel interpretation. What could be more attractive to these students who love change than this educational approach that demands flexibility and innovation? Here students will be able to spin a strong thread between individual interests, curriculum and future careers.

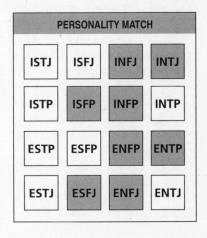

In the following listing of college majors it is important to remember that students can fit into any college and can be successful in any major. We have found that the Personality Types below fit very well at this college. The course-of-study chosen for each Personality Type corresponds to MBTI® research and is presented as an example favorable for that type.

INFJ and freedom of expression go together like hand in glove. At Sarah Lawrence there will be no shortage of conversations questioning the status quo and examining the ills of society. The Conference System pairs student and professor, biweekly, to discuss the most meaningful way to complete the course. The INFJ, who needs to explore the depth of one particular author like Wordsworth rather than survey three or four similar texts, will find the course in **Writing** and the course titled The Writer's Life an ideal combination to focus on one particular author.

INFP can be quiet and is very often passionate. They develop and explore their unique inner vision or belief system. Here at Sarah Lawrence they are likely to reach for a personal understanding of a subject by discussion with other students. Undergraduates who are equally observant and willing to work at defining values will happily join their conversation. INFPs will admire and approve of SLC's wide-ranging focus in the **Biology** department. In this department, INFP can explore the limits and boundaries of human health while preparing for graduate study in physical therapy.

INTJ who is analytical and future-oriented will want to take advantage of the Conference Courses for advanced students. This type will precisely prepare for approval from their Don and the Committee on Student Work. The Division of Science and Math will provide a curriculum that stretches INTJ's passion at tackling big problems. Their process in tackling may be a fuzzy gestalt or clearly defined; their intellectual predisposition surely finds a perfect home in the **Science Third Program**. It helps INTJ interface their solution penchant with mathematical concepts and perspectives.

ENTP thrives on a wide-ranging knowledge and tension in the debating scene. This logical type would enjoy sparking debates that contrast the idealism prevalent on this campus versus reality in contemporary American life. The interdisciplinary nature of the course work at SLC meets ENTP's need for variety. It wouldn't be hard to imagine ENTPs signing up for the **History** courses like The Idea of a Balance of Power. Since their primary interests often focus on laws and principles, the combination of philosophy and recent historical events is dynamite.

ENFP might get the greatest benefit from the Don system at SLC. The Don must provide the structure necessary for this type's free-roaming intellect, yet the Don will be pleasantly surprised and rewarded by ENFPs' typical warmth, enthusiasm and caring. SLC's Early Childhood Center is more than capable of firing up ENFP's imagination. Observation along with study in child development will fire up ENFP's insights. Interaction with the children comes naturally for this fun-loving type. The required meetings with ENFP's Don will help bring the insight and meaning to the experience.

ISFP will accept introspective debate at SLC when the subjects are centered on serving others or nature. Their strong practical bent will be attracted to community partnerships and service learning in the **Chemistry** department that combine course readings with volunteering in the surrounding community. ISFPs must secure a strong sense of personal worth during life's travels. They typically reach this through action and hands-on activity.

ESFJ is usually orderly and down to earth. This type might be amused by some of the expansive ideas that float through and around the Sarah Lawrence campus. ESFJs are almost always focused on the people around them. Giving and receiving energy and affirmation is a natural activity. Their passion lies in serving others. SLC interfaces service-learning with the reality-based major **Science, Technology and Society**. Undergraduates perform on-site internships within the community about real-world problems that are influenced by science. This type of learning is excellent for ESFJs. They will further enjoy understanding how society influences and shapes science.

ENFJ is another good bet for this campus. This imaginative idealist who demands harmony prefers and must have diversity of perspectives and peoples. They weave imagination and options together by listening to all perspectives with objectivity and caring. They value the viewpoints of others. The concentration in **Public Policy** at SLC offers a wealth of sociology courses that start with the exploration of difficult societal themes like promoting peace. ENFJs graduating in this discipline will excel at verbal presentations, often changing the perspectives of their audience.

STANFORD UNIVERSITY

520 Lasuen Mall
Stanford, CA 94305-3005
Website: www.stanford.edu
Admissions Telephone: 650-723-2091
Undergraduates: 6,854; 3,549 Men, 3,305 Women
Graduate Enrollment: 8,438

Physical Environment

Imagine 8,000 acres in northern California, eye-pleasing Spanish architecture and a lake with many walking, biking and hiking trails. Stanford appeals to students who like the outdoors, which is not hard to do in this **idyllic climate** of southern San Francisco Bay. Easy to get to from the airport, a student can take the BART to an above-ground train with a stop at the campus. **Bicycles** however, are the transportation vehicle of choice for those who want to make the most of their time. That is virtually everyone at this very selective institution. The Bicycle Undergrads create vehicle jams along with the skateboard crowd and other wheels around the rotunda, jokingly dubbed "the death circle." We can attest to the fact that it is wise to stay out of their way.

Students typically live on campus. Not bound to any house systems, they can live in any of the resident halls. During busy times one recalls media images of China with so many bikers pedaling energetically to their destination. Bike parks are a social meeting place. Sorority and fraternity houses offer residential options for their members. The **outdoor café** by the main library is another social stop for students who need a perk in between the long hours of study. The new Arillage Family Dining Commons features a Culinary Studio and cooking classes. Not to be undervalued for lack of gastronomic relief, the library houses a **huge, invaluable research collection** of books in the humanities and social sciences. Did we mention bicycles?

Social Environment.

Stanford students look attractive, **sporty** and sociable. They dress well, on the preppy side, and look cool on their skateboards, with iPods, attired in shorts. No doubt students from cold climates feel unencumbered and relaxed here. Sixty percent of students who attend Stanford come from other states than California, however there is little time for state and home town banter. These students are **serious** about their studies and their future. They understand the **research culture** that prevails here. After getting accepted, students (who were in the top eight percent of their class) must be focused on taking advantage of the research opportunities especially in the social sciences, either by researching an idea of their own or helping professors with their research. This may be why students are up at two in the morning discussing an idea, whether or not it will ever see the light of day. For Stanford undergrads, it's important to get these **ideas out in the open** and discuss them. Students mix and match various classes to define their major. For example, a student studied Product Design and enrolled in an interdisciplinary program called "IDEA," which requires **connective thinking** to link design with the Biology major. Featured at 107 participating universities, Stanford provides access to this platform for students to generate emerging individual thoughts beyond the impact of current faculty interests and research. Bravo Stanford - and the other 20 universities in our book that elect this approach to educating tomorrow's leaders.

Compatibility with Personality Types and Preferences

Stanford University is a superb educational institution for the undergraduate student on a mission to excel. Since all students on campus seem to fit this definition, the determination in the air is more than considerable. Fast-moving undergrads on bikes mirror the precise, linear thinking on this campus (T). The typical high school graduate arrives at Stanford with a well-developed passion for a special topic or subject. Within their passion, undergrad students ask 'How does this occur?' and 'What next is important to discover?' As juniors and seniors in high school, these students were incurably curious. Now at Stanford, they actively jump into the chance to experiment, study and inundate their minds with knowledge. As students on this casual but intense campus, they are likely to be open and excited about exploring (N) while accumulating a solid foundation of hard facts (S) in their chosen field. The faculty and administration expect and enhance this daily, weekly, semester after semester investment (J) of personal/physical energy. Who fits in well here? The bright student who packs the day with class, study, research, student activity meetings, professor appointments, more classes and guest lectures and tops it off with roomie dialogues on that last lecture of the evening. Flexibility and individual choice highlights residential planning by the administration. Stanford loyalties are to the ideas and the knowledge forged within the student body or campus organizations.

Underlying the campus energy and productivity is confidence. Students do not second guess their interests, commitment or ability to secure that exceptional Stanford education. Professors pursue their directed research at the graduate level and welcome the interested, prepared undergraduate who inquires about it. At the same time, there are seemingly endless options to design and execute mini-research with the curriculum of the undergraduate degree. Research grants and other resources needed to pursue and define new knowledge are available to the motivated undergraduate. This type of research can often be accomplished within a quarter or two and suits the young, confident learner who wants to cram as much as possible into those four short years.

The university takes the mini-research a step further by offering a rather unique co-term program. Co-term allows undergraduates to apply for graduate school and take grad course work during the undergraduate years. The distinct advantage is flexibility and freedom (P) to pursue an academic interest through courses simultaneously at upper and lower levels. The productive, determined Stanford undergraduate is met with a willing

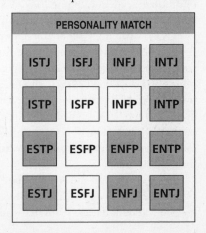

PERSONALITY MATCH

ISTJ	ISFJ	INFJ	INTJ
ISTP	ISFP	INFP	INTP
ESTP	ESFP	ENFP	ENTP
ESTJ	ESFJ	ENFJ	ENTJ

administration and a faculty dedicated to expanding knowledge utilizing student curiosity and perseverance as the primary tool.

In the following listing of college majors it is important to remember that students can fit into any college and can be successful in any major. We have found that the Personality Types below fit very well at this college. The course-of-study chosen for each Personality Type corresponds to MBTI® research and is presented as an example favorable for that type.

ENFP with their broad range of interests might enjoy the freedom that exists within **Material Science and Engineering**. The degree at Stanford puts exceptional research options at the disposal of the undergrad. ENFPs are passionate about their sense of the possible. They apply their gut instincts to just about any subject. The elbow room within this discipline and the possibilities of emerging applications of materials calls loudly to persuasive, fun-loving ENFP. This department especially concentrates on nanotechnology. It also calls up the need for dreamers and those who brainstorm and invent their way through to solutions and new discoveries.

ISFJ can mix together their fabulous factual memory and ability to accurately recall the context of a social activity. The **Linguistics** major at Stanford will make use of both of these assets. It also doesn't hurt that language systems are highly structured which appeals to this type. Learning in this discipline tends to take advantage of language labs where sensory activity like computer-assisted instruction and audio and visual presentations are typical and also favored by ISFJs. At Stanford, the undergraduate has access to the comprehensive social research mechanisms available in the Humanities Center. Students must concentrate in an area such as Language Structures or Language and Society. ISFJs will explore the extensive body of research housed on this campus through the lens of their typical social acumen.

INFJ typically hopes to delve into complex projects or work that benefits others and the major in **Symbolic Systems** at Stanford fits the bill. This major seems packed with abstract possibilities, yet it is a very grounded degree growing out of the disciplines of language, mathematics and objective information. INFJs will be successful at extracting meaning from language systems and creative in transferring those meanings to computational theory and utility. The degree crosses several traditional academic boundaries of knowledge. This type is both competent and comfortable crossing into new territories.

INTJ with high school or community experience in theater could find the Bachelor of Arts in **Drama** at Stanford very compelling. It includes a considerable component of theory, critical study and production. INTJs who declare this major must also select one of seven emphases. This type likes the freedom and integration found in the Directing emphasis. The in-depth study of theater's role throughout literature and history will very likely appeal to INTJs. Given the considerable coursework in production, staging, performing and directing, the INTJ will have the tools to let their fertile minds fly while creating original performances, possibly for the senior project.

ISTP could find the **Art Practice** major at Stanford calling out to the maverick side of their personality. This type often wants to experiment and push technical, mechanical boundaries. ISTPs have an abundance of original thinking and creativity when it comes to their passions. The artistically-talented ISTP who wants to work with metals, glasses and solid materials will quickly utilize the scientific equipment available on this research campus. Their dreams can be formed into arts media through discovery and combination of the physical properties found within common or rare earth elements. Stanford's engineering, geology and chemistry labs stand at the ready for the budding ISTP three-dimensional artist.

ISTJ looks with interest and appreciation at the objective nature of the Stanford major in **Geophysics**. The curriculum is arranged so that graduates can directly enter the work force or move on to graduate studies. This is a practical feature that appeals to ISTJs. The discipline will make good use of their spectacular memory for details and admirable powers of concentration. ISTJ will gladly step up individual research utilizing facilities in the Center for Computational Earth & Environmental Science. If there is a daunting competency to be reached for, step aside for the ISTJs, they are up for Rock Physics. They do not leave much to chance and their data banks of personal knowledge are notable, if not eye-watering.

INTP has the patience and insight to secure solutions to the technical problems which compose much of the advanced curriculum in **Product Design**. Stanford offers this unusual major within the School of Engineering. The course work is an interesting blend of art, psychology, math and mechanical engineering. The Product Design coursework focuses on benefiting society through adaptive practices, systems and equipment. The graduate with this degree will have knowledge and skills to plow through dilemmas in work and living environments. Products in this sense can be revolutionary; think of Velcro. INTP is just the type to get absorbed in a societal need and come up with a winning patent.

ESTP has a set of skills primed for action. ESTPs are driven to be productive in the present situation and time frame. Although the major in **Aeronautics and Astronautics** will require a focus on the future, the day to day work environment is stimulating and oriented toward observable events, in particular, observable dilemmas such as how to recycle life sustaining chemicals or how to move around in light gravity on a planet surface. These 'how' questions are a specialty of Stanford's approach to education and it is also a favorite ESTP word. The department assumes that each student will pursue a graduate degree in the field. The research equipment at this campus is extensive and will support ESTP's penchant for troubleshooting, acute observation and flexibility.

ENTP with an interest in politics will jump right into the problem solving offered by the senior seminar in **Public Policy**. This major appeals to ENTPs because of the high stakes decision making in a local and regional government. ENTPs are comfortable with the world of power and influence. Stanford's curriculum specifically engages the bay area community to provide policy analyses for community issues in commerce, public services and social services. Stanford undergraduates get firsthand experience with success or not so successful analytic problem solving. Bright, quick ENTP will be right at home sitting at the table, generating concepts for the group to review.

ESTJ will bring their strong reasoning and practical approaches to the curriculum in **Energy Resources Engineering**. Stanford has carved out a research niche in the search for energy production utilizing evolving engineering methods. The intersection between geology, energy and engineering is a firm yet emerging discipline. ESTJ has an administrative mind and will strongly identify with the focus for efficiency in this career field.

ENFJ is inclined to gather large views of historical movements as well as the reasons behind them. The Stanford degree in **History** is a broad three-dimensional approach taking in time, the world's geographical regions and a selected topic. More than likely, competent, composed ENFJ will put this education to good use with a follow on Master's Degree to attain expertise in their chosen field. Undergraduate research will center on the amazing collection of social science research at the Green Library. ENFJs are likely to forge personal relationships within the community of librarians and assistants as they secure a foundation in their concentration. All this prepares ENFJs to move forward with the graduate degree and a career in advocacy and influential leadership. Idealists at heart, ENFJs will seek out the educational path that also capitalizes on their engaging, compelling style.

ENTJ will probably like the **Earth Systems Program** that is chock full of complexity and relevance. These two should dominate the discipline if this type is going to happily expend energy within a career field. ENTJ's competitive, sharp instincts will hone productive thoughts between human activity and the earth environment. Stanford shapes this degree with the critical question, 'What should be measured within the air, land and organisms of the planet?' This seems to comprise the first two undergraduate years of study. Thereafter the question of 'How to measure and gain relevant meaning?' launches the ENTJ on a demanding quest for the remaining two years on campus. This type's natural inclination to apply logic while searching for new associations and meanings is ideal for the increasing importance of Earth's ecological systems.

SWARTHMORE COLLEGE

500 College Avenue
Swarthmore, PA 19081-1390
Website: www.swarthmore.edu
Admissions Telephone: 610-328-8300, 800-667-3110
Undergraduates: 1,510; 741 Men, 769 Women

Physical Environment

The Swarthmore campus is a beautiful **arboretum** that reveals itself slowly, with walking trails behind stone buildings and an outdoor amphitheater surrounded by woods. There are no frills in the architecture here. The buildings' **clean lines** are appealing for their **simplicity**. Intellectual students who have spent much time in the outdoors, pondering nature, are attracted to Swarthmore. The thick woods and sheer beauty of the trees have a calming effect; most favored are the outdoor amphitheater and endless discussions about **life and philosophy** while sitting on the white Adirondack chairs randomly located around the campus.

The ethos of this campus pushes through with uncluttered buildings and grounds conducive to thinking about learning and creating community. Students eat together in Sharples Dining Hall, located in the center of campus. Dining services caters to undergrads who want to picnic before the weather closes in with delightful, delicious-looking picnic baskets to go. The Swarthmore **Friends Meeting Place** speaks of tolerance among people of all faiths and races. Almost all students live on campus or in school-sponsored housing. There is room indoors and outdoors for **introspection**, reflection and conversation too. When students want a faster pace, the nearby train takes students to the "city of brotherly love," Philadelphia, where some volunteer with initiatives to benefit the inner city.

Social Environment

A Swarthmore education requires students to **exert their minds** and so that they may comprehend and impact contemporary society. At the same time, these students are highly involved in activities other than academic. The clubs and organizations range from Amnesty International to Mother Puckers' women's ice hockey, Muslim, Jewish and Catholic students' association, to the Ten Commandments Leadership and Learning Fellowship. The Swarthmore Conservative Union, a former student organization, Swarthmore Republicans and Swarthmore Students Supporting Life seem to have little presence on this campus.

Swarthmore students tolerate some level of dissent within themselves. There is a high level of racial and ethnic awareness on this campus. These students seek their diversions in athletic, religious, literary and political fields. The Peaslee **Debate** Society is well-known for winning many parliamentary debates against other Ivy League colleges. Swarthmore students must have or develop the ability to think on their feet and come up with a reply to an argument as it is being made.

Students here write well and quite a bit. Even students enrolling for engineering, an unexpected major at this liberal-arts college, write a great deal and learn engineering within the context of a liberal arts education. They also practice public speaking through getting involved in theatre classes and productions. Students here are usually anti-war and shun public demonstrations of their ideas. Swarthmore honors the **concept of pacifism** and exposure to people from other countries and races. Some service projects reach into local neighborhoods while most activism is directed through on-campus activities. Students here are **absorbed in learning** and focused on sharpening their minds—service is balanced with other educational goals and one of the components.

It goes without saying that students are up to the academic rigors of this education. The Honors Program further challenges students by offering a sequence of courses and field work. The relationship between a student and professor is like the meeting of two bright lights. Students take the intellectual risks inherent in pursuing a challenging course of study. Some opt for a senior Honors Study with faculty members. Students can take classes within their consortium of colleges which include other nearby highly selective colleges.

Compatibility with Personality Types and Preferences

Swarthmore College is thorough and studied. Critical discussions form around the concepts of education, purpose and country. These conversations among faculty and students evolve and reformulate within the whole student body. Swarthmore is Quaker in origin and outlook. The college environment places high value on human life (F) by connecting those lives to purpose and utility within society. This transcends the curriculum and activities on the campus. Random activity has little use at Swarthmore and spontaneity is measured (T) and judged by its outcome or product. The minds of the students are frequently in overdrive as a result. Education is truly the winding path that you travel (P) and knowledge is information that you gather along the way. Swarthmore educators really fine tune the art of the question. In fact, there is a sequence of courses offered that center on the process of interpretation (N). To minimize excessive wear and stress on emotional stamina, the administration maintains a very functional environment. Directions and expectations are clear and simple in reference to curriculum requirements and major advising. Residential life is quite community-oriented and intimately connected with learning. Relationships within the college culture are key learning vehicles also. Alumni, faculty, administrators and undergraduates form a whole body that remains intact with the historical and very active Quaker values.

In the following listing of college majors it is important to remember that students can fit into any college and can be successful in any major. We have found that the Personality Types below fit very well at this college. The course-of-study chosen for each Personality Type corresponds to MBTI® research and is presented as an example favorable for that type.

PERSONALITY MATCH

ISTJ	ISFJ	INFJ	INTJ
ISTP	ISFP	INFP	INTP
ESTP	ESFP	ENFP	ENTP
ESTJ	ESFJ	ENFJ	ENTJ

INFP has iron will and iron values which could come in pretty handy with a minor of **Environmental Studies**. The Swarthmore catalog still starts the description for this minor with the statement that there are profound changes occurring in our earthly habitat. Undergraduates are expected to develop their own beliefs in respect to environmental issues confronting mankind. This values-oriented campus will surely assist INFPs as they do so in combination with their major. Expression of the inner self is critical for this type yet their private nature doesn't easily permit opportunities. This type could convey their deeply held beliefs by strongly advocating for environmental practice within their chosen career field.

INFJ is thoughtful and can be reserved. However when it's fun time, they get out their goof-meters and enjoy themselves with others. Their silly humor will go a long way in the sobering subject of **Economics.** This major at Swarthmore College very much focuses on scarcity, decision making and the ethics of how resources are distributed to the public. INFJs go over complicated ideas many times to search out something they missed and reconcile those ideas with their own values. Within this field, the INFJ graduate can follow their hearts and help bureaucracies refine procedure to distribute resources in an efficient way.

INTJ has the backup systems and mental software so to speak to sign up for Swarthmore College's minor in **Interpretation Theory.** This unusual collection of courses sharpens skill in intellectual analysis through a pointed look at history. It nicely combines with any other major on campus. The purpose of the minor is to understand the world. This is no small task and INTJ is not likely to shrink from it. This type's attraction to principles and ideas will come in handy too. They are likely to participate in many of the performing arts and lecture activities that abound on this campus.

ISFJ especially likes the facts and can handle a great volume of information. The major in **Mathematics and Statistics** at Swarthmore can serve up plenty. ISFJs are also rather sensitive types and will approve of this major, assuming they like numbers. It is especially appealing because the degree has great social utility with its emphasis on applied statistics. ISFJs are at liberty to select course work from any of the social sciences to pair with this major. On graduation, this type will be in the perfect position to provide all kinds of statistical data to nonprofits and organizations serving humanity.

ISFP can start studies at Swarthmore College with satisfaction in the special major in **Education Studies.** It is very similar to a major/minor in concept. The action-oriented ISFP will look forward to and enjoy the practicum in the classroom. They will likely select a major that takes advantage of their interest and empathy for others. Swarthmore has great flexibility and most of the social science majors include hands-on service learning. It is a win-win for the ISFP if the major and minor offers instruction out of the classroom and places them in the middle of the action with others.

INTP is likely to find the **History** minor at Swarthmore College a perfect counterpoint to a degree in **Engineering.** Swarthmore College is one of the few institutions that frees up space for engineering majors to secure a minor in a non-science subject. INTPs, endlessly curious and easily preoccupied with thought, are likely to take the college up on that offer. INTPs will be able to draw conclusions in the sciences and find meaning in historical patterns. That is just the buzz for INTP.

ENFP with an artistic bent will relate to the student and faculty community within Swarthmore's Art department. They will warm to the one-on-one relationship between student and faculty in this department. Another positive for this type is the interdisciplinary course work in the **Studio Art** major at Swarthmore. Of course, the major offers the foundational art courses in visual expression. However, here students also look through the artist lens as they take courses in history, religion, psychology and politics. ENFPs will delight in submitting the required written essay that explores the meaning of an artistic work in its historical context.

ENTP has the curiosity to declare **Peace and Conflict Studies** as a minor. ENTP's intuition will be on call as they analyze conflict and look for resolution. This type also will appreciate the freedom of exploring and taking courses in this interdisciplinary minor. They usually find it difficult to commit to just one major field of study. This minor gives ENTP an anchor from which to explore other disciplines exercising their insight by integrating the minor. This type likes to take a chance and could easily sign up for courses on a whim. In this way, enthusiast ENTP will consider several majors. Imagination, in the end, will direct the selection of their major.

ESFJ is likely to make a very comfortable home on the Swarthmore campus. Their strong desire for harmony and loyalty to the organization will be compatible with college perspectives. The major in **Religion** is studied through the lens of community and cultures. This type is really curious about others and enjoys listening to and learning of their ways. Once ESFJs gather in this basic understanding which they quickly commit to memory, they respect and seek to understand the culture and religious ways of others. Swarthmore College offers a a special curriculum in **Education** with an option to secure teaching credentials at K-12 schools. Teaching religion at an independent or for that matter Quaker school could be a dream job for ESFJs. They will likely be active participants in all the Swarthmore traditions, perhaps even taking over a leadership role in festivals.

ENFJ is a bit of an idealist and they will find much support and encouragement for their idealism at Swarthmore. At the same time, the faculty and administration admire practicality which is evident in the **Public Policy** minor. This interdisciplinary minor draws on economics, political analysis and quantitative analysis as well as direct experience in the field. It is a demanding minor and offers the ENFJ a skill set to combine with their strong oratory skills. It naturally combines with other subjects that contribute to the welfare of others which is important to the ENFJ. In many ways, Swarthmore College honors the inclinations of this type.

SYRACUSE UNIVERSITY

200 Cruise-Hinds Hall
Syracuse, NY 13244
Website: www.syracuse.edu
Admissions Telephone: 315-443-3611
Undergraduates: 13,504; 5,942 Men, 7,562 Women

Physical Environment

An aerial view of Syracuse University shows a campus at the crossroads of highways 690 and 81 in greater Syracuse, with a population of approximately 700,000. This location has contributed to the considerable growth of this university which was chartered in 1870 by the Methodist Episcopal church. This location in the **center of upper New York State** and the convenient travel by highways brings in large numbers of undergraduates from populated areas of New York, Pennsylvania and the New England states. They are comfortable with indoor living in the winter when they wake up to **heavy blankets of snow**. These students have the **stamina** to walk back and forth from their residence halls on the perimeter of campus to their classrooms. The sub-arctic environment serves up fun with sledding, ice-skating or skiing. Taken together with the distance and climate, students here do not over-focus on the design element of their wardrobe.

Syracuse has a variety of both historic and new buildings that are spread over 200 acres. Although many buildings have a charming exterior, in places the campus feels almost like a large, state university. The residence hall options are **multi-story towers of brick** and cinderblock built in the 50s and 60s. Updated and renovated, the dorm rooms include the typical suite-style, singles and doubles. Huntington Hall, housing the School of Education, underwent a significant face lift and continues to sponsor the well known lecture series, Landscapes in Urban Education. This series featured a presentation titled, Our Schools Suck, on March 3, 2011, by the authors of the book by the same title. Among the several controversies swirling in contemporary America, public education is often in the public square and Syracuse University adds much to the conversation.

The nearly **50,000-seat athletic dome** calls to high school students who want a university with a strong school spirit. Basketball and football games are really the starter soup for the social life at Syracuse. Students love to support their teams, painting their faces orange and wearing orange sports gear. More than devoted sports fans, they are also energetic intramural players.

Social Environment

Syracuse University has **nine schools and colleges**. Students identify with the **practical nature** of the curriculum in each. The largest first-year enrollment is in the College of Arts and Sciences. Much smaller enrollments occur in the Engineering and Computer Sciences, Human Services and Health Professions, Visual and Performing Arts, Whitman School of Management and Newhouse School of Public Communications. This last school is by far the most selective, having graduated many well-known sports journalists and actors.

There are many **different types** and groups of people at Syracuse, with approximately half coming from New York State and the remaining 6,000 from foreign countries, cities and rural communities. There are artistic free-thinkers in the School of Arts and Sciences, nurturers who enter the helping professions and decision-makers likely to be enrolled in the business school. The common denominator is that they enjoy group interaction. They get together often for the many parties and social events. Fraternities and sororities are a well-established tradition here and 20 percent of the students join a **Greek organization**. Between the 32 honors societies and strong public communications program, many students are exceptional in their writing abilities and oral expression. They like to discuss politics and current events and debate their ideas often outside the classroom.

Students here tend to be **service-minded** and usually want to work in the community of Syracuse. Each school and college has a connection to specific parts of the city. The Center for Public and Community Service oversees a strong service learning program for the surrounding neighborhoods.

Students rank comfortably in the top quarter of their class and have strong standardized scores. Those students who have the higher qualifications and artistic talent gravitate to the nationally recognized schools, such as Newhouse or the Visual and Performing Arts. These students tend to be more focus-driven as they enter a well-defined track of study. On the other hand, many students in the College of Arts and Sciences benefit from the process of searching for a major, often enrolling as undeclared.

Compatibility with Personality Types and Preferences

Since Syracuse University is larger than most private universities and colleges, it has distinct social environments within its richly resourced campus community. Several of the selective schools, such as the Newhouse School of Public Communications, appeal to the creative types focused on possibilities (N). However, other schools and colleges within the university tend toward guided logical practice (T) in preparation for graduation and the coming world of work. Certainly there is a hardy soul in the Syracuse undergraduates who emerge to conquer both the weather and the intellectual demands of the curriculum. The administration's educational philosophy predisposes the curriculum to meet the needs of the American workplace. The student who wants to develop skills and acquire a specific knowledge base (S) will not be disappointed with the Syracuse curriculum.

The faculty is equally dedicated to enhancing student talents and individual values. A key feature of this is the strong emphasis on serving others (F), especially the citizens and businesses of greater Syracuse along with communities in New York State. The resilient Syracuse undergrads are very comfortable extending their helping hand in a myriad of innovative ways developed by the schools and colleges at the university. Above all, the Syracuse community and Syracuse

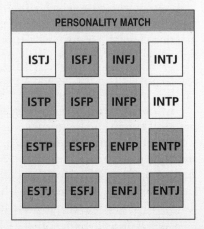

undergraduate student body is civically engaged (E).

In the following listing of college majors it is important to remember that students can fit into any college and can be successful in any major. We have found that the Personality Types below fit very well at this college. The course-of-study chosen for each Personality Type corresponds to MBTI® research and is presented as an example favorable for that type.

ISTP with an interest in design or arts definitely is going to smile when they see that Syracuse offers **Metalsmithing**. Since it is offered at the introductory, intermediate and advanced level, ISTPs will be in their element as they construct and weld that last piece of silver in the senior portfolio for graduation. This type will easily acquire the technical expertise involved in this skill/art. They are likely to join and take leadership in the metalsmithing club on campus, perhaps adding a few robotic pieces of jewelry.

ESTP is pretty realistic and the minor in **Forensic Science** will be interesting. The basic concepts of scientific principles are examined in this minor. The more robust curriculum in the integrated learning major of forensic science interfaces well with majors in the social or physical sciences such as chemistry, biology or psychology. Study in this discipline offers ESTP career options in medicine, science, engineering and the social sciences. This type might move forward into the exciting world of investigating criminal behavior.

ESFJ fits well into the world of business when the career involves direct, daily interaction with customers. The major in **Real Estate** at Syracuse will likely support many of ESFJ's inclinations for career options. The newly emerging mixed commercial/residential villages appeal to community building with this type. Whitman School of Management assures financial astuteness with a solid management core in finance, marketing, accounting and corporate mechanisms.

ESTJ likes to be organized. Careers that involve data compilation in traditional work environments, such as government departments, are a natural for this type. Syracuse, together with the State University of New York, jointly offers a degree in **Environmental Science and Forestry.** Undergraduates can also pursue a teacher certificate in the sciences for 7-12th grade. Decisive ESTJs can navigate between these two universities to capture the practical information needed to comprehend our national forests and the paper products produced.

ENTP who can be entrepreneurial with ease might enjoy declaring a major **in Entrepreneurship and Emerging Enterprises**. This type is naturally drawn to new business ventures. ENTPs are innovative, quick to spot a trend and enjoy the idea of pulling together a start up businesses or hybrid strategic partnerships. The course titled Consulting in Entrepreneurial Practice brings java computing analysis to emerging financial enterprise start ups. This can nicely inject a bit of reality for ENTP who may be overly optimistic in these types of environments.

ISFJ could look closely at the **Music Education** major. Five emphases within the major allow for classic instrumental emphasis or a choral/elementary emphasis. With either choice the ISFJs will like closely connecting with their students in the classroom. This type is well-suited for a faculty position in public or independent schools. The school of music at Syracuse also offers degrees in music industry, music performance composition all of which support this type's dedication and thorough preparation for a career in music.

ISFP with a flair for apparel should look into the **Fashion Design** degree at Syracuse. It is well-complimented with the Fiber Arts and Textile Arts and Fashion Design curriculum, also in the College of Visual and Performing Arts. This type enjoys both independence and handiwork. Piecing together their own creations on paper through to production and sale in clothing stores will be exciting and rewarding for ISFPs. Syracuse has an exceptionally rich curriculum in the hand-crafted arts. Many talented students in other fields such as metalsmithing will surround ISFPs.

ESFP will surely want to look at the **Retailing/Management** degree. This curriculum allows for elective courses outside of the management curriculum and ESFP is likely to pursue design courses in the College of Visual and Performing Arts. The dynamite combination makes for business savvy and design savvy retailers. ESFP's ease with persuasion and dynamic, fast-moving environments could mean a smooth transition into retail business on graduation. The course in Visual Merchandising and Store Planning will certainly appeal to their eye for flair and design.

INFP always seeks meaning and a connection between their educational studies and personal growth. The degree at Syracuse in **Social Work** has good bones for this type. The career field demands close relationships with clients. INFPs are quite comfortable with intimacy while they provide caring and guidance for those in distress. The school prepares graduates with administrative and policy knowledge as well as a grounding in the concept of promoting human dignity. INFPs surely will agree with this.

ENFP in the **Advertising** degree at Syracuse is a desirable combination. This type is drawn to possibilities in the fast-paced, dynamic world of marketing through creative, artistic images. ENFPs will delight in combining the visual imagery with the words to broadcast a persuasive message. The undergraduate major selection is flexible but leans one of two ways, management or creative design. ENFPs are likely to follow their creative minds into the latter.

ENTJ is not likely to shrink from the complexities in the degree at Syracuse titled **Supply Chain Management**. It sounds a bit dry, but it can be a high risk, hard-driving discipline. The curriculum could be interdisciplinary with elective courses chosen in statistics, communications, probability, alliances, transportation and more. They address the business factors of risk, marketing, transportation, inventory and time/distance in distributing the inventory. It is the hard-charging, multitasking ENTJ who handles it all.

INFJ has that ability to juggle complicated ideas and connect them in a meaningful way with people. The degree in **Linguistics** at Syracuse pulls together knowledge from many areas such as anthropology, geography, sociology, languages and psychology. This degree is excellent for the INFJs who know they will pursue graduate studies. It can be paired with a minor in **Classics** which studies a nation's culture, institutions and underlying values. INFJs will be adept at these two abstract, interdisciplinary fields. The total package would be excellent for careers in law or with international NGOs.

ENFJ is very well-suited for the Syracuse **Inclusive Elementary and Special Education** Teacher Prep program. This type is fulfilled when performing activities that help others grow and succeed. The education field has several key features that appeal to ENFJs. Diversity is high on this list with ENFJs placing harmony within the environment as their first priority.

TUFTS UNIVERSITY

Office of Admissions
419 Boston Avenue
Medford, MA 02155
Website: www.tufts.edu
Admissions Telephone: 617-627-3170
Undergraduates: 5,150; 2,524 Men, 2,626 Women
Graduate Students: 2,534

Physical Environment

Tufts University is located on a small rise in the Medford-Somerville area and is accessible by the subway that travels to and from Boston. From the subway stop, it is a bus or 20-minute walk to campus. The heart of campus is encircled with mostly red-brick buildings around "the green" and "President's lawn" which students cross regularly on their way to class. On a sunny and warm day students lay on the grass or sit by a tree in the quad studying. In winter they may be studying in the Tisch Library or sledding down the hill in front of it, or taking in the **view of Boston** from the roof. Tufts' outdoor monument is a **cannon** that changes colors and messages overnight. Some are social and political in nature while others are more lighthearted.

The residence halls are assigned by lottery each year with preference given to freshmen and sophomores. Upperclassmen are likely to live off campus. Additionally, there are 15 theme houses for students of like interests and 13 Greek chapter houses with off-campus housing. There are many great eateries adjacent to campus for undergraduates, such as Buddy's Truck stop, a diner in a silver 1929 Worcester lunch-car that brings back the 60s era with all the nostalgia. This environment appeals to students who want **sophistication**, a top name university near a large city, without the intrusive impact of traffic and congestion. The surrounding neighborhoods primarily consist of modest houses built in the mid 19th century to house the growing labor market for industrialization. The university shares significant campus resources with the neighborhoods well advertised on the website link titled, "Neighbor."

Social Environment

High achieving, intellectual students are attracted to Tufts' rigorous academics in the arts and sciences, engineering and pre-professional sciences. Entering freshman score at the top range on standardized tests. A Tufts' education is for those who enjoy analyzing facts, observing what is and imagining what can be. Similar to the story of Johnny Appleseed, the trailblazer in mid-1800s, most Tufts students are confident their future will become fruitful. They are typically curious and motivated to take risks with the idea of discovering something new with practical value. Liberal Arts students may opt for a pass/fail grade in an elective subject they know little about, just to stretch their thinking and improve their **reasoning** ability.

Students who like **visual imagery** will enjoy Tufts' propensity to communicate via photographs and artistic design, although it is less apparent on the Tufts website recently. It is formally part of the curriculum through the partnership between Tufts and the **School Museum of Fine Arts** in Boston. The new Center for Scientific Visualization allows researchers from multiple disciplines to reimagine their own work in this different medium. Students here find value in presenting what they observe. In this way, the viewers are free to react as they may, since passion is trumped by curiosity and reason on this campus.

The university mission is to create and transmit knowledge. Undergraduates at Tufts connect the dots between past events and the present day. They ponder what could be. They form groups to discuss the latest and greatest scientific discoveries. They are open to each others' **novel interpretations.** Many arrive with well-developed **leadership** abilities and will move on to graduate studies. Many will seek professions in medicine, allied health and veterinary science where they will apply their learning in a practical way. Practice will mix with **imagination** and these graduates will be quite open to emerging frontiers in their fields. Students enjoy arts-oriented or service-oriented activities here. There is a vibrant musical and **theatrical core** of campus performances for and by undergraduates. The hefty academic loads leave little time to indulge in casual socializing.

Compatibility with Personality Types and Preferences

Tufts University is taking scientific research into the emerging world of visual imagery and visual utility. The lines are blurring between technology, art, science and visual applications on this university campus. To be sure, a lot of Tufts research remains oriented to the fundamental properties of basic molecular research. However, within their laboratories there seems to be an outward momentum (E) directed by the faculty and administration. Tufts research results are frequently translated for the general community of citizenry through visual expression. Video, photography and manipulated images produced by faculty and students seem to carry the weight of an essay about new found knowledge.

The novel (N) discoveries from the Tufts laboratories often convey a particular technology and its application to the human community (F), through visual media. Perhaps this is best illustrated by the home webpage of the Tufts website in late 2008: A holographic piece of art glass. It draws the viewer into an interior layer of color and pattern that is pleasing to look at but it is actually mapping chemical data and location for a biological organism. This visual imagery occurred through the use of common silk and lasers in the lab. It sends a non-threatening, appealing message about emerging technology (P) that will potentially be used in medicine and environmental disasters. The neutral reputation of lasers and the comfortable presence of silk in our lives projects an optimism that many viewers will relate to. It is typical of the students and faculty at this research-oriented university. On the department's website, in late 2011, a scary intravenous bag and tube is substituted with a comforting spool of red silk thread, suspended above the prone patient, with a thin thread dropping down to the wrist. The cartoon makes you smile. American medicine - excellent, despite political commentary to the contrary.

Tufts also reaches out locally and internationally through its social and scientific research. The university has a decades' long interest in child development. Research in this area finds its way to and from the Tufts New England Medical Center in their Floating Hospital for children receiving treatment. Undergraduates also travel off campus to observe and understand other ethnic groups. Internships and co-ops here are oriented to comprehend or document other cultures. Visual record keeping (S) is a favorite choice to capture and bring home the meaning of experiences abroad. Undergraduates of Tufts are precise observers, confident in technological application and ready to risk activity and energy that may not immediately appear purposeful. They are innovators for society through the medium of technology.

In the following listing of college majors it is important to remember that students can fit into any college and can be successful in any major. We have found that the Personality Types below fit very well at this college. The course-of-study chosen for each Personality Type corresponds to MBTI® research and is presented as an example favorable for that type.

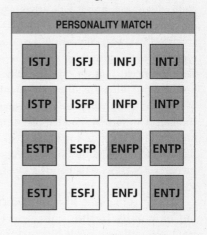

INTJ can be oriented to creative design. This type is very good at dreaming up new systems that solve three dimensional problems. Tufts University offers a curriculum that includes the elements of engineering with the functional elements of human habitation. The BS degree in **Engineering in Architecture Studies** prepares graduates for advanced study in architecture or design. The very thorough and often technically competent INTJ will be drawn to state of the art innovation seen in much modern architecture. Metals, glass and polymers are all rather exotic substances to use in construction. Their use requires engineering expertise and a distinct absence of conventional models. INTJ has these both in abundance.

ISTP could hook up with the **Computer Engineering** degree almost like a robot being connected to a joystick. The two simply go together. Tufts University offers an excellent environment for getting prepared to tackle computer applications for the next 30 or 40 years. On this campus, ISTP will be nudged toward experimentation as well as ethical application. Undergraduates work in teams and also solo. ISTP is fine with either approach. This type brings a desire for efficiency to their work and study. They avoid fussy stuff and will find the tools, logic and principles they seek to get to the end of the tunnel with the least effort expended. This is a nice trait to have in the workplaces that direct and control our limited resources through software.

ISTJ will find the second major in **Biotechnology** suitable for pairing up with a traditional major in the social or physical sciences. The precise nature of the physical applications in biotechnology appeal to this type. They can bring their tremendous concentration and retention powers to bear in the lab experiments. The ISTJ can also explore several career tracks through this coursework. ISTJs could be attracted to medical practice, health administration, research or diagnostic skills in the realm of the pure sciences. At Tufts, this type will be surrounded by innovative thinking and novel internships. This will provide the encouragement they need to continue exploring options until it is clear which direction they will pursue.

ESTP loves to solve a problem that requires people plus machines as elements of the solution. They are pretty good at it too. Tufts University offers the very unusual **Human Factors** major in the five-year Bachelor of Science degree. It is a very versatile degree. This type often boasts a good sense of the aesthetics, likes to move into the center of action and typically is very much at ease with people. All of these skills will become major strengths as they design products for work, recreation or daily living. Both client and ESTP will enjoy the projects focusing on safety, appearance and efficiency.

ENFP is naturally enthusiastic and Tufts is a place of optimism. Both this type and their enthusiasm will be a wonderful gift to bring to the studies in **Child Development**. It is an exceptionally strong program with its research foundation, history of children's studies and many options for internships. ENFPs love to help other people and they are quite creative in this art. They are excellent long-range thinkers, comfortable and happy with big abstract ideas, ready with a smile or a bit of humor. They are ideal for spontaneous work with children in stressful environments like inner city neighborhoods, refugee camps or disaster areas. This degree nicely prepares ENFP, who demands a satisfying lifetime career, for graduate work in child studies.

ENTP is one who likes to predict future trends. The major at Tufts University in **Community Health** is just right for this. It draws together collected knowledge from very different fields like political science and engineering plus others. ENTP is a big thinker, ready to embrace these concepts and reformulate them into health perspectives. This type will especially be attracted to the side of the major that deals with policy and planning for large health systems. Faculty in all majors at Tufts will encourage undergraduates to visit and observe other cultures. ENTPs with their boundless need for new experiences can learn to trust their intuition and creativity in distant locations while pondering mass delivery of preventive health care.

ESTJ likes to organize and analyze. This type is comfortable with systems of logic and fact. They could excel at using systems to bring products to the market, straighten out unproductive organizations or develop a technological interface that advances medical practice. The degree in **Biomedical Engineering** is a good choice because it offers the option of developing technology for emerging medicinal procedures. This type prefers to work toward objective goals. How much more logical and objective does it get than developing assistive devices for surgical insertion in the human body? Tufts extensive presence in the health care field provides the needed prompting for this traditional, conservative type to keep exploring this growing field.

ENTJ can productively ponder the future of continental Africa after educational exploration of its many distinct regions. Attracted to the complexity and hugeness of the continent, ENTJ is fine with pulling that knowledge from several departments on campus. **Africa in the New World** is a minor that would easily combine with majors in the physical or social sciences. This type has long term vision to help human communities move forward. Tufts' approach to off-campus learning experiences is ideal for African study. The faculty embraces observation and places much faith in research technology. The confident ENTJ doesn't need much more than this to launch a rewarding international career.

TULANE UNIVERSITY

Office of Admissions
6823 St. Charles Avenue
New Orleans, LA 70118
Website: www.tulane.edu
Admissions Telephone: 504-865-5731
Undergraduates: 5,993; Men, 3,371 Women
Graduate Students: 5,133

Physical Environment

Few people can think of **New Orleans** and not conjure up images of the devastation left by Hurricane Katrina in the fall of 2005. Students who were on their way to Tulane were directed to return to their homes. Other colleges throughout the nation accepted displaced Tulane students while the university got back on its feet, and this it did. Tulane came back even stronger with significantly larger numbers at the start of this decade.

The new Tulane has re-invented itself. It has trimmed down some programs such as engineering, which has merged with the department of sciences. Tulane continues to invest in **research**, especially at the graduate level. This graduate level of instruction quickly seeps down to undergraduate courses, thus exposing undergrads to challenging concepts early on.

Undergraduate students may take the St. Charles Avenue trolley to get to campus from downtown. They will pass through Gibson Hall, which houses the admission office. It's distinguishable by its **Romanesque architecture** of stone over brick, built in the 1800s. Across the street from this building, which is referred to as "Uptown Campus," the **arboretum** gives the students an opportunity to connect with nature when they want a break from studying. The Spanish moss hanging from the trees amplifies the Southern ambiance.

Another building competes for attention on this campus. It's the Lavin-Bernick Center, an impressive modern structure that is the hub of campus and central meeting place for students. This is an eco-friendly building with lots of windows, energy-saving water walls, and space galore for students to hang out. Students sit on comfy sofas in lounges that look out onto lush trees. After all, this is the **Big Easy**, and students like to chill. **Student organizations** have their offices here. Weatherhead Hall, opened in fall 2011, is a living and learning community for sophomores and honor students. First and second-year students must live on campus. It is not uncommon for faculty members and their families to get involved with students, an extension of the campus/city community feel at Tulane.

Social Environment

An important statistic here is that about 70 percent of students come from outside the state of Louisiana. Many come from the **Northeast, followed by the South Atlantic and the Midwest.** They can be seen walking in flip-flops and reveling in the warm weather. Prior to Katrina, they came to Tulane and New Orleans because they were looking for a different experience. The atmosphere has changed since

Hurricane Katrina. While today's students still come for the quality of the education, the weather and the fun atmosphere, they also come for **Civic Engagement**.

In high school, these were highly sociable students who enjoyed giving back to the community. At Tulane they become even more **civic-minded**. They get course credit for their work, but many continue even after the incentive of the credit is gone. Eager undergrads, wanting to impact the campus and the city, will also climb the ladder of fraternity and sorority organizations where they can learn to manage people with access to university-allocated resources. **Elected student leadership** within the collegiate community is very active on this campus.

Service forms a nuclei of social life on campus and Tulane students actively support CACTUS, an extensive network of projects that benefit the New Orleans community, **Literacy work** is a popular choice. The extensive interaction between undergrads and the community receives strong oversight from the university. This commitment assures well-planned activities that work for those giving and those receiving. As a result, there is lots of back and forth between students and administration.

Tulane's message is clear: be a leader, be **engaged and be successful**. Those students with **emotional power and resiliency** do well here. It comes in most handy as students readily join the Mardi Gras celebrations and the vibrant, sophisticated city life as often as studies and commitment will allow.

Compatibility with Personality Types and Preferences

Tulane University is very much a reflection of its unique association with New Orleans, a city that blended cultural influences for centuries and carries a European aura. Alongside this fascinating historical culture, Tulane's well-regarded graduate schools developed and mirrored the organization of formal European universities in past centuries. This academic philosophy prompts the graduate school research perspectives to translate downward to the undergraduate curriculum. Students at Tulane quickly get a wide exposure (N) to advanced concepts and observation of how those ideas travel in today's mainstream organizations. The university's emphasis on utilization of knowledge also moves into the concepts of leadership for the undergraduate student population. Undergraduate students prepare, through active leadership on campus and in the New Orleans neighborhoods, to translate their recently accrued knowledge out into the larger American community of business and government.

Freshmen happily adopt the casual dress needed for the climate while they prepare for the formal, corporate worlds of policy, business, government and the professions. For this reason, there is a precise order (T) to the coursework in the educational majors and minors. There also is a clear set of core courses designed to assure competencies (S) for all graduates of the university. These competencies in writing, foreign language, public service, mathematics and humanities drive the message home that graduates accomplish much within their span of influence in the world.

There is a natural alliance between Tulane's curriculum and the demands of an advanced economy. Social and extracurricular activity at this university very much prompts connection to the outer world. (E). Undergraduates do not suffer from tunnel vision on this campus. The university mirrors the experience of city life and complex city politics. It can do so because minutes away one finds the professional sophistication of New Orleans and the socio-economic needs of its neighborhoods. Tulane administration is mindful of these juxtapositions (F). It seeks to prepare graduates for transition within all societies for the purposes of leadership and progress. Successful Tulane students are typically characterized by their predisposition to thoughtful reflection about society.

In the following listing of college majors it is important to remember that students can fit into any college and can be successful in any major. We have found that the Personality Types below fit very well at this college. The course-of-study chosen for each Personality Type corresponds to MBTI® research and is presented as an example favorable for that type.

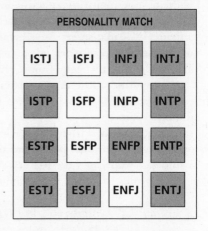

INFJ is often happy developing strategies to address pervasive health problems within neighborhood communities. The five-year BS/MS degree in **Global and Community Health** is ideal for this occupational interest. INFJ will easily commit to the nature of this field and appreciate the demand to create new approaches to communicable disease. The need for this work is increasing as fast as the population is growing on Earth. INFJ is most satisfied working in career fields such as this because of the extreme need. The major is unusual and receives robust support in tandem with Tulane's perspective toward graduating accomplished professionals.

INTJ prefers to be involved with original, emerging activities. Creative occupations such as architecture and design can easily work for this type if they have artistic talent. Tulane University offers a minor in **Architectural Studies**. The major in **Engineering Physics** would make a nice companion for this minor if INTJ has tolerance for additional semesters beyond the four years. As 21st century design calls for cantilevered structures with glass, metal and the use of new materials, it will be the INTJ who understands their strength and physical properties. This major and minor combination is quite attractive for designs that fit the needs of human habitation. This is all very appealing stuff to INTJ whose vision works handily with large, complicated systems.

ISTP will enjoy the **Biomedical Engineering** degree at Tulane University because of the independent research options. The graduate programs reveal many strands of research in this growing field. Undergraduates are required to design a year-long research project of their own. This type lights their own fire once they identify their mechanical passion somewhere within the research labs! At the same time, the school requires students to work on a team-designed project. This, too, fits in well with ISTP who enjoys working with others of similar interest and often becomes the go-to person when the project hits a snag.

INTP will need to satisfy their curiosity in reference to the **Health Informatics** major offered at Tulane University. They like to mix, match and invent computer programs that might constructively organize the millions of data files associated with public and private health service. There really is no level of information management that is too complex or vast for this type as long as they have access to powerful computing resources. This major is well-situated in Tulane's School of Public Health and undergraduates have access to a wealth of knowledge resident in the faculty at this prestigious, forward-thinking medical school.

ESTP can find the finance world enticing with its inherent elements of risk and investment. The major in **Finance** at Tulane University has a good selection of coursework that surveys these two critical concepts. The focus on professional preparation also appeals to ESTP who is usually socially savvy. This type can successfully promote products or services with ease through their negotiation skills at the conference table. Tulane's strong graduate programs in the business school will pique the interest of undergraduate ESTPs who could charm their way into socializing and informally learning from the graduates.

ENFP isn't often drawn to business careers but the major in **Management** in Tulane's business school could really appeal to this type. Social issues mix with business concerns as products and services move to market. At times, the issues threaten to derail the company or product line. Within this major, ENFPs must select one of two career tracks, consulting or entrepreneurship. The consulting track is the likely ENFP choice since it focuses on ethics, negotiations and conflict resolutions. It will be valuable for sorting through corporate mergers and acquisitions. As such, it is a skill needed by major consulting firms and this would offer ENFP plenty of travel and excitement.

ENTP could be attracted to the course sequence in **Environmental Health Sciences** at Tulane because it features a focus in disaster management along with toxicology. Preparation for any number of environmental crises is appealing to ENTP who instinctively improvises. Throw in their typical confidence and you have the potential for a very capable disaster manager. ENTP prefers to be in the power circles while focusing on policy planning for the future. This sequence of courses will fill up their disaster skills tool box. Regional and state governments will offer multiple internship options and career options which are stimulating for this type.

ESFJ will delight in combining two fields not often paired together at the undergraduate level. The major in **Psychology and Early Childhood Education** is so appealing to this sensitive, caring type. The precise psychological coursework focused on the individual is an excellent companion to the generalized educational studies applicable to the classroom. Tulane University pairs the major with the option for teacher certification. This type will find career satisfaction in traditional community organizations such as preschools and outreach programs for children. Tulane's strong interface with the city neighborhoods provides excellent service learning options also.

ESTJ often moves into positions of authority during their career. Tulane University is an excellent undergraduate environment for this purpose. ESTJ often has a realistic career plan and commonly utilizes the undergraduate degree to gain access to professional studies for their chosen field. The major titled **Legal Studies in Business** has several advantages for this purpose. It is a curriculum that offers specific, realistic preparation for quite a few fields such as real estate and insurance. ESTJ could also use it to enter law school or as an operations manager in a legal firm. Regardless, this type is excellent at focusing on goals: theirs or the firm's!

ENTJ is quite comfortable in leadership positions. Tulane's emphasis on leadership in extracurricular activities will give this type a chance to secure several positions of authority during the four years on campus. The degree in Management with a major in **Marketing** will allow them to move into the business world they typically enjoy. Coursework emphasizes planning and management of products or services in retail markets. This curriculum has the added benefit of preparing ENTJ for their long term career options. This type has vision that extends far forward so consulting to national and international companies might be on a career horizon for ENTJ. Their natural networking ability also comes in very handy in this field.

UNION COLLEGE

Office of Admissions
Schenectady, NY 12308
Website: www.union.edu
Admissions Telephone: 518-388-6122
Undergraduates: 2,170; 1,116 Men, 1,054 Women

Physical Environment

Union College is a long-established college that for over 200 years has educated **historical figures** such as William H. Seward, Abraham Lincoln's Secretary of State and U.S. President Chester A. Arthur. The beauty of this campus dates back to the late 1700s, when it was founded as a non-denominational college, which must have taken some courage in those days. A most unique building on campus is **Nott Memorial**, a site for many cultural events, and easily recognizable for its **16 sides and Russian-like architecture**

Dedicated May 2011, the Peter Irving Center seeks to increase the **interface between teaching and research** with IBM's donation of Intelligent Cluster computing capabilities. This exceptional facility and the Butterfield Hall renovation, including a scanning electron microscope, reveals the confidence and expectation by the admi. istration for their undergraduate students. The Lippman Hall renovation completed in 2011 supports the social sciences on campus.

Union College is located in Schenectady, a 30-minute drive from the Albany airport. This town is up and coming and although students tend to stay on campus, the town center is within walking distance. They can take the pedestrian walk to the neat little cafes, restaurants and theatre. The Schenectady area is not on the Snow Belt so it gets an average of **three good snow storms** each year and the rest is just northeastern weather.

A popular campus hub is Reamer Center which is home to many student organizations and the dining room. Also, students like to socialize in the cave-like Old Chapel, where there's a coffee bar with internet access, games and room for dances. Students here like their sports, the gymnasium, ball courts, hockey rink and pool accommodate these interests.

Social Environment

The social environment at Union College can be described in one word: **community**. This campus is for students who want to connect with their peers and their professors, learn a lot and form a warm, welcoming community. These are very **social students** who get involved in many activities. Each student is assigned to a **"Minerva house"** which puts on event after event. This gives students the opportunity to both lead and be entertained. Another benefit of the Minerva houses is that students improve their skill at planning and collaboration. There are parties held by fraternity and sorority houses. Undergraduates form a tight-knit community that supports one another's differences, invites discussion and will bring this sense of community to their future work places. The Union educational experience **includes**

a study abroad period, and for some, this becomes a selfless effort to help that has much in common with the Peace Corps.

The campus is one of a select few liberal arts colleges with an **interesting engineering** program grounded in intellectual discourse. It's for students who want that well-rounded education that is structured and traditional with a core of general education requirements. The core includes history, science, math and study abroad to gain exposure to other cultures. The vast majority of students ranked in the top quarter of their high school graduating class. Union College also attracts students who have an interest in pre-professional fields such as medicine. Many students who graduate with a Bachelor's degree will go on to obtain an MBA, which they can complete right on campus. Other students volunteer overseas and continue to grow in their convictions that the world can be changed for the better and everyone ought to pitch in. There is an implicit expectation that students will keep in touch with each other after they graduate from Union College.

Compatibility with Personality Types and Preferences

Students and faculty at Union College reach out, intending to latch on to the future (N) of ideas and concepts. Together, they form a community that prefers to integrate current knowledge by crossing boundaries and disciplines. As a result, personal connections are quite vital at Union College. Friendships and mentoring are viewed as a primary foundation for learning (F). Integrating knowledge through analysis and discovery is the other side of the balanced coin.

Undergraduates here carry the responsibility to be prepared for change in the coming century and thus must remain open (P) and able to respond to evolution in their chosen field. The individual departments offer a wide selection of coursework for exploration. This breadth in the curriculum encourages students to continue sampling the field beyond the foundation, often into the junior and senior years. The curriculum always interfaces the social and human context with the technical and scientific concepts. Student-centered research is designed to teach undergraduates how to interpret data and concepts. It features traditional mentoring, advising and investigative methodologies. Therefore, undergrads assertively seek out concepts that can attain success in the marketplace of ideas.

Similarly, the residential life here is vibrant and thoughtfully planned (J). Education invariably crosses the boundary with the residential life programming. The international study program is designed for overseas academic study that reveals foreign cultural perspectives as applied to the academic subject. The international sites are selected for this purpose and not chosen to meet other objectives such as travel or service. The educational balance between innovation and social community begins in Schenectady and translates to the regional, national and international learning communities. Integrated knowledge is uppermost at Union College and the administration's humane perspective is very much a part of this integration.

In the following listing of college majors it is important to remember that students can fit into any college and can be successful in any major. We have found that the Personality Types below fit very well at this college. The course-of-study chosen for each Personality

Type corresponds to MBTI® research and is presented as an example favorable for that type.

INFP is one to join up and support a cause or select a career field that advances a particular social issue. The degree at Union College in **Psychology** is nicely tailored to the needs of this type. The curriculum provides a survey of the numerous directions this evolving science is moving toward. It is really important for INFP to interface their work with their ideals. INFP can focus on human behavior in any of several areas: learning, personality, developmental, language and the list keeps growing as this field matures. INFP

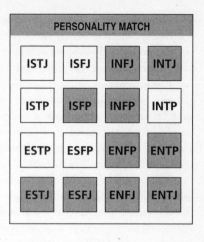

PERSONALITY MATCH

is likely to seek and gain admission for the Honors degree in this major.

INFJ is a thoughtful type and a darn good fit for Union College. The degree in **Philosophy** calls for study of developmental growth in young adults. During four years on campus, undergraduates have matured in ability to wrestle with ethics and human behavior. The curriculum in philosophy is constructed in a sequence that grows in complexity right along with the undergraduates. INFJs will consider the honors thesis in preparation for graduate study in law, health or the social sciences.

INTJ is an ideal type to declare a minor within an emerging field. New knowledge seems to live in the two realms of precision and imagination. It will be the INTJ who can connect these two in **Nanotechnology** at Union College. As could be expected, this department developed a curriculum that is representative of Union's academic philosophy. Students will acquire basic information about the properties of matter. They will also spend considerable time in relationship with peers and faculty supporting research studies and searching for resolutions. It is a complex thinking activity. However, INTJ is up to it.

ISFP usually can handle change and in fact enjoys changing it up for a good reason. Union College, of the same predisposition, incorporates the inevitability of change within their educational philosophy. The degree in **Computer Science** at this campus has several attributes that are attractive to ISFPs. Union College values the concept of relationship within the American community. This lends a social context to technical knowledge and that works for values driven ISFP.

ENFP has a very large horizon when it comes to selecting subjects of interest, however, the major selected by this type must offer abstraction and variety. The major in **Geology** can deliver both. At Union College, the current state of the art in understanding Earth's geographic formations is paired with world news of tsunamis and earthquakes in the Pacific Rim. This major is very much about connecting the past, present and the future with abstract, big pictures. ENFP is all for that.

ENTP might be intrigued by the thought of a career in teaching astronomy. Should ENTP have mathematical acumen and interest, the major in **Astronomy** at Union College explores career options for this discipline. This a must for ENTP who must keep options open by hook or crook. This ingenious type might by pass teaching astronomy in high school to reach for a law career in patent work for space hardware. On the other hand, an advanced degree in human health research oriented to the human body in space is a career option. ENTP is attracted to possibilities and Union College is devoted to preparing graduates for the innovative future.

ESFJ wants to support productive partnerships within a community through current business and government practice. The curriculum in **Science, Medicine and Technology in Culture** is available as a minor or major that could support any of ESFJ's favored career choices in the health sciences, education or social sciences. For the ESFJ captured by the physical sciences, the minor will provide perspective that points to a pure science major such as physics.

ESTJ has the tenacity and determination to deal with the issues surrounding worldwide demands for energy. Union College has just the program to prepare ESTJs for this challenging environment with their unique minor in **Energy Studies.** The course Heat, Light and Astronomy will alert Union graduates to the possibility of future energy production in space. This type will like the recommended study abroad in New Zealand for this minor.

ENFJ is rewarded by understanding and helping others to realize individual potential. The major in **Anthropology** at Union College surveys specializations within this discipline. ENFJs are decisive and organized. The help and mentoring of faculty will be critically important as ENFJ chooses a focus within this expansive curriculum. This type will want the advantage of a warm, mentoring relationship to craft a post-graduate plan. The department curriculum includes coursework in anthropological medicine, environmental anthropology, economic anthropology, urban anthropology, anthropology and religion, psychological anthropology and several more.

ENTJ will find the major in **Neuroscience** at Union College offers three tracks in studying the human brain: bioscience, cognitive or computational. Should they like the idea of moving toward psychiatry, the cognitive track will work. If they like the idea of becoming a medical researcher or medical doctor, the bioscience track will work. If its computational neuroscience, careers in artificial intelligence are calling. With any choice, this type will bring a flair for the corporate world to their career through private practice or consulting work. ENTJ always has that little touch of entrepreneurship buried within their career plans.

THE UNIVERSITY OF CHICAGO

Office of Admission
5801 S. Ellis Avenue
Chicago, Illinois 60637
Website: www.uchicago.edu
Admissions Telephone: 773-702-8650
Undergraduates: 4,000; 2,120 Men, 1,880 Women

Physical Environment

The University of Chicago is located on the south side of Chicago in the **Hyde Park** area, which flanks Lake Michigan. In this neighborhood of approximately 45,000 residents there is a mixture of single family homes, apartment buildings, an occasional run-down house and historic edifices under the care of the local preservation society. Many of the 35 residential houses located in 10 residence halls are located in this neighborhood. Prospective students may not be aware of how the physical layout of the campus affects the daily pedestrian commute on this campus. Four residence halls are located off campus with a 15-minute walk to reach the academic quads. Bus service delivers students to and from campus. In 2009, the South Campus Residence Hall was opened and it serves somewhat as a student center with its late night quick-stop market and gathering spaces. Midway Pleasance, bisecting the campus, is halfway through updating the streetscape, featuring safety improvements for pedestrians.

The University of Chicago's circa-1890s original campus consists of a **neo-Gothic rectangular** structure, replete with gargoyles and all, built along several city blocks that enclose a large rectangular yard, the main quadrangle. The massive stone walls lend a feeling of intellectual inclusiveness. There is a sense of freedom to explore in a cerebral and spiritual sense here. The Joe and Rika Mansueto Library, opened in October 2011, sports automatic book retrieval in shelves 50 feet high. It is modern to the extreme and the architectural space reminds one of the Apple store in New York City. The architecture forms an interesting juxtaposition of layers and heights.

Set against the futuristic skyline of Chicago's impossibly high skyscrapers, the architectural past, present and imagined future seem to blend intellectually. The campus environment is a bastion of **rational thought**. Here there is everything for the **brilliant, quiet** student. For curious, intellectually-aggressive first year students, knowledge and **pursuing research** are tandem activities. The undergraduate education starts with classic foundations, often around an oval Harkness table rather than class or lecture hall. It prompts the students to prepare and conduct the lesson supplemented by faculty oversight. In this challenging way, students forge a deep level of inquiry that will surely open multiple research avenues in academic pursuit during the upperclass years.

Social Environment

Students admitted to University of Chicago find the campus is greatly extended into the city with its reputation for modern American culture. Chicago is a labyrinth of humanity and undergrads quickly find that the campus community is a safe anchor from which to explore the city. Students quickly generate connections among bright peers and **stimulating professors**. Many of them already know their academic major. They seek the body of knowledge that they **absolutely must know** in order to continue life. To that end they work hard and love it. **Intellectual passion** is rampant on campus. With that said, sports don't dominate the social scene but intramural teams are robust and very active. Each residence hall has multiple teams plus schedules, location and equipment is very accessible. Active fraternities and sororities contribute to the social and service activities.

These students enjoy **occasional breaks off campus** visiting ethnic, socio-economic, artistic, blues and jazz clubs, but a lot of the action is on campus with interesting student clubs like Juggling Enriching Lives Like Yours. So, who fits in well here? What does a potential University of Chicago applicant look like as a high school student? They have a strong transcript with the most advanced high school courses. They expect to build a **comprehensive body of knowledge** that will become a jumping-off point for further academic study. Many are **reserved** in comparison to typical high school personalities. As undergrads their lunch time conversation could include discussions on corruption in Chicago politics and the state of Illinois. During dinner these same students may return with facts and references to illuminate this problematic trend in American legislative bodies, yet political activism is not the typical style here. These undergrads are more likely to file the information away and act on it later from within the power circles they will enter in future decades. First-year students learn to cope with the urban environment, building confidence as they move through **tough academics** and also pick up city social skills. These **extremely bright** students thrive on intensity.

Compatibility with Personality Types and Preferences

University of Chicago is an analytical machine (T) with soft, fuzzy edges. It's a nice combination actually. They honor tradition (J) and history in a number of ways which can serve to soften the hard edge of logic on this campus. However, the graduate research relentlessly seeks the new truths that seem to pop up with the passing of each decade. The list of scientific discoveries at U Chicago, such as carbon-14 dating, attests to this. University of Chicago students are cool with reading historical texts and speculating on what was meant by the author of those texts (N). This interesting way of looking in the past for possibilities is a hallmark of the university, as well as a contradiction. These students arrive as freshman with the belief that the next four years will intensely look to the future to develop their understanding of the world, yet U Chicago sees much wisdom in the past. Undergraduates will learn to look for novel ideas (P) in all time and space mediums. They will come to connect this personal understanding with the past and

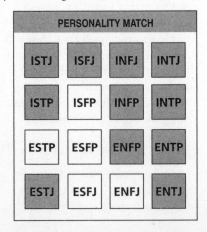

PERSONALITY MATCH

ISTJ	ISFJ	INFJ	INTJ
ISTP	ISFP	INFP	INTP
ESTP	ESFP	ENFP	ENTP
ESTJ	ESFJ	ENFJ	ENTJ

the future forming a starter soup for intellectual endeavors in graduate school. The curriculum pulls from across disciplines, honoring wisdom, no matter the age it was developed. University of Chicago draws students who are conservative in some ways, and anxiously curious and driven to add their own layer to humankind's accumulated wisdom.

In the following listing of college majors it is important to remember that students can fit into any college and can be successful in any major. We have found that the Personality Types below fit very well at this college. The course-of-study chosen for each Personality Type corresponds to MBTI® research and is presented as an example favorable for that type.

INFJ who has a spiritual bent will very much be interested in the **Religion and Humanities** major at University of Chicago. The thoroughness with which this major is designed is pretty impressive and definitely appeals to INFJ's attraction to philosophy and human values. Four major areas help build a foundation for upper level courses. First, U Chicago approaches the basic complexity of studying religion. Second, the department helps the student acquire one of several strategies to comprehend historical religious texts. Next, students focus on the community of believers and how they self-interpret their religion. And lastly, specific religious texts are reviewed. With this preparation, INFJ will find many satisfying days of study throughout the four years.

ENFP smiles broadly when they see that U Chicago offers a program of study in **Big Problems**. It is not a major but combines nicely with the many interests typical of the wide ranging ENFPs. As foretold, Big Problems are essentially defined as unsolvable. U Chicago brings together courses that help undergraduates learn how to approach the enormous complexity with optimism and skill intended to make a positive difference. ENFPs will have no trouble stretching their imaginations wide enough to comprehend the enormity and love the long-range projections that go along with the program.

INFP sometimes has a chivalrous streak. The major required course sequence in **Civilization Studies** at U Chicago is a good bet if they want to explore the helping fields in the social sciences but aren't sure which to pursue. By studying past successful civilizations, INFPs ferret out questions and answers that led to the betterment of that ancient citizenry. In the process, it is not hard to imagine this ingenious type contemplating ancient knowledge for applications to present-day societies.

ENTJ who likes numbers is going to really enjoy the **Applied Mathematics** major at U Chicago. This department is at the forefront of leading edge mathematics. Faculty actively promote the evolution of modern day math usage in disciplines across society. ENTJs with their visionary mind and interest in reality will like the three-course requirement in one of the physical sciences. By combining the efficiency of advanced math with a physical science, ENTJ will access and secure leadership positions within industry. This type might otherwise exercise leadership as a professor of mathematics who mentors and organizes graduates to solve industrial problems.

INTJ will find lots of room to maneuver with the **Physics** major at U Chicago. The administration and department philosophies strongly support interdisciplinary application. INTJs will first get grounded in the fundamental studies of matter, energy and force. This can be followed with further technical courses that move in the direction of medical, atmospheric or environmental sciences. INTJs love the rapid, spontaneous nature of discovery in technology and will likely be inventing stuff themselves after further graduate studies.

ENTP might initially find the **Law, Letters and Society** major at U Chicago revealing a very structured view of society. It could bump up against this type's wish for spontaneity with intellectual competence. As ENTP moves through the sequence of coursework and research, they will gain clarity on how society is organized, shaped and controlled through the application of laws. This very abstract nature of study is sufficiently complex to keep ENTP from getting bored. The required course selection will also be a good lesson in control for the freewheeling ENTP.

INTP absolutely likes to come up with something original. It really gets their juices going. The interdisciplinary program in **Creative Writing** here is a perfect approach to writing for this type who is passionate about their major. U Chicago expects those who take these writing courses to apply their writing expertise to their major field of study. INTP is just fine with this idea and will approve of new writing styles designed to turn the apple cart around, whatever apples are in their major.

ESTJ has a penchant for seeking out and doing away with the illogical and inefficient. This is a great characteristic if you intend to major in **Economics.** The math and the modern economy are the focus. The marketplace is explored through mathematical theories of supply and demand such as game theory, auctions and econometrics. Since this type is a natural administrator with the toughness needed to run regulatory offices, the course Regulation of Vice is a fine preparation for careers in government and its interface with the corporate world.

ISTJ is going to get the facts straight and every one of the facts will be in that straight line. You can count on it. The major in **Geophysical Sciences** is a good bet with its scientific data that ISTJs can apply with their tremendous powers of concentration. ISTJs may struggle with the individualized nature of the curriculum. Undergraduates in this department at U Chicago start tailoring their studies immediately by following their interests. This type is inclined to survey approaches to education, yet they can count on much congeniality with peers and faculty in finding that niche of interest that will become their major focus. Once identified, ISTJ's strengths come back into play big time.

ISFJ who is attracted to nursing, as they can easily be, can pursue the major in **Biological Sciences** here. It will be an ideal preparation for the medical field or perhaps a professor of nursing. The department does not introduce studies from other disciplines into this major, beyond the general education requirements of the University itself. Rather there is a sound commitment to educate undergraduate students with a realistic understanding of the physical nature of this science.

ISTP is often accurate with the numbers and always likes to add reality to whatever they study. The major in **Statistics** is a good choice for this type, yet ISTPs with their little touch of humor will need more than just numbers to keep them engaged. At U Chicago, there is choice to combine the statistics major with any other field in the natural or social sciences. This type is likely to move toward the physical sciences, however, since they are often technically quite competent.

UNIVERSITY OF MIAMI

Office of Admission
P.O. Box 248025
Coral Gables, FL 33124-4616
Website: www.miami.edu
Admissions Telephone: 305-284-4323
Undergraduates: 9,640; 4,693 Men, 4,947 Women
Graduate Students: 4,676

Physical Environment

The university is only a few miles from downtown Miami and less than **20 minutes from South Beach,** the most popular beach in Florida. Students experience beach life at its best, along with vibrant night life and outdoor restaurants. U Miami is a magnet for students who like warm weather, appreciate the **Latin American, Cuban flavor** and look forward to improving their high school Spanish in the city.

The university is surrounded by the residential neighborhoods of Coral Gables with a metro rail stop five minutes walking distance from campus that students can take downtown. The university boasts its own hospital the Jackson Memorial Medical Center, which houses graduate programs and the medical school. Also, UM has a school of **marine and atmospheric science** on Biscayne Bay. Students who love to explore, hands-on, the world of marine life will look forward to Spring 2013 when a major research facility will open dedicated to understanding the interface between the oceans and human health.

The University occupies much of its 260 acres with many buildings surrounding a large lake. The campus feels city-like when the visitor first arrives and tries to find a parking spot. The "Hurricane" shuttle service takes students around campus and to the "Hurricanes" football games. The university's team plays in the Sun Life Stadium along with the Miami Dolphins, adding to the "professional" aura of this top 20 ranking collegiate football team.

First year students must live on campus and can't bring cars, so they have time to get acquainted with the **large physical plant and their walking shoes**. There are six chapter houses for fraternities and none for sororities. They often join forces when planning social events and parties. Residence Halls are coed and operate traditionally with men and women on alternate floors. This arrangement reflects the administrations awareness and solid programming for the first year challenges away from home. University Village is the largest housing complex on the edge of campus for upperclassmen and grad students. **Benches and outdoor chairs** abound on campus in lovely outdoor landscaped places. The Whitten University Center now sports enhanced spaces like an outdoor, lakeside performance stage. In 2011, construction started on a new student activities center. There are only two dining halls on this large campus, located on opposite sides. Most first year students are on the meal plan while upper class students go off campus more often or rent an apartment with friends. Sprinkled throughout are the Subways, Wendy's, etc.

Social Environment

Students who attend U of Miami are academically **high achieving** and arrive with high grades and high standardized test scores. Seventy percent of those admitted were in the top 10 percent of their high school graduating class. They may come from across the United States, but all appreciate the warm weather. The majority comes from Florida and New York, followed by California, Texas, the Midwest and Atlantic seaboard. First-year classes can be large, especially the **general education classes**. Upper-level classes have fewer students, some with as few as 20 students or less.

There is **peer counseling** here which means that an upperclass student helps an incoming student to pick classes, to set up their time schedule wisely and to get the inside scoop about courses. U Miami has an active career center and alumni network for students looking for jobs. The curriculum specifies service learning in the course descriptions and much of the volunteer effort is focused on conducting surveys in the community. The research environment on the campus is not especially accessible to undergraduate students. However, with perseverance upperclassmen with solid applications can join in current faculty research at U Miami's excellent facilities. The future marine science center will likely be a research facility where staff and students are reluctant to close the door and go home.

In this large university it helps if students have lived away from home for some time and can take charge of their activities. Some students participate in Greek life just to quickly gain a cohesive set of friends for socializing. Others like to take their time to find their niche at the university or in the city. Students are open to **multi-cultural experiences**. Upon graduation some students decide to remain in Miami while others follow their careers across the country.

Compatibility with Personality Types and Preferences

University of Miami in Florida is a large presence in the collegiate liberal arts world. It is a large campus and has the big undergraduate student numbers to rival a mid-sized state university. The educational curriculum boasts many majors not frequently found at independent institutions. U Miami has the extra advantage of appealing to single-minded high school grads who know exactly what they want to be when they grow up. Undergraduate energy on this campus tends to move in two directions: one is negotiating the demanding, dynamic curriculum and the other is the big, wide city life. Students who like this university come to terms with the city's social intensity in their own way. Some embrace it with vigor; others sample it as needed for a break from the demanding academics. Regardless of social inclinations, students here are on the ball, paying attention, pursuing a goal (S). The campus is geared for analytic learning with expectations for precise content (T) by both the professors and students in the classroom.

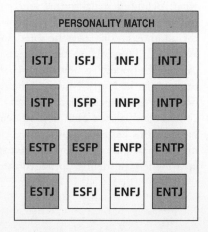

PERSONALITY MATCH

ISTJ	ISFJ	INFJ	INTJ
ISTP	ISFP	INFP	INTP
ESTP	ESFP	ENFP	ENTP
ESTJ	ESFJ	ENFJ	ENTJ

Fuzziness is reserved for pillows in the dormitory. It is an ideal campus for the socially adept who can take advantage (E) of the exciting international culture, yet show up in class the next day prepared. It is also just right for the socially quieter types who often keep their nose in the books, yet want to experiment with new social venues in college. For these latter types, it is great to drop into the city anonymously for an evening of observation with a friend or two. Undergraduates who keep their academics as the first priority do quite well at this energetic, assertive campus. They become productive, astute citizens in the workforce which is a pretty darn good paraphrase of the U Miami mission statement.

In the following listing of college majors it is important to remember that students can fit into any college and can be successful in any major. We have found that the Personality Types below fit very well at this college. The course-of-study chosen for each Personality Type corresponds to MBTI® research and is presented as an example favorable for that type.

INTJ sometimes finds higher education in academia an enticing career goal. This type thrives in educational atmospheres where peers are also interested in tough subjects. The INTJs really love to pull together theoretical, abstract information and throw it into an operating system or useable concept. U Miami offers a double major in **Marine Science** that is paired with one of the other physical sciences: geology, biology, chemistry, physics or computer science. Visionary INTJs will have no trouble seeing the connections between these disciplines during their undergraduate years. After graduation, advanced degrees for academic teaching/research posts or government and industry might call out to this type.

ISTP loves to discover the how and why of things. The **Audio Engineering** degree at U Miami is an accredited degree and comes with all the demands and privileges of a bachelor of science in engineering. The fun part for ISTP is that this option is highly integrated with the robust School of Music at this university. ISTPs will secure the code or get a door key for access to the audio labs at all times of night. The options for utilizing this degree are greater than one might think: medical instrumentation, analog/digital industrial applications and the obvious music entertainment industry.

ISTJ can utilize the curriculum track in **Health Science General** to explore and possibly prepare for a career in the medical field—perhaps veterinary services. This type is outstanding at noticing the facts and details, including listening carefully to the owners or their four-legged patients. ISTJs are typically conscientious, thoughtful and competent and possess fabulous memories for techniques and procedures. They are comfortable in offering services that require repetitive use of the skills. Mastery of content is their forte and they will be prepared for admission to professional schools.

INTP could like the major in **Ecosystem Science and Policy**. This curriculum also requires a second major selected from the physical sciences or math. The senior capstone course interfaces science and policy as it applies to a verifiable ecosystem, perhaps the Everglades. INTPs on our planet earth will not back away from such heavy, theoretical and critical issues. In fact, this type is energized by problems of this complexity. They typically need time to think over their reaction/answer. Identification of their second major will evolve out of this introspective process. Fast-paced, fact-based, University of Miami may put a little rush on them, yet this major and the campus social life are ideal for this type. INTPs often become absorbed in study and only occasionally want to head out for a social break.

ESTP is often a natural at promoting goals through spontaneous, quick-thinking action in their lighthearted way. This predisposition might become a full-blown career after completing the major in **Public Relations** within the very strong School of Communication at University of Miami. ESTPs accurately read the tea leaves and will enjoy learning the craft of developing a consistent, targeted message. Spontaneity once again comes into play as ESTP dreams up all the various vehicles to get the message out to the audience.

ESFP might dust off their fifth grade recorder or hang onto that marching band horn to look closely at the unusual major, **Music Therapy**, offered at U Miami. This type is often attracted to the helping professions in education and health care. At the same time, many have proficiency or at least an interest in the performing arts. Therefore, this major should click with a few ESFPs. The requirement for good communication skills needed in this field also comes naturally to this type. The well-provisioned School of Music at U Miami is also accredited through therapeutic organizations, giving the graduate strong credibility in the marketplace. This growing discipline is exploring treatments for difficult personality constructs such as autism.

ENTP tends to be a risk-taker who might look favorably at going into business. A few courses in **Entrepreneurship** selected together with the business advisors at the business school is ideally situated with nearby international, dynamic Miami. The school encourages a competitive focus with the annual business plan competition. Naturally assertive, ENTPs will be comfortable looking for partners to enter this contest. Likely ENTP will pair up with a peer in their major discipline and put an entrepreneurial angle to a research study. Although not known for their practicality, their creativity often sparkles.

ESTJ and the concept of authority go quite nicely together. It is a serious and honorable business for this type to make decisions, supervise and issue guidance with a solid foundation of skills and knowledge. The major in **Management** at U Miami is well-positioned to sharpen that foundational set of skills. The international flavor of Miami alerts traditional ESTJs to new possibilities in commerce. ESTJs will study the thorough business curriculum, but note that internships and professional mentoring seem to be reserved for the graduate students. After consideration, this type may opt for a minor in business which is also possible.

ENTJ likes to be high on the list for efficient on-time arrivals. This often capable administrator likes to develop an innovative and on-time leadership style. University of Miami School of Business is well paired with the School of Nursing in offering the major in **Health Sector Management and Policy**. ENTJs will recognize that this degree would give them entry points to executive positions in medicine, health insurance or health administration. Miami's educational philosophy prepares citizens for the future and ENTJs are masters at strategic planning. This degree, this type, leads to multiple entry points for the future.

UNIVERSITY OF PENNSYLVANIA

Office of Admissions
1 College Hall
Philadelphia, PA 19104-6376
Website: www.upenn.edu
Admissions Telephone: 215-898-7507
Undergraduates: 9,580; 4,708 Men, 4,882 Women
Graduate Students: 8,676

Physical Environment

U Penn is located in busy and bustling West Philadelphia, a few blocks from the Schuylkill River. The university's surrounding neighborhoods have many **ethnic shops and restaurants** along narrow streets. Upperclass students with confidence in their city skills ride their bikes to and from off-campus apartments should they decide to rent a room in these neighborhoods. Once on campus, they are assisted by the Penn Connect design that 'friendlies' this urban campus for pedestrians. The campus offers a park-like setting and an interesting **mélange of historic buildings** in Federal, Colonial, Romanesque and Modern vertical style. Shoemaker Green, completed in fall 2012, is a reclaimed open space on campus that will serve to improve ground water and reduce heat intensity during the summer months. College Hall was the first building in 1872 to be constructed on U Penn's campus and the statue of Ben Franklin in front of the entrance was there to witness it. An immediate sense of **American history** attracts high school students who may have elected American history over European history in their advanced high school classes.

The **teaching hospital** on campus with its emergency ambulances reminds premed students that there are many opportunities for internships. The University Museum evokes images of monks chanting in the night because of the Romanesque architectural detail. The extremely varied architecture, representing so many periods on this campus, enhances study and draws students interested in applied art and classical studies. The libraries are housed separately by subject and are clearly designated for either undergraduate or graduate use. U Penn is a very organized place indeed.

Most students are housed in the College Houses, essentially **tall dormitory towers**. The inside perimeter of these residences and the evolving campus design provide a comfortable enclosure and contrast to the city. The nearby Penn track is handy enough for most students to exercise on campus. Students sit or sunbathe outside in good weather. The towers suit students who are comfortable with functionality. Most often, students meet in dorm halls, while they change classes and in the central corridor of this compact campus. U Penn students arrive comfortable with the **city landscape** or become quickly attuned to it.

Social Environment

The very large majority of U Penn students are valedictorians of their high school graduation class. They were likely to be athletes and/or the **movers and shakers** who initiated service projects through their high school clubs for their hometown community. They tend to come from all over the U.S. and around the world, since **geographical diversity** is a draw on campus and in Philadelphia.

Students who apply to U Penn are competitive and proud to have reached their goal of entering an Ivy League university. Students of many faiths find much awareness and respect on campus for their religious and ethnic perspectives. Here students value hard work and hard play. Greek life is alive with scholarship, service and social activities. The fraternity parties are popular. Students tend to dress with awareness of the latest city trends as they often hail from professional and highly educated families. Once students reach upperclass status and gain city skills, they flock off campus for socializing with other undergraduates from nearby selective colleges in favorite Philadelphia watering holes.

Academically, undergraduates are self-directed and more than capable of holding their own in the large student body while tackling a very **difficult curriculum**. Their well-developed inclination to be **goal-driven** is usually reflected in their educational studies and the prospective career fields they expect to enter. Students like clear course expectations and they appreciate faculty who probe deeply and precisely into advanced coursework on this **Ivy campus**. Undergraduates like to know why they are studying a specific subject along with the more tangible effects of that knowledge. They incorporate many aspects of their U Penn experience from vibrant Philadelphia, training in the research labs to lectures of the Pulitzer Prize winning faculty. The historical architecture reminds U Penn graduates of the transience of time and the need to get on with individual pursuits.

Compatibility with Personality Types and Preferences

University of Pennsylvania is unique among the Ivys in a number of categories. Probably the singular and most important factor is that of Ben Franklin, founder. His lifetime achievements influenced a foundation of practicality and innovation that is holistically in place today. Three hundred years later, as one looks closely at the course of studies available to undergraduate students, you will see a curriculum of which he would likely approve. U Penn excels at real world applications of knowledge (S). The new Translationanal Research Center is more than over the top. It's hard to turn a phrase that describes it. Although few undergraduates will travel through the entryways, the atmosphere of excellence and discovery pervades the stellar sciences at Penn. In fact, the educational philosophy is defined in part as being a 'repository of knowledge.' This would make sense to their historic founder, who played a pivotal role in the survival of this nation during the Revolutionary period.

Undergraduates at U Penn like the concept that you gather all the known information and then see how it can be applied. This type of knowledge can be advanced into the near future for the benefit of society as well

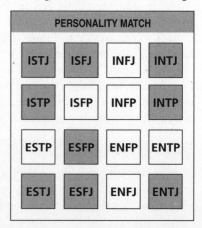

PERSONALITY MATCH			
ISTJ	ISFJ	INFJ	INTJ
ISTP	ISFP	INFP	INTP
ESTP	ESFP	ENFP	ENTP
ESTJ	ESFJ	ENFJ	ENTJ

as the bank account of the innovator. It is most important to understand how things work and how they will be used at U Penn. The favorite learning tool for this is logical analysis (T). Students drawn to U Penn are exceptionally fine logical thinkers. The happy student at U Penn knows that the universe is predictable (J) and will be evolving for the better as soon as they graduate and get out in the marketplace!

In the following listing of college majors it is important to remember that students can fit into any college and can be successful in any major. We have found that the Personality Types below fit very well at this college. The course-of-study chosen for each Personality Type corresponds to MBTI® research and is presented as an example favorable for that type.

ISTJ at U Penn will want to look into the Huntsman Program to utilize their excellent memory for foreign languages in an environment that requires accuracy and efficiency. A language like **Russian** combined with the **International Studies and Business** curriculum is an excellent choice for the business world, a comfortable place for ISTJ. This type can make the tough decisions and cut through to the core with precision. That includes summoning up amazing concentration while conducting business in a second language with aggressive, savvy East European entrepreneurs.

ISFJ can work one on one and do very well at satisfying a client's needs. Add this to their natural appreciation for fine design and you have a concentration in **Real Estate.** U Penn's Wharton School of Business and Management is always in the top five. Undergraduates reap the benefits of its presence on campus. Upon graduation, ISFJ is likely to join a brokerage and pick up the experience needed to move into top firms. An alternative might be to branch out and serve the real estate market in the U.S. or internationally. This reflective type prefers to serve others and might be found developing affordable housing in third world countries in a few years. Ben Franklin would approve.

INTJ is quite the visionary and prefers to work in areas where originality and new ideas rule. U Penn's major in **Digital Media Design** could be a good one if paired with some level of artistic talent. This four-year degree resides in the Engineering School of Applied Science. INTJs have the determination to create new expression and ways of communication. They love to work independently and often hold themselves to the very high standard. Only a few types would be willing to secure a Bachelor of Science in Engineering with the goal of going into graphics. Yet when you throw in virtual reality, then INTJs are on board. The U Penn graduate in this field will probably move toward virtual programming that helps apply practical knowledge without the risk of physical failure. Ben Franklin has a smile on his face.

ISTP might want to take up a career in the military. As a member of the Navy Reserve Officer Corps at U Penn, there will be rewarding financial scholarship to apply to tuition. This type is a natural troubleshooter when it comes to practical problems. The Economics degree with a concentration in **Actuarial Science** might open up challenging and rewarding career tracks in weapons development. This type's comfort with machines and moving parts supplements their pragmatic accuracy with numbers and details. This degree and those characteristics are true assets while evaluating risks inherent to billion dollar weapon system contracts.

INTP likes to take on studies that might seem beyond the pale to others. Neuroengineering and genetic engineering fit nicely into the category of possible majors for this type. They possess a rampant curiosity for new fields. U Penn's research facilities in the **Bioengineering** field are more than pretty special. Once again we have the Ben Franklin perspectives influencing the curriculum of this Ivy. After all, how much more practical does it get than working on the artificial heart that could become reality in the near future? No abstractions here, it either beats on time or it's not working. INTPs could spend years perfecting the instrumentation with their exceptional skills in long-range planning.

ESFP absolutely gets the real world of 'what's happening now.' There is no fuzzy-headed, wanderlust thread through their observation of the day. U Penn's Wharton School of Business concentration in **Insurance and Risk Management** will take advantage of this skill. It also provides this type with people interaction which they thrive on. The variety of risk assessments within the field of insurance also work perfectly for ESFPs who are excellent communicators. Their ability to recall and juggle large amounts of data allows them to be productive in this exacting science. The major in economics with this concentration prepares ESFP to tackle city-wide assessments such as those generated in New Orleans as a result of Hurricane Katrina.

ESFJ easily travels well in the world of **Nursing.** U Penn's objective within the nursing school is to activate research designs that improve nursing practices. ESFJ values this goal because it involves serving patients as individuals. Priority one for this type is maintaining a healthy, well-functioning, caring environment. U Penn's degree in nursing has an interdisciplinary nature with human health decisions viewed through ethical, wellness and community perspectives, as well as treatment regimes. This type has the curiosity to touch base with all patients and staff during their nursing daily routines. The U Penn nursing graduate is surely headed for decision making at the most encompassing levels of health in our society.

ESTJ is very good at spotting inefficient and impractical habits. With this natural inclination, they function well as civil servants in city, state or national government. Implementing policy while interacting with the public is a critical skill. Fortunately, competent decision making tends to be ESTJ's work style. They simply cut through confusion or inefficiency if at all possible. With the U Penn major in **Urban Studies** this type has the knowledge and credibility to wield authority in some of the most demanding municipal environments. It would be ESTJs, with a U Penn degree in this major, that possess the competence to excel at city planning for Detroit, Los Angeles, Miami or DC.

ENTJ could look at the fine management degrees in U Penn's Wharton School and settle on **Health Care Management and Policy**. This field offers the complexity and big picture that ENTJs need for satisfaction. It also offers the potential for a spiraling climb to the top in an industry that seems to be very good at spiraling. This type has the acumen to develop successful plans in complex environments. The medical fields of today include artificial hearts, indigent services, technical diagnostics, knowledge of litigation and above all, execs who bring a sense of honesty. ENTJs, with a U Penn degree in this field, will have each and every one of these skills and talents.

UNIVERSITY OF REDLANDS

1200 East Colton Avenue
Redlands, CA 92373
Website: www.redlands.edu
Admissions Telephone: 800-455-5064
Undergraduates: 2,410; 1,060 Men, 1,350 Women

Physical Environment

Located in the **small town** of Redlands, about 60 miles east of the Pacific Ocean, this campus is accessible via Ontario International or Los Angeles airport. The environment visually centers and encourages students to focus on the delicate balance between nature and man. Students can easily access the mountains for recreation. The campus is spacious but not remote. Downtown Redlands is nearby and offers the familiar college-oriented pizza palaces. However, the campus is the primary social gathering place and the comfortable dining hall stands out as where students meet. They cross this trendy cafeteria many times during the day and plan their late afternoon and evening activities.

Redlands' first building, a Baptist Chapel, was strategically located on top the highest hill surrounded by orange groves with striking views of the San Bernardino Mountains. The administration understood then and now the **nature of space** and how it plays a critical factor in **shaping human activity**. They located the cafeteria in the middle of the campus next to the new science quad, library and sports complex. Renovation of the library in 2011 includes the much desired 24-hour study lounge. The sports complex is extensive and includes an outdoor pool for water polo. At this university many students are athletically-inclined and talented. The new Center for the Arts expands the artistic and creative spaces on campus.

On one side of the quad by the chapel, the Johnston School for Integrative Studies is almost a second college within the Redlands campus. Students selected for this program tend to more alternative ways. The Johnston School is a cohesive living-and-learning community since Johnston students take classes in the same residence halls where they live. Johnston students chart their own course of study through an independent educational contract that leads to award of their degree at graduation.

Social Environment

Student life is integrated with academic life. The aim of the university is to develop students capable of making wise choices in a complex social world. The university hosts a vibrant **Greek community** with chapter houses for the local sororities and fraternities on campus. Students are both **physically fit** and clean cut for the most part. Many activities such as Health and Fitness Week were initiated by students to get everyone involved. Students want the emphasis on service learning much as they did in their hometowns during high school. At the same time there is an **entrepreneurial focus** that seeps down from the business school encouraging undergraduates to be successful as well as passionate. As a result, students tend to be responsible, seek traditional security and hope to benefit society. Seventy percent of the students ranked in the top 25 percent of their high school graduating class.

The prevailing political view here is toward non-violent activism with five student organizations solely devoted to promoting awareness and policy for those across the world living in poverty. There is also an underlying and quiet tolerance of all world religions. The service community is also quite active with membership in national chapters devoted to raising awareness of destitute populations. U Redlands undergraduates regularly raise monies to support programs in Africa. The Johnston School attracts more vocal and politically active students. Johnston students may choose to study abroad in Rwanda, instead of Italy, in order to better understand a troubled region's ethnic conflict. All students keep an eye on Darfur, Burma, Palestine, Israel, Iran, Iraq, Afghanistan and other the hot spots in the world. Most Redlands students care about **social change, sustainable development** and finding new solutions to old problems.

Compatibility with Personality Types and Preferences

University of Redlands does a great job blending order, structure (S), creativity and openness (N) into a strong, consistent campus culture. The environment is comfortable and feels healthy and optimistic. The administration and faculty devote most of their effort and resources toward the learning experience. The social experience or social fabric on this campus takes its direction from the academic life. Students socialize "early and often" while their gatherings (F) are also likely to have more than a shade of beneficial activity within. This nicely reflects part of the college mission to develop "circular diversity." There is just a hint of the Quaker morality on this campus. In decades past, the founders hoped to educate students who would come to appreciate other cultures by studying established formal belief systems from around the world. The administration and faculty hold this cross cultural foundation as uppermost while guiding the student population through their educational studies. At the same time, American culture and heritage is valued and studied for its historical richness and underlying national strengths.

PERSONALITY MATCH			
ISTJ	ISFJ	INFJ	INTJ
ISTP	ISFP	INFP	INTP
ESTP	ESFP	ENFP	ENTP
ESTJ	ESFJ	ENFJ	ENTJ

In the following listing of college majors it is important to remember that students can fit into any college and can be successful in any major. We have found that the Personality Types below fit very well at this college. The course-of-study chosen for each Personality Type corresponds to MBTI® research and is presented as an example favorable for that type.

ENTP should like the mix of finance and economics. This could lead to a career in investments and U of Redlands offers a BS in **Financial Economics**. There is a strong math requirement for this degree which includes freshman level calculus and one sophomore level math class, followed by a junior level elective in "Mathematical Economics." With this preparation, ENTP will attain the skills to move across the spectrum of the financial markets, following their keen intuition and entrepreneurial spirit.

ENFJ is an excellent fit on the Redlands campus. The major in **Government** is particularly rich with national perspectives, reflecting Redland's comfort level with American heritage. Learning outcomes for undergraduates seem to pop in the curriculum with freshness in this major. You can get your head around this statement taken from the major's website - 'Discover the origins of government and how they are structured.'

ENFP who is interested in the people of other cultures will gain much from the major in **Anthropology** at Redlands. The excellent department in Asian Studies explores very distinct cultures and historical medieval roots. Warm-hearted ENFP might imagine delivering social services for the rural populations in the poorer Pacific Rim nations. The Redlands faculty in this department supports one-of-a-kind study abroad for this very purpose. The faculty mentoring for ENFP's Plan of Study gently guides this type toward completing a curriculum that is relevant and has meaning to current needs within the national community.

INFP is another excellent fit at University of Redlands. In **Creative Writing**, the English department focuses on the creative process rather than a specific genre such as poetry, short stories or writing for the theater. Exceptionally vision-driven, INFPs seek to find their own tune to march to in the collegiate years. The major in creative writing offers an avenue to express their closely held values. The department regularly bumps up its visiting speakers lecture series. INFP will incorporate their thoughts with noted writers and that is just fine with INFP.

INFJ, the deep thinker, will find plenty to ponder in the **Religious Studies** department here. It is supported by a strong study abroad experience that prompts students to elect a geographic location at the historical seat of a world religion. At Redlands, the Religious Studies major is particularly reflective with courses like "Buddhist Literary Imaginations" and "The Historical Search for Jesus." This type will refine their internal belief system with passion and move confidently into a career path that takes advantage of their precise thinking and ethical perspective.

ESFJ wants to efficiently help others, preferably with direct or at least tangible results. The degree in **Communicative Disorders** here fits this description. At Redlands there is a carefully defined curriculum within each major. In addition to the speech and hearing body of knowledge, students must also have interpersonal skills to gain admission to the major and be successful on the job. It is likely that ESFJ will pass these requirements with flying colors since they are warm and enjoy situations where they can better get to know individuals.

ESFP would find the degree in **Business Administration** at U Redlands just the right mix between objective study and humane perspectives. This campus is remarkably encouraging of experiential learning through the internship, study abroad and travel abroad options in May and the summer. The business department presents the basic business skills in a thorough manner. ESFPs need and crave action so their typical gift of gab with sound business practices might make for VP of Sales within five years at local or regional business concerns.

ISFP can definitely find a place at U Redlands and it might just be the **Biology** major which includes a more formal approach to premed advising than many small liberal arts colleges offer. The course titled 'Observations in the ER' allows ISFP students to watch others excel at their own talent—taking quick decisive action in crisis situations. Since this type also is a free spirit and prefers freedom of action in the work place, perhaps they would rather be outside, not quite so confined as an emergency room. U Redlands department in biology is also helping undergrads explore the nature of insects and the diseases they carry to our food crops. Small scale research projects in the California fruit orchards are so doable here.

ISFJ can be generous, giving, helpful and thoughtful. These are ideal characteristics for patient elementary teachers. At Redlands, the preparation for **Teacher Education** is one of the best around. In part, this is because California certification requirements are stricter than many other states. At the same time, Redlands culture is one of understanding and appreciating others, so it is not surprising that they offer the Master of Education. This makes it efficient for the ISFJs who want to complete certification after graduation with the baccalaureate degree. U Redlands has a program that leads to this goal with one more year on campus. Those who follow this path graduate with a Masters in Education and are more than ready for the classroom.

UNIVERSITY OF RICHMOND

28 Westhampton Way
Richmond, VA 23173
Website: www.richmond.edu
Admissions Telephone: 804-289-8640
Undergraduates: 2,999; 1,369 Men, 1,630 Women

Physical Environment

U Richmond started out as a Baptist seminary in the 1800s with Westhampton College for women added in 1914 on the other side of the lake. Located in a middle class suburb of Richmond, the university grounds reveal a **landscaped valley** reminiscent of a country club. The 350 acres of campus are separated by a **ten-acre lake** in the middle. The student center is strategically built as a bridge over this lake, thus connecting the two sides of campus. In this building students exercise or eat at Tyler's Grill while taking in the views of the water and woods. It's no surprise why this campus is often cited as one of the most beautiful in the U.S.

In the late 80s, an alumnus donated $20 million which was used to erect the building that would house the **Jepson School for Leadership**. This unique program defines leadership through the lens of the humanities. Annual forums at the Jepson School focus on world trends. 2010's Forum addressed the difficult concept of The Common Good. A quick look at the forums over the past 20 years reveals many critical issues facing the world. Corruption in elected governments has not been a topic. However, it may be in coming forums as a result of increasing revelations about high ranking U.S. officials in the 21st century. Queally Hall, an important addition to the Robins School of Business, includes a finance trading room. Similarly, a $35 million building helped the Bio-Science program expand in faculty and majors, such as neuroscience. High school students who like lengthy discussions with their lab science chemistry teacher are attracted to U Richmond because of this facility.

Fraternity and sorority meeting houses, lodges and cottages, serve as gathering places and are not residential. Some residence halls are coed. There are many **athletic** fields and a sports complex supporting NCAA Division I teams. This smaller university now is pulling in more accomplished athletes.

Social Environment

The **Honor Code** is a defining experience for a U Richmond student. First year women sign an honor contract during a public ceremony called Proclamation Night, while first year men are similarly "incorporated" on Investiture Night. The administration supports these **historic collegiate traditions** in several ways including the male and female separation of student governments, dean of student offices and honor code administration for each. Generally, the student body is fine with observing this traditional organization with education and extracurriculars totally coed.

Students rank in the top quarter of their high school class and they very much enjoy the intellectual atmosphere here. Students, well prepared by their gender specific residential colleges, have the luxury to explore societal roles without distraction. The U Richmond bubble can be an affirming intellectual cocoon. Many students go in for smart, casual clothing. Although most enter without a declared major, they have a deep love for the liberal arts. U Richmond has a core curriculum of knowledge types: numerical, experimental, behavioral, expressive and temporal/spatial.

In order to understand the type of student who does well at U Richmond, one could look to the experiences that students share inside these beautiful buildings. Students have the ability to take an idea and the **abstraction** of it and move it forward. They examine many concepts from different perspectives and then fit their understanding together within their declared major of study. They are broad in approach and also intent in respect to their liberal arts studies. They **pull down the barriers** between the liberal arts subjects and pure science and research.

The business and journalism majors, however, are viewed as academic disciplines that are comprised of **skill and craft preparation** for a career. Students in these disciplines experience a different educational perspective, a bit outside of the humanities undergraduate student population. Their studies are more finely tuned for competence in a career field.

Another student experience at U Richmond is that of undergraduates who want to pursue leadership studies in the Jepson School. They compete in an admission process for those selective programs relating to leadership. These students like theories and quickly absorb the connections between sociological aspects of leadership. Students are encouraged to double major and double minor in two other liberal arts subjects.

Compatibility with Personality Types and Preferences

University of Richmond can be viewed as a study in contrast. Warm, southern grace coexists with a classical, time-honored format for education, yet the administration reacts quickly to the pulse of emerging trends in modern America. The Jepson School of Leadership offering leadership studies is a good example. Richmond's overall academic philosophy also leans toward the interdisciplinary approach of acquiring knowledge (N). On the other hand, logical, traditional wire diagram organization (T) is reflected in the two residential colleges—Richmond College for the men and Westhampton College for the women. The school's honor code, student government and academic rules are administered separately through these two colleges based on gender. And so it goes, back and forth, two distinct educational philosophies ruling, depending on the particular department. Some majors are best described as transformative, bold and innovative. Others are conventional in their course curriculum. Above all, U Richmond is an intellectual environment that places the highest priority on acquiring knowledge with traditional respect for the historical institutional practices and codes.

In the following listing of college majors it is important to remember that students can fit into any college and can be successful in any major. We have found that the Personality Types below fit very well at this college. The course-of-study

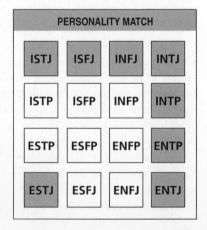

PERSONALITY MATCH

ISTJ	ISFJ	INFJ	INTJ
ISTP	ISFP	INFP	INTP
ESTP	ESFP	ENFP	ENTP
ESTJ	ESFJ	ENFJ	ENTJ

chosen for each Personality Type corresponds to MBTI® research and is presented as an example favorable for that type.

ISTJ who appreciates the tried and true could go for the **Accounting** major. The mind of a typical ISTJ is almost computer-like. Their ability to take in and utilize data will be perfect for this traditional discipline. ISTJs often are rather private individuals who appreciate the confidentiality required in the objective world of accounting. This type sees the asterisks and actually reads the fine print at the bottom of the page. U Richmond undergraduate study in the business curriculum is equally precise.

ISFJ talented in the arts will do well in Richmond's strong **Studio Arts** department. Undergraduate students will be exposed to a broad spectrum of art techniques and mediums. At the conclusion of four years, ISFJs entering career tracks in the arts will have a strong collection of work for their portfolio. U Richmond's thoroughness appeals to ISFJ's nature to answer the call of duty and be mindful of good design in their surroundings.

INFJ can be attracted to business if the emphasis is people-oriented in actual practice on the job. Because of this, the **Management** concentration in the Robins School of Business works for them. The curriculum allows the INFJ to acquire concepts and skills in organizational development and organizational design. Combined with a major in business administration, INFJs are likely to excel as a consultant or specialist in the 'people' end of enterprise, including marketing on occasion.

INTJ is an independent, quiet leader more often than not. Richmond has two rather nice options for this type who likes to think both big and original. The **Military Science and Leadership** program allows INTJ to explore the art required to lead military forces without military commitment. At the start of the junior year, this type can accept or decline a second lieutenant commission in the Army Reserves, complete with government financial aid. The INTJ who also chooses the **International Studies Concentration in Africa** has an eye to the future. The strategic value of this continent to the world will assure either a military or civilian career with decades-long fascination and opportunity.

INTP gets the intellectual freedom they need in the study of **Economics** at Richmond in the Arts and Sciences program. They can opt for the standard course work or specialize in business economics, international economics, economic history, public policy or quantitative economics. This wide-ranging discipline really suits independent, pattern-oriented INTP with plenty of options and wiggle room to exercise their global curiosity.

ENTP who looks closely at the **Rhetoric and Communication Studies** just may declare the major immediately. The coursework should be very attractive to this type. Argumentation and Debate alone will pull them in. Add in a minor in **Leadership Studies** and you will have a very competent, powerful ENTP change agent. The major is rarely offered and harkens back to the traditional educational perspectives of the university. Courses will be invaluable to ENTPs who can experience difficulty expressing their original thoughts.

ENTJ will find the **Marketing** concentration very handy for their entrepreneurial spirit. Richmond's robust school of business is nicely supplemented with the school of leadership and students are eligible to pursue a minor in leadership. ENTJs will find this combination very attractive because of their inclination to take charge. The refined business practices explored in the Richmond curriculum will give ENTJ the finesse to go along with lead positions after arriving on the job.

ESTJ has what it takes to make an effective parole officer, and Richmond has the corresponding **Criminal Studies** degree. This type likes to manage with gusto. The degree objectively focuses on the goals of supporting society and helping the troubled individuals within the penal system. ESTJ has the personality to serve both of these 'clients' at the same time. The Victim Assistance Academy in downtown Richmond is an unusual resource not often available to students entering this career track. As an undergraduate degree, it can lead to immediate employment or be a strong stepping stone to graduate study in criminal justice, public administration, social work, sociology or law. Ever mindful, practical ESTJ will narrow down the choice early in their studies at U Richmond.

UNIVERSITY OF SOUTHERN CALIFORNIA

University Park
Los Angeles, CA 90089
Website: www.usc.edu
Admissions Telephone: 213-740-2311
Undergraduates: 17,500; 8,192 Men, 9,308 Women
Graduate Students: 19,500

Physical Environment

The USC undergraduate campus is in the **center of Los Angeles**. This humming and thriving city pulses at an eclectic pace. To love USC is to love Los Angeles and all that it offers, and Los Angeles loves the USC Trojans. This setting pulls in students who can step with zest into the very large USC campus and the glitzy L.A. city life. The many nearby diversions like the beaches, high end shopping, the giant legendary film-production houses and much more require prospective students to become familiar with **public transportation options**. It takes approximately one-and-a-half hours to travel by metro train and metro bus from the LAX airport to the campus. Once on campus, the **compact**, modern, multi-storied academic buildings demand a similar familiarity with transportation routes for pedestrian and bike paths.

Modern residence halls have created guaranteed space for every freshman and returning sophomores. Parking spaces on campus are not guaranteed and available on a first-come-first-served basis. That, along with the weather, explains why campus is jam-packed with **bicycles**. Even those with cars will find it near impossible to drive to class. The Greek houses embody the exceptional school spirit on this campus. Sports facilities, as well as the new sports complex, support their national reputation as an **athletic powerhouse**. The weather and emphasis on sports encourages lively activity on campus at all hours of the day and night. This 155-acre enclosed campus gives students fertile ground to mature into young adults and develop a **vibrant**, smart social life.

The research labs are designed for a faculty that is **innovative** and **independent**. The universities' fundamental purpose of **searching for knowledge** tolerates extra-large faculty personalities which coexist with pushing into the unknown. The Broad Center for Regenerative Medicine opened in Fall 2010 houses 11 research labs and 200 researchers. This is just one of the research facilities at USC. WOW.

Social Environment

This body of approximately 17,000 undergraduates is made up of very creative, **dynamic,** curious students who ranked in the top 10 percent of their high school class. There are typically 250 National Merit Achievement scholars each year. USC students come with many ethnic, international, religious and socio-economic backgrounds. Because of this, many students quickly attain polished social skills if they did not arrive with them already. This experience, plus the lack of extended cold weather, translates into an intellectual freedom best described as eagerness and anticipation.

The pre-professional programs and business school pull in practical types who value traditional careers that are in demand. Here also, the student who ran his own scientific experiments in the basement is rewarded with access to USC's **amazing research labs**. The cinematic arts department draws Hollywood hopefuls who want to intern in the nearby Hollywood film industry that offers these opportunities.

This campus attracts those who get along well in a large community filled with very different talents and social styles. There are "geeks," in the best sense of the word and "party animals" in the funniest sense. There are quiet and withdrawn students who find hiding places in the labs where they go to deescalate and chase after knowledge.

This university is **exceptionally well-managed**. The 1994 Strategic Plan is remarkable for its foresight in respect to the campus and even the Pacific oceanic basin!! Service staff, faculty and administrators seem to support a humming campus. It shows in a number of ways, most obvious is their superb athletic performance. The undergraduate student body responds to this exceptional environment. The dormitories are contemporary in design with built in **utility.** The residential life policies are clear and simplify this high density living environment. There is a PDF file on all topics at USC! The administration intends to reserve student emotional energies for learning and playing. In the evening, students are outside, talking, walking and playing pickup games. Students are **optimistic** and healthy to the casual observer. Those who gain the most out of this USC experience are independent learners, **self-directed**, imaginative and goal-driven.

Compatibility with Personality Types and Preferences

Wow is the word that comes to mind when thinking of this large university. Also independence, dynamic and invention crowd into a good description. At USC, intellectual and physical energy combine and the product mirrors thriving, spontaneous Los Angeles. In some ways, the city and the campus are the same since the USC community proudly admires and frequently interfaces with the culture and resources of the city (E). In addition to this distinct LA influence, educational philosophies also drive and impact this huge collegiate community. These USC philosophies include a magnetic-like attraction to the unknown (N). There seems to be an institutional mandate to push the boundaries of human knowledge. The mandate is naturally achieved through the exceptional research resources on the several USC campuses that include the physical laboratories and the world class faculty. The undergraduate students themselves are expected to actively push forward. Their vehicle for this process is through the coursework of the undergraduate degrees (S) which are unique and large in number. At the same time, the majors are dwarfed by the extraordinary list of minors offered, many of them also unusual. A review of the catalog reveals that critical thinking (T) and logical disciplined approaches to learning are primary vehicles of energy on this exceptional campus. Of equal importance,

PERSONALITY MATCH			
ISTJ	ISFJ	INFJ	INTJ
ISTP	ISFP	INFP	INTP
ESTP	ESFP	ENFP	ENTP
ESTJ	ESFJ	ENFJ	ENTJ

the positive undergraduate student body interface with the administration is mirrored in the undergraduate concern for others within the larger community. The Engemann Student Health Center projected to open in 2013 will attest to this. This predisposition for noticing and caring about others seems to extend to visitors, employees, academics and other individuals who find themselves on this campus for a few hours or a career (F).

In the following listing of college majors it is important to remember that students can fit into any college and can be successful in any major. We have found that the Personality Types below fit very well at this college. The course-of-study chosen for each Personality Type corresponds to MBTI® research and is presented as an example favorable for that type.

ESFJ will readily understand the purpose of the degree in **Health Promotion and Disease Prevention Studies**. This type is typically very responsible and readily supports following the rules. As they learn more about preventative health through the course Theoretical Principles of Health Behavior, they will relate to the "shoulds" and "should nots." Their empathy for others encourages them to seek answers in courses like Social Exclusion, Social Power and Deviance. Their loyal natures will likely assure them of continued upward momentum within larger health organizations.

INFJ is quietly persistent and powerful with their gift of insight. The **Biophysics** undergraduate degree on this campus is going to utilize each of these INFJ talents. Introduction to Quantum Mechanics and Its Applications is a course that challenges and launches INFJs into the world of graduate school. Follow on graduate classes could be in biology, physics or medical school. INFJ will summon up the hours, personal drive and values needed to select the most productive graduate program.

INTJ who is attracted to both the creativity of computer science and the unforgiving nature of physics won't have to choose between the two with the USC undergraduate degree in **Physics/Computer Science**. Its solid coursework in math, computing and physics nicely prepares the senior for the Final Project. This particular area of study also helps INTJ refine their scientific insight while reality reigns in their most out-of-this-world ideas.

INFP can drop into the **Health and Humanity** undergraduate degree and search for life's meaning throughout the four collegiate years. They can clarify their personal contribution to the field by taking courses in the modules of bioethics, aging, ethnicity, the mind and biology. This type might select the thematic module titled Health and Aging or Health and the Mind. The very abstract nature of these topics allows INFPs to focus on human potential and that is very comfortable for this type.

INTP is drawn to complicated patterns. They seek out complex, large systems with data and hope to further develop a particular strand within that knowledge. They think about riddles and word puzzles a lot. The unusual minor at USC in **Operations and Supply Chain Management** introduces this type to the world of numerical volume. Think what could happen if all 4,000 fuel pumps on all the 737 airliners started leaking in the same month across the nation. How should you then make repairs and prevent a possible airplane crash, without disrupting the airline schedules? INTP can handle this type of crisis scheduling and also stand up to the intense pressure that always surrounds these decisions.

ENFP is loath to make a decision too early for their undergraduate degree. In the **Policy, Planning and Development** degree they will take elective coursework among the fields of health, sustainable planning and real estate development, law and social innovations. After graduation, this type might just work in each area through multiple career progressions. This will keep ENFP's need for variety and interest appropriately satisfied.

ENTP with a flair for business will position themselves well with the interdisciplinary minor in **Cultures and Politics of the Pacific Rim**. It might pair up with a major in communication or business and give this type the elbow room they typically like to have as they charge into their studies with abandon. Their ability to see into the future is spot on if they have developed the intellectual discipline to support their insight. USC will help them with the discipline part. ENTP will reciprocate with originality in essays for courses like Global Strategy for the Communications Industry.

ENTJ who is not majoring in business but wants to pick up the basic tools will like the minor in **Organizational Leadership and Management** at USC. There are three classes this type will like: Power, Politics and Influence, Designing and Leading Teams and The Art and Adventure of Leadership. This last course is probably their motto and they should wear it on a T-shirt.

ENFJ has a vibrant humor that connects easily with their audience. The undergraduate degree in **Communication** will allow ENFJs to discover and develop their natural charisma. Their fine sense at verbally reaching out to people through formal presentations is an advantage. The course in Public Speaking reflects USC's acknowledgement of the importance and art of presentation. Formal, traditional curricula combined with the most modern and evolving techniques will be enticing for this future oriented type.

ESFP won't miss a beat reporting for the 6-o'clock news. This type could take advantage of the undergraduate degree in **Cinematic Arts: Film and Television Production**. The high-storied buildings in downtown Los Angeles boldly marked with their ABC and network signage remind the student that USC is the perfect location to study communications. Both the production classes in cinema techniques and the courses with cultural analyses are included in the impressive course offerings for this undergraduate degree.

ESTP is going to thrive with the day-to-day action of a career in real estate. USC has a specialty in **Real Estate** among its many useful specializations within the Business Administration major. The city of Los Angeles offers a natural extension to the campus and this curriculum. An hour drive around L.A. reveals the many, many different types of human habitats that fit within the definition of real estate. It will take a GPS, good driving skills and about 10 months to understand this metropolis. ESTP can handle the drive with skill, acquire LA acumen and professionally move on to any other American metropolis.

ISTP can select a minor in **Management Consulting** and be successful in certain business environments. They would be good at helping businesses that offer practical services or products. This type will make a judgment by using their strong logical, analytic skills. They will work hard, seeking solutions in a production environment. Although they are not natural business consultants, ISTPs can be exceptionally effective in an industrial setting.

UNIVERSITY OF TAMPA

401 West Kennedy Boulevard
Tampa, FL 33606-1490
Website: www.ut.edu
Admissions Telephone: 813-253-6211, 888-MINARET
Undergraduates: 6,051; 2,621 Men, 3,430 Female

Physical Environment

Imagine leaving the business district of Tampa, crossing the bridge of **the inter-coastal waterway** and then coming upon a palace with wrap-around verandahs, honeycombed archways and minarets on the roof that evoke images of Arabian Nights. Historic Plant Hall, U Tampa's admissions and administration center, formerly a luxury hotel, features **Russian architecture**. This is Florida, where vacations and surprises come together. This location holds a special attraction. It attracts many students who are tired of cold winters. Students, returning from Thanksgiving break, want to wear flip-flops in November as they board a plane for Florida.

Modern residential halls that were completed in the first decade of 2000 include suite-style halls reserved for upperclassmen. Dormitories are spacious and similar to that aspired to by young urban professionals. Brevard Hall is one of the most popular and much coveted by upperclass students because of this community-style living and the views of the **waterfront** and the minarets.

The campus is well into a major construction phase of new facilities. The Student Health Center is a bonus not easily matched by most colleges of similar size. The newest UT nursing laboratories include sophisticated simulation equipment. The new academic building completed in 2010 dramatically expanded the life science curriculum and programs.

Within the humming and active academic spaces, the John H. Sykes College of Business has a **financial trading room** and brings in students interested in business, Wall Street investment and Tampa internships. Students here are travel-savvy and they get off campus easily and often. Travel by airplane, city transportation, urban living and Floridian culture are the variables that shape these four years of college.

Social Environment

University of Tampa is a good fit for those students who need to develop strong academic skills and are motivated to do so. They will find the room to grow and develop as undergraduates. Those with learning differences will find the professors and faculty supportive. First year students experience an intensive, solid program in **writing** that introduces the reasoning skills needed on this reality-based, hands-on campus. Newly completed, Skyes Chapel is a center for campus spirituality.

The social experience at U of Tampa has many faces. Students come from New England and the Midwest and there is a large Hispanic and African American minority. International students, Asian Americans and Native American Indians are also representative of the student body which makes for fun ethnic celebrations and traditions. The Greek fraternities and sororities are popular with 20 percent of the student body joining. Most social activities are held on campus since the immediate surrounding neighborhood is comprised of conference hotels. College baseball, basketball, crew and cheerleading bring athletic-minded students to this year-round summer climate.

Approximately half of the students rank in the top quarter of their high school class. These students take advantage of **the practical education** in the pursuit of the good careers and rise up to their professor's clear expectations. Students who are attracted to the idea of **learning through research** will appreciate the options here at UT. The faculty strongly mentors through the art of research study and students can find credit and noncredit work in the campus laboratories. This includes business research which fewer small liberal arts colleges pursue.

Compatibility with Personality Types and Preferences

The students at U Tampa are just a bit more on the city sophisticate side than the typical first year student in college. The international presence of the city draws students from many differing backgrounds and they blend their outlooks and expectations giving a futuristic edge to this campus. At U Tampa, there is a strong focus on attaining work experience and skills to move successfully and directly into the future workplace. As a result, practical yet cutting-edge knowledge (S) is quite the fashion at U Tampa. The faculty is devoted to providing high quality experiential learning. To this end, there is an attraction to technology and the faculty assertively introduces its use within the curriculum.

With a greater number of cultural perspectives on this campus, there is a familiar awareness of others and a sensitivity that translates into serving the community. The educational atmosphere combines new trends in society-at-large with common sense. The faculty is mindful of the international presence in the city and brings a global perspective to the curriculum along with use of technology. It all serves to encourage orderly (J), methodical perspectives within the highly useful academic majors at U Tampa.

In the following listing of college majors it is important to remember that students can fit into any college and can be successful in any major. We have found that the Personality Types below fit very well at this college. The course-of-study chosen for each Personality Type corresponds to MBTI® research and is presented as an example favorable for that type.

PERSONALITY MATCH

ISTJ	ISFJ	INFJ	INTJ
ISTP	ISFP	INFP	INTP
ESTP	ESFP	ENFP	ENTP
ESTJ	ESFJ	ENFJ	ENTJ

ISTJ will like the direct nature of instruction in the **Criminology** major, especially the Criminology Scholars' Program. This very exacting type prefers to cover all the bases. The annual Scholars Seminar presented by a respected practitioner in the field could find this type sitting in the front row, diligently taking notes. The major combines nicely with the minor in **Law and Justice** for a comprehensive preparation in the criminology career field.

ESTP with an interest in athletics could excel in the field of **Sport Management**. This career field will exercise their talents in problem solving. Tampa's Sport Management curriculum provides undergraduate students with a good exposure to all of the academic disciplines that intersect the billion dollar sports industry—finance, economics, media, fund raising, event management, stadium management, legal issues and the list goes on.

ESFP will like the variety and action in the **Marine Science** major. U Tampa is alert to employment trends in this major and requires a double major. Students must add either biology or chemistry. ESFPs, often possessing a vibrant personality, would be ideal ambassadors for endangered animals or exceptional animal trainers at Sea World. This combination of science, education and entertainment plays to their strengths.

ESTJ could be very comfortable with the major titled **Financial Services Operations and Systems**. At U Tampa, the focus is toward a comprehensive exposure to the markets and regulating institutions. The course titled Data Mining and Informatics introduces a highly useful forensic skill. Since ESTJs are natural administrators, they will be more than capable of directing action in the fast-paced financial world.

ESFJ could go for the **Exercise Science** degree. It is centered on individual physical fitness. This type's strong sense of responsibility and genuine caring for others fits in nicely with this degree. It is ideal for immediate, meaningful employment in exercise studios, gyms and Pilates classes. The degree can also be a solid stepping stone for graduate studies in allied health fields, also a favorite occupation for this type.

ENFJ often builds consensus with ease. Their attraction to the possible and their strong people-based values interface nicely with the major in **Government and World Affairs**. Nongovernmental organizations will tap ENFJs' strengths sending them out to serve in underdeveloped countries. Turning the Possible into the Probable is the motto on their T-shirt.

ISFJ, often appreciative of design, could be a good match for the certificate in **Arts Administration and Leadership** at U Tampa. This type's fine sense of space and color will be an asset in design worlds. With this certificate and a major in **Management of Information Systems** multiple careers and employers emerge such as the Smithsonian, Caesars Palace in Las Vegas, Disney World, Hilton Hotels and architectural firms. Each of these organizations has heavy reliance on design and computers to maintain and operate their client-centered environments. This is good because ISFJ is client-centered too.

VALPARAISO UNIVERSITY

Office of Admission
Valparaiso, IN 46383-6493
Website: www.valpo.edu
Admissions Telephone: 219-5011; 888-468-2576
Undergraduates: 2,692; 1,217 Men, 1,475 Women
Graduates: 1,100

Physical Environment

Valparaiso means "Vail of paradise." Students refer to their school as simply "Valpo." This university is surrounded by a **1960s neighborhood** of simple homes, each different than the other, and well-cared yards. The campus buildings are **striking, functional and flat** on the horizon. Its straight lines remind us of Frank Lloyd Wright's architecture. The Fites Engineeering Innovation Center, opened in fall 2011, is primarily designed for undergraduates with labs and learning spaces. A newly-built student union centralizes student services and reflects the no frills, practical nature of the administration.

The nearby, large new library sends a clear message about the **importance of academics** and intellectual work. Students arrive with an appreciation for the traditional visual arts and the center for the arts encourages them to continue their creative work. The Chapel of the Resurrection, built on a rock, has a Midwestern, prairie-style architecture to it. It's a clear **moral reference point** on this campus, where the chapel marks the physical and emotional center. It is a metaphor for the strong role that Christianity plays at Valpo. Many students attend the optional daily services since 36 percent are Lutheran and 20 percent are Catholic.

Midwestern values of efficiency and hard work are alive and well at Valparaiso University. Two-thirds of the student body is from the Midwest and plains states with many from New York, California, Colorado and Texas. Students must live on campus the first three years. They are from traditional families and are comfortable with this arrangement and like the affordable education. Greek life is also traditional with fraternity and sorority members living in chapter houses off and on campus One-third of the undergraduates are affiliated with **Greek organizations** and take on very large community service initiatives. As with the other traditional values on this campus, Greek life calls to brotherhood and sisterhood that supports community building.

Athletics are really big at Valpo. They strongly support their sports teams in the traditional collegiate style. Slightly less than 20 percent of the students here are involved in competitive athletics at this Division I University. When the campus starts to close in, students take the bus to Chicago or travel to the near-by beaches of Lake Michigan in the early fall or late spring.

Social Environment

Students here want a big school experience with lots of professional and club sports while still learning in small classrooms with attentive professors. Valpo pulls in students who will pay close attention to securing a job on graduation. Students are attracted to the **pre-professional** programs in business, engineering and nursing, yet students also like the core of liberal arts classes which allows for more abstract discussion. If they did not have it in high school they will certainly get abstraction and searching for human purpose in their first two years at this campus. The two required religion courses, with one focusing on Christianity, are the basis of the **ethical underpinnings** on this Lutheran campus. The global leaders living and learning community prompts students to include awareness of other cultures and values in their individual careers and goals. The Christ College is for honors students and campus leaders. Their participation in campus-wide student activities is significant and **fun-centered**.

Who does well at Valpo? Students who were very involved in high school activities and probably took some **leadership initiatives**. Those students who preferred to study with others. Those who joined volunteer service clubs in high school to fundraise or tutor. They were likely participants in their church youth groups, organizing fun and service weekend activities. This college environment is well-interfaced with **common sense** and the attention given to the undergraduate experience.

Those students who want to become ethical contributors to society, graduate and move on to traditional careers do well here. These graduates value fair play on the fields and hard work in the company conference room.

Compatibility with Personality Types and Preferences

Two abstract principles consistently hover over the Valparaiso University campus. Faith and learning move together within this realistic community and within each individual student. Faith and learning, evolutionary in nature, are constantly adapting in response to modern society. How better to bring modern American society to campus than through the freshman students moving into dormitories each August? Learning takes off for first year students with expectations that undergraduates will ethically define their understanding of the world. Despite this very conceptual expectation, Valparaiso is quite grounded in the here and now. The educational philosophy strongly supports out of classroom learning experiences (S) where students participate directly in field experiences. Technology is embraced and ever present on the campus along with faith. Student organizations and student behavior adopt a consistent emphasis on service and caring (F), yet the campus is full of activity and fun also. At Valpo, students are interacting with each other on a continual basis (E). The arts, athletics, service, learning, spiritual study and dorm confabs can all be silly or serious. In this lighthearted and honest environment, the administration expects both faith and learning will develop serving both the graduating students and the Valpo campus that they will shape in the passing four years. Valpo is not static in any sense of the word.

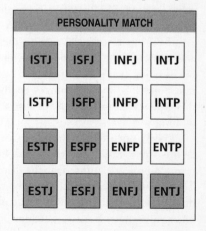

PERSONALITY MATCH

ISTJ	ISFJ	INFJ	INTJ
ISTP	ISFP	INFP	INTP
ESTP	ESFP	ENFP	ENTP
ESTJ	ESFJ	ENFJ	ENTJ

In the following listing of college majors it is important to remember that students can fit into any college and can be successful in any major. We have found that the Personality Types below fit very well at this college. The course-of-study chosen for each Personality Type corresponds to MBTI® research and is presented as an example favorable for that type.

ENTJ is busy preparing for leadership at reality-based Valparaiso. The major in **American Studies** orients itself to the philosophical underpinnings of American society. The ENTJ who wants to move into a career associated with government will have a very sound understanding of America as founders, Washington, Franklin, Adams, hoped it would become. This type enjoys teaching and helping others through their knowledge. It is easy to imagine an ENTJ sitting on the bench of our United States court system.

ESTJ could use the knowledge gained in Valpo's **Actuarial Sciences** major with a career in corporate finance or insurance. This type is comfortable with environments that combine facts with the expectation of decision. The world of high finance definitely fits this description. ESTJ is not fatigued by the responsibilities of supervising others. In fact, they are quite comfortable with traditional settings that require decisive action.

ESTP is a natural for Valpo's **Sports Management** major. The element of entertainment in professional sports fits this dynamic personality type well. This major requires a minor or double minor in **Fundamentals of Business** or **Business Administration**. Two classes in particular, the Psychology of Sport and Sport and Society, will help ESTPs understand their role in management as a promoter or as the organizational guru within the multimillion dollar professional teams. Yet the strong business curriculum keeps ESTP grounded in financial detail.

ESFP takes kindly to helping others through mentoring and informal advising. The concentration in **Criminology** is a good choice for this type who is sympathetic to young children and adolescents. The course in Urban Sociology is going to find on-the-go ESFPs wandering the streets of nearby Chicago. Here they will find excellent opportunities for internships with Chicago's many ethnic populations and value systems. ESFP is often especially skilled at reducing tensions within troubled relationships which is perfect for this field.

ISFP has a technical side to their personality and Valpo has the right degree and approach for this type who would like to get a degree in **Civil Engineering**. ISFPs enjoy being out of doors. The practical courses in geotechnical, structural transportation, water resources engineering and environment protection appeal to this type. ISFPs prefer to leave abstraction stuck between the pages of books located on library shelves.

ENFJ, not often attracted to the discipline of economics, might look twice at the Valpo major **International Economics and Cultural Affairs.** The senior research project can interface the distribution of resources with the social outcomes. This should appeal to ENFJs who would enjoy championing altered systems of distribution to achieve positive outcomes. At Valpo, there will be a solid discussion on exactly what a 'positive outcome' looks like. Millennials will come to understand, as each generation does, there are limits to social engineering. Valpo especially will help undergraduates search for solutions through theological, moral reasoning while exploring the limits of courts, government and social programs.

ISTJ will like the field of accounting because it is so very fact-based. This type is literally a mastermind with data. They can excel in this profession because of their own thoroughness and follow through. The Bachelor of Science in **Accounting** has room for more electives since it requires additional coursework beyond the fourth year of study. For impatient ISTJs, although there are few, the Bachelor of Business Administration with an accounting major is more focused and is completed in four years.

ISFJ has the touch to be empathetic with the people they supervise. When you combine this with their wry sense of humor, the **Management** major in Valpo's college of business is a nice choice. After all who wouldn't want a boss like this? The ISFJ brings these special talents to the world of business. It is likely to move them toward staff positions where they are advising employees on the nature of their performance or work output. This will appeal to ISFJ.

ESFJ is often gifted with the art of communication and a strong desire to pay attention to organize and retain facts. The major at Valparaiso in **Marketing** has a nice element that is not always emphasized in this highly persuasive field – that of loyalty. This university is strong in weaving values and the ethical perspective throughout its campus and curriculum. Caring ESFJs will find this is just the right approach to marketing and business for their style.

VANDERBILT UNIVERSITY

2201 West End Avenue
Nashville, TN 37325
Website: www.vanderbilt.edu
Admissions Telephone: 800-288-0432
Undergraduates: 6,817; 3,162 Men, 3,655 Women
Graduate Students: 6,082

Physical Environment

At the edge of a vibrant city, a mile from downtown Nashville, **Commodore Vanderbilt** started this institution that students call "Vandy." His mission was to "strengthen ties between geographical areas" at a time when the world seemed larger. Vanderbilt embraces the American nation and studying abroad is important because it strengthens America's ability to interact successfully with other cultures. The Commodore wanted this college to be intellectually at the center of the region and a thriving nation and with powerful **connections** to industry. With its **relentless drive for excellence**, Vanderbilt remains within a smaller number of fine universities that continue to respect traditions from the American past yet incorporate innovative 21st Century attitudes and knowledge. True to its founder, the university is a bold institution advocating for a strong, lasting and united America.

The university campus is an **arboretum** with beautiful trees, huge magnolias and oaks, tying together a varied architecture, from Victorian to the 60ish and to the modern. The recently-built Peabody School of Education and Blair School of Music are at one end of the campus. The **sprawling campus** encourages students to form smaller, cohesive communities centered around their school or major field of study.

All freshmen live in the Ingram Commons within one of 10 houses. For sophomores, juniors and seniors, the university supports learning-living communities often based on academic interests and sponsored by academic departments. Others are theme-oriented residence options like the Mayfield learning lodges which afford the opportunity to live and work together on service learning projects. The surrounding neighborhoods are comparatively safe and attractive. The community receives the students warmly in their many restaurants, pubs and coffee shops with lattes and ice-cream by the curb-side. The Grand Ole Opryland influence is strong in town and students never know which famous country singer they might run into.

Social Environment

Vandy's admission process is highly selective. The Vandy student is **bright, high-performing** and expectant of a professional career. **Academic demands** are considerable for the undergraduate students. Extensive faculty research establishes an ever-present educational standard that seeps into the undergraduate curriculum. Academic probation is best avoided as hand wringing and sad eyes are not listed as viable pathways to get back into good academic standing. **Independence, resilience and perseverance** are valuable characteristics for prospective students. The Honor code and university regulations are well respected and applied evenly.

The Blair School of Music is for students who want to pursue **music performance**, teaching or the musical arts. This last major consists of equal preparation in performance, literature and musical theory. Founded in 1964 when Blue Grass and country music were already well established, the Blair School connects well with Nashville's booming music industry. It reflects Vanderbilt's desire to educate students to a high level of accomplishment. Blair graduates will bring musical awareness and appreciation to their communities, as the Commodore would have wanted. During his lifetime, music performance was the primary form of entertainment. The Blair School echoes the overall Vanderbilt heritage, providing an education that is functional, artistic and rational. It applies to each of Vanderbilt's outstanding colleges and schools.

Many undergraduates come from well-funded public or independent schools. They bring a core of familiar experiences and activities typical of their high school years. Undergrads often **socialize around a cause or service activity** and put forth full effort while having **fun.** They are likely to generate club sponsored projects that raise funds for the local needy communities. A majority of students hail from Tennessee, followed by Texas, and as many or more are valedictorians or salutatorians.

There is a **predisposition to go Greek**. The Vandy social life offers a traditional atmosphere with many Greek-sponsored social activities. But non-Greeks find plenty of affiliations through their living and learning communities, academic interests, sports and cause-related interests. The students strongly support the Vanderbilt athletic teams. The Commodores are winning games in the tough SEC football conference and students love the renovated stadium. The mild winter weather, recreational social activities, as well as southern manners make for a comfortable, pleasant campus environment.

Compatibility with Personality Types and Preferences

Vanderbilt students often move through their four years of studies on campus expecting to acquire a rational, all-encompassing knowledge of their chosen discipline. The Vanderbilt educational philosophy supports this drive for excellence. Acquiring and refining knowledge (T) is critically important and these students understand and appreciate this goal. The pursuit of excellence may squeeze out time for a broader survey of global issues; however, this trade-off leads to exceptionally focused, competent graduates. Students become ready to lead and push the frontiers in their discipline both in the national and global community. The faculty and student body is supportive of strength and power emanating from knowledge. In this way Vandy graduates will become pillars at many American institutions.

The student body is quite active (E) and well-organized around favorite political causes which tend to reflect traditional American values such as registering voters in the immediate neighborhoods. The student body also solidly steps out and makes their views known on controversial subjects such as abortion, as in past participation while marching in Washington, DC pro-life movements. The predominant feeling on campus supports the American historical perspective toward human community. This is reminiscent of those values raised in the ancient texts and held by Commodore Vanderbilt. It certainly supports the unique Peabody College of Educational and

Human Development. Classic, (J) traditional values really mesh within the student body of civically-minded young adults who were active in high school service and will remain so throughout life.

In the following listing of college majors it is important to remember that students can fit into any college and can be successful in any major. We have found that the Personality Types below fit very well at this college. The course-of-study chosen for each Personality Type corresponds to MBTI® research and is presented as an example favorable for that type.

PERSONALITY MATCH			
ISTJ	ISFJ	INFJ	INTJ
ISTP	ISFP	INFP	INTP
ESTP	ESFP	ENFP	ENTP
ESTJ	ESFJ	ENFJ	ENTJ

ISTJ is a natural administrator who will want to secure an exceptionally fine preparation for leadership should they pursue a career in the K-12 schools. The ideal major for this purpose is at Vanderbilt. **Human and Organizational Development** looks at public policy and human development. It gives this type needed practice and experience with broad-based approaches to problem solving in demanding career paths such as school principal or superintendent of schools.

ISTP could find the **Biomedical Engineering** curriculum at Vandy to be full of fascinating lab courses. The Medical Imaging course will be a fun challenge for this type through its study of technical absorption, reflection and scattering of energy. The precise nature of this degree and its technical methods appeals to the unemotional side of ISTPs. The utility of diagnosing and treating illness speaks to the real life practicality that is necessary for this type to stay interested.

ESTJ can pick up management credentials at Vandy through the minor in **Scientific Computing**. It combines with the **Biomedical Engineering** degree and prepares this type to follow their inclination to take charge while clearing up shades-of-gray thinking. Given this, the course in Program and Project Management is going to be excellent for their other inclination to root out inefficiency and remember virtually all aspects of a project.

ISFJ is a gentle soul and will be most welcome in the **Child Studies** major. At Vandy, students study the entire world of the child from developmental psychology, language, learning to the family. Fascination with human development will engage the very rich inner world and personal perspectives of this type. Their dependability is also spot on for a career in this field, lending an element of stability to the intense, variable activity of American childhood.

INFP is often considerate as well as adaptable. They may be drawn to the field of education and especially to children struggling in the classroom. The degree at Vanderbilt in **Early Childhood Education** could appeal to INFP's desire to seek out and support human potential. As a double major with Child Studies, it addresses current educational innovation. Often times childhood services are now inclusive of both parents and the child in the preschool years. INFP's insight is considerable and will discern family weaknesses in child-rearing while creating activities to bolster parenting skills.

ENFP will look for exciting possibilities across the Vanderbilt curriculum and could settle on engineering. The degree in **Engineering Science** offers flexibility to pursue a specialization. ENFPs will look at Transportation Engineering because of the promise and the need of improved travel networks. The course in Transportation Systems Engineering will push this type's intuition into creativity. The exacting details of an engineering degree, however, may tax this spontaneous type.

INTJ will find the **Mathematics** department at Vandy offering a great preparation for advanced study in a demanding profession like astronomy and upper level undergraduate courses with impossible course titles like Error-Correcting Codes and Cryptography. This will come in handy when America finally returns to the moon, assuming we do not wish to share our advanced technology under globalization paradigms.

INTP has characteristics reminiscent of the triple "i"—intense, internal, intuition. They will help this type move rather smoothly through a degree in **Chemistry** at demanding Vandy. The physical facilities and labs are outstanding prompting free thinking and conceptual schemes, one after the other. INTPs will need to be mindful of the very structured nature of the science departments at Vandy. Creativity is fine here, accidents that could have been prevented and being late are not so well appreciated.

ENTJ will jump right into Game Theory with Economic Applications. This course has the entrepreneurial bent and is sufficiently complex to keep ENTJ's busy mind engaged. This course is an elective in the **Economics** degree which might also fit into Vandy's unusual concentration in Economics and History. Leave it to this type to understand the intriguing nature of combining these two subjects.

WABASH COLLEGE

P.O. Box 352
Crawfordsville, IN 47933
Website: www.wabash.edu
Admissions Telephone: 765-361-6225
Undergraduates: 871 Men

Physical Environment

Wabash College is located in the middle of **rural Indiana**. The Indianapolis airport is 45 miles away with farms and fields of corn and soy bean in between. Wabash College is thriving with exceptional alumni support and a strong endowment left by the Eli Lilly pharmaceutical company. The small town of Crawfordsville is surrounded by modest neighborhoods and some old Victorian homes, a bit reminiscent of Norman Rockwell's America. In winter the temperatures can fall to minus 10 degrees Fahrenheit. It keeps Wabash students moving around a lot especially on the weekends when they occasionally visit the **six nearby co-ed colleges** or join the frequent off-campus learning on location across the world.

On campus the Chapel is the gathering place for students and faculty on Thursday morning. It is not mandatory to attend, but **legendary Wabash Alumni** always bring in a big crowd. Speakers may present cultural lectures or students themselves may present their research on a variety of subjects. At times it's a talk on **character development**, such as what it means to be a **Wabash man.**

The **athletic center** is nothing short of spectacular with its Olympic-size pool, lots of exercise equipment and weight rooms. It is a magnet for athletic students. In March 2011, the new baseball stadium opened with an inaugural game. It is the latest swell addition to the athletic facilities. Wabash College has many **fraternities** with houses that function as residential halls. Fraternities and clubs spur friendly rivalries and the men generate a great deal of camaraderie within the student body as a result of social traditions.

Trippett Hall is the visitors' center and office of the Center of Inquiry in the Liberal Arts. The center conducts research to strengthen liberal arts education. Wabash College students are the beneficiaries of such research because the professors here implement the best educational practices as evidenced by the Center. Across the way is the Malcolm X Institute which hosts its own social club comprised of Wabash students of **all ethnic backgrounds**. They discuss Wabash happenings along with race relations in America on a weekly basis, always in a casual way, and always with food, typically the ever-present college pizza.

Social Environment

At a time when distinctly fewer men than women are enrolling in college as well as professional schools, Wabash College presents a fine counterpoint, Guy Friendly and Guy Promoting. Wabash offers intriguing information for those institutions who intend to address this negative trend in the coming decades. At Wabash, college boys will become men over the course of the four years along with an appreciation of the **role of men** in the larger American society. For starters, there is an ongoing discussion about what it means to be a Wabash man. It necessarily spills over into ethical behaviors with the student body and with extracurricular activities with women. Casual conversation on this campus ranges from sports to women to ethics. Students and faculty here tend to value historical college traditions. There is study hall in the fraternity houses and residence halls each evening during the week.

Many young men seek out Wabash College because they had **traditional,** somewhat conservative lifestyles at home. High school athletes appreciate Wabash. Socially outgoing guys appreciate Wabash. Students who were leaders in high school clubs appreciate Wabash. Eagle scouts appreciate Wabash. Guys who want to study physics by building and throwing armored spears like Wabash. Those who like to stay involved and are enthusiastic see the Wabash community holding these same values. Professors engage students in **pointed discussions** that often become enthusiastic, **ongoing debates**. Successful students prepare carefully for class. On the occasions a student doesn't come prepared they discover that on this small campus there is no place to hide. The **Gentlemen's Code**, the Wabash men, understand there is little to be gained without serious intellectual effort. Here they learn to formulate their thoughts and express their opinions.

Athletes are the central focus of the campus during the week and some weekends. Thirty percent of students who come here play one or two sports in the NCAA III conference. Wabash college football, wrestling, baseball and basketball teams are hotbeds for young men intent on toning up their muscles and physical agility.

The college also sports an impressive drama department and large performing theatre; guys can experiment with **forms of expression through the arts**. Well-provisioned art studios provide new avenues for thought. This is an intentional community of people who care for each other. Professors take a personal interest in advising their students well beyond career and grades.

Wabash College attracts those looking for a high caliber liberal arts education. The great majority graduated in the top quarter of their high school class and the college boasts a very respectable number of men who achieved perfect and near perfect standardized test scores.

Compatibility with Personality Types and Preferences

Wabash College has done a great job of incorporating learning styles with moral behavior into a strong mix that serves a variety of undergraduate men. The administration of this guys-only college really understands the perspectives of their entering freshmen. Professors promote the idea of abstract thinking and its value to the incoming students in first year courses. New students quickly hear about humane concepts (F), awareness and analytic thinking. The values associated with athletics, sportsmanship and giving-it-your-best, are in practice across the campus. The Gentlemen's Rule calls for students to act with responsibility at all times and to be accountable at all times. Faculty and administration carefully build the Wabash community through these moral codes and expectations of personal behavior.

As undergraduates progress toward graduation, they learn through trial and error (T) how one is expected to honor the Wabash community and prepare for citizenship in (E) the larger society. Faculty in all departments elect to make considerable use of experiential (S) learning. All undergraduate students travel frequently to locations within the U.S. and overseas through their courses. Professors make great use of the short four-to-five day trips to connect students to the world beyond campus. This observation and fact-based learning is featured in foreign language and political science courses especially. The faculty also invokes use of abstract conceptual learning (N), which is featured in Wabash's classics curriculum. The curriculum nicely meets the educational preferences of these two opposite learners: the hands-on, give-me-the-facts student and the abstract discussion-based learner. Students who are attracted to Wabash are confident that this single-gender environment will give them the best of both worlds—the caring world that builds community and the traditional guy world that loves athleticism and power.

In the following listing of college majors it is important to remember that students can fit into any college and can be successful in any major. We have found that the Personality Types below fit very well at this college. The course-of-study chosen for each Personality Type corresponds to MBTI® research and is presented as an example favorable for that type.

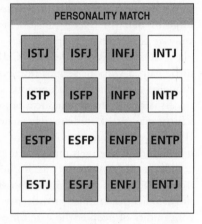

INFP pretty much has to have their personal values lined up with daily living. They rarely bend their behavior code. Wabash College is a brilliant light when it comes to ethical behavior. As a result, INFPs are likely to feel good about this campus. The major in **Philosophy** can offer this type the chance to bring congruence to their inner values. The curriculum includes a wide range of topics with unfamiliar perspectives. Students refine their own points of view through discourse and intense study of the classical texts. The Pre-Law advising on campus supports the philosophy major who might want to pursue a legal career in advocating for the disadvantaged. This surely meets the needs of INFPs. They will find like-minded guys to have fun with and probably get active in campus publications.

INFJ is a creative type, supporting change for improving the lives of others. The **German** major with **Allied Health Sciences** advising at Wabash College offers INFJs uncommon career possibilities. This will attract INFJs who love to think about the future and will carefully review the decision as to which path to follow after their years at Wabash. The familiarity with a foreign language further expands their linguistic thinking as well as opens up research options in Europe and around the globe. All of this sounds downright exciting to the typical INFJ interested in the sciences. They are likely to find a fraternity or club or both that share their values and jump right in connecting their ideals with service projects.

ISTJ is going to love studying **History** at Wabash College because it clearly points to five areas of competence for its graduates. This makes good sense for this type who values accuracy. The History major combined with **Pre-Law** advising provides a clear career track for this realistic type. The department offers a curriculum that focuses on analytical skills, interpretation and oral/written expression. These are the tools of the historian and the lawyer. The former seeks to recover meaning from documents and the latter seeks to change a current practice or event. ISTJs are likely to find like-minded friends on campus, revealing their wry humor while participating in select social activities on campus. Expect the homecoming float to sport some humorous feature.

ISFJ with their typical well-developed sense of color, space and utility will find Wabash College is well-placed to provide a major in **Studio Art** or **Art History.** ISFJs who may be lacking the talent but possess the artistic sensibilities can elect the Art History major. It will be bolstered by the strong curriculum in the classics. Both majors concentrate on visual expression of abstract ideas. Not to worry about how to translate this concept into a career because Wabash has a pre-professional concentration in **Business**. ISFJs can gain both of these skill sets here. They might join the Malcolm X discussion and pizza fests because this type is typically aware of and often concerned for others.

ISFP likes to work with their hands and enjoy the outdoors. ISFPs can get out the shovels for the major in **Classics** at Wabash College with archeological digs in Greece and Jordan. The curriculum focuses on Greek and Roman ancient literature, history, art and archeology. With this major, ISFPs might want to look into the **Teacher Education** concentration. Wabash assures undergraduate students have multiple experiences in the classroom early and reflect on the experience by submitting a sophomore portfolio for admission to the program. The emphasis on fun at this college is also ideal for this type who will look for organizations to join with a solid record of service activities.

ESTP likes to take calculated risks for the most part and this translates into spontaneity on the Wabash campus. It comes alive on the weekends with full-hearted fun and activity associated with the athletic teams and the social fraternities. Academically, ESTPs are brilliant observers of what is, i.e. reality. The major in **Physics** is a strong possibility for this hands-on type. The conceptual thinking on this campus may be a bit off-putting for this type. However, the athleticism, multi-cultural perspectives, social community and alumni presence are very appealing to this natural straight shooter. The major in physics can smooth ESTP into the graduate world of law, engineering, teaching and computer programming. This type will be in the first row at athletic events cheering and leading the fans. They also might be on the various teams since they are often physically coordinated.

ENFP can be a very compassionate soul and the study of **Religion** at Wabash College just might appeal. The department has an excellent national reputation. Theology professors come from across the country each summer to explore methods of religious study with the financial support of the Lilly Endowment. At Wabash, enthusiasm for the classics easily supplements comprehending ancient religious texts. Professors actively mentor students in this major that can lead to further theological studies and the worlds of medicine, law and business. ENFP's insight will find a home in the Wabash curriculum. They will also find plenty of fun which is a daily requirement, similar to a vitamin supplement, for ENFPs. They are likely to join one of the fraternities and may join the Sphinx Club of students supporting the historical, social traditions of Wabash.

ENTP will be front and center when it comes to discerning conversation. They crave the social debate and can become stressed without this source of energy. The classic major in **Rhetoric** with a concentration in **International Studies** is ideal for this type. The major explores how the mass media impacts mass consciousness. In doing so, ENTPs will seek understanding of social institutions and organizations as they pressure society to adopt their peculiar version of reality. As a spontaneous thinker, ENTPs must guard against articulating their unformed thoughts. The coursework in this major rewards seconds spent in deconstructing positions put forth in the public square. As ENTPs master this time delay processing, they can become powerful personalities with their creativity and long-range thinking in play. The additional work in international studies will open doors for possible careers. Ingenious ENTPs will spot lots of career options. Their difficulty will be in selecting one or two.

ESFJ will like studying **Biology** at Wabash College. The science building, opened in 2002, has all the bells and whistles to support an experiential, lab-driven curriculum. The department has a particular interest in molecular biology which well prepares students to move forward to graduate study. ESFJs want to find harmony and companionship in their environment. Wabash College works socially and academically for this type. The immersion and experiential learning options on and off campus offer practical skills. The large number of spirit-filled organizations offer traditional options to participate and lead.

ENFJ will like the independence that comes with a career in **Psychology** and the opportunities to help others one on one. The department in psychology at Wabash College has well incorporated the leaps in psychological therapy over the past 30 years. Their curriculum focuses on the scientific research that is becoming critical as the field moves forward with new discoveries about behavior and the brain. ENFJs will find the preparation needed for admission to the increasingly competitive PhD studies in this field. ENFJ has a natural inclination toward generating concepts. Faculty in this department push students to generate and answer significant questions. There is emphasis in the department to select undergraduate research that is meaningful to the larger community and not only the undergraduate. ENFJ may need to ponder the utility of their proposed research and assure it has applicability to agendas other than their own.

ENTJ will find the sequence of courses in **Business** to their liking as generally this type has an entrepreneurial side. Their desire for leadership and long-range planning seems to naturally fit into the business world, yet much of leadership today, even in the business world, requires political acumen. At Wabash College the **Political Science** major is a solid choice for an ENTJ looking to read the political tea leaves. The department gives good exposure to four areas: American politics, comparative politics, international politics and political theory. With a foundational heads-up in the political world and business world, this type is ready to enter any number of challenges in the post-graduate world of academia or work. ENTJs will support Wabash athletic events and likely be a leader in any number of other organizations that provide them leadership opportunities such as the fraternities.

WAKE FOREST UNIVERSITY

1834 Wake Forest Road
Winston-Salem, NC 27109
Website: www.wfu.edu
Admissions Telephone: 336-758-5201
Undergraduates: 4,591; 2,215 Men, 2,376 Women
Graduate Students: 2,405

Physical Environment

Wake Forest University was founded by the Baptists in 1834 in Wake county, North Carolina and moved in 1950 to the **heavily-forested area** of Winston-Salem. Wake Forest has a strong **Christian heritage** through its former affiliation with the Baptist religion. Now the university exemplifies the values associated with that Christian heritage and the campus appeals to students who want to belong to a cohesive community. Residential living on campus is enhanced by the new student social activities center adjacent to the forest. Very student-centric, **The Barn** opened in fall 2011 and is a classic A-frame structure with a metal roof reminiscent of the one story mid-1800s Appalachian feed barns. It is perfect for its location and purpose of hosting student-hosted parties.

Nostalgia aside, rigorous academics may be why students have nicknamed this university "work forest." First and second year students are required to live on campus and this fosters strong circles of friendship. 2013 may bring the requirement for juniors also to live on campus. **Night owls** are attracted to "Campus Ground," a student-run coffee house that stays open late. Study spaces are currently tight on campus. Finals week brings extra designated spaces, for example students can study in the dining hall or certain academic buildings temporarily available. South Hall, a new dorm opened in fall 2011, is part of a construction program on campus that is generating new spaces and renovating older facilities. Under construction in 2011-12, Farell Hall is scheduled to open in summer 2013 and will house the business school. Kirby Hall will then acquire the expanded social science departments and expanded programs.

Social Environment

Wake Forest attracts students of good character who have a strong **sense of duty**. They accomplish what needs to be done as frank and genuine individuals. Wake Forest appeals to students who want to communicate with well-known leaders in politics and civic organizations. Students here value work that produces tangible results. They also expect strong career advising on this campus to help them with internships and job opportunities. Most students are naturally **ambitious** and competitive and enjoy the professors who support them in their plans for research and **career exploration**.

They are confident, **gregarious** and physically active as well as disciplined. Students work very hard during the week but relax on the weekend. They enjoy pranks and humor and are not above wrapping trees with toilet paper to celebrate a sports victory. They bring this **spirit to athletic games** and love their mascot the Demon Deacon, who is very distinctive in a black and yellow tie. Wake Forest students are typically trustworthy, high achieving, competent, and fun-loving. Parties are plentiful on and off campus with guidance provided via the interfraternity council and the collegiate administration and staff.

Compatibility with Personality Types and Preferences

Wake Forest is a campus where a humane vision is appreciated and discerned throughout the curriculum. The administration and faculty have strongly focused curriculum development and advising at the academic department level for undergraduate students. Independent thought and analysis is a vehicle for reaching truths within introductory and advanced course work. Through study and discussion undergraduates look to secure skills and knowledge. It is an educational atmosphere where professors are mentors and friends and undergraduates appreciate the supportive academic environment. Logical analysis (T) and an emphasis on service for others interfaces this academic community.

Faculty encourage students to prepare for difficult issues that will be raised in the senior year courses. Critical reading, thinking and writing push students to develop personal values and explore ethical positions. Students often learn through inquiry that utilizes inductive reasoning. This process requires the movement of particular information to general understanding. Think of Wake Forest as a well-balanced community of learning with room for big picture folks (N), the here-and-now reality types (S), and those orderly planners (J).The strong social and athletic traditions in residential life on campus help the undergraduate's transition from high school to successful collegiate student. In fact, the campus honors many of the vibrant, fun collegiate stuff of the old classic movies.

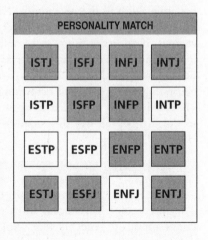

In the following listing of college majors it is important to remember that students can fit into any college and can be successful in any major. We have found that the Personality Types below fit very well at this college. The course-of-study chosen for each Personality Type corresponds to MBTI® research and is presented as an example favorable for that type.

ENTJ will feel comfortable with the wide range of financial courses in the **Economics** major. The Economics of Entrepreneurship course studies economic theory in comparison with the actions of successful entrepreneurs, past and present. This type will be at ease in the uncertain world of economics. The curriculum will give ENTJs practice at applying their insight and strategic planning. It will be an invaluable learning experience for this type who will likely move into a professional environment such as law, business, medicine or government as an expert advisor.

ISTJ will really appreciate the extensive course selection in the **Biology** Department. There are just a few survey courses in the freshmen and sophomore year. ISTJs will approve of the variety and intensity of subjects offered in junior and senior year. The course in Insect Biology might appeal to this type because the level of detail would be distinct, voluminous and organized. ISTJs are attracted to comprehensive, demanding classification systems in the animal kingdom.

ESFJ places well being high on any priority list. The course in Physiology of Exercise could easily be an elective of choice for this reason. This curriculum will affirm ESFJ's people-centered focus and prepares undergraduates for entry into professional schools in the health sciences. It examines both the benefits and potential risk as the body responds to various exercise programs. Wake Forest has a strong emphasis on all aspects of safety across the campus. It shows clearly in this **Health and Exercise Science** degree.

ISFJ should look at the courses in the **Anthropology** department at Wake Forest. The curriculum could be preferable for this type who is patient with the details and empathetic. Students have the opportunity to volunteer or secure work study at the WFU museum for Anthropology. This hands-on learning allows ISFJs to examine the process of exhibit preparation. Their sense of loyalty will ensure the exhibit's worthiness in serving the membership and public.

ISFP often has affinity with nature and the interdisciplinary minor in **Environmental Studies** could easily draw attention from ISFPs. This minor has a social policy tract that could lead to a satisfying career where idealism is honored in conservancy organizations. The second tract in the minor explores scientific paradigms as applied to the physical environment.

ESTJ will be drawn to the business school major in **Finance**. Among the several management courses, Strategic Management will appeal to their drive for setting goals and making decisions. Competition will be acceptable to this type with their ability to make tough calls when necessary. ESTJs are likely to enjoy the computer modeling of business competitions.

ENFP will relate to Wake Forest on the very first day. Outgoing, active participation is the norm on campus and this type will be first in line on game day. Should the **Psychology** major draw them in, a favorite class could be Altered States of Consciousness. This course offers the novelty that captures ENFP's attention. Their exceptional insight will be an advantage in this course. The study of dreams, meditation and hypnosis could also help them with self-introspection as opposed to exclusively focusing on friends.

ENTP is often drawn to concepts in **Political Science**. At Wake Forest, the major examines this unpredictable field—just think of the United Nations. Nevertheless, the subject is likely to be fascinating for ENTPs. On this campus they will be rewarded with both variety and intensity of study—American Politics, Comparative Politics, International Politics and Political Theory. Choosing one of these specializations will make for a difficult decision for ENTPs. The introductory course in each should help with the decision.

INFP just might sign up for the minor in **Linguistics** at Wake Forest. The overview, history and structure of romance languages will be of interest to many students of this personality preference.

INFJ values independence and social harmony. It is a perfect fit for Wake Forest. Within the Department of **Religion,** INFJs will find a solid foundation of survey courses in the major world religions. Beyond this level, INFJ will find a fascinating selection of topics viewed through religious perspectives. The department offers a rich study in Christian texts and history. The inquiry will surely trigger personal introspection by INFJs.

INTJ often will find idle speculation leads to something definite in the way of an idea that can be put into action. This consistent thinker often excels in research. The major in **Chemistry** at Wake Forest is ideally oriented toward research. Put this together with a follow on career path that includes research and development in the pharmaceutical industry and the whole picture could be intriguing for many INTJs.

WASHINGTON AND LEE UNIVERSITY

116 North Main Street
Lexington, VA 24450-0303
Website: www.wlu.edu
Admissions Telephone: 540-463-8710
Undergraduates: 1,758; 877 Men, 881 Women
Graduates: 414

Physical Environment

Washington and Lee University is located in the **quaint and historical town** of Lexington, population 7,000, close to the George Washington National Forest and surrounded by farm land and horse country. The beauty of the nearby Appalachian Mountains, the campus itself and the picturesque horse country appeal to the students who attend W&L. However, nearby Washington, DC is of greater importance to students attracted to W&L, who typically are looking for **power internships** in communications, business and politics.

The campus is built on a hill overlooking the town of Lexington. Students enter through traditional southern wrought iron gates to look up through **an impressive row of white columns** framing the lines of red brick academic buildings. Each year, incoming students walk though these gates onto the brick walkway embossed with the Latin motto "non incautus futuri," not unmindful of the future. The Colonnade Project is infusing modern technologies into these stately structures in five phases, with Newcomb Hall completed in 2010 and Payne Hall in 2011.

Campus architecture is all the more remarkable because of George Washington's 20,000 shares of James River canal stock, bequested as seed money to the university. At the bottom of this hill, Confederate hero General Robert E. Lee is buried with his horse. This historically rich campus of national importance calls out to students who appreciate history and liked advanced United States history courses in high school.

The newer section of campus was developed on top of the ridge and reflects the futuristic side of Washington and Lee with high technology and very up-to-date athletic facilities. Accomplished high school athletes are attracted to the university because of the excellent sports facilities. Students meet in the Elrod commons, the library, the ivy covered classroom buildings and Greek houses. Freshmen and sophomores are required to live on campus. Thereafter students rent apartments or houses in town which are readily available.

The profound sense of American tradition and community is apparent to all who walk the campus. Yet now the historical American presence on this campus is juxtaposed with other worldly views. W&L students, along with other members of the millennial generation, are presently drawn to the Middle East, Africa and Pacific Basin cultures and geographies.

Social Environment

W&L students are eager to learn the concepts, knowledge and expectations that give them a head start in **pivotal career fields**. They are high-achieving, expressive, ambitious and hard-working. Many typically come from socially and historically powerful families. Students like to be challenged by a **rigorous academic** curriculum and faculty at W&L is more than happy to oblige. Study in these small liberal arts classes is **intense and individual**. Students easily settle into academic mentoring relationships with their professors. There is an expectation of **conversational engagement**. The 'speaking tradition' and Honor System are prompts in a social environment that is finely tuned to each individual and their position within contributing to the overall community.

Students at W&L expect to sharpen their **intellectual acumen** through the broad exposure and exploration within the core curriculum. The interdisciplinary study of governing is designed for students who will pursue careers within international or national legislative bodies. The student body here forms close ties. As graduates, they will have access to the distinguished W&L alumni network, which combines the old with the new.

Honorable relationships in the **traditional southern sense** of honesty, pride and graciousness are respected by students here. As a result, the **Greek system** is exceptionally strong on this campus. They hold many parties and events, socials and formal dances that keeping the town's drycleaners busy. They will value much of what is good within their family and community histories, but realize and want to be part of the evolving future. Service learning is typically focused on issues of poverty and sustainability and interfaced throughout the curriculum.

Compatibility with Personality Types and Preferences

Clarity of thinking, originality (N), analysis, precision and attention to current societal trends do a good job of characterizing the Washington and Lee academic environment. Logic and the art of concentrated thinking (T) are in demand on this campus. Incoming undergraduate students are encouraged to adopt the W&L value of honoring intellectual inquiry. Seminars, courses and clubs all offer guideposts in respect to current day practices and issues. The Mock Convention is an intense two year effort by the student body to predict the presidential candidate of the sitting minority national political party. On this campus, the undergraduate student forms an individual amalgam of knowledge complete with the persuasive communication abilities needed to place it in the public square. Successful students here are keen and assertive.

Change arrives regularly at W&L. Most notably in the past few years there is a greater global and multidisciplinary approach to many majors. As with most collegiate curriculums this is observed in the multidisciplinary approach to a single subject. At W&L it is observed in the history curriculum which now offers sophomore courses that were formerly upper level and reserved for the history majors. The dropping of upper level content allows elective course access by students

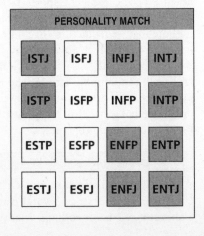

PERSONALITY MATCH

ISTJ	ISFJ	INFJ	INTJ
ISTP	ISFP	INFP	INTP
ESTP	ESFP	ENFP	ENTP
ESTJ	ESFJ	ENFJ	ENTJ

majoring in other subjects. Such courses as Anthropology of American History blend these two subjects together. Courses within the Americas are reduced, while content is increased in the opposite hemisphere. At W&L undergraduates are grounded in the leading-edge present. Students here don't often miss new trends in society or find themselves unaware of academic or social movements.

In the following listing of college majors it is important to remember that students can fit into any college and can be successful in any major. We have found that the Personality Types below fit very well at this college. The course-of-study chosen for each Personality Type corresponds to MBTI® research and is presented as an example favorable for that type.

ENTJ is an exceptionally fine fit for Washington and Lee. Direct, decisive and conceptual, they will be drawn to the Williams School of **Commerce, Economics and Politics**. Among the exciting entrepreneurial projects within the school is the W&L Student Consulting. This group of business students advises client companies on a variety of strategies to increase market profitability. On an earlier webpage, it portrayed an old fashioned pen and ink drawing of modern forged metal gears and chess pieces symbolizing critical thinking. How W&L!

ENFJ would likely approve of the overview of W&L's major in **Foreign Language Education**. Research within this major is focused on learning strategies. The multiple methods and approaches to understanding foreign language occupy much of the undergraduates' experience in this department. The department worked together with the Commonwealth of Virginia to extended the benefits of research and resources to foreign language teachers across the state.

ENFP who is stimulated by difficulties and enthusiastic in solving them is quite welcome on this campus. ENFPs can usually excel in any major that captures their imagination. The interdepartmental major in **Neuroscience** could serve a couple of functions for this type who likes to carefully examine all the exciting possibilities. The major offers research in the several disciplines of biology, chemistry, psychology, mathematics and the computational sciences. Once the research concentration is selected, ENFP will be passionate with their chosen subject.

INFJ could quietly bring metaphor and symbolic representation to some of the nuts and bolts logic that travels so easily on this campus. Should they disagree with a particular statement or direction of discourse, which they are likely to do, it may be done with a touch more grace than some of their more direct and dispassionate classmates. The **Medieval and Renaissance Studies** major is ideal for this student's exceptional insight as will be applied to human populations during the 1300s to the 1600s. If any type can find purpose and meaning in medieval customs and society, it will be the INFJ.

INTJ brings skeptical analysis to the classroom and will quickly challenge any information that doesn't fit into their emerging perspective. Of all the types, this one will have the least appreciation for the tradition and custom that W&L emphasizes. The INTJ takes nothing for granted. If this type needs to rearrange the principles of **Physics** and the basics of nature, so be it. W&L faculty would likely permit and enjoy the ensuing mayhem—for a short time.

ENTP can be comfortably assertive on this campus. With strong ideas and big personas in abundance at W&L, ENTPs will receive the intellectual stimulation they crave. The **Mock Trial** could give ENTPs the jury box audience in which to put forth their courtroom litigation strategies. Quick thinkers, assertive and outspoken, this type will likely perform well and perhaps win the competition if they do not procrastinate.

INTP is intellectually curious and contemplative. Their powerful minds may be underestimated when they are typically reserved in the classroom. However, faculty at W&L will spot intellectual potential and draw out this type. INTPs and the courses in **Philosophy** are likely to connect and become a minor or possibly a major. This type will push for personal clarity and truth through their individual study when examining philosophers. The faculty will support them in the truest sense once past the foundational courses.

ISTJ comfortably masters large volumes of fact and they take whatever extra steps necessary to be accurate. ISTJs won't be overwhelmed with the intensity of the W&L free flow of ideas; rather, their natural tendency is to endure until all is said and done. They gain well-deserved respect for their perseverance and mastery of the subject. The **Pre-Law Studies** is a sequence of courses that offer an overview of the legal systems in our nations. The overview focuses on familiar subjects through the lens of current political trends.

ISTP is likely to find a good home in a technical and statistical field of interest like the W&L **Environmental Studies** major. It requires direct observation of phenomena in the field. This type would identify with environmental capstone projects that involve redeveloping the degraded slopes along stream beds. W&L practicality and technology is featured in this major. Technical gadgets involving measurement will appeal to the university and the ISTPs.

WASHINGTON UNIVERSITY IN ST. LOUIS

One Brookings Drive
St. Louis, MO 63130-4899
Website: www.wustl.edu
Admissions Telephone: 800-638-0700, 314-935-6000
Undergraduates: 6,816; 3,408 Men, 3,408 Women
Graduates: 7,179

Physical Environment

Wash U is located in St. Louis approximately five miles from the mighty Mississippi River and famous Arch. The campus is just west of city limits and is accessible by Metro which begins at the airport. Students board at Skinker station, a few blocks from the university, and go shopping or out to Forest Park, in nice weather. It was the location of the 1904 World's Fair, and now hosts museums, the zoo, planetarium and many athletic fields. The mock statue of Rodin's Thinker offers good luck to students who touch it as they walk to class.

The university has purchased many of the properties on the perimeter of the undergraduate Danforth campus to renovate and upgrade structures. Brookings Hall houses Wash U's admissions office and is the most photographed edifice on campus. Appearing much as a European castle with its gates open, it influences other structures on campus to follow in the same design. The **mixture of these classical buildings along with modern facilities** is striking but in 2011-12 you may have not seen them for all the construction cranes, scaffolding and obstacles utilized to add three new engineering facilities and the new dining facility. Now, Wash U will turn its attention to the Olin Business school with the construction of two new buildings completed by the end of 2013.

The weather here is unpredictable. Students say they may go to class at 8 AM in shorts and T-shirts and by the time they get out of class it's snowing. Wash U is built on top of a hill and can get very windy in the winter. Most conveniently there are many places on campus where students can warm up with hot chocolate and coffee. The modern library has rectangular glass panels and houses the enticing coffee shop, "Whispers." It is often packed with students who are studying or hanging out between classes. Another favorite place on campus is the Holmes lounge, because of its **strikingly gorgeous ceiling,** heavily inlaid with carvings and the comfy leather chairs. This building dates back to 1904 when the city hosted the first World's Fair. Students here grab a wrap and a drink at the nearby café and listen to a speaker or enjoy some quiet company. The Danforth University Center also has an interesting ceiling with colored panels, and visitors note that ceilings are an interesting feature on this campus. The Center offers a-la-carte, and a second, sit-down restaurant.

Social Environment

When first-year students arrive to Washington University's Danforth campus, they come with **stellar high school transcripts and standardized test scores**. Maybe they were the **quiet, very accomplished** types in high school who were less interested in participating in sports than intellectual discussions and extra-curricular activities.

They ponder the optional Wash U pass/fail grade options but each department sets its own guidelines. There is some academic competition on campus. The university attracts many pre-professional students who work hard to gain admission in prestigious schools of law, medicine and business. **Plentiful research opportunities** and supportive faculty extend across the schools and colleges at this university and many undergrads expect to engage in research.

Students look **neat** and conservative in their jeans and sweatshirts, plugged into their iPods or cell-phones, heavy knapsack on the back. Many bring their bikes here so they can get off campus to their sports practice on time. When the weather is nice, students like to play a game of flag football in their quad. They are students who look at life through an **intellectual lens** and a good number drift toward Geek. There is a nice and easy flow of interaction between students. One-third of the students join **Greek life** and become really involved in it. After the first year on campus, undergrads can choose from classic dorm-style residence halls or live in the many renovated houses adjacent to the campus managed by the university.

In the first year, students are encouraged to socialize with their peers on their floor. The first-year experience is strongly programmed, and it offers uncertain students a chance to relax and unstress from the **academic load**. **Strong friendships** form during this first year that remain in place through graduation on this campus. For some, it's hard to break out of that bubble and get to know other students. Students tend to come from the North East, West coast and down south, with wide ranging geographic representation.

Compatibility with Personality Types and Preferences

Washington University consistently ensures its academic environment supports the central focus of their mission—teaching, scholarship and service. Like-minded students thoroughly enjoy Wash U. It reflects their wish to grow in understanding of themselves (I) and become active and appreciative of giving back. Faculty and administration support a stable community with a strong undercurrent that highlights the responsibilities inherent in teaching and learning - the two way street. The research laboratories at the University serve two purposes well. Advancing knowledge with new findings and the invitation to undergraduates to participate are equally important. Teacher and student collaboration is common on campus. Students who excel at this university come to learn from faculty and the expansive curriculum.

Exceptionally bright students who are predisposed to analysis and objective thinking (T) excel here. Academic activity is ever present in the classes, in the extracurricular clubs and the social gathering of friends. Faculty soften the academic edges with individual encouragement and collaborative and team learning. Mentoring students is a high priority for faculty. The student-professor relationship often moves into the research labs and grows within the academic structure (J) of research. Graduates are focused on achievement and move easily onto excellent graduate programs as well as influential positions in business.

In the following listing of college majors it is important to remember that students can fit into any college and can be successful in any major. We have found that the Personality Types below fit very well at this college. The course-of-study chosen for each Personality

Type corresponds to MBTI® research and is presented as an example favorable for that type.

INFP will find the major in **Urban Studies** at Washington University absolutely in synch with their desire to study and work for a greater cause. Students in this major find a broad curriculum cataloging ills and issues within American urban settings. The department is vigilant in review of the difficulties surfacing in large American metropolitan cities. Juniors are encouraged to apply for the senior honors program. INFP is likely to do this and naturally develop a well-supported thesis proposal. It will be presented in good written form and likely get approval from one of the core faculty members. Wash U social life is sufficiently intellectual for this type, too.

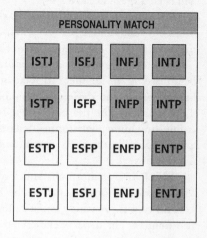

INFJ is drawn to creating new ideas to say the very least. The minor in **Bioinformatics** is an unusual course of study offered within the engineering department at Washington University. It is an emerging field that will afford this type with many opportunities for pushing the envelope. This minor combines nicely with a degree in computer science, biology or engineering. Creative INFJ will likely choose one of these three by honoring their inclination to help others. INFJ might zero in on implanted electronic devices that monitor diabetic levels in the blood stream.

INTJ is attracted to complex, tough problems. The major in **Operations and Supply Chain Management** offers a peek at the complexity of moving pieces around the globe to support manufacturing and service operations. Business competition is intense under free trade and globalization trends. These types of competitive environments get INTJ enthusiastically in the game. They may appear quietly in the game but the reality is that their participation is evident after they generate a solution. Their self-contained nature adds all the more power to their internal thinking.

ISTP likes investigation and the major in **Archeology** requires a good bit of speculating. Students in this major learn about the nature and meaning of artifacts as they travel to study collections in major museums across the country. This type also likes to be outdoors because of the freedom and activity that comes with leaving the desk and hard drive behind. At Wash U, they can expand their preparation for this career by selecting a study abroad experience that takes them into active archeological digs. The emphasis on academics over social learning on campus appeals to this type.

ISTJ relates well to the goals of the **Health Care Management** major at Washington University. Graduates are expected to think precisely and develop useful frameworks that address problems. Both of these activities come easily to ISTJ. This type prefers to gather all the facts and assess them objectively to reach an overall position. The financial mechanisms in national health care are under constant scrutiny, and it is the ISTJ who can answer the numbers questions. This type has a quiet humor and will find themselves in demand with friends who also hit the books and need a break occasionally.

ISFJ should not be surprised by the intellectual approach to **Fashion Design** at Wash U. After all, this is a very intense academic environment. The graduates of this major bring skill and confidence to fashion creation in the rapidly changing apparel industry. ISFJ is typically aware of design in their immediate environment. It could be an easy jump for them to focus on fashion apparel. Work after graduation will be developing and delivering desirable fashion options that serve retail customers. This career honors the type's own belief in creating and maintaining a pleasing, comforting human environment. Their typical attention to detail is perfect and they are very good at repetitive routine evidenced in the seasonal delivery of spring and fall fashions.

ENTP is ever ingenious and looking to come up with original ideas and will find plenty of room for each in the **Earth and Planetary Sciences** major at Wash U. This type is constantly available for intellectual discussion and that fits so well on this campus. The department encourages students to participate in research studies, including geobiology. This appeals to ENTP who prefers a challenge and normally feels up to just about any challenge that comes their way. This demanding subject and equally demanding university will not disappoint them. The political advocacy on campus will delight this type who is always ready to debate—on either or both sides!

ENTJ attracted to the idea of business will find the major in **Economics** at Wash U quite interesting. The department infuses the curriculum with mathematical models applied to national problems such as inflation and government decision making. This university is very much focused on the social issues that are reported in the national media and national debates. ENTJs have a strong analytical mind which they can put to use while moving through the curriculum in this major. It will be this type who sees through the confusion and searches out the facts in order to form their own perspective.

INTP has the curiosity and time to speculate about the unusual elements to be found in the **Geobiology** undergraduate certificate at Washington University. INTPs will use their insight and intense curiosity in the labs, amplifying their understanding of this emerging discipline. The unknowns within the planet's historical record will definitely catch the attention and generate academic interest in this type. INTPs will approach those unknowns as if they were puzzles to be solved and time is no obstacle, there will be decades to find the answers.

WESLEYAN UNIVERSITY

237 High Street
Middletown, CT 06459
Website: www.wesleyan.edu
Admissions Telephone: 860-685-3000
Undergraduates: 2,837; 1,378 Men, 1,467 Women

Physical Environment

Named in honor of John Wesley, the founder of the Methodist Church, Wesleyan University is located mid-way between Hartford and New Haven, off old Route 66, which weaves though the quaint and sleepy town of Middletown. In this setting students use their creativity to find a wide variety of things to do on and off campus. Some enjoy volunteering in town. The university spreads out on a hill where a mixture of eighteenth century **New England brownstones** and modern buildings creates an eclectic feel. The Andrus quad is a common meeting place for students who want to play a casual game of Frisbee, barefoot, on a sunny day, and it's also where formal games of football and baseball are played. The residence halls are a mixture of buildings from the 60s, **contemporary structures** and **Victorian homes**. The Arts Center consists of a series of modern buildings that are startling in their difference from the remainder of the campus architecture and surrounding town. It's an abrupt change for this campus that seems to infer that it's not wedded to the past. This architecture is as varied, bold and **discussion-provoking** as Wesleyan students are individually different and vocal themselves. Renovation of the squash courts generated space for academic offices and the career resource offices. The Usdan Center is central to the campus energy. It is the meeting place for all who spend their days in this intellectual environment. Students have many pleasant architectural spaces for gathering, dining and learning.

Social Environment

Wesleyan students mirror the multi-ethnic population of New York City, two-and-a-half hours distant by car. They are likely to engage in any activity that holds their interest. They are also warm and very supportive of each other and enjoy their friendships. In the classroom there is no excessive competition for grades. Greatly involved in the life of the mind, they are **articulate and outspoken** about their **beliefs.** They pretty much seek **solutions** to problems that affect society and the world in general. All are centered on content and knowledge as key ingredients of their individual development. AP and IB high school coursework only served to whet their appetite and spike their GPAs and standardized test scores.

Passions are accepted, supported and expected within the student body. They tend to be **fairly counterculture** and enroll to fine tune their opinions in this free-thinking campus environment. Students here might ask questions like: Is this electricity efficiently produced? Can our campus budget support labor or products from Rwanda? Many would seek to dissuade use of poorly paid labor in under-developed countries for the benefit of industrialized nations. They intend to be informed about local and national politics and will put in time reading their favored websites for that purpose. However, activism is just one of many pursuits and not the most popular. Conversation at Usdan, club meetings, sports spectating, playing on Cardinals pick up teams and sporting red hoodies consume the **'Wes' social focus** on any given day.

Compatibility with Personality Types and Preferences

Wesleyan is a college for the creative (N) students who want to search for truths through exact and precise dialogue. The student who arrives on campus with a questioning predisposition will find plenty of company. Though these opinions are likely to be tested as contemporary events impact society, the campus culture is comfortable with that process. Students are encouraged to develop their own core beliefs about the world around them. The undergraduate degree observes human endeavor in pure sciences, material property and society. Armed with that information, Weslies must then apply it to their own life and their own activity in leisure or business. The people-centered folks (F) will find much energy directed toward the state of humanity. Practical considerations are put aside to value abstraction and ideals on this campus. The undergraduate curriculum explores human endeavor in the pure sciences, use of national resources and social constructs in society.

PERSONALITY MATCH			
ISTJ	ISFJ	INFJ	INTJ
ISTP	ISFP	INFP	INTP
ESTP	ESFP	ENFP	ENTP
ESTJ	ESFJ	ENFJ	ENTJ

In the following listing of college majors it is important to remember that students can fit into any college and can be successful in any major. We have found that the Personality Types below fit very well at this college. The course-of-study chosen for each Personality Type corresponds to MBTI® research and is presented as an example favorable for that type.

INFJ is often well-prepared in the classroom and will be rewarded for going the extra mile in gathering ideas for a deeper class discussion. Students must complete a cultural immersion within this major. The coursework in **Psychology** presented at this university includes social and cultural interface with the discipline. However, it is well-focused in the traditional focus of psychological illness and psychological development. INFJ will appreciate the emphasis on mastering analytic methods for grad school.

INTJ applies analytical power to find underlying themes and might enjoy the major in **Government** at Wesleyan. The course Politics of Terrorism should prove a good challenge for this type so comfortable with the impossible. Their approach to this major will center on ideas and principles. INTJs, bypassing emotional agendas put forth in the public square, will bring incisive observations into the class discussions.

ENTP will egg on the discussion, debate style, in the interdisciplinary major called **Science in Society**. This major will appeal to their predisposition to gather and synthesize knowledge. The major studies the application of scientific advances within society. The courses tend to lean toward abstraction even though the observable events are studied. ENTPs will weave their own understanding and bring personal significance to the four years in this major. Post-graduate work in health care administration could be on ENTP career horizons.

ISTJ at Wesleyan is likely to appreciate the **American Studies** major because it pulls together knowledge of the United States through a hemispheric perspective. The curriculum includes knowledge as seen through the perspectives of other disciplines such as anthropology, history, religion and sociology. This gathering of separate chunks of knowledge must then be placed into the overall ISTJ's understanding of the American experience. It is the preferred way to learn for this type. Separate units of knowledge combine to form one comprehensive whole.

INFP interested in writing will apply their demanding expectations of self to the major in **English** at Wesleyan University. Admission to this major is selective and creative INFPs have the will that secures a nod of approval. In fact, this insightful soul is likely to pursue the degree with honors. INFPs best express themselves through mediums that place distance between their deeply held values and others. The medium of the written word is ideal. Among the extraordinary courses at Wesleyan in English, there are ten courses in writing alone, a testimony to the strength of the thinking that goes on at this campus.

ENFP will find the **Art History** major at Wesleyan ideal because it approaches art through cultural history. Rather than overly focusing on the visual art techniques and style, this type will prefer to take advantage of their strong insight while finding the human story in paintings. Art and Identity in the U.S. previously offered would draw in ENFP. Perhaps Frank Lloyd Wright: Myth and Fact can do the same.

ENFJ will appreciate the **African American Studies** major because of its interdisciplinary approach. Literature, music, dance, civil rights, black power, black president are all studied as identity milestones and experience within the African American community. ENFJs are often fascinated with other people. They bring their objectivity and passion to the studies.

INTP will like the pure pursuit of science in the **Molecular Biology and Biochemistry** major. This type could easily be attracted to study which focuses on the transmission of genetic information. Despite the yawning title of this project, Transcriptional Regulation of rRNA metabolism related genes in yeast, INTPs could be absorbed in the lab, arriving late to dinner and oblivious to the clean up clatter in the dining hall.

ENTJ is a strategic planner and might enjoy **Economics** at Wesleyan University. This major prepares for post-graduate study in business, law and the public sector. ENTJs like these active professions. Much of the curriculum is devoted to quantitative methods and analysis in the worlds of finance. There is also room for some coursework in broader perspectives such as scarcity in society and internationally, Latin American Economic Development. This practical type then gets to delve into senior level thesis and tutorial. Students will critique their own economic perspectives while seeking practical application.

WILLIAMS COLLEGE

Office of Admission
800 Main Street
Williamstown, MA 01267
Website: www.williams.edu
Admissions Telephone: 413-597-2211
Undergraduates: 2,032; 985 Men, 1,048 Women

Physical Environment

Nestled at the base of mountain ranges in the north-west corner of Massachusetts, Williams College is close to the Appalachian Trail, just a few miles from Vermont. The Berkshire mountains appeal to hikers, skiers-snowboarders and those who love rocks and geology. The 450-acre college includes 132 buildings, which are brand-new in some places and well worn by the severe weather in others. Recent structures have been erected in architectural styles predominantly modern such as the concrete dorm next to the playing fields. Route 2 passes through the campus, and with quiet time and imagination one can hear the clip clopping of 19th century horse and buggies.

Today Route 2 is utilized as a main thoroughfare to and from Williamstown, nearby cultural museums and tourist recreation. Students here love this campus with its occasional quirky buildings maintained with a thrifty New England budget. The Kellogg House, 200 years old, is being renovated as well as relocated to expand space for the environmental science center. Its proud history is also well worn since it has served multiple faculty and purposes in its two centuries. Hollander and Schapiro Halls are new academic buildings opened in 2010 for the humanities and social sciences. Coming up in 2014 will be a new library with all the 24 hour bells, whistles and café.

Students are drawn to the quiet, rolling mountains and valleys because of the **enveloping feel** of the fresh air, the exceptional outdoor physical recreation and the two excellent art museums, one on campus and the other in Williamstown. The Williams College Art Museum holds many **original paintings and artifacts**. Students interested in art history are likely to be drawn to the pleasant combination of beautiful Berkshire landscape and the fine art. The art collection offers pieces from several specific points in time representative of the historical art discipline. Many prospective students also note the theatre and dance building, called the '62 Center.' **Performing arts** are a key component on this campus both as a major and as a vital form of entertainment for the student population.

The extensive Science Complex pulls in many pre-med, pre-vet and science-loving students. The Athletics complex is very large as indoors training and sports supplement the outdoor activity during study breaks. In the center of campus the Jewish Religious Center probably calls to prospective students who value an atmosphere of openness and tolerance both in and outside the classroom. The **student center** is the major hub for eating and socializing and the undergraduates remain long after finishing their meal, next to their forgotten dishes piled up on tables. The town itself, just a few blocks down on Route 2, has several small establishments that cater to visiting parents and Williams employees.

Social Environment

Students who like Williams College seem to have a natural instinct that steers them toward one of the **varied social groups** on this campus. Each student brings unique talents to their incoming class. The community changes as the classes and individuals pass through reflecting their **individual and collective values**. In a way, it's like earlier times, when all neighbors got together to raise a barn. It's easier to collaborate on a project than to do it all by oneself. Once the barn is constructed all returned home taking new knowledge of their community and leaving behind a solid structure. Students here are similarly helpful within their small intimate circle of friends and ready to work together on a larger campus venue when a 'community barn is about to be raised.'

Intellectual boundaries are pretty permeable when it comes to ideas and debate here at Williams College. Students share their knowledge and teach one another with the support of professors who **labor quite devotedly** to educate the undergraduates. **Tutorials** are an example of this social construct. Two students work together with a professor and forge ahead seeking exceptional clarity and depth. It's intensive and sometimes fatiguing as students challenge each other to rise higher in the next "class" as the professor eggs them on. About one-fourth of the students participate in Tutorials. Students engage in time-honored winter conversation, fashioning their thoughts during **long evenings** in the public spaces on campus.

For recreation there's the excitement of the games and their purple cow mascot. Students here are exuberant at game time and very comfortable painting their faces purple. Some undergraduates are strivers who love the range of liberal arts. They are drawn to the college's prominent reputation in New England. Many students here were popular in their high school and bring that confidence with them. All in all, Williams College appeals to students who value tradition and want to continue an intellectual journey that connects community with responsibility.

Compatibility with Personality Types and Preferences

Williams College can be viewed as a time capsule of American history. This campus brings a sense of the passing days standing still. This concept has value in the charged up world of 21st century young adults. Students who prefer college days with more traditional mentoring and a good buffer distancing them from the contemporary scene will find this campus a good bet. Students attracted to Williams are likely wanting a very close (F), directed experience with their professors and department advisor. Academic philosophy on this campus seems to interface trendy multicultural approaches in collegiate education without putting fundamental knowledge of the discipline at risk. There is a notable specificity within Williams courses. These bright undergraduates are expectant of

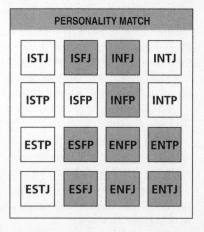

PERSONALITY MATCH			
ISTJ	ISFJ	INFJ	INTJ
ISTP	ISFP	INFP	INTP
ESTP	ESFP	ENFP	ENTP
ESTJ	ESFJ	ENFJ	ENTJ

a top notch educational experience and it is there for the taking. In fact, excellence is an uppermost value on this campus, delivered by the devoted faculty and demanded by the undergraduates.

Students attracted to Williams College would expect to graduate with superior analytical skills. They would also be approving of personal codes of behavior that mirror some of the colonial New England ideals. Education at Williams College is a process (P) rather than a goal. The process is very much paired with the sense of Williams' campus community, an educational community where discussion, collaboration and earnest exploration (N) is the daily norm. Students must bring a lot of energy (E) to the intensity, reflection and deep interface (I) with fellow students and faculty. These students are expressive and academically engaged with each other. Here at Williams, the more reserved undergraduates excel at the one-on-one relationship. The long, insular winters are well-punctuated with many Williams College traditions that occasionally lighten the atmosphere with fun and provide a break from the academic heavy lifting on this campus.

In the following listing of college majors it is important to remember that students can fit into any college and can be successful in any major. We have found that the Personality Types below fit very well at this college. The course-of-study chosen for each Personality Type corresponds to MBTI® research and is presented as an example favorable for that type.

ENFP would do well to take advantage of the varied, in depth offerings of the **History** department. Williams College has extensive tradition and foundation with historic America. The advanced courses in United States history offer some illuminating lenses through which to survey America: American Way of War, America and the Sea to Technology and Science in American Culture. Of course, Williams College offers the familiar lenses of ethnicity and gender as applied to our history. But they also offer penetrating historical perspectives less often encountered in today's best educational institutions. ENFPs love to be inspired and creative. How about combining this major with a journalistic career in historical perspectives and current social trends?

ENTP would do well to pursue the **Leadership Studies** track at Williams College. The faculty offers a collection of courses that explore the power relationships between leaders and followers. Since ENTPs are drawn to the worlds of power, they often find themselves in positions of authority and seek rapport. At the same time, these creative thinkers can become tongue-tied when trying to express their vision. The course in Art of Presidential Leadership exposes ENTPs to strategies and they will likely select a few for their own tool box.

ESFJ frequently moves into the world of health care. At Williams College, the **Biology** department offers a balanced course of studies that prepare graduates for advanced degrees in the life sciences. This type's strong organization skills and the close advising on this campus will assure that ESFJs sample all the career options prior to graduation. This is important because this type makes decisions with careful deliberation and with a desire to be of value to others and society. The Williams tutorial is also likely to really appeal to this type who values harmony and close working relationships.

ENFJ can be a compassionate personality, so the study of **Psychology** is likely to resonate. The field has expanded considerably within the last thirty years. The department has a strong emphasis in developmental, cognitive and social psychology with less emphasis in the biological determinants of human behaviors. ENFJs could naturally seek admission to PhD programs in social research with this background.

ISFJ often is a stickler for technical accuracy. They can put this skill to good use in a scientific career and Williams College has a unique concentration in **Maritime Studies** that pairs up easily with another science major of choice. This concentration offers several perspectives on maritime naval power, ocean studies and literature welling up from the literary depths. If ISFJs would rather major in the social sciences they can still pair up with Maritime Studies. They are likely to enjoy the study of the classic epic, *The Old Man and the Sea*. Williams College is just the place to value and study literary classics of all ages.

ENTJ has the characteristics and style needed and necessary to be a credible expert and consultant. Their propensity for long-range planning is just the right stuff for a degree in **Geosciences.** The department offers a focus on interacting global systems and really hones in on the oceans and water circulation. Since geosciences is so wide-ranging and requires exacting resources, faculties at liberal arts colleges will often select areas of specialization beyond the foundational course work. At Williams College, one of the specializations moved toward oceanography and is nicely supplemented with the unusual concentration in maritime studies. ENTJs need to have an intellectually satisfying sort of work and Williams College is well prepared to launch them into this critical field laden with discovery.

INFJ likes to study complex problems very closely and at a steadied pace that is free of the pressures of strict time schedules. The degree in **Political Economy** at Williams College certainly offers both. It ties public policy together with economic resources at an unhurried pace of study on this campus that reminds a casual visitor of a time capsule. INFJs are likely to thrive with the tutorials that pair a professor with student in debate and elocution for the semester. This unusual degree requires a willing, powerful thinker and INFJ often has both these, but also a dose of stubborn. INFJ may chaff at the structured curriculum in this major, but will hear that that undergraduate passion does not necessarily lead to mastery of a major or discipline.

INFP will possibly be drawn to the **Theatre** major at Williams College. This department views dramatic performance as an interpretive tool that utilizes the story line for a purpose. Aside from their typical appreciation of the arts, INFPs love to tell their story and present their original thoughts through another medium. They are not figuratively or literally 'talking heads.' With their creative spirit in overdrive a combination of drama and therapy could emerge. Williams College students in theater typically double major. INFPs might go for a double major: theater/psychology.

ESFP has the enthusiasm and spontaneity to spin a degree in **Classics** into a high end service in floral landscapes and floral interior design. ESFPs would refer to antiquity and classical concepts of design that allow this type to offer innovation in their interior and exterior botanical landscapes. The classics department is exceptionally credible since it pairs up with Williams College's deep appreciation for historical tradition. The college's own art museum supplements the on-campus courses in this major. Williams offers a nice selection of coursework in botany to add the practical flair to this career goal.

YALE UNIVERSITY

38 Hillhouse Avenue
New Haven, CT 06520
Website: www.yale.edu
Admissions Telephone: 203-432-9316
Undergraduates: 5,282; 2,617 Men, 2,665 Women
Graduate Students: 6,251

Physical Environment

Yale is the **second oldest private institution** of higher education in the nation and has been at its present location in downtown New Haven since 1716. The neighborhood houses a mixture of clothing stores, museums, art galleries, city offices and ethnic restaurants. Yale and New Haven have evolved together over the centuries. The Yale residential colleges have been in continuous renovation since 1996. Most recently, Morse College finished its 'redo' featuring a small theater, an underground courtyard and other fab spaces for dance, exercise, art and music. Located closer to the center of campus, the new health center opened in August 2010. City streets and campus tend to blur together and Yale students remain aware of their surroundings.

The Yale campus displays **three centuries of architecture**, from the red-brick, Georgian style of Connecticut Hall to the Gothic Harkness Memorial Tower to the ultra-modern glass-and-metal Malone engineering building. Undergraduate students reside in one of **12 houses**, located in the most central and well-traveled areas of the campus. The university intends to increase by two more residential colleges by 2013. Yale is the originating point of the **Harkness table**, an exceptional teaching practice that honors its namesake professor. Harkness classrooms feature a signature oval table that is designed to be conducive to discussion. Students must come prepared to teach the class while the professor guides their discussion. It is designed for receiving feedback, face-to-face from peers.

The 12 residential colleges become **cohesive communities** of approximately 300 students each. The bonds of friendship that develop in a house are part of the Yale experience. The Master of each house facilitates students' **social and academic gatherings**, most of which are designed for smaller groups of 10 to 40 students with similar cultural and academic interests.

Social Environment

Yale students are **very aware.** Period. Of many things--politics, health, art, math formulas, space, history, cancer, wealth, power, networks, ibuprofen, zinnias, the Mississippi River. Not a conclusive list, it is best understood of as an infinitive recitation of important nouns. Three recent United States presidents graduated from Yale. Circles of power and feedback enhance and re-enhance the institution. Politically, Yalies have traditionally leaned to the right except for the last decade, when the Iraq war and economic downturn have made this side less appealing to their perspective.

When they are vocal, Yalies are respectful if not tactful. If they have any complaints they tend to voice them with "I" statements that carefully express personal views, avoiding the manipulation so common in our public square today. Undergraduates are **socially sophisticated** for the most part. Yale residential life revolves around the performing **arts events** on campus and afternoon English tea at the Master's house, or maybe foosball, or maybe knitting club, or maybe…. These are weekly events when artists and political figures are invited to the residential college living spaces to converse with undergraduates about their work over tea, foosball or knitting. These soirees mimic the amazing **intellectual depth** found on this campus.

Greek Life is quiet, and there are many opportunities to volunteer and network socially. There is folklore and fact about the secret societies such as skull and bones, to which many American politicos belong. When it comes to service, Yale students focus on **international outreach** and global issues. Locally, they volunteer with not-for-profit organizations such as the United Way and the Housing Authority of New Haven as part of a program called "Community Based Learning Initiative." Service learning can extend to research projects studying increased communication between local citizens and the campus through art, drama and historical presentations. Three-quarters of Yale students are involved with **literacy work**. The university strongly supports this through funding and volunteer opportunities. These and other initiatives are intended to improve relations between the university and the city of Hartford.

Compatibility with Personality Types and Preferences

Yale University reserves its premier role for undergraduate students. The educational experience at the college is tailored for the aggregate student body. The individual student is educated with a view toward the whole student body moving forward to populate new intellectual frontiers. With less focus on finding a common thread within the individuals admitted, there is intellectual variety and a distinct need for unique talents with personal perspective. The vast resources at Yale College are positioned to meet all academic interests. Each student is assured that the materials and educational presence are in place to develop their comprehension. Students are brought into the academic fold and expected to become part of Yale's short and long term intellectual community. Nevertheless, the Ivory Tower is not much in evidence. There is a fair amount of intellectual jostling with demand by the students to further shape their academic experience and goals. Undergraduates must scramble within the curriculum availability for the combination of the studies they should secure. They must invoke flexibility (P) when Rarified Underwater Basket Weaving 201 is filled for the semester. Serendipity has a place on this campus. Yale graduates are expected to become influential and acknowledged intellectuals negotiating societies' limitations early in their careers.

With that said, you will see that the Yale environment includes all personality types. Strands of study and knowledge which occur as discussion (T) or independent study at smaller fine liberal arts colleges become full-fledged programs or courses at Yale. The private students (I) will find it possible to select programs and studies with small numbers of like-minded peers. Faculty within their major will happily collaborate in studied research offering that isolated, preferred single point focus. In this way and other educational practices, the campus is looking inward. Intellectual resources, emotional resilience and energy are not diverted away from the student body, yet the student who derives energy from others (E) will find that Yale educational philosophies expect interaction and collaboration. This mixing it up is honored as the best way to advance the whole student population. Yale faculty expects and intentionally benefits from this collaboration with students. The resultant reciprocal learning with students brings knowledge of current trends within society to the campus gestalt.

The student who arrives expectantly looking for relationships to replace hometown friends now dispersed across the collegiate landscape (F) will find solace in 12 residential colleges, essentially small communities. Friendships quickly develop within each of these residences which are populated to be more or less identical in makeup. All the activities of a small community are present and active in each of the 12. It allows the individual student a larger number of casual, yet valuable acquaintances while saving most of their energy for intense academic activity. Throughout four years, students will find encouragement to relate their knowledge to the larger world of their academic discipline. Yale provides that encouragement through professorial mentoring within the residential colleges. Students must use their imagination (N) to propose and identify the experiences that will push them forward in their discipline. As a result, there is considerable informal interface with the exceptional faculty within the residences.

Yale resources include collections of specimens and artifacts that mirror world class museums. Three centuries of collecting has positioned their historical archives to be topped only by the collections of advanced nation states while equal to or beyond their peer Ivy institutions. The archival vaults have to be a delight for the student who prefers to see, touch, listen and smell (S) while learning. The science laboratories are equipped beyond wild wishes to support undergraduate proposals with a disciplined approach (J) in research design. Indeed, there is not a learning preference that is not very well-supported at Yale.

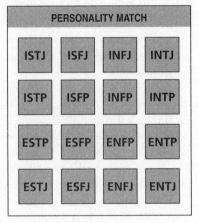

In the following listing of college majors it is important to remember that students can fit into any college and can be successful in any major. We have found that the Personality Types below fit very well at this college. The course-of-study chosen for each Personality Type corresponds to MBTI® research and is presented as an example favorable for that type.

INFP can be driven by their personal beliefs. Often this is a private journey that leads INFPs down some pretty creative paths. During their upperclassman years, this type will want to move ahead in spite of any scheduling or limiting obstacles. They are likely to be relentless in pursuing knowledge for their vision of how the world could be improved. The **Yale Summer Session** gives them a little lagniappe, Louisiana talk for an extra slice of bread, to squeeze in a needed course prior to graduation. Their ease with writing can be put to good use in these more concentrated classes. INFPs can be creative at the art of overachieving.

INFJ occasionally enters the dynamic world of business. At Yale, INFJs will learn how to bring their people focus into the entrepreneurial world through the **Engineering and Applied Sciences** program of study. It offers three educational tracks for the non-science major who wishes to move into the world of business. INFJs will have their big-picture-glasses on during all the course work and can quickly spot an opportunity to bring advanced science into the practical world. This program is perfect for INFJs who can major in any social science of their choice which, of course, will connect the dots between people and values.

INTJ will probably ponder the **Special Divisional Major** at some point through the first years at Yale. INTJs are bent on translating their visions into reality. At the same time, they are pretty original and their novel ideas can be difficult to understand. It is possible that even Yale may not have the direction of academic study they require. In this case, INTJs can present their request to the appropriate faculty committee and hopefully be given the go ahead. This type has the persistence and personal strength to follow the process through to the decision. Should it not come out in their favor, the vision will still live on, perhaps, now altered to assure success next time.

INTP will constantly be delighted and absorbed with the major in **Physics and Philosophy**. How much more complicated could it get? For this type, that is just what they need to keep their intense search for clarity at bay or at least occupied. INTPs see the world through patterns and expect those patterns to provide utility at some level, even if it is an abstract level. At Yale, this type can rely on others to lay down a social schedule and they will show up. When they find others interested in their philosophical patterns at the residential college soirees, it will be hard to get in a word edgewise.

ISTP is going to be a first class participant in the **Aerial Robotics Research Group** at Yale. This club plays around with machines in the air that are directed and powered by computers and people on the ground. ISTPs will only play with machines if they do something practical or interesting. This type will see that the group fulfills both qualifications; the undergraduate student membership is looking toward both commercial and military utility. ISTPs will become charter members, especially if a little friendly competition evolves with other like-minded college techies.

ISTJ is swell at picking up huge amounts of specific data and storing it for immediate or future use. Once gathered this type enjoys analysis and formulation in useful categories and concepts. ISTJs are a natural for **Archeological Studies** at Yale. Their senior thesis, required for this major, will be a comprehensive study through logical analysis of their individual observations on an archeological find. ISTJs will devote months to this work and it will likely have practical implications for further research in the field.

ISFJ with an artistic talent has the dedication, starting with day one, to develop a portfolio of studio art work in the freshman and early sophomore years. This reflective, gentle type will find the art department assertively moving into new expressive forms such as Art Wiki—interactive web art for all. The **Art** major explores all modern day and traditional studio arts. ISFJs will bring their excellent visual memories to the forefront in any medium they choose. Their typical sensitivity for others will find a home within this community of fellow students and faculty. They will thrive in the residential house system and support the house Master's efforts to bring the arts into their residence.

ISFP prefers to actively and directly work with information. The major in **Near Eastern Languages and Civilizations** has a component of archeology mixed into the studies. Visits to Egypt for immersion learning and the chance to visit sites of ancient civilizations enliven the major for this type. ISFPs also really appreciate the chance to gather information off campus away from traditional academic environments. It is very relaxing for this type. The artistic nature of much Egyptian archeology also appeals to ISFPs. They relate to this discipline which carries visual meaning as do many of the familiar ancient hieroglyphics incorporated through the centuries into current day symbols.

ESTP is quick to get the picture and will like the courses of instruction centered on **Operations Research**. These courses teach elements of optimization, efficiency and calculation as applied to complex systems in business and government. ESTPs can pick from four subfields within the course work: mathematical programming, stochastic processes, game theory or production/inventory control. This whole arena has elements of risk within the reality of day-to-day operations. This type is right at home and ready to jump in, armed with a Yale education, there will be solutions— with fun added in to relieve any boring moments.

ESFP will be sporting a smile after a few hours of introduction to the residential colleges. The options for fun and friends will be pretty enticing for this social type. Along the same lines, the program of study in **Sociology** department should be quite appealing. There are a couple of approaches to the major. One is called the nonintensive and the other, the intensive. Their social schedule permitting, ESFPs will move in one direction or the other. The major in sociology meets their need for variety and activity. Students quickly become involved in researching behavior and outcomes. ESFPs actually like to move into disorganized environments to bring order and meaning. Therefore most study in this discipline makes sense to them.

ENFP who likes science and math might get the nod to enter Yale's **Perspectives on Science and Engineering** lecture series and discussion for freshmen students. This is a survey course designed to expose the interdisciplinary nature of the sciences. ENFPs can keep up with the speakers because their minds move very quickly when it comes to charting new courses. They may not arrive on time or remember to bring their laptop to tap notes, but when they leave the class they will be full of energy and dreaming of possibilities for their future studies in the coming years.

ENTP is fascinated by the world and quite capable of finding multiple shades of meaning through their expansive insight. The language courses in **Polish** hold multiple advantages for this creative type. Their interest in political science will likely come to surface at Yale also. Their comfort level in big settings with important players is an asset when leveled with a little needed humility. Fortunately, Yale offers multiple lessons in humility. ENTPs only have to think about the resurgent Russia and its former satellites to see the utility in speaking a little Polish on the international stage.

ESFJ is forever curious about others. This type is more than capable of collecting and cataloging information for future benefit on behalf of people and their organizations. Whatever curriculum ESFJs move toward at Yale, it is likely to involve community action, either formal or informal. The course in **Study of the City** at Yale has advantages for this type. American cities are attempting to serve all populations and they have multiple programming needs. This course offers a look at those needs and explores solutions through hands-on activities, usually enjoyed by the ESFJ.

ESTJ often hones in on challenges, preferably those that exist in the real world rather than an Ivory Tower. They will be right at home here at Yale. The dynamic, hard to predict field of **Economics** offers the somewhat chaotic environments they like to straighten out. This type could specialize in the methods and skills that capture data trends within the national economies around the world. ESTJs will especially enjoy the department's Seminars that emphasize class interaction, writing and reading professional articles. ESTJ's natural inclination for leadership in this active environment will likely come forth.

ENFJ will find the **Agrarian Studies Program** at Yale University intriguing because it approaches land study through the lens of human potential. The courses focus on the third world and less developed, emerging nations. Undergraduate students learn through discussion and conversation with members of many different departments at the university. Development of agrarian communities forms the foundation for this program. ENFJs will likely find themselves overseas to get firsthand knowledge of cultures within impoverished environments. After graduation, this gifted public speaker will likely bring forward their new found understanding to interested audiences at regional and national levels.

ENTJ has the competitive drive to hang in there for the valuable fifth year of the **Public Health** degree at Yale. This type will be happy with the combination BA-BS and the Masters level degree awarded on completion. Their desire for leadership and natural penchant for planning are ideal for the challenges of health service in American society. ENTJ's entrepreneurial spirit will not let idealism rule to the point of putting real action in jeopardy—again, a very desirable characteristic for a career in public health. Clearly, the prestige of graduation from Yale is also not lost on this type who brandishes a leadership style that features change and creativity.

CHAPTER 6

THE TABLES OF COLLEGES AND MAJORS RECOMMENDED FOR PERSONALITY TYPES

In this chapter you will see a comprehensive listing of the colleges and majors assessed in this book that are compatible with your Personality Type. It is important to understand that this list is not exclusive and students can be successful at any college. Our basic premise is that the colleges within these tables represent collegiate environments that are excellent fits for the indicated Personality Type and characteristic learning style.

The reader is reminded within each of the 82 college descriptions that the Personality Type information provided is supplemental and it is best used in conjunction with other factors such as size, distance from home, social environment, admission and financial considerations, etc.

Sixteen Personality Types and Colleges

ISTJ
American University
Amherst College
Beloit College
Boston College
Boston University
Brandeis University
Butler University
California Institute of Technology
Claremont Colleges–Pomona
Claremont Colleges–Scripps
College of Charleston
College of Wooster
Columbia University
Connecticut College
Dartmouth College
Davidson College
Denison University
Duke University
Emory University
Florida Southern College
Furman University
George Washington University
Georgetown University
Georgia Institute of Technology
Hamilton College
Harvard University
Johns Hopkins University
Kalamazoo College
Kenyon College
Lynchburg College
Marquette University
Massachusetts Institute of Technology
Middlebury College
Northeastern University
Northwestern University
Notre Dame University
Oberlin College
Princeton University
Roanoke College
Rollins College
Saint Louis University
Stanford University
Tufts University
University of Chicago
University of Miami
University of Pennsylvania
University of Richmond
University of Tampa
Valparaiso University
Vanderbilt University

Wabash College
Wake Forest
Washington and Lee University
Washington University
Wesleyan University
Yale University

ISFJ
Amherst College
Bates College
Beloit College
Boston College
Brandeis University
Butler University
Case Western Reserve University
Claremont Colleges–Pitzer College
Claremont Colleges–Scripps
Colby College
Colgate University
College of Wooster
Columbia University
Connecticut College
Davidson College
Denison University
Elon University
Emory University
Florida Southern College
Furman University
Georgetown University
Georgia Institute of Technology
Guilford College
Harvard University
Haverford College
Johns Hopkins University
Kalamazoo College
Kenyon College
Lynchburg College
Marquette University
Muhlenberg College
Northeastern University
Notre Dame University
Occidental College
Pepperdine University
Princeton University
Redlands University
Roanoke College
Rollins College
Saint Louis University
Salve Regina University
Stanford University
Swarthmore College
Syracuse University
Tufts University
University of Chicago
University of Pennsylvania

University of Richmond
University of Tampa
Valparaiso University
Vanderbilt University
Wabash College
Wake Forest
Washington University
Williams College
Yale University

INFJ

Agnes Scott College
Amherst College
Bates College
Beloit College
Bowdoin College
Brown University
Carleton College
Case Western Reserve University
Claremont Colleges–Claremont McKenna
Claremont Colleges–Harvey Mudd
Claremont Colleges–Pitzer College
Claremont Colleges–Pomona
Colgate University
College of Charleston
College of Wooster
Columbia University
Connecticut College
Davidson College
Denison University
Duke University
Emory University
Florida Southern College
Furman University
Georgetown University
Guilford College
Hamilton College
Hampshire College
Harvard University
Haverford College
Hendrix College
Kalamazoo College
Lawrence University
Massachusetts Institute of Technology
Middlebury College
New York University
Oberlin College
Occidental College
Princeton University
Redlands University
Salve Regina University
Sarah Lawrence College
Stanford University
Swarthmore College
Syracuse University

Tulane University
Union College
University of Chicago
University of Richmond
University of Southern California
Wabash College
Wake Forest
Washington and Lee University
Washington University
Wesleyan University
Williams College
Yale University

INTJ

Agnes Scott College
American University
Amherst College
Bates College
Bowdoin College
Brown University
California Institute of Technology
Carleton College
Case Western Reserve University
Claremont Colleges–Claremont McKenna
Claremont Colleges–Harvey Mudd
Claremont Colleges–Pomona
Claremont Colleges–Scripps
Columbia University
Connecticut College
Dartmouth College
Duke University
Emory University
George Washington University
Georgetown University
Hamilton College
Hampshire College
Harvard University
Hendrix College
Johns Hopkins University
Lawrence University
Massachusetts Institute of Technology
Middlebury College
New York University
Northwestern University
Oberlin College
Occidental College
Princeton University
Sarah Lawrence College
Stanford University
Swarthmore College
Tufts University
Tulane University
Union College
University of Chicago
University of Miami

University of Pennsylvania
University of Richmond
University of Southern California
Vanderbilt University
Washington and Lee University
Washington University
Wesleyan University
Yale University

ISTP

American University
Amherst College
Boston College
Boston University
Bowdoin College
Brandeis University
California Institute of Technology
Carleton College
Case Western Reserve University
Claremont Colleges Harvey Mudd
Claremont Colleges–Pomona
Claremont Colleges–Scripps
Columbia University
Connecticut College
Dartmouth College
Davidson College
Emory University
George Washington University
Georgia Institute of Technology
Hamilton College
Harvard University
Johns Hopkins University
Kenyon College
Marquette University
Massachusetts Institute of Technology
New York University
Northeastern University
Princeton University
Saint Louis University
Salve Regina University
Stanford University
Syracuse University
Tufts University
Tulane University
University of Chicago
University of Miami
University of Pennsylvania
University of Southern California
Vanderbilt University
Washington and Lee University
Washington University
Yale University

ISFP

Bates College

Beloit College
Boston University
Bowdoin College
Brandeis University
Brown University
Butler University
Case Western Reserve University
Claremont Colleges–Pitzer College
Colby College
College of Charleston
College of Wooster
Davidson College
Denison University
Elon University
Florida Southern College
Furman University
Guilford College
Hampshire College
Harvard University
Haverford College
Hendrix College
Kalamazoo College
Kenyon College
Lynchburg College
New York University
Northeastern University
Pepperdine University
Princeton University
Redlands University
Roanoke College
Rollins College
Saint Louis University
Salve Regina University
Sarah Lawrence College
Swarthmore College
Syracuse University
Union College
University of Southern California
Valparaiso University
Wabash College
Wake Forest
Yale University

INTP

Agnes Scott College
American University
Amherst College
Bates College
Bowdoin College
Brown University
California Institute of Technology
Carleton College
Case Western Reserve University
Claremont Colleges–Harvey Mudd
Claremont Colleges–Pitzer College

Claremont Colleges–Pomona
College of Wooster
Columbia University
Connecticut College
Dartmouth College
Davidson College
Duke University
Emory University
Georgetown University
Hamilton College
Hampshire College
Harvard University
Haverford College
Hendrix College
Lawrence University
Massachusetts Institute of Technology
Middlebury College
Northwestern University
Oberlin College
Occidental College
Princeton University
Stanford University
Swarthmore College
Tufts University
Tulane University
University of Chicago
University of Miami
University of Pennsylvania
University of Richmond
University of Southern California
Vanderbilt University
Washington and Lee University
Washington University
Wesleyan University
Yale University

INFP

Agnes Scott College
Bates College
Beloit College
Bowdoin College
Brandeis University
Brown University
Carleton College
Case Western Reserve University
Claremont Colleges–Harvey Mudd
Claremont Colleges–Pitzer College
Claremont Colleges–Pomona
Colgate University
College of Wooster
Columbia University
Davidson College
Denison University
Duke University
Elon University

Florida Southern College
Guilford College
Hampshire College
Harvard University
Haverford College
Hendrix College
Lawrence University
Massachusetts Institute of Technology
Oberlin College
Occidental College
Pepperdine University
Princeton University
Redlands University
Saint Louis University
Sarah Lawrence College
Swarthmore College
Syracuse University
Union College
University of Chicago
University of Southern California
Vanderbilt University
Wabash College
Wake Forest
Washington University
Wesleyan University
Williams College
Yale University

ESTP

American University
Boston College
Boston University
Butler University
California Institute of Technology
Case Western Reserve University
Claremont Colleges–Claremont McKenna
Colby College
College of Charleston
Columbia University
Dartmouth College
Denison University
Elon University
Florida Southern College
Furman University
George Washington University
Georgetown University
Georgia Institute of Technology
Hamilton College
Harvard University
Johns Hopkins University
Kenyon College
Lynchburg College
Marquette University
Massachusetts Institute of Technology
Muhlenberg College

New York University
Notre Dame University
Northeastern University
Princeton University
Roanoke College
Rollins College
Saint Louis University
Salve Regina University
Stanford University
Syracuse University
Tufts University
Tulane University
University of Miami
University of Southern California
University of Tampa
Valparaiso University
Wabash College
Yale University

ESFP

Agnes Scott College
American University
Boston College
Boston University
Brandeis University
Brown University
Butler University
Case Western Reserve University
Claremont Colleges–Harvey Mudd
Claremont Colleges–Pitzer College
Colby College
Colgate University
College of Charleston
College of Wooster
Denison University
Elon University
Florida Southern College
Furman University
George Washington University
Georgetown University
Georgia Institute of Technology
Guilford College
Hampshire College
Harvard University
Kenyon College
Lynchburg College
Marquette University
Massachusetts Institute of Technology
Muhlenberg College
New York University
Northeastern University
Northwestern University
Redlands University
Rollins College
Saint Louis University

Salve Regina University
Syracuse University
University of Miami
University of Pennsylvania
University of Southern California
University of Tampa
Valparaiso University
Williams College
Yale University

ENFP

Agnes Scott College
Bates College
Beloit College
Boston College
Boston University
Bowdoin College
Brown University
California Institute of Technology
Carleton College
Case Western Reserve University
Claremont Colleges–Harvey Mudd
Claremont Colleges–Pitzer College
Claremont Colleges–Pomona
Colgate University
College of Wooster
Columbia University
Dartmouth College
Denison University
Elon University
Florida Southern College
Furman University
George Washington University
Georgetown University
Guilford College
Hampshire College
Harvard University
Haverford College
Hendrix College
Johns Hopkins University
Lawrence University
Massachusetts Institute of Technology
Muhlenberg College
New York University
Northwestern University
Occidental College
Princeton University
Redlands University
Salve Regina University
Sarah Lawrence College
Stanford University
Swarthmore College
Syracuse University
Tufts University
Tulane University

Union College
University of Chicago
University of Southern California
Vanderbilt University
Wabash College
Wake Forest
Washington and Lee University
Wesleyan University
Williams College
Yale University

ENTP

Agnes Scott College
American University
Amherst College
Bates College
Boston College
Bowdoin College
Brown University
California Institute of Technology
Carleton College
Case Western Reserve University
Claremont Colleges–Claremont McKenna
Claremont Colleges–Pomona
Colgate University
College of Charleston
College of Wooster
Columbia University
Connecticut College
Dartmouth College
Duke University
George Washington University
Georgetown University
Georgia Institute of Technology
Guilford College
Hamilton College
Hampshire College
Harvard University
Haverford College
Hendrix College
Johns Hopkins University
Lawrence University
Massachusetts Institute of Technology
Middlebury College
New York University
Northwestern University
Notre Dame University
Oberlin College
Occidental College
Princeton University
Redlands University
Sarah Lawrence College
Stanford University
Swarthmore College
Syracuse University

Tufts University
Tulane University
Union College
University of Chicago
University of Miami
University of Richmond
University of Southern California
Wabash College
Wake Forest
Washington and Lee University
Washington University
Wesleyan University
Williams College
Yale University

ESFJ

Agnes Scott College
American University
Bates College
Beloit College
Boston College
Brandeis University
Brown University
Butler University
Claremont Colleges–Claremont McKenna
Claremont Colleges–Pitzer College
Claremont Colleges–Pomona
Claremont Colleges–Scripps
Colgate University
College of Wooster
Columbia University
Davidson College
Denison University
Elon University
Florida Southern College
Furman University
Georgetown University
Guilford College
Harvard University
Haverford College
Kalamazoo College
Lawrence University
Lynchburg College
Marquette University
Muhlenberg College
New York University
Northeastern University
Notre Dame University
Occidental College
Pepperdine University
Princeton University
Redlands University
Roanoke College
Saint Louis University
Salve Regina University

Sarah Lawrence College
Swarthmore College
Syracuse University
Tulane University
Union College
University of Pennsylvania
University of Southern California
University of Tampa
Wabash College
Wake Forest
Williams College
Yale University

ESTJ

American University
Amherst College
Boston College
Boston University
Brandeis University
Butler University
California Institute of Technology
Claremont Colleges–Claremont McKenna
Claremont Colleges–Pomona
Claremont Colleges–Scripps
Colby College
College of Charleston
Dartmouth College
Davidson College
Duke University
Elon University
Emory University
Florida Southern College
Furman University
George Washington University
Georgetown University
Georgia Institute of Technology
Hamilton College
Harvard University
Johns Hopkins University
Kalamazoo College
Kenyon College
Lynchburg College
Marquette University
Massachusetts Institute of Technology
Muhlenberg College
New York University
Northeastern University
Northwestern University
Notre Dame University
Pepperdine University
Princeton University
Roanoke College
Rollins College
Saint Louis University
Syracuse University

Stanford University
Tufts University
Tulane University
Union College
University of Chicago
University of Miami
University of Pennsylvania
University of Richmond
University of Tampa
Valparaiso University
Vanderbilt University
Wake Forest
Yale University

ENFJ

Agnes Scott College
Amherst College
Bates College
Beloit College
Bowdoin College
Brandeis University
Brown University
Butler University
Case Western Reserve University
Claremont Colleges–Claremont McKenna
Claremont Colleges–Harvey Mudd
Claremont Colleges–Pitzer College
Claremont Colleges–Scripps
Colby College
Colgate University
College of Wooster
Columbia University
Connecticut College
Dartmouth College
Davidson College
Denison University
Duke University
Elon University
Emory University
Florida Southern College
Furman University
Georgetown University
Georgia Institute of Technology
Guilford College
Hampshire College
Harvard University
Haverford College
Hendrix College
Kalamazoo College
Lawrence University
Lynchburg College
Marquette University
Middlebury College
Muhlenberg College
New York University

Northeastern University
Notre Dame University
Occidental College
Pepperdine University
Princeton University
Redlands University
Roanoke College
Saint Louis University
Salve Regina University
Sarah Lawrence College
Stanford University
Swarthmore College
Syracuse University
Tufts University
Union College
University of Southern California
University of Tampa
Valparaiso University
Wabash College
Washington and Lee University
Wesleyan University
Williams College
Yale University

ENTJ

American University
Beloit College
Boston College
Boston University
Bowdoin College
Brandeis University
Butler University
California Institute of Technology
Carleton College
Claremont Colleges–Claremont McKenna
Claremont Colleges–Pomona
Claremont Colleges–Scripps
Colgate University
College of Charleston
Columbia University
Connecticut College
Dartmouth College
Duke University
Elon University
Emory University
George Washington University
Georgetown University
Georgia Institute of Technology
Hamilton College
Harvard University
Johns Hopkins University
Kalamazoo College
Lawrence University
Lynchburg College
Marquette University

Massachusetts Institute of Technology
Middlebury College
Muhlenberg College
New York University
Northeastern University
Northwestern University
Notre Dame University
Oberlin College
Occidental College
Pepperdine University
Princeton University
Roanoke College
Rollins College
Saint Louis University
Stanford University
Syracuse University
Tulane University
Union College
University of Chicago
University of Miami
University of Pennsylvania
University of Richmond
University of Southern California
Vanderbilt University
Wabash College
Wake Forest
Washington and Lee University
Washington University
Wesleyan University
Williams College
Yale University

Personality Types and College Majors

ISTJ

ISFJ

Computer Science 70, 116, 196, 255, 264
Creative Writing 314
Critical Theory 243
Earth and Planetary Sciences 185
Earth Sciences 129
Earth, Atmosphere and Planetary Sciences 223
East Asian Studies 251
Economics 125, 329
Economics and Mathematics 149
Ecosystem Science and Policy 317
Engineering Physics 94
Engineering, History 291
Evolutionary Biology 141
Geobiology 362
Geology 56
Health Informatics 305
International Health 165
Jazz 120
Mathematics 102
Molecular Biology and Biochemistry 365
Neuroscience 211
Operations and Supply Chain Management 333
Philosophy 101, 178, 358
Physics 43, 87, 133
Physics and Philosophy 373
Product Design 287
Psychology 101
Theater Studies 228

INFP

African American Studies 55
Art 90
Biology 282
Civilization Studies 313
Cognitive Science 211
Community Health 79
Comparative Study of Religion 187
Creative Writing 325
Drama and Theater Arts 119
Early Childhood Education 344
Educational Studies 43, 138
English 116, 365
Environmental Studies 291
Environmental Economics 107
Forensic Accounting 174
Fine Arts 193
Gerontological Studies 94
Health and Humanity 333
Health Pre-Medicine 181
History 59
Human Services 144
Irish Studies 236

Language and Culture 262
Linguistics 353
Linguistics and Cognitive Science 101
Multimedia Design 258
Music 70
Neuroscience 132, 251
Nutrition and Dietetics 275
Philosophy with Law 348
Physics 51, 101
Psychology 141, 195, 309
Religion 153
Religious Studies 94
Science Technology and Society 223
Social Work 296
Sociology 255
Studio Art 74
Summer Session 372
Theater 369
Theater and Dance 101
Urban Design 361

ESTP

Accounting 239
Administrative Science 105
Advertising 67
Aeronautics and Astronautics 287
Aviation Management 275
Asian and Middle Eastern Studies 129
Athletic Training 161, 269
Broadcast and New Media 145
Business Administration 340
Business Economics Management 87
Civil Engineering 170, 224
Computer Science 236
Construction Engineering and Management 219
Criminology 84
Cultural and Historic Preservation 279
Dance 137, 272
Economic Crime Prevention and Investigation 215
Environmental Science and Public Policy 186
Environmental Geosciences 247
Environmental Studies 177
Finance 232, 305
Financial Economic Sequence 99
Forensic Science 295
Fundamentals of Business 340
Game Theory 87
Global Logistics and Transportation 112
Human Factors and Engineering Psychology 300
Information Technology 157

ESTJ

ENFJ

Health and Society 60
History 288
History and Classics 150
Human Development 105
Human Services and American Sign
   Language 240
International Economics and Cultural
   Affairs 340
Language and Linguistics 75
Middle/Secondary Education 84
Museum Studies 216
Peace, Conflict and Social Justice Studies
   193
Plant Biology 141
Political Journalism Certificate 276
Preprofessional Studies 247
Psychology 71, 130, 154, 256, 350, 368
Public Administration 146
Public Policy 292
Public Policy-Sociology 282
Public Relations 259
Rhetoric 55
Romance Languages and Literature 186
Special Education 296
Sociology 134, 235
Social Welfare & Justice 220
Victim Services 220
Writing and Rhetoric 108

ENTJ

Advertising 259
African Studies Program 167, 300
Aerospace Engineering 170
American Studies 340
Applied Mathematics 313
Asian Traditions 231
Astrophysics 108
Athletic Training 216
Australian Studies 272
Biomedical Engineer 276
Biomedical Engineering 142
Botany 125
Business 350
Chemical Engineering 87
Civil Engineering 93
Cognitive Science 256
Commerce, Economics & Politics 357
Corporate Reporting and Analysis 63
Earth Systems 288
Economics 52, 146, 352, 362, 365
Economics History 345
Engineering Management Systems 121
Entrepreneurship and Management 200
Environmental Studies 229

European and Mediterranean Studies 235
Film, TV and Theater 247
Geosciences 369
Global Health and Health Policy 265
Government 178
Health Care Management and Policy 322
Health Sector Management and Policy 318
Human Development 105, 204
Information Systems 240
International Business 84
International Relations 269
Italian 102
Japanese Language and Literature 162
Legal Studies 102
Management 224
Marketing 306, 329
Mathematics and Economics 71
Mathematics, Economics 212
Mathematics Specialty in Statistics 67
Neurobiology 189
Neuroscience 75, 310
Organizational Leadership and
   Management 334
Physics 251
Political Science 48
Political Science with Business 350
Psychology 60, 90, 149
Public Health 375
Public Relations 220
Russian Area Studies 130
Science Technology Society 102
Supply Chain Management 296
Transportation and Logistics 244

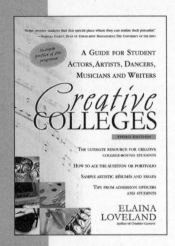

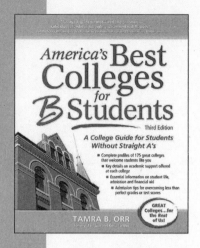

AMERICA'S BEST COLLEGES FOR B STUDENTS: A COLLEGE GUIDE FOR STUDENTS WITHOUT STRAIGHT A'S

- Complete profiles of 175 great colleges that welcome students like you

- Key details on academic support offered at each college

- Essential information on student life, admission and financial aid

- Admission tips for overcoming less than perfect grades or test scores

---

America's Best Colleges for B Students

ISBN: 978-1-61760-000-5

Price: $19.95

Get your copy at bookstores nationwide or from www.supercollege.com

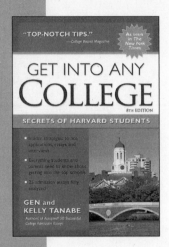

LEARN HOW TO GET INTO
THE COLLEGE OF YOUR DREAMS

- A complete, step-by-step guide to acing college applications, essays, interviews and more

- How to get free cash for college

- Tips for 9th-12th graders

- How to raise your SAT and ACT scores

- Secrets to writing an irresistible essay

- How to create a stunning application

- Tips for mastering the interview

- Proven methods for parents to give your student an edge

Get into Any College

ISBN: 978-1-61760-006-7

Price: $16.95

Get your copy at bookstores nationwide or from www.supercollege.com

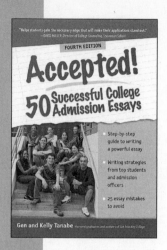

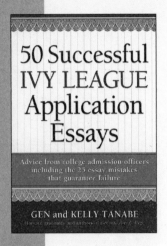

CRAFT A WINNING ESSAY FOR AN IVY LEAGUE COLLEGE

- How to select the best topic

- What Ivy League admissions officers want to see in your essay

- The 25 mistakes that guarantee failure

- The top tips from Ivy League students on how to write a successful essay

---

50 Successful Ivy League Application Essays

ISBN 13: 978-1-932662-40-5

Price: $14.95

Get your copy at bookstores nationwide or from www.supercollege.com

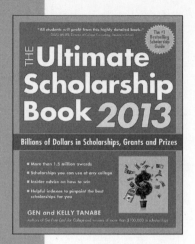

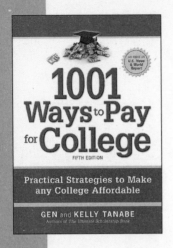

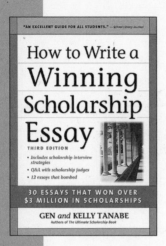

GET MORE TOOLS AND RESOURCES FOR COLLEGE AT SUPERCOLLEGE.COM

Visit www.supercollege.com for more free resources on college admission, scholarships and financial aid. And apply for the SuperCollege Scholarship.

ABOUT THE AUTHORS

ROSALIND P. MARIE has pursued a lifelong interest in education as a School Psychologist and independent educational advisor. Her background includes counseling, testing and parent support at public and independent schools in Idaho and Alabama. In 1995, Marie opened an independent consulting service advising parents and students seeking admission to boarding school, college or therapeutic programs. She has served on regional and national boards in the fields of education and presents at psychological and educational conferences. Marie holds a Master's degree in Psychology, Counseling and Guidance and an Educational Specialist Degree in School Psychology. Retired from the United States Air Force Reserves in 2000, she lives in Huntsville, Alabama with husband John and too many pets.

C. CLAIRE LAW founded Educational Avenues® after working in college admission and financial aid at Carleton University in Canada, the Art Institutes in Atlanta, Bryant University where she served as the Director of International Admission and AMS-Education Loan Trust, a Sallie Mae lender. Law has a Master's degree in Human Development from the University of Rhode Island. She's on the faculty at UC-Irvine Extension where she teaches online classes required for the "Independent Educational Consultant" Certificate. Prompted by her daughter's college admission process, she became an MBTI® certified professional and began using personality type to better match students with colleges. She resides on Daniel Island, South Carolina with her husband Chip and cat Bobbi.